An Introduction to the
Analysis of Algorithms

3rd Edition

An Introduction to the
Analysis of Algorithms

3rd Edition

Michael Soltys

California State University Channel Islands, USA

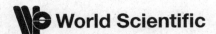 World Scientific

NEW JERSEY · LONDON · SINGAPORE · BEIJING · SHANGHAI · HONG KONG · TAIPEI · CHENNAI · TOKYO

Published by

World Scientific Publishing Co. Pte. Ltd.
5 Toh Tuck Link, Singapore 596224
USA office: 27 Warren Street, Suite 401-402, Hackensack, NJ 07601
UK office: 57 Shelton Street, Covent Garden, London WC2H 9HE

Library of Congress Cataloging-in-Publication Data
Names: Soltys, Michael, 1971–   author.
Title: An introduction to the analysis of algorithms / Michael Soltys,
    California State University Channel Islands, USA.
Description: 3rd edition. | New Jersey : World Scientific, [2018] |
    Includes bibliographical references and index.
Identifiers: LCCN 2018002035 | ISBN 9789813235908 (hardback : alk. paper)
Subjects: LCSH: Algorithms--Textbooks.
Classification: LCC QA9.58 .S63 2018 | DDC 518/.1--dc23
LC record available at https://lccn.loc.gov/2018002035

British Library Cataloguing-in-Publication Data
A catalogue record for this book is available from the British Library.

For any available supplementary material, please visit
http://www.worldscientific.com/worldscibooks/10.1142/10875#t=suppl

Desk Editor: Amanda Yun

Printed in Singapore

To my family

Preface

If he had only learnt a little
less, how infinitely better he
might have taught much more!

Charles Dickens [Dickens
(1854)], pg. 7

This book is a short introduction to the analysis of algorithms, from the point of view of proving algorithm correctness. The quote above refers to Mr. M'Choakumchild, a caricature of a teacher in Charles Dickens' *Hard Times*, who chokes the minds of his pupils with too much information. We will avoid M'Choakumchild's mistake, and make a virtue out of brevity.

Our theme is the following: how do we argue mathematically, without a burden of excessive formalism, that a given algorithm does what it is supposed to do? And why is this important? In the words of C.A.R. Hoare:

> As far as the fundamental science is concerned, we still certainly
> do not know how to prove programs correct. We need a lot of
> steady progress in this area, which one can foresee, and a lot of
> breakthroughs where people suddenly find there's a simple way
> to do something that everybody hitherto has thought to be far
> too difficult[1].

Software engineers know many examples of things going terribly wrong because of program errors; their particular favorites are the following two[2]. The blackout in the American North-East during the summer of 2003 was due to a software bug in an energy management system; an alarm that

---

[1] From *An Interview with C.A.R. Hoare*, in [Shustek (2009)].

[2] These two examples come from [van Vliet (2000)], where many more instances of spectacular failures may be found.

should have been triggered never went off, leading to a chain of events that climaxed in a cascading blackout. The Ariane 5, flight 501, the maiden flight of the rocket in June 4, 1996, ended with an explosion 40 seconds into the flight; this $500 million loss was caused by an overflow in the conversion from a 64-bit floating point number to a 16-bit signed integer.

When Richard A. Clarke, the former National Coordinator for Security, asked Ed Amoroso, head of AT&T Network Security, what is to be done about the vulnerabilities in the USA cyber-infrastructure, Amoroso said:

> Software is most of the problem. We have to write software which has many fewer errors and which is more secure[3].

Similarly, Fred D. Taylor, Jr., a Lt. Colonel in the United States Air Force and a National Security Fellow at the Harvard Kennedy School, wrote:

> The extensive reliance on software has created new and expanding opportunities. Along with these opportunities, there are new vulnerabilities putting the global infrastructure and our national security at risk. The ubiquitous nature of the Internet and the fact that it is serviced by common protocols and processes has allowed anyone with the knowledge to create software to engage in world-wide activities. However, for most software developers there is no incentive to produce software that is more secure[4].

Software security falls naturally under the umbrella of software correctness.

While the goal of program correctness is elusive, we can develop methods and techniques for reducing errors. The aim of this book is modest: we want to present an introduction to the analysis of algorithms—the "ideas" behind programs, and show how to prove their correctness.

The algorithm may be correct, but the implementation itself might be flawed. Some syntactical errors in the program implementation may be uncovered by a compiler or translator—which in turn could also be buggy— but there might be other hidden errors. The hardware itself might be faulty; the libraries on which the program relies at run time might be unreliable, etc. It is the main task of a programmer to write code that works given such a delicate, error prone, environment. Finally, the algorithmic content of a piece of software might be very small; the majority of the lines of code could be the "menial" task of interface programming. Thus, the ability to argue correctly about the soundness of an algorithm is only one of many facets of the task at hand, yet an important one, if only for the pedagogical reason of learning to argue rigorously about algorithms.

---

[3]See page 272 in [Clarke and Knake (2011)].
[4]Harvard Law School National Security Journal, [Fred D. Taylor (2011)].

We begin this book with a chapter of preliminaries, containing the key ideas of induction and invariance, and the framework of pre/post-conditions and loop invariants. We also prove the correctness of some classical algorithms, such as the integer division algorithm, and Euclid's procedure for computing the greatest common divisor of two numbers.

We present three standard algorithm design techniques in eponymous chapters: greedy algorithms, dynamic programming and the divide and conquer paradigm. We are concerned with correctness of algorithms, rather than, say, efficiency or the underlying data structures. For example, in the chapter on the greedy paradigm we explore in depth the idea of a *promising partial solution*, a powerful technique for proving the correctness of greedy algorithms. We include online algorithms and *competitive analysis*, as well as randomized algorithms with a section on *cryptography*.

Algorithms solve problems, and many of the problems in this book fall under the category of *optimization problems*, whether cost minimization, such as Kruskal's algorithm for computing minimum cost spanning trees—section 2.1, or profit maximization, such as selecting the most profitable subset of activities—section 4.4.

The book is sprinkled with problems. Most problems are theoretical, but many require the implementation of an algorithm; we suggest the Python 3 programming language for such problems. The reader is expected to learn Python on their own; see for example, [Dierbach (2013)] or [Downey (2015)][5]. One of the advantages of Python is that it is easy to start writing small snippets of code that work—and most of the coding in this book falls into the "small snippet" category. The solutions to most problems are included in the "Answers to selected problems" at the end of each chapter. The solutions to most of the programming exercises will be available for download from the author's web page[6].

The intended audience of this book are graduate and undergraduate students in Computer Science and Mathematics. The presentation is self-contained: the first chapter introduces the aforementioned ideas of pre/post-conditions, loop invariants and termination. The last chapter, Chapter 9, Mathematical Foundations, contains the necessary background in Induction, Invariance Principle, Number Theory, Relations and Logic. The reader unfamiliar with discrete mathematics is encouraged to start with Chapter 9 and do all the problems therein.

---

[5]The PDFs of earlier versions, up to 2.0.17 at the time of writing, are available for free download from Green Tea Press, http://greenteapress.com/wp/think-python.

[6]http://www.msoltys.com.

This book draws on many sources. First of all, [Cormen *et al.* (2009)] is a fantastic reference for anyone who is learning algorithms. I have also used as reference the elegantly written [Kleinberg and Tardos (2006)]. A classic in the field is [Knuth (1997)], and I base my presentation of online algorithms on the material in [Borodin and El-Yaniv (1998)]. I have learned greedy algorithms, dynamic programming and logic from Stephen A. Cook at the University of Toronto. Section 9.3, a digest of relations, is based on lectures given by Ryszard Janicki in 2008 at McMaster University. Section 9.4 is based on logic lectures by Stephen A. Cook taught at the University of Toronto in the 1990s.

I am grateful to Ryan McIntyre who proof-read the 3rd edition manuscript, and updated the Python solutions, during the summer of 2017.

As stated at the beginning of this Preface, we aim to present a concise, mathematically rigorous, introduction to the beautiful field of Algorithms. I agree strongly with [Su (2010)] that the purpose of education is to cultivate the "yawp":

> I sound my barbaric *yawp* over the root(top)s of the world!

which are words of John Keating, quoting a Walk Whitman poem ([Whitman (1892)]), in the movie *Dead Poets Society*. This *yawp* is the deep yearning inside each of us for an aesthetic experience ([Scruton (2011)]). Hopefully, this book will supply a yawp or two.

Contents

Chapter 1

Preliminaries

> It is commonly believed that more than 70% (!) of the effort and cost of developing a complex software system is devoted, in one way or another, to error correcting.
>
> Algorith., pg. 107 [Harel (1987)]

1.1 What is correctness?

To show that an algorithm is correct, we must show somehow that it does what it is supposed to do. The difficulty is that the algorithm unfolds in time, and it is tricky to work with a variable number of steps, i.e., while-loops. We are going to introduce a framework for proving algorithm (and program) correctness that is called *Hoare's logic*. This framework uses induction and invariance (see Section 9.1), and logic (see Section 9.4) but we are going to use it informally. For a formal example see Section 9.4.4.

We make two assertions, called the *pre-condition* and the *post-condition*; by correctness we mean that whenever the pre-condition holds *before* the algorithm executes, the post-condition will hold *after* it executes. By *termination* we mean that whenever the pre-condition holds, the algorithm will stop running after finitely many steps. Correctness without termination is called *partial correctness*, and *correctness* per se is partial correctness *with* termination. All this terminology is there to connect a given problem with some algorithm that purports to solve it. Hence we pick the pre and post condition in a way that reflects this relationship and proves it true.

1

These concepts can be made more precise, but we need to introduce some standard notation: Boolean connectives: $\wedge$ is "and," $\vee$ is "or" and $\neg$ is "not." We also use $\rightarrow$ as Boolean implication, i.e., $x \rightarrow y$ is logically equivalent to $\neg x \vee y$, and $\leftrightarrow$ is Boolean equivalence, and $\alpha \leftrightarrow \beta$ expresses $((\alpha \rightarrow \beta) \wedge (\beta \rightarrow \alpha))$. $\forall$ is the "for-all" universal quantifier, and $\exists$ is the "there exists" existential quantifier. We use "$\Rightarrow$" to abbreviate the word "implies," i.e., $2|x \Rightarrow x$ is even, while "$\not\Rightarrow$" abbreviates "does not imply."

Let A be an algorithm, and let $\mathcal{I}_A$ be the set of all *well-formed* inputs for A; the idea is that if $I \in \mathcal{I}_A$ then it "makes sense" to give I as an input to A. The concept of a "well-formed" input can also be made precise, but it is enough to rely on our intuitive understanding—for example, an algorithm that takes a pair of integers as input will not be "fed" a matrix. Let $O = A(I)$ be the output of A on I, if it exists. Let α_A be a pre-condition and β_A a post-condition of A; if I satisfies the pre-condition we write $\alpha_A(I)$ and if O satisfies the post-condition we write $\beta_A(O)$. Then, partial correctness of A with respect to pre-condition α_A and post-condition β_A can be stated as:

$$(\forall I \in \mathcal{I}_A)[(\alpha_A(I) \wedge \exists O(O = A(I))) \rightarrow \beta_A(A(I))]. \tag{1.1}$$

In words: for any well formed input I, if I satisfies the pre-condition and $A(I)$ produces an output (i.e., terminates), then this output satisfies the post-condition.

Full correctness is (1.1) together with the assertion that for all $I \in \mathcal{I}_A$, $A(I)$ terminates (and hence there exists an O such that $O = A(I)$).

Problem 1.1. *Modify (1.1) to express full correctness.*

A fundamental notion in the analysis of algorithms is that of a *loop invariant*; it is an assertion that stays true after each execution of a "while" (or "for") loop. Coming up with the right assertion, and proving it, is a creative endeavor. If the algorithm terminates, the loop invariant is an assertion that helps to prove the implication $\alpha_A(I) \rightarrow \beta_A(A(I))$.

Once the loop invariant has been shown to hold, it is used for proving partial correctness of the algorithm. So the criterion for selecting a loop invariant is that it helps in proving the post-condition. In general many different loop invariants (and for that matter pre and post-conditions) may yield a desirable proof of correctness; the art of the analysis of algorithms consists in selecting them judiciously. We usually need induction to prove that a chosen loop invariant holds after each iteration of a loop, and usually we also need the pre-condition as an assumption in this proof.

1.1.1 *Complexity*

Given an algorithm $\mathcal{A}$, and an input x, the running time of $\mathcal{A}$ on x is the number of steps it takes $\mathcal{A}$ to terminate on input x. The delicate issue here is to define a "step," but we are going to be informal about it: we assume a Random Access Machine (a machine that can access memory cells in a single step), and we assume that an assignment of the type $x \leftarrow y$ is a single step, and so are arithmetical operations, and the testing of Boolean expressions (such as $x \geq y \wedge y \geq 0$). Of course this simplification does not reflect the true state of affairs if for example we manipulate numbers of 4,000 bits (as in the case of cryptographic algorithms). But then we redefine steps appropriately to the context.

We are interested in *worst-case complexity*. That is, given an algorithm $\mathcal{A}$, we let $T^{\mathcal{A}}(n)$ to be the maximal running time of $\mathcal{A}$ on any input x of size n. Here "size" means the number of bits in a reasonable fixed encoding of x. We tend to write $T(n)$ instead of $T^{\mathcal{A}}(n)$ as the algorithm under discussion is given by the context. It turns out that even for simple algorithms $T(n)$ maybe very complicated, and so we settle for asymptotic bounds on $T(n)$.

In order to provide asymptotic approximations to $T(n)$ we introduce the *Big O* notation, pronounced as "big-oh." Consider functions f and g from $\mathbb{N}$ to $\mathbb{R}$, that is, functions whose domain is the natural numbers but can range over the reals. We say that $g(n) \in O(f(n))$ if there exist constants $c, n_0 \in \mathbb{N}$ such that for all $n \geq n_0$, $g(n) \leq cf(n)$, and the *little o* notation, $g(n) \in o(f(n))$, which denotes that $\lim_{n\to\infty} g(n)/f(n) = 0$. We also say that $g(n) \in \Omega(f(n))$ if there exist constants c, n_0 such that for all $n \geq n_0$, $g(n) \geq cf(n)$. Finally, we say that $g(n) \in \Theta(f(n))$ if it is the case that $g(n) \in O(f(n)) \cap \Omega(f(n))$. If $g(n) \in \Theta(f(n))$, then $f(n)$ is called an *asymptotically tight bound* for $g(n)$, and it means that $f(n)$ is a very good approximation to $g(n)$. Note that in practice we will often write $g(n) = O(f(n))$ instead of the formal $g(n) \in O(f(n))$; a slight but convenient abuse of notation.

For example, $an^2 + bn + c = \Theta(n^2)$, where $a > 0$. To see this, note that $an^2 + bn + c \leq (a + |b| + |c|)n^2$, for all $n \in \mathbb{N}$, and so $an^2 + bn + c = O(n^2)$, where we took the absolute value of b, c because they may be negative. On the other hand, $an^2 + bn + c = a((n + c_1)^2 - c_2)$ where $c_1 = b/2a$ and $c_2 = (b^2 - 4ac)/4a^2$, so we can find a c_3 and an n_0 so that for all $n \geq n_0$, $c_3 n^2 \leq a((n + c_1)^2 - c_2)$, and so $an^2 + bn + c = \Omega(n^2)$.

Problem 1.2. *Find c_3 and n_0 in terms of a, b, c. Then prove that for $k \geq 0$, $\sum_{i=0}^{k} a_i n^i = \Theta(n^k)$; this shows the simplifying advantage of the Big O.*

1.1.2   *Division*

What could be simpler than integer division? We are given two integers, x, y, and we want to find the quotient and remainder of dividing x by y. For example, if $x = 25$ and $y = 3$, then $q = 3$ and $r = 1$. Note that the q and r returned by the division algorithm are usually denoted as $\text{div}(x, y)$ (the *quotient*) and $\text{rem}(x, y)$ (the *remainder*), respectively.

Algorithm 1.1 Division

Pre-condition: $x \geq 0 \wedge y > 0 \wedge x, y \in \mathbb{N}$

  1: $q \leftarrow 0$
  2: $r \leftarrow x$
  3: **while** $y \leq r$ **do**
  4:         $r \leftarrow r - y$
  5:         $q \leftarrow q + 1$
  6: **end while**
  7: **return** q, r

Post-condition: $x = (q \cdot y) + r \wedge 0 \leq r < y$

We propose the following assertion as the loop invariant:

$$x = (q \cdot y) + r \wedge r \geq 0, \tag{1.2}$$

and we show that (1.2) holds after each iteration of the loop. Basis case (i.e., zero iterations of the loop—we are just before line 3 of the algorithm): $q = 0, r = x$, so $x = (q \cdot y) + r$ and since $x \geq 0$ and $r = x$, $r \geq 0$.

Induction step: suppose $x = (q \cdot y) + r \wedge r \geq 0$ and we go once more through the loop, and let q', r' be the new values of q, r, respectively (computed in lines 4 and 5 of the algorithm). Since we executed the loop one more time it follows that $y \leq r$ (this is the condition checked for in line 3 of the algorithm), and since $r' = r - y$, we have that $r' \geq 0$. Thus,

$$x = (q \cdot y) + r = ((q + 1) \cdot y) + (r - y) = (q' \cdot y) + r',$$

and so q', r' still satisfy the loop invariant (1.2).

Now we use the loop invariant to show that (if the algorithm terminates) the post-condition of the division algorithm holds, *if* the pre-condition holds. This is very easy in this case since the loop ends when it is no longer true that $y \leq r$, i.e., when it is true that $r < y$. On the other hand, (1.2) holds after each iteration, and in particular the last iteration. Putting together (1.2) and $r < y$ we get our post-condition, and hence partial correctness.

To show termination we use the least number principle (LNP). We need to relate some non-negative monotone decreasing sequence to the algorithm; just consider $r_0, r_1, r_2, \ldots$, where $r_0 = x$, and r_i is the value of r after the i-th iteration. Note that $r_{i+1} = r_i - y$. First, $r_i \geq 0$, because the algorithm enters the while loop only if $y \leq r$, and second, $r_{i+1} < r_i$, since $y > 0$. By LNP such a sequence "cannot go on for ever," (in the sense that the set $\{r_i | i = 0, 1, 2, \ldots\}$ is a subset of the natural numbers, and so it has a least element), and so the algorithm must terminate.

Thus we have shown full correctness of the division algorithm.

Problem 1.3. *What is the running time of algorithm 1.1? That is, how many steps does it take to terminate? Assume that assignments (lines 1 and 2), and arithmetical operations (lines 4 and 5) as well as testing "$\leq$" (line 3) all take one step.*

Problem 1.4. *Suppose that the precondition in algorithm 1.1 is changed to say: "$x \geq 0 \wedge y > 0 \wedge x, y \in \mathbb{Z}$," where $\mathbb{Z} = \{\ldots, -2, -1, 0, 1, 2, \ldots\}$. Is the algorithm still correct in this case? What if it is changed to to the following: "$y > 0 \wedge x, y \in \mathbb{Z}$"? How would you modify the algorithm to work with negative values?*

Problem 1.5. *Write a program that takes as input x and y, and outputs the intermediate values of q and r, and finally the quotient and remainder of the division of x by y.*

1.1.3 *Euclid*

Given two positive integers a, b, their *greatest common divisor*, denoted as $\gcd(a, b)$, is the greatest integer that divides both. Euclid's algorithm, presented as algorithm 1.2, is a procedure for finding the greatest common divisor of two numbers. It is one of the oldest know algorithms; it appeared in Euclid's *Elements* (Book 7, Propositions 1 and 2) around 300 BC.

Note that to compute $\text{rem}(n, m)$ in lines 1 and 3 of Euclid's algorithm we need to use algorithm 1.1 (the division algorithm) as a subroutine; this is a typical "composition" of algorithms. Also note that lines 1 and 3 are executed from left to right, so in particular in line 3 we first do $m \leftarrow n$, then $n \leftarrow r$, and finally $r \leftarrow \text{rem}(m, n)$. This is important for the algorithm to work correctly, because when we are executing $r \leftarrow \text{rem}(m, n)$, we are using the newly updated values of m, n.

Algorithm 1.2 Euclid

Pre-condition: $a > 0 \wedge b > 0 \wedge a, b \in \mathbb{Z}$

1: $m \leftarrow a \; ; \; n \leftarrow b \; ; \; r \leftarrow \operatorname{rem}(m, n)$
2: **while** $(r > 0)$ **do**
3:         $m \leftarrow n \; ; \; n \leftarrow r \; ; \; r \leftarrow \operatorname{rem}(m, n)$
4: **end while**
5: **return** n

Post-condition: $n = \gcd(a, b)$

To prove the correctness of Euclid's algorithm we are going to show that after each iteration of the while loop the following assertion holds:

$$m > 0, n > 0 \text{ and } \gcd(m, n) = \gcd(a, b), \tag{1.3}$$

that is, (1.3) is our loop invariant. We prove this by induction on the number of iterations. Basis case: after zero iterations (i.e., just before the while loop starts—so after executing line 1 and before executing line 2) we have that $m = a > 0$ and $n = b > 0$, so (1.3) holds trivially. Note that $a > 0$ and $b > 0$ by the pre-condition.

For the induction step, suppose $m, n > 0$ and $\gcd(a, b) = \gcd(m, n)$, and we go through the loop one more time, yielding m', n'. We want to show that $\gcd(m, n) = \gcd(m', n')$. Note that from line 3 of the algorithm we see that $m' = n, n' = r = \operatorname{rem}(m, n)$, so in particular $m' = n > 0$ and $n' = r = \operatorname{rem}(m, n) > 0$ since if $r = \operatorname{rem}(m, n)$ were zero, the loop would have terminated (and we are assuming that we are going through the loop one more time). So it is enough to prove the assertion in Problem 1.6.

Problem 1.6. *Show that for all $m, n > 0$, $\gcd(m, n) = \gcd(n, \operatorname{rem}(m, n))$.*

Now the correctness of Euclid's algorithm follows from (1.3), since the algorithm stops when $r = \operatorname{rem}(m, n) = 0$, so $m = q \cdot n$, and so $\gcd(m, n) = n$.

Problem 1.7. *Show that Euclid's algorithm terminates, and establish its Big O complexity.*

Problem 1.8. *How would you make the algorithm more efficient? This question is asking for simple improvements that lower the running time by a constant factor.*

Problem 1.9. *Modify Euclid's algorithm so that given integers m, n as input, it outputs integers a, b such that $am + bn = g = \gcd(m, n)$. This is called the* extended Euclid's algorithm. *Follow this outline:*

(a) *Use the LNP to show that if $g = \gcd(m, n)$, then there exist a, b such that $am + bn = g$.*

(b) *Design Euclid's extended algorithm, and prove its correctness.*

(c) *The usual Euclid's extended algorithm has a running time polynomial in $\min\{m, n\}$; show that this is the running time of your algorithm, or modify your algorithm so that it runs in this time.*

Problem 1.10. *Write a program that implements Euclid's extended algorithm. Then perform the following experiment: run it on a random selection of inputs of a given size, for sizes bounded by some parameter N; compute the average number of steps of the algorithm for each input size $n \leq N$, and use* gnuplot[1] *to plot the result. What does $f(n)$ —which is the "average number of steps" of Euclid's extended algorithm on input size n—look like? Note that size is not the same as value; inputs of size n are inputs with a binary representation of n bits.*

1.1.4 *Palindromes*

Algorithm 1.3 tests if a string is a *palindrome*, which is a word that read the same backwards as forwards, e.g., madamimadam or racecar.

In order to present this algorithm we need to introduce a little bit of notation. The *floor* and *ceil* functions are defined, respectively, as follows: $\lfloor x \rfloor = \max\{n \in \mathbb{Z} | n \leq x\}$ and $\lceil x \rceil = \min\{n \in \mathbb{Z} | n \geq x\}$, and $\lfloor x \rceil$ refers to the "rounding" of x, and it is defined as $\lfloor x \rceil = \lfloor x + \frac{1}{2} \rfloor$.

Algorithm 1.3 Palindromes

Pre-condition: $n \geq 1 \wedge A[0 \ldots n-1]$ is a character array

1: $i \leftarrow 0$
2: **while** $(i < \lfloor \frac{n}{2} \rfloor)$ **do**
3:      **if** $(A[i] \neq A[n - i - 1])$ **then**
4:          **return** F
5:      **end if**
6:      $i \leftarrow i + 1$
7: **end while**
8: **return** T

Post-condition: return T iff A is a palindrome

---

[1]Gnuplot is a command-line driven graphing utility (http://www.gnuplot.info). Also, Python has a plotting library matplotlib (https://matplotlib.org).

Let the loop invariant be: after the k-th iteration, $i = k + 1$ and for all j such that $1 \leq j \leq k$, $A[j] = A[n - j + 1]$. We prove that the loop invariant holds by induction on k. Basis case: before any iterations take place, i.e., after zero iterations, there are no j's such that $1 \leq j \leq 0$, so the second part of the loop invariant is (vacuously) true. The first part of the loop invariant holds since i is initially set to 1.

Induction step: we know that after k iterations, $A[j] = A[n-j+1]$ for all $1 \leq j \leq k$; after one more iteration we know that $A[k+1] = A[n-(k+1)+1]$, so the statement follows for all $1 \leq j \leq k+1$. This proves the loop invariant.

Problem 1.11. *Using the loop invariant argue the partial correctness of the palindromes algorithm. Show that the algorithm terminates.*

It is easy to manipulate strings in Python; a segment of a string is called a *slice*. Consider the word `palindrome`; if we set the variables s to this word,

```
s = 'palindrome'
```

then we can access different slices as follows:

```
print s[0:5]      palin
print s[5:10]     drome
print s[5:]       drome
print s[2:8:2]    lnr
```

where the notation `[i:j]` means the segment of the string starting from the i-th character (and we always start counting at zero!), to the j-th character, including the first but excluding the last. The notation `[i:]` means from the i-th character, all the way to the end, and `[i:j:k]` means starting from the i-th character to the j-th (again, not including the j-th itself), taking every k-th character.

One way to understand the string delimiters is to write the indices "in between" the numbers, as well as at the beginning and at the end. For example

$$_0p_1a_2l_3i_4n_5d_6r_7o_8m_9e_{10}$$

and to notice that a slice `[i:j]` contains all the symbols between index i and index j.

Problem 1.12. *Using Python's inbuilt facilities for manipulating slices of strings, write a succinct program that checks whether a given string is a palindrome.*

1.1.5 *Further examples*

In this section we provide more examples of algorithms that take as integers as input, and manipulate them with a while-loop. We also present an example of an algorithm that is very easy to describe, but for which no proof of termination is known (algorithm 1.6). This supports further the notion that proofs of correctness are not just pedantic exercises in mathematical formalism but a real certificate of validity of a given algorithmic solution.

Problem 1.13. *Give an algorithm which takes as input a positive integer n, and outputs "yes" if $n = 2^k$ (i.e., n is a power of 2), and "no" otherwise. Prove that your algorithm is correct.*

Problem 1.14. *What does algorithm 1.4 compute? Prove your claim.*

Algorithm 1.4 See Problem 1.14

1:   $x \leftarrow m \; ; \; y \leftarrow n \; ; \; z \leftarrow 0$
2:   **while** $(x \neq 0)$ **do**
3:        **if** $(\mathrm{rem}(x, 2) = 1)$ **then**
4:           $z \leftarrow z + y$
5:        **end if**
6:        $x \leftarrow \mathrm{div}(x, 2)$
7:        $y \leftarrow y \cdot 2$
8:   **end while**
9:   **return** z

Problem 1.15. *What does algorithm 1.5 compute? Assume that a, b are positive integers (i.e., assume that the pre-condition is that $a, b > 0$). For which starting a, b does this algorithm terminate? In how many steps does it terminate, if it does terminate?*

Algorithm 1.5 See Problem 1.15

1:   **while** $(a > 0)$ **do**
2:        **if** $(a < b)$ **then**
3:           $(a, b) \leftarrow (2a, b - a)$
4:        **else**
5:           $(a, b) \leftarrow (a - b, 2b)$
6:        **end if**
7:   **end while**

Consider algorithm 1.6 given below.

Algorithm 1.6 Ulam's algorithm

Pre-condition: $a > 0$

  $x \longleftarrow a$

  while last three values of x not $4, 2, 1$ **do**

    if x is even **then**

        $x \longleftarrow x/2$

    else

        $x \longleftarrow 3x + 1$

    end if

  end while

This algorithm is different from all the algorithms that we have seen thus far in that there is no known proof of termination, and therefore no known proof of correctness. Observe how simple it is: for any positive integer a, set $x = a$, and repeat the following: if x is even, divide it by 2, and if it is odd, multiply it by 3 and add 1. Repeat this until the last three values obtained were $4, 2, 1$. For example, if $a = 22$, then one can check that x takes on the following values: $22, 11, 34, 17, 52, 26, 13, 40, 20, 10, 5, 16, 8, \mathbf{4}, \mathbf{2}, \mathbf{1}$, and algorithm 1.6 terminates. It is conjectured that regardless of the initial value of a, as long as a is a positive integer, algorithm 1.6 terminates. This conjecture is known as "Ulam's problem,"[2] and despite decades of work no one has been able to solve this problem.

In fact, recent work shows that variants of Ulam's problem have been shown undecidable. We will look at undecidability in Chapter 9, but [Lehtonen (2008)] showed that for a very simple variant of the problem where we let x be $3x + t$ for x in a particular set A_t (for details see the paper), there simply is no algorithm whatsoever that will decide for which initial a's the new algorithm terminates and for which it does not.

Problem 1.16. *Write a program that takes a as input and displays all the values of Ulam's problem until it sees $4, 2, 1$ at which point it stops. You have just written an almost trivial program for which there is no proof of termination. Now do an experiment: compute how many steps it takes to reach $4, 2, 1$ for all $a < N$, for some N. Any conjectures?*

---

[2]It is also called "Collatz Conjecture," "Syracuse Problem," "Kakutani's Problem," or "Hasse's Algorithm." While it is true that a rose by any other name would smell just as sweet, the preponderance of names shows that the conjecture is a very alluring mathematical problem.

1.2 Ranking algorithms

The algorithms we have seen so far in the book are classical but to some extent they are "toy examples." In this section we want to demonstrate the power and usefulness of some very well known "grown up" algorithms. We will focus on three different ranking algorithms. Ranking items is a primordial human activity, and we will take a brief look at ranking procedures that range from the ancient, such as Ramon Llull's, a 13-th century mystic and philosopher, to old, such as Marquis de Condorcet's work discussed in Section 1.2.3, to the state of the art in Google's simple and elegant PageRank discussed in the next section.

1.2.1 *PageRank*

In 1945, Vannevar Bush wrote an article in the Atlantic Monthly entitled *As we may think* [Bush (1945)], where he demonstrated an eerie prescience of the ideas that became the World Wide Web. In that gem of an article Bush pointed out that information retrieval systems are organized in a linear fashion (whether books, databases, computer memory, etc.), but that human conscious experience exhibits what he called "an associative memory." That is, the human mind has a semantic network, where we think of one thing, and that reminds us of another, etc. Bush proposed a blueprint for a human-like machine, the "Memex," which had ur-web characteristics: digitized human knowledge interconnected by associative links.

When in the early 1990s Tim Berners-Lee finally implemented the ideas of Bush in the form of HTML, and ushered in the World Wide Web, the web pages were static and the links had a navigational function. Today links often trigger complex programs such as Perl, PHP, MySQL, and while some are still navigational, many are transactional, implementing actions such as "add to shopping cart," or "update my calendar."

As there are now billions of active web pages, how does one search them to find relevant high-quality information? We accomplish this by ranking those pages that meet the search criteria; pages of a good rank will appear at the top — this way the search results will make sense to a human reader who only has to scan the first few results to (hopefully) find what he wants. These top pages are called *authoritative* pages.

In order to rank authoritative pages at the top, we make use of the fact that the web consists not only of pages, but also of *hyperlinks* that connect these pages. This hyperlink structure (which can be naturally modeled by a

directed graph) contains a lot of latent human annotation that can be used
to automatically infer authority. This is a profound observation: after all,
items ranked highly by a user are ranked so in a subjective manner; exploit-
ing the hyperlink structure allows us to connect the subjective experience
of the users with the output of an algorithm!

More specifically, by creating a hyperlink, the author gives an implicit
endorsement to a page. By mining the collective judgment expressed by
these endorsements we get a picture of the quality (or subjective perception
of the quality) of a given web page. This is very similar to our perception
of the quality of scholarly citations, where an important publication is cited
by other important publications. The question now is how do we convert
these ideas into an algorithm. A seminal answer was given by the now
famous PageRank algorithm, authored by S. Brin and L. Page, the founders
of Google — see [Brin and Page (1998)]. PageRank mines the hyperlink
structure of the web in order to infer the relative importance of the pages.

Consider Figure 1.1 which depicts a web page X, and all the pages
$T_1, T_2, T_3, \ldots, T_n$ that point to it. Given a page X, let $C(X)$ be the number
of distinct link that leave X, i.e., these are links anchored in X that point
to a page outside of X. Let $PR(X)$ be the page rank of X. We also employ
a parameter d, which we call the *damping factor*, and which we will explain
later.

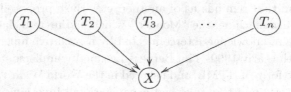

Fig. 1.1   Computing the rank of page A.

Then, the page rank of X can be computed as follows:

$$PR(X) = (1 - d) + d \left[\frac{PR(T_1)}{C(T_1)} + \frac{PR(T_2)}{C(T_2)} + \cdots + \frac{PR(T_n)}{C(T_n)} \right]. \qquad (1.4)$$

We now explain (1.4): the damping factor d is a constant $0 \leq d \leq 1$, and
usually set to .85. The formula posits the behavior of a "random surfer"
who starts clicking on links on a random page, following a link out of that
page, and clicking on links (never hitting the "back button") until the
random surfer gets bored, and starts the process from the beginning by
going to a random page. Thus, in (1.4) the $(1 - d)$ is the probability of

choosing X at random, while $\frac{PR(T_i)}{C(T_i)}$ is the probability of reaching X by coming from T_i, normalized by the number of outlinks from T_i. We make a slight adjustment to (1.4): we normalize it by the size of the web, N, that is, we divide $(1 - d)$ by N. This way, the chance of stumbling on X is adjusted to the overall size of the web.

The problem with (1.4) is that it appears to be circular. How do we compute $PR(T_i)$ in the first place? The algorithm works in stages, refining the page rank of each page at each stage. Initially, we take the egalitarian approach and assign each page a rank of $1/N$, where N is the total number of pages on the web. Then recompute all page ranks using (1.4) and the initial page ranks, and continue. After each stage $PR(X)$ gets closer to the actual value, and in fact converges fairly quickly. There are many technical issues here, such as knowing when to stop, and handling a computation involving N which may be over a trillion, but this is the PageRank algorithm in a nut shell.

Of course the web is a vast collection of heterogeneous documents, and (1.4) is too simple a formula to capture everything, and so Google search is a lot more complicated. For example, not all outlinks are treated equally: a link in larger font, or emphasized with a "`<STRONG>`" tag, will have more weight. Documents differ internally in terms of language, format such as PDF, image, text, sound, video; and externally in terms of reputation of the source, update frequency, quality, popularity, and other variables that are now taken into account by a modern search engine. The reader is directed to [Franceschet (2011)] for more information about PageRank.

Furthermore, the presence of search engines also affects the web. As the search engines direct traffic, they themselves shape the ranking of the web. A similar effect in Physics is known as the *observer effect*, where instruments alter the state of what they observe. As a simple example, consider measuring the pressure in your tires: you have to let some air out, and therefore change the pressure slightly, in order to measure it. All these fascinating issues are the subject matter of Big Data Analytics.

Problem 1.17. *Consider the following small network:*

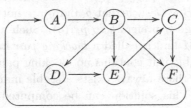

*Compute the PageRank of the different pages in this network using (1.4)
with damping factor $d = 1$, that is, assuming all navigation is done by
following links (no random jumps to other pages).*

Problem 1.18. *Write a program which computes the ranks of all the pages
in a given network of size N. Let the network be given as a 0-1 matrix,
where a 1 in position (i, j) means that there is a link from page i to page
j. Otherwise, there is a 0 in that position. Use (1.4) to compute the page
rank, starting with a value of $1/N$. You should stop when all values have
converged — does this algorithm always terminate? Also, keep track of all
the values as fractions a/b, where $\gcd(a, b) = 1$; Python has a convenient
fractions library:* `import fractions`*.*

1.2.2   *A stable marriage*

Suppose that we want to match interns with hospitals, or students with
colleges; both are instances of the *admission process problem*, and both
have a solution that optimizes, to a certain degree, the overall satisfaction
of all the parties concerned. The solution to this problem is an elegant
algorithm to solve the so called "stable marriage problem," which has been
used since the 1960s for the college admission process and for matching
interns with hospitals.

An instance of the *stable marriage problem* of size n consists of two
disjoint finite sets of equal size; a set of *boys* $B = \{b_1, b_2, \ldots, b_n\}$, and a set
of *girls* $G = \{g_1, g_2, \ldots, g_n\}$. Let "$<_i$" denote the ranking of boy b_i; that
is, $g <_i g'$ means that boy b_i prefers g over g'. Similarly, "$<^j$" denotes
the ranking of girl g_j. Each boy b_i has such a ranking (linear ordering)
$<_i$ of G which reflects his preference for the girls that he wants to marry.
Similarly each girl g_j has a ranking (linear ordering) $<^j$ of B which reflects
her preference for the boys she would like to marry.

A *matching* (or *marriage*) M is a 1-1 correspondence between B and
G. We say that b and g are *partners* in M if they are matched in M and
write $p_M(b) = g$ and also $p_M(g) = b$. A matching M is *unstable* if there
is a pair (b, g) from $B \times G$ such that b and g are not partners in M but b
prefers g to $p_M(b)$ and g prefers b to $p_M(g)$. Such a pair (b, g) is said to
block the matching M and is called a *blocking pair* for M (see figure 1.2).
A matching M is stable if it contains no blocking pairs.

It turns out that there always exists a stable marriage solution to the
matching problem. This solution can be computed with the celebrated

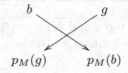

Fig. 1.2   A blocking pair: b and g prefer each other to their partners $p_M(b)$ and $p_M(g)$.

algorithm due to Gale and Shapley ([Gale and Shapley (1962)]) that outputs a stable marriage for any input B, G, regardless of the ranking[3].

The matching M is produced in stages M_s so that b_t always has a partner at the end of stage s, where $t \leq s$. However, the partners of b_t do not get better, i.e., $p_{M_t}(b_t) \leq_t p_{M_{t+1}}(b_t) \leq_t \cdots$. On the other hand, for each $g \in G$, if g has a partner at stage t, then g will have a partner at each stage $s \geq t$ and the partners do not get worse, i.e., $p_{M_t}(g) \geq^t p_{M_{t+1}}(g) \geq^t \ldots$. Thus, as s increases, the partners of b_t become less preferable and the partners of g become more preferable.

At the end of stage s, assume that we have produced a matching

$$M_s = \{(b_1, g_{1,s}), \ldots, (b_s, g_{s,s})\},$$

where the notation $g_{i,s}$ means that $g_{i,s}$ is the partner of boy b_i after the end of stage s.

We will say that partners in M_s are *engaged*. The idea is that at stage $s+1$, b_{s+1} will try to get a partner by *proposing* to the girls in G in his order of preference. When b_{s+1} proposes to a girl g_j, g_j accepts his proposal if either g_j is not currently engaged or is currently engaged to a less preferable boy b, i.e., $b_{s+1} <^j b$. In the case where g_j prefers b_{s+1} over her current partner b, then g_j breaks off the engagement with b and b then has to search for a new partner.

Problem 1.19. *Show that each b need propose at most once to each g.*

From problem 1.19 we see that we can make each boy keep a bookmark on his list of preference, and this bookmark is only moving forward. When a boy's turn to choose comes, he starts proposing from the point where his bookmark is, and by the time he is done, his bookmark moved only forward. Note that at stage $s+1$ each boy's bookmark cannot have moved beyond the girl number s on the list without choosing someone (after stage

---

[3]In 2012, the Nobel Prize in Economics was awarded to Lloyd S. Shapley and Alvin E. Roth "for the theory of stable allocations and the practice of market design," i.e., for the stable marriage algorithm.

Algorithm 1.7 Gale-Shapley

1: Stage 1: b_1 chooses his top g and $M_1 \longleftarrow \{(b_1, g)\}$
2: **for** $s = 1, \ldots, s = |B| - 1$, Stage $s + 1$: **do**
3:      $M \longleftarrow M_s$
4:      $b^* \longleftarrow b_{s+1}$
5:      **for** b^* proposes to all g's in order of preference: **do**
6:          **if** g was not engaged: **then**
7:              $M_{s+1} \longleftarrow M \cup \{(b^*, g)\}$
8:              end current stage
9:          **else if** g was engaged to b but g prefers b^*: **then**
10:             $M \longleftarrow (M - \{(b, g)\}) \cup \{(b^*, g)\}$
11:             $b^* \longleftarrow b$
12:             repeat from line 5
13:         **end if**
14:     **end for**
15: **end for**

---

s only s girls are engaged). As the boys take turns, each boy's bookmark is advancing, so some boy's bookmark (among the boys in $\{b_1, \ldots, b_{s+1}\}$) will advance eventually to a point where he must choose a girl.

The discussion in the above paragraph shows that stage $s + 1$ in algorithm 1.7 must end. The concern here was that case (ii) of stage $s+1$ might end up being circular. But the fact that the bookmarks are advancing shows that this is not possible.

Furthermore, this gives an upper bound of $(s+1)^2$ steps at stage $(s+1)$ in the procedure. This means that there are n stages, and each stage takes $O(n^2)$ steps, and hence algorithm 1.7 takes $O(n^3)$ steps altogether. The question, of course, is what do we mean by a step? Computers operate on binary strings, yet here the implicit assumption is that we compare numbers and access the lists of preferences in a single step. But the cost of these operations is negligible when compared to our idealized running time, and so we allow ourselves this poetic license to bound the overall running time.

Problem 1.20. *Show that there is exactly one girl that was not engaged at stage s but is engaged at stage $(s + 1)$ and that, for each girl g_j that is engaged in M_s, g_j will be engaged in M_{s+1} and that $p_{M_{s+1}}(g_j) <^j p_{M_s}(g_j)$. (Thus, once g_j becomes engaged, she will remain engaged and her partners will only gain in preference as the stages proceed.)*

Problem 1.21. *Suppose that* $|B| = |G| = n$. *Show that at the end of stage* n, M_n *will be a stable marriage.*

We say that a pair (b, g) is *feasible* if there exists a stable matching in which b, g are partners. We say that a matching is boy-*optimal* if every boy is paired with his highest ranked feasible partner. We say that a matching is boy-*pessimal* if every boy is paired with his lowest ranking feasible partner. Similarly, we define girl-*optimal/pessimal*.

Problem 1.22. *Show that our version of the algorithm produces a boy-optimal and girl-pessimal stable matching. Does this mean that they ordering of the boys is irrelevant?*

Problem 1.23. *Implement algorithm 1.7.*

1.2.3 *Pairwise Comparisons*

A fundamental application of algorithmic procedures is to choose the best option from among many. The selection requires a ranking procedure that guides it, but given the complexity of the world in the Information Age, the ranking procedure and selection are often done based on an extraordinary number of criteria. It may also require the chooser to provide a justification for the selection and to convince someone else that the best option has indeed been chosen. For example, imagine the scenario where a team of doctors must decide whether or not to operate on a patient [Kakiashvili *et al.* (2012)], and how important it is to both select the optimal course of action and provide a strong justification for the final selection. Indeed, a justification in this case may be as important as selecting the best option.

Considerable effort has been devoted to research in search engine ranking [Easley and Kleinberg (2010)], in the case of massive amount of highly heterogeneous items. On the other hand, relatively little work has been done in ranking smaller sets of highly similar (homogeneous) items, differentiated by a large number of criteria. Today's state of the art consists of an assortment of domain-specific *ad hoc* procedures, which are highly domain dependent: one approach in the medical profession [Kakiashvili *et al.* (2012)]; another in the world of management [Koczkodaj *et al.* (2014)], etc.

Pairwise Comparisons (PC) has a surprisingly old history for a method that to a certain degree is not widely known. The ancient beginnings are often attributed to a thirteenth century mystic and philosopher Ramon

Lull. In 2001 a manuscript of Llull's was discovered, titled *Ars notandi, Ars eleccionis, and Alia ars eleccionis* (see [Hägele and Pukelsheim (2001); Faliszewski *et al.* (2010)]) where he discussed voting systems and prefigures the PC method. The modern beginnings are attributed to the Marquis de Condorcet (see [Condorcet (1785)], written four years before the French Revolution, and nine years before losing his head to the same). Just as Llull, Condorcet applied the PC method to analyzing voting outcomes. Almost a century and a half later, Thurstone [Thurstone (1927)] refined the method and employed a psychological continuum with the scale values as the medians of the distributions of judgments.

Modern PC can be said to have started with the work of Saaty in 1977 [Saaty (1977)], who proposed a finite nine-point scale of measurements. Furthermore, Saaty introduced the *Analytic Hierarchy Process* (AHP), which is a formal method to derive ranking orders from numerical pairwise comparisons. AHP is widely used around the world for decision making, in education, industry, government, etc. [Koczkodaj (1993)] proposed a smaller five-point scale, which is less fine-grained than Saaty's nine-point, but easier to use. Note that while AHP is a respectable tool for practical applications, it is nevertheless considered by many [Dyer (1990); Janicki (2011)] as a flawed procedure that produces arbitrary rankings.

Let $X = \{x_1, x_2, \ldots, x_n\}$ be a finite set of objects to be ranked. Let a_{ij} express the numerical preference between x_i and x_j. The idea is that a_{ij} estimates "how much better" x_i is compared to x_j. Clearly, for all i, j, $a_{ij} > 0$ and $a_{ij} = 1/a_{ji}$. The intuition is that if $a_{ij} > 1$, then x_i is preferred over x_j by that factor. So, for example, Apple's Retina display has four times the resolution of the Thunderbolt display, and so if x_1 is Retina, and x_2 is Thunderbolt, we could say that the image quality of x_1 is four times better than the image quality of x_2, and so $a_{12} = 4$, and $a_{21} = 1/4$. The assignment of values to the a_{ij}'s are often done subjectively by human judges. Let $A = [a_{ij}]$ be a *pairwise comparison matrix*, also known as a *preference matrix*. We say that a pairwise comparison matrix is *consistent* if for all i, j, k we have that $a_{ij}a_{jk} = a_{ik}$. Otherwise, it is *inconsistent*.

Theorem 1.24 (Saaty). *A pairwise comparison matrix A is consistent if and only if there exist $w_1, w_2, \ldots, w_n$ such that $a_{ij} = w_i/w_j$.*

Problem 1.25. *Note that the w_i's that appear in Theorem 1.24 create a ranking, in that x_j is preferable to x_i if and only if $w_i < w_j$. Suppose that A is a consistent PC matrix. How can you extract the w_i's from A?*

In practice, the subjective evaluations a_{ij} are seldom consistent, which poses a set of problems ([Janicki and Zhai (2011)]), namely, how do we: (i) measure inconsistency and what level is acceptable? (ii) remove inconsistencies, or lower them to an acceptable level? (iii) derive the values w_i starting with an inconsistent ranking A? (iv) justify a certain method for removing inconsistencies? An inconsistent matrix has value in that the degree of inconsistency measures, to some extent, the degree of subjectiveness of the referees. But we need to be able to answer the questions in the above paragraph before we can take advantage in a meaningful way of an inconsistent matrix.

Problem 1.26. *[Bozóki and Rapcsák (2008)] propose several methods for measuring inconsistencies in a matrix (see especially Table 1 on page 161 of their article). Consider implementing some of these measures. Can you propose a method for resolving inconsistencies in a PC matrix?*

1.3 Answers to selected problems

Problem 1.1. $(\forall I \in \mathcal{I}_A)[\exists O(O = A(I)) \wedge (\alpha_A(I) \rightarrow \beta_A(A(I)))]$. This says that for any well formed input I, there is an output, i.e., the algorithm A terminates. This is expressed with $\exists O(O = A(I))$. Also, it says that if the well formed input I satisfies the pre-condition, stated as the antecendent $\alpha_A(I)$, then the output satisfies the post-condition, stated as the consequent $\beta_A(A(I))$.

Problem 1.2. Clearly,

$$an^2 + bn + c \ge an^2 - |b|n - |c| = n^2(a - |b|/n - |c|/n^2) \qquad (1.5)$$

$|b|$ is finite, so $\exists n_b \in \mathbb{N}$ such that $|b|/n_b \le a/4$. Similarly, $\exists n_c \in \mathbb{N}$ such that $|c|/n_c^2 \le a/4$. Let $n_0 = max\{n_b, n_c\}$. For $n \ge n_0$, $a - |b|/n_0 - |c|/n_0^2 \ge a - a/4 - a/4 = a/2$. This, combined with (1.5), grants:

$$\frac{a}{2}n^2 \le an^2 + bn + c$$

for all $n \ge n_0$. We need only to assign c_3 the value $a/2$ to complete the proof that $an^2 + bn + c \in \Omega(n^2)$.

Next we deal with the general polynomial with a positive leading coefficient. Let

$$p(n) = \sum_{i=1}^{k} a_i n^i = n^k \sum_{i=1}^{k} a_i/n^{k-i},$$

where $a_k > 0$. Clearly $p(n) \leq n^k \sum_{i=1}^{k} |a_i|$ for all $n \in \mathbb{N}$, so $p(n) = O(n^k)$. Moreover, every a_i is finite, so for each $i \in \mathbb{N}$ such that $0 \leq i \leq k - 1$, $\exists n_i$ such that $a_i/n^{k-i} \leq a_k/2k$ for all $n \geq n_i$. Let n_0 be the maximum of these n_i's. $p(n)$ can be rewritten as $n^k(a_k + \sum_{i=0}^{k-1} a_i/n^{k-i})$, so

$$p(n) \geq n^k(a_k - \sum_{i=0}^{k-1} a_i/n^{k-i}).$$

We have shown that for $n \geq n_0$, $\sum_{i=0}^{k-1} a_i/n^{k-i} \leq a_k - k(a_k/2k) = a_k/2$, so let $c = a_k/2$. For all $n \geq n_0$, $p(n) \geq (a_k - a_k/2)n^k = cn^k$. Thus, $p(n) = \Omega(n^k)$.

We have shown that $p(n) \in O(n^k)$ and $p(n) \in \Omega(n^k)$, so $p(n) = \Theta(n^k)$.

Problem 1.3. The while loop starts with $r = x$, and then y is subtracted each time; this is bounded by x (the slowest case, when $y = 1$). Each time the while loop executes, it tests $y \leq r$, and recomputes r, q, and so it costs 3 steps. Adding the original two assignments ($q \leftarrow 0, r \leftarrow x$), we get a total of $3x + 2$ steps. Note that we assume that x, y are presented in binary (the usual encoding), and that it takes $\log_2 x$ bits to encode x, and so the running time is $3 \cdot 2^{\log_2 x} + 2$, i.e., the running time is *exponential* in the length of the input! This is not a desirable running time; if x were big, say 1,000 bits, and y small, this algorithm would take longer than the lifetime of the sun (10 billion years) to end. There are much faster algorithms for division such as the Newton-Raphson method.

Problem 1.4. The original precondition (under which the algorithm is correct) is:

$$x \geq 0 \wedge y > 0 \wedge x, y \in \mathbb{N}$$

where $\mathbb{N} = \{0, 1, 2, \dots\}$. So in the first case our work has already been done for us; any member of $\mathbb{Z}$ which is ≥ 0 is also in $\mathbb{N}$ (and any member of $\mathbb{N}$ is in $\mathbb{Z}$), so these preconditions are equivalent. Given that the algorithm was correct under the original precondition, it is also correct under the new one. In the second case it is not correct: consider $x = -5$ and $y = 2$, so initially $r = -5$, and the loop would not execute, and $r \geq 0$ in the post-condition would not be true.

Problem 1.6. First observe that if u divides x and y, then for any $a, b \in \mathbb{Z}$ u also divides $ax + by$. Thus, if $i|m$ and $i|n$, then

$$i|(m - qn) = r = \text{rem}(m, n).$$

So i divides both n and $\text{rem}(m, n)$, and so i has to be bounded by their greatest common divisor, i.e., $i \leq \gcd(n, \text{rem}(m, n))$. As this is true for every i, it is in particular true for $i = \gcd(m, n)$; thus $\gcd(m, n) \leq \gcd(n, \text{rem}(m, n))$. Conversely, suppose that $i|n$ and $i|\text{rem}(m, n)$. Then $i|m = qn + r$, so $i \leq \gcd(m, n)$, and again, $\gcd(n, \text{rem}(m, n))$ meets the condition of being such an i, so we have $\gcd(n, \text{rem}(m, n)) \leq \gcd(m, n)$. Both inequalities taken together give us $\gcd(m, n) = \gcd(n, \text{rem}(m, n))$.

Problem 1.7. Let r_i be r after the i-th iteration of the loop. Note that $r_0 = \text{rem}(m, n) = \text{rem}(a, b) \geq 0$, and in fact every $r_i \geq 0$ by definition of remainder. Furthermore:

$$\begin{aligned} r_{i+1} &= \text{rem}(m_{i+1}, n_{i+1}) \\ &= \text{rem}(n_i, r_i) \\ &= \text{rem}(n_i, \text{rem}(m_i, n_i)) \\ &= \text{rem}(n_i, r_i) < r_i. \end{aligned}$$

and so we have a decreasing, and yet non-negative, sequence of numbers; by the LNP this must terminate. To establish the complexity, we count the number of iterations of the while-loop, ignoring the swaps (so to get the actual number of iterations we should multiply the result by two).

Suppose that $m = qn + r$. If $q \geq 2$, then $m \geq 2n$, and since $m \leftarrow n$, m decreases by at least a half. If $q = 1$, then $m = n + r$ where $0 < r < n$, and we examine two cases: $r \leq n/2$, so n decreases by at least a half as $n \leftarrow r$, or $r > n/2$, in which case $m = n + r > n + n/2 = 3/2n$, so since $m \leftarrow n$, m decreases by $1/3$. Thus, it can be said that in all cases at least one element in the pair decreases by at least $1/3$, and so it can be said that the running time is bounded by k such that $3^k = m \cdot n$, and so by $O(\log(m \cdot n)) = O(\log m + \log n)$. As inputs are assumed to be given in binary, we can conclude from this that the running time is linear in the size of the input.

A tighter analysis, known as Lamé's theorem, can be found in [Cormen *et al.* (2009)] (theorem 31.11), which states that for any integer $k \geq 1$, if $a > b \geq 1$ and $b < F_{k+1}$, where F_i is the i-th Fibonacci number (see Problem 9.5), then it takes fewer than k iterations of the while-loop (not counting swaps) to run Eucild's algorithm.

Problem 1.8. When $m < n$ then $\text{rem}(m, n) = m$, and so $m' = n$ and $n' = m$. Thus, when $m < n$ we execute one iteration of the loop only to swap m and n. In order to be more efficient, we could add line 2.5 in algorithm 1.2 saying **if** $(m < n)$ **then** swap(m, n).

Problem 1.9. (a) We show that if $d = \gcd(a, b)$, then there exist u, v such that $au + bv = d$. Let $S = \{ax + by | ax + by > 0\}$; clearly $S \neq \emptyset$. By LNP there exists a least $g \in S$. We show that $g = d$. Let $a = q \cdot g + r$, $0 \leq r < g$. Suppose that $r > 0$; then

$$r = a - q \cdot g = a - q(ax_0 + by_0) = a(1 - qx_0) + b(-qy_0).$$

Thus, $r \in S$, but $r < g$—contradiction. So $r = 0$, and so $g|a$, and a similar argument shows that $g|b$. It remains to show that g is greater than any other common divisor of a, b. Suppose $c|a$ and $c|b$, so $c|(ax_0 + by_0)$, and so $c|g$, which means that $c \leq g$. Thus $g = \gcd(a, b) = d$.

(b) Euclid's extended algorithm is algorithm 1.8. Note that in the algorithm, the assignments in line 1 and line 8 are evaluated left to right.

Algorithm 1.8 Extended Euclid's algorithm

Pre-condition: $m > 0, n > 0$
1:   $a \leftarrow 0$; $x \leftarrow 1$; $b \leftarrow 1$; $y \leftarrow 0$; $c \leftarrow m$; $d \leftarrow n$
2:   **loop**
3:         $q \leftarrow \mathrm{div}(c, d)$
4:         $r \leftarrow \mathrm{rem}(c, d)$
5:         **if** $r = 0$ **then**
6:            stop
7:         **end if**
8:         $c \leftarrow d$; $d \leftarrow r$; $t \leftarrow x$; $x \leftarrow a$; $a \leftarrow t - qa$; $t \leftarrow y$; $y \leftarrow b$; $b \leftarrow t - qb$
9: **end loop**

Post-condition: $am + bn = d = \gcd(m, n)$

We can prove the correctness of algorithm 1.8 by using the following loop invariant which consists of four assertions:

$$am + bn = d, \quad xm + yn = c, \quad d > 0, \quad \gcd(c, d) = \gcd(m, n). \qquad \text{(LI)}$$

The basis case:

$$am + bn = 0 \cdot m + 1 \cdot n = n = d$$
$$xm + yn = 1 \cdot m + 0 \cdot n = m = c$$

both by line 1. Then $d = n > 0$ by pre-condition, and $\gcd(c, d) = \gcd(m, n)$ by line 1. For the induction step assume that the "primed" variables are the result of one more full iteration of the loop on the "un-primed" variables:

$$a'm + b'n = (x - qa)m + (y - qb)n \qquad \text{by line 8}$$
$$= (xm - yn) - q(am + bn)$$
$$= c - qd \qquad \text{by induction hypothesis}$$
$$= r \qquad \text{by lines 3 and 4}$$
$$= d' \qquad \text{by line 8}$$

Then $x'm = y'n = am + bn = d = c'$ where the first equality is by line 8, the second by the induction hypothesis, and the third by line 8. Also, $d' = r$ by line 8, and the algorithm would stop in line 5 if $r = 0$; on the other hand, from line 4, $r = \text{rem}(c, d) \geq 0$, so $r > 0$ and so $d' > 0$. Finally,

$$\gcd(c', d') = \gcd(d, r) \qquad \text{by line 8}$$
$$= \gcd(d, \text{rem}(c, d)) \qquad \text{by line 4}$$
$$= \gcd(c, d) \qquad \text{see problem 1.6}$$
$$= \gcd(m, n). \qquad \text{by induction hypothesis}$$

For partial correctness it is enough to show that if the algorithm terminates, the post-condition holds. If the algorithm terminates, then $r = 0$, so $\text{rem}(c, d) = 0$ and $\gcd(c, d) = \gcd(d, 0) = d$. On the other hand, by (LI), we have that $am + bn = d$, so $am + bn = d = \gcd(c, d)$ and $\gcd(c, d) = \gcd(m, n)$.

(c) On pp. 292–293 in [Delfs and Knebl (2007)] there is a nice analysis of their version of the algorithm. They bound the running time in terms of Fibonacci numbers, and obtain the desired bound on the running time.

Problem 1.11. For partial correctness of algorithm 1.3, we show that if the pre-condition holds, and *if* the algorithm terminates, then the post-condition will hold. So assume the pre-condition, and suppose first that A is *not* a palindrome. Then there exists a smallest i_0 (there exists one, and so by the LNP there exists a smallest one) such that $A[i_0] \neq A[n - i_0 + 1]$, and so, after the first $i_0 - 1$ iteration of the while-loop, we know from the loop invariant that $i = (i_0 - 1) + 1 = i_0$, and so line 4 is executed and the algorithm returns F. Therefore, "A not a palindrome" $\Rightarrow$ "return F."

Suppose now that A *is* a palindrome. Then line 4 is never executed (as no such i_0 exists), and so after the $k = \lfloor \frac{n}{2} \rfloor$-th iteration of the while-loop, we know from the loop invariant that $i = \lfloor \frac{n}{2} \rfloor + 1$ and so the while-loop is not executed any more, and the algorithm moves on to line 8, and returns T. Therefore, "A is a palindrome" $\Rightarrow$ "return T."

Therefore, the post-condition, "return T iff A is a palindrome," holds. Note that we have only used part of the loop invariant, that is we used the fact that after the k-th iteration, $i = k + 1$; it still holds that after the k-th iteration, for $1 \leq j \leq k$, $A[j] = A[n - j + 1]$, but we do not need this fact in the above proof.

To show that the algorithm terminates, let $d_i = \lfloor \frac{n}{2} \rfloor - i$. By the pre-condition, we know that $n \geq 1$. The sequence $d_1, d_2, d_3, \ldots$ is a decreasing sequence of positive integers (because $i \leq \lfloor \frac{n}{2} \rfloor$), so by the LNP it is finite, and so the loop terminates.

Problem 1.12. It is very easy once you realize that in Python the slice [::-1] generates the reverse string. So, to check whether string s is a palindrome, all we do is write s == s[::-1].

Problem 1.13. The solution is given by algorithm 1.9

Algorithm 1.9 Powers of 2
___
Pre-condition: $n \geq 1$
  $x \leftarrow n$
  while $(x > 1)$ **do**
    if $(2|x)$ **then**
      $x \leftarrow x/2$
    else
      stop and return "no"
    end if
  end while
  return "yes"
Post-condition: "yes" $\iff$ n is a power of 2

Let the loop invariant be: "x is a power of 2 iff n is a power of 2."

We show the loop invariant by induction on the number of iterations of the main loop. Basis case: zero iterations, and since $x \leftarrow n$, $x = n$, so obviously x is a power of 2 iff n is a power of 2. For the induction step, note that if we ever get to update x, we have $x' = x/2$, and clearly x' is a power of 2 iff x is. Note that the algorithm always terminates (let $x_0 = n$, and $x_{i+1} = x_i/2$, and apply the LNP as usual).

We can now prove correctness: if the algorithms returns "yes", then after the last iteration of the loop $x = 1 = 2^0$, and by the loop invariant n is a power of 2. If, on the other hand, n is a power of 2, then so is every x, so eventually $x = 1$, and so the algorithm returns "yes".

Problem 1.14. Algorithm 1.4 computes the product of m and n, that is, the returned $z = m \cdot n$. A good loop invariant is $x \cdot y + z = m \cdot n$.

Problem 1.17. We start by initializing all nodes to have rank $1/6$, and then repeatedly apply the following formulas, based on (1.4):

$$\mathrm{PR}(A) = \mathrm{PR}(F)$$
$$\mathrm{PR}(B) = \mathrm{PR}(A)$$
$$\mathrm{PR}(C) = \mathrm{PR}(B)/4 + \mathrm{PR}(E)$$
$$\mathrm{PR}(D) = \mathrm{PR}(B)/4$$
$$\mathrm{PR}(E) = \mathrm{PR}(B)/4 + \mathrm{PR}(D)$$
$$\mathrm{PR}(F) = \mathrm{PR}(B)/4 + \mathrm{PR}(C)$$

The result is given in figure 1.3.

	0	1	2	3	4	5	6	...	17
A	0.17	0.17	0.21	0.25	0.29	0.18	0.20		0.22
B	0.17	0.17	0.17	0.21	0.25	0.29	0.18		0.22
C	0.17	0.21	0.25	0.13	0.14	0.16	0.19	...	0.17
D	0.17	0.04	0.04	0.04	0.05	0.06	0.07		0.06
E	0.17	0.21	0.08	0.08	0.09	0.11	0.14		0.11
F	0.17	0.21	0.25	0.29	0.18	0.20	0.23		0.22
Total	1.00	1.00	1.00	1.00	1.00	1.00	1.00	...	1.00

Fig. 1.3 Pagerank convergence in Problem 1.17. Note that the table is obtained with a spreadsheet: all values are rounded to two decimal places, but column 1 is obtained by placing $1/6$ in each row, column 2 is obtained from column 1 with the formulas, and all the remaining columns are obtained by "dragging" column 2 all the way to the end. The values converged (more or less) in column 17.

Problem 1.19. After b proposed to g for the first time, whether this proposal was successful or not, the partners of g could have only gotten better. Thus, there is no need for b to try again.

Problem 1.20. b_{s+1} proposes to the girls according to his list of preference; a g ends up accepting, and if the g who accepted b_{s+1} was free, she is the new one with a partner. Otherwise, some $b^* \in \{b_1, \ldots, b_s\}$ became disengaged, and we repeat the same argument. The g's disengage only if a better b proposes, so it is true that $p_{M_{s+1}}(g_j) <^j p_{M_s}(g_j)$.

Problem 1.21. Suppose that we have a blocking pair $\{b, g\}$ (meaning that $\{(b, g'), (b', g)\} \subseteq M_n$, but b prefers g to g', and g prefers b to b'). Either b

came after b' or before. If b came before b', then g would have been with b or someone better when b' came around, so g would not have become engaged to b'. On the other hand, since (b', g) is a pair, no better offer has been made to g after the offer of b', so b could not have come after b'. In either case we get an impossibility, and so there is no blocking pair $\{b, g\}$.

Problem 1.22. To show that the matching is boy-optimal, we argue by contradiction. Let "*g is an optimal partner for b*" mean that among all the stable matchings g is the best partner that b can get.

We run the Gale-Shapley algorithm, and let b be the first boy who is rejected by his optimal partner g. This means that g has already been paired with some b', and g prefers b' to b. Furthermore, g is at least as desirable to b' as his own optimal partner (since the proposal of b is the first time during the run of the algorithm that a boy is rejected by his optimal partner). Since g is optimal for b, we know (by definition) that there exists some stable matching S where (b, g) is a pair. On the other hand, the optimal partner of b' is ranked (by b' of course) at most as high as g, and since g is taken by b, whoever b' is paired with in S, say g', b' prefers g to g'. This gives us an unstable pairing, because $\{b', g\}$ prefer each other to the partners they have in S.

Yes, this means that the ordering of the boys is immaterial, because there is a unique boy-optimal matching, and it is independent of the ordering of the boys.

To show that the Gale-Shapley algorithm is girl-pessimal, we use the fact that it is boy-optimal (which we just showed). Again, we argue by contradiction. Suppose there is a stable matching S where g is paired with b, and g prefers b' to b, where (b', g) is the result of the Gale-Shapley algorithm. By boy-optimality, we know that in S we have (b', g'), where g' is not higher on the preference list of b' than g, and since g is already paired with b, we know that g' is actually lower. This says that S is unstable since $\{b', g\}$ would rather be together than with their partners.

1.4   Notes

This book is about proving things about algorithms; their correctness, their termination, their running time, etc. The art of mathematical proofs is a difficult art to master; a very good place to start is [Velleman (2006)].

On page vii we mentioned the North-East blackout of 2003. At the time the author was living in Toronto, Canada, on the 14th floor of an apartment building (which really was the 13th floor, but as number 13 was outlawed in Toronto elevators, after the 12th floor, the next button on the elevator was 14). After the first 24 hours, the emergency generators gave out, and we all had to climb the stairs to our floors; we would leave the building, and scavenge the neighborhood for food and water, but as refrigeration was out in most places, it was not easy to find fresh items. In short, we really felt the consequences of that algorithmic error intimately.

In the footnote to Problem 1.10 we mention the Python library `matplotlib`. Below we provide a simple example, plotting the functions $f(x) = x^3$ and $h(x) = -x^3$ over the interval $[0, 10]$ using this library:

```
import matplotlib.pyplot as plt
import numpy as np

def f(x):
    return x**3
def h(x):
  return -x**3

Input = np.arange(0,10.1,.5)
Outputf = [f(x) for x in Input]
Outputh = [h(x) for x in Input]

plt.plot(Input,Outputf,'r.',label='f - label')
plt.plot(Input,Outputh,'b--',label='h - label')
plt.xlabel('This is the X axis label')
plt.ylabel('This is the Y axis label')
plt.suptitle('This is the title')
plt.legend()
plt.show()
```

Of course, `matplotlib` has lots of features; see the documentation for more complex examples.

The palindrome `madamimadam` comes from Joyce's *Ulysses*. We discussed the string manipulating facilities of Python in the section on palindromes, Section 1.1.4, but perhaps the most powerful language for string manipulations is Perl. For example, suppose that we have a text that contains hashtags which are words of characters that start with '#', and we wish to collect all those hashtags into an array. One trembles at the prospect of having to implement this in, say, the C programming language, but in Perl this can be accomplished in one line:

```
@TAGS = ($TEXT =~ m/\#([a-zA-Z0-9]+)/g);
```

where $TEXT contains the text with zero or more hashtags, and the array @TAGS will be a list of all the hashtags that occur in $TEXT without the '#' prefix. For the great pleasure of Perl see [Schwartz *et al.* (2011)].

Search engines are complex and vast software systems, and ranking pages is not the only technical issue that has to be solved. For example, parsing keywords to select relevant pages (pages that contain the keywords), before any ranking is done on these pages, is also a challenging task: the search system has to solve many problems, such as *synonymy* (multiple ways to say the same thing) and *polysemy* (multiple meanings), and many others. See [Miller (1995)].

Section 1.2.2 is based on §2 in [Cenzer and Remmel (2001)]. For another presentation of the Stable Marriage problem see chapter 1 in [Kleinberg and Tardos (2006)]. The reference to the Marquis de Condorcet in the first sentence of section 1.2.2 comes from the PhD thesis of Yun Zhai ([Zhai (2010)]), written under the supervision of Ryszard Janicki. In that thesis, Yun Zhai references [Arrow (1951)] as the source of the remark regarding the Marquis de Condorcet's early attempts at pairwise ranking. There is a wonderfully biting description of Condorcet and his ideas in Roger Kimball's *The Fortunes of Permanence* [Kimball (2012)], pp. 237–244. Condercet may have given us the method of Pairwise Comparisons, but he was a tragic figure of the Enlightenment: he promised *"perfectionnement même de l'espèce humaine"* ("the absolute perfection of the human race"), but his utopian ideas were the precursor of countless hacks who insisted on perfecting man whether he wanted it or not, ushering in the inevitable tyrannical excesses that are the culmination of utopian dreams.

Professor Thomas L. Saaty (Theorem 1.24) died on August 14, 2017. He was a distinguished professor at the University of Pittsburghs Katz School of Business. The government of Poland gave Prof. Saaty a national award after its use of his theory AHP for making decisions resulted in the country initially not joining the European Union.

Chapter 2

Greedy Algorithms

> It may be profitable to you to
> reflect, in future, that there
> never were greed and cunning
> in the world yet, that did not
> do too much, and overreach
> themselves.
>
> D. Copperfield, [Dickens (1850)]

Greedy algorithms are algorithms prone to instant gratification. They make choices that are *locally optimum*, hoping that they will lead to a *global optimum* at the end. An example of a greedy procedure is the dispensing of change by a convenience store clerk. In order to use the fewest coins possible, the clerk gives out the coins of the highest value for as long as possible, moving on to the next lower denomination when that is no longer possible, and repeats.

Greediness is a simple strategy that works well with some computational problems but fails with others. In the case of cash dispensing, if we have coins of value $1, 5, 25$ the greedy procedure always produces the smallest possible number of coins, but the same is not true for $1, 10, 25$. Just consider dispensing 30, which greedily is $25, 1, 1, 1, 1, 1$, while $10, 10, 10$ is optimal.

2.1 Minimum cost spanning trees

We represent finite graphs with adjacency matrices. Given a directed or undirected graph $G = (V, E)$, its *adjacency matrix* is a matrix A_G of size $n \times n$, where $n = |V|$, such that entry (i, j) is 1 if (i, j) is an edge in G, and it is 0 otherwise.

An adjacency matrix itself can be easily encoded as a string over $\{0, 1\}$. That is, given A_G of size $n \times n$, let $s_G \in \{0, 1\}^{n^2}$, where s_G is simply the concatenation of the rows of A_G. We can check directly from s_G if (i, j) is an edge by checking if position $(i - 1)n + j$ in s_G contains a 1.

An *undirected graph* G is a pair (V, E) where V is a set of *vertices*, or *nodes*, and $E \subseteq V \times V$ and $(u, v) \in E$ iff $(v, u) \in E$, and $(u, u) \notin E$. The *degree* of a vertex v is the number of edges touching v. A *path* in G between v_1 and v_k is a sequence $v_1, v_2, \ldots, v_k$ such that each $(v_i, v_{i+1}) \in E$. G is *connected* if between every pair of distinct nodes there is a path. A *cycle* is a simply closed path $v_1, \ldots, v_k, v_1$ with $v_1, \ldots, v_k$ all distinct, and $k \geq 3$. A graph is *acyclic* if it has no cycles. A *tree*, by definition, is a connected acyclic graph. A *spanning tree* of a connected graph G is a subset $T \subseteq E$ of the edges such that (V, T) is a tree. In other words, the edges in T must connect all nodes of G and contain no cycles.

If G has a cycle, then there is more than one spanning tree for G, and in general G may have many spanning trees, but each spanning tree has the same number of edges.

Lemma 2.1. *Every tree with n nodes has exactly $n - 1$ edges.*

Problem 2.2. *Prove lemma 2.1. (Hint: first show that every tree has a leaf, i.e., a node of degree one. Then show the lemma by induction on n.)*

Lemma 2.3. *A graph with n nodes and more than $n - 1$ edges must contain at least one cycle.*

Problem 2.4. *Prove lemma 2.3.*

It follows from lemmas 2.1 and 2.3 that if a graph is a tree, i.e., it is acyclic and connected, then it must have $(n - 1)$ edges. If it does *not* have $(n - 1)$ edges, then it is either not acyclic, or it is not connected. If it has less than $(n - 1)$ edges, it is certainly not connected, and if it has more than $(n - 1)$ edges, it is certainly not acyclic.

It is natural to assign costs to edges in a graph, as edges may represent distances, bandwidth, or costs of getting from A to B in general. Let $c(e)$ denote the cost of edge e, where $c(e)$ is a non-negative real number. The total cost of a graph G, $c(G)$, is the sum of the costs of all the edges in G. We say that T is a *minimum cost spanning tree (MCST)* for G if T is a spanning tree for G and given any spanning tree T' for G, $c(T) \leq c(T')$.

Given a graph $G = (V, E)$, and a cost function c associated with the edges in E, we want to find a MCST. It turns out, fortuitously, that an obvious greedy algorithm—known as Kruskal's algorithm—works. The algorithm is: sort the edges in non-decreasing order of costs, so that $c(e_1) \leq c(e_2) \leq \ldots \leq c(e_m)$, and add the edges one at a time, except when including an edge would form a cycle with the edges added already.

Algorithm 2.1 Kruskal

1: Sort the edges: $c(e_1) \leq c(e_2) \leq \ldots \leq c(e_m)$
2: $T \longleftarrow \emptyset$
3: **for** $i : 1..m$ **do**
4:      **if** $T \cup \{e_i\}$ has no cycle **then**
5:          $T \longleftarrow T \cup \{e_i\}$
6:      **end if**
7: **end for**

But how do we test for a cycle, i.e., execute line 4 in algorithm 2.1? At the end of each iteration of the for-loop, the set T of edges divides the vertices V into a collection $V_1, \ldots, V_k$ of *connected components*. That is, V is the disjoint union of $V_1, \ldots, V_k$, each V_i forms a connected graph using edges from T, and no edge in T connects V_i and V_j, if $i \neq j$. A simple way to keep track of $V_1, \ldots, V_k$ is to use an array $D[i]$ where $D[i] = j$ if vertex $i \in V_j$. Initialize D by setting $D[i] \longleftarrow i$ for every $i = 1, 2, \ldots, n$.

To check whether $e_i = (r, s)$ forms a cycle within T, it is enough to check whether $D[r] = D[s]$. If e_i does not form a cycle within T, then we update: $T \longleftarrow T \cup \{(r, s)\}$, and we merge the component $D[r]$ with $D[s]$ as shown in algorithm 2.2.

Algorithm 2.2 Merging components

$k \longleftarrow D[r]$
$l \longleftarrow D[s]$
for $j : 1..n$ **do**
     if $D[j] = l$ **then**
         $D[j] \longleftarrow k$
     end if
end for

Problem 2.5. *Given that the edges can be ordered in m^2 steps, with, for example, insertion sort, what is the running time of algorithm 2.1? For a short discussion of sorting algorithms see the Notes (Section 2.5).*

Problem 2.6. *Write a program that implements algorithm 2.1 with algorithm 2.2 for keeping track of connected components. Assume that the input is given as an $n \times n$ adjacency matrix.*

We now prove that Kruskal's algorithm works. It is not immediately clear that Kruskal's algorithm yields a spanning tree, let alone a MCST. To see that the resulting collection T of edges is a spanning tree for G, assuming that G is connected, we must show that (V, T) is connected and acyclic.

It is obvious that T is acyclic, because we never add an edge that results in a cycle. To show that (V, T) is connected, we reason as follows. Let u and v be two distinct nodes in V. Since G is connected, there is a path p connecting u and v in G. The algorithm considers each edge e_i of G in turn, and puts e_i in T *unless* $T \cup \{e_i\}$ forms a cycle. But in the latter case, there must already be a path in T connecting the end points of e_i, so deleting e_i does not disconnect the graph.

This argument can be formalized by showing that the following statement is an invariant of the loop in Kruskal's algorithm:

$$\text{The edge set } T \cup \{e_{i+1}, \ldots, e_m\} \text{ connects all nodes in } V. \tag{2.1}$$

Lemma 2.7. *Algorithm 2.1 outputs a tree T provided that G was connected.*

Problem 2.8. *Prove Lemma 2.7 to show that given a connected G, algorithm 2.1 outputs a T that is both connected and acyclic. In order to prove that T is connected, show that (2.1) is a loop invariant. In the induction step, show that if (2.1) holds after execution i of the loop, then $T \cup \{e_{i+2}, \ldots, e_m\}$ connects all nodes of V after execution $(i + 1)$ of the loop. Conclude by induction that (2.1) holds for all i. Finally, show how to use this loop invariant to prove that T is connected. How can you argue that T is acyclic?*

Problem 2.9. *Suppose that $G = (V, E)$ is not connected. Show that in this case, when G is given to Kruskal's algorithm as input, the algorithm computes a spanning forest of G. Define first the notions of a connected component and spanning forest. Then give a formal proof using the idea of a loop invariant, as in problem 2.8.*

To show that the spanning tree resulting from the algorithm is in fact a MCST, we reason that after each iteration of the loop, the set T of edges can be extended to a MCST using edges that have *not yet* been considered. Hence after termination, all edges have been considered, so T must itself be a MCST. We say that a set T of edges of G is *promising* if T can be extended to a MCST for G, that is, T is promising if there exists a MCST T' such that $T \subseteq T'$.

Lemma 2.10. " *T is promising*" *is a loop invariant for Kruskal's algorithm.*

Proof. The proof is by induction on the number of iterations of the main loop of Kruskal's algorithm. Basis case: at this stage the algorithm has gone through the loop zero times, and initially T is the empty set, which is obviously promising (the empty set is a subset of any set).

Induction step: We assume that T is promising, and show that T continues being promising after one more iteration of the loop.

Notice that the edges used to expand T to a spanning tree must come from those not yet considered, because the edges that have been considered are either in T already, or have been rejected because they form a cycle. We examine by cases what happens after edge e_i has been considered:

Case 1: e_i is rejected. T remains unchanged, and it is still promising. There is one subtle point: T was promising before the loop was executed, meaning that there was a subset of edges $S \subseteq \{e_i, \ldots, e_m\}$ that extended T to a MCST, i.e., $T \cup S$ is a MCST. But after the loop is executed, the edges extending T to a MCST would come from $\{e_{i+1}, \ldots, e_m\}$; but this is not a problem, as e_i could not be part of S (as then $T \cup S$ would contain a cycle), so $S \subseteq \{e_{i+1}, \ldots, e_m\}$, and so S is still a candidate for extending T to a MCST, even *after* the execution of the loop. Thus T remains promising after the execution of the loop, though the edges extending it to a MCST come from a smaller set (i.e., not containing e_i).

Case 2: e_i is accepted. We must show that $T \cup \{e_i\}$ is still promising. Since T is promising, there is a MCST T_1 such that $T \subseteq T_1$. We consider two subcases.

Subcase a: $e_i \in T_1$. Then obviously $T \cup \{e_i\}$ is promising.

Subcase b: $e_i \notin T_1$. Then, according to the Exchange Lemma below, there is an edge e_j in $T_1 - T_2$, where T_2 is the spanning tree resulting from the algorithm, such that $T_3 = (T_1 \cup \{e_i\}) - \{e_j\}$ is a spanning tree. Notice that $i < j$, since otherwise e_j would have been rejected from T and thus would form a cycle in T and so also in T_1. Therefore $c(e_i) \leq c(e_j)$, so $c(T_3) \leq c(T_1)$, so T_3 must also be a MCST. Since $T \cup \{e_i\} \subseteq T_3$, it follows that $T \cup \{e_i\}$ is promising.

This finishes the proof of the induction step. $\qquad\square$

Consider the graph in figure 2.1, and a run of Kruskal's algorithm represented in figure 2.2, starting in the top-left graph, continuing right, then next row of graph, going left to right, ending in the bottom-right corner with the resulting MCST.

Fig. 2.1 All edges have cost 1.

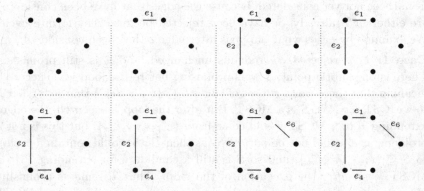

Fig. 2.2 Run of Kruskal's algorithm on graph in Figure 2.1.

Initially, in the top-left corner, we have no edges and $T = \emptyset$, and in each iteration we consider the next edge, resulting in the following:

Iteration	Edge	Current T	MCST extending T
0		$\emptyset$	$\{e_1, e_3, e_4, e_7\}$
1	e_1	$\{e_1\}$	$\{e_1, e_3, e_4, e_7\}$
2	e_2	$\{e_1, e_2\}$	$\{e_1, e_2, e_4, e_7\}$
3	e_3	$\{e_1, e_2\}$	$\{e_1, e_2, e_4, e_7\}$
4	e_4	$\{e_1, e_2, e_4\}$	$\{e_1, e_2, e_4, e_7\}$
5	e_5	$\{e_1, e_2, e_4\}$	$\{e_1, e_2, e_4, e_7\}$
6	e_6	$\{e_1, e_2, e_4, e_6\}$	$\{e_1, e_2, e_4, e_6\}$
7	e_7	$\{e_1, e_2, e_4, e_6\}$	$\{e_1, e_2, e_4, e_6\}$

Note that the algorithm considers the edges in the order of their indices, i.e., $e_1, e_2, e_3, e_4, e_5, e_6, e_7$, and that the cost of all these edges is 1. (Thus, any ordering of these edges would yield a MCST, but not necessarily the same MCST as the canonical ordering.)

Lemma 2.11 (Exchange Lemma). *Let G be a connected graph, and let T_1 and T_2 be any two spanning trees for G. For every edge e in $T_2 - T_1$ there is an edge e' in $T_1 - T_2$ such that $T_1 \cup \{e\} - \{e'\}$ is a spanning tree for G. (See figure 2.3.)*

Fig. 2.3   Exchange lemma.

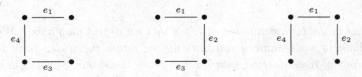

Fig. 2.4   Example of the exchange lemma: the left-most and the middle graphs are two different spanning trees of the same graph. Suppose we add edge e_4 to the middle tree; then we delete e_3 and obtain the right-most spanning tree.

Problem 2.12. *Prove this lemma. (Hint: let e be an edge in $T_2 - T_1$. Then $T_1 \cup \{e\}$ contains a cycle—can all the edges in this cycle belong to T_2?)*

Problem 2.13. *Suppose that edge e_1 has a smaller cost than any of the other edges; that is, $c(e_1) < c(e_i)$, for all $i > 1$. Show that every MCST for G includes e_1.*

Problem 2.14. *Before algorithm 2.1 proceeds, it orders the edges in line 1, and presumably breaks ties—i.e., sorts edges of the same cost—arbitrarily. Show that for every MCST T of a graph G, there exists a particular way of breaking the ties so that the algorithm returns T.*

Problem 2.15. *Write a program that takes as input the description of a grid, and outputs its MCST. An n-grid is a graph consisting of n^2 nodes, organized as a square array of $n \times n$ points. Every node may be connected to at most the nodes directly above and below (if they exist), and to the two nodes immediately to the left and right (if they exist). An example of a 4-grid is given in figure 2.5.*

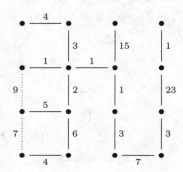

Fig. 2.5   An example of a 4-grid. Note that it has $4^2 = 16$ nodes, and 17 edges.

What is the largest number of edges that an n-grid may have? We have the following node-naming convention: we name the nodes from left-to-right, row-by-row, starting with the top row. Thus, our 4-grid is described by the following adjacency list:

$$4 : (0, 1; 4), (1, 5; 3), (2, 6; 15), (3, 7; 1), (4, 5; 1), (5, 6; 1), \ldots \qquad (2.2)$$

where the first integer is the grid size parameter, and the first two integers in each triple denote the two nodes that describe an edge, and the third integer, following the semicolon, gives the cost of that edge.

When given as input a list of triples, your program must first check whether the list describes a grid, and then compute the MCST of the grid. In our 4-grid example, the solid edges describe a MCST. Also note that the edges in (2.2) are not required to be given in any particular order.

Your program should take as input a file, say `graph.txt`*, containing a list such as (2.1). For example,* 2:(0,1;9),(2,3;5),(1,3;6),(0,2;2) *and it should output, directly to the screen, a graph indicating the edges of a MCST. The graph should be "text-based" with "***" describing nodes and "−" and "|" describing edges. In this example, the MCST of the given 2-grid*

would be represented as:
```
 * *
 | |
 *-*
```

2.2   Jobs with deadlines and profits

We have n jobs, each of which takes unit time, and a processor on which we would like to schedule them sequentially in as profitable a manner as possible. Each job has a profit associated with it, as well as a deadline; if a job is not scheduled by its deadline, then we do not get its profit. Because each job takes the same amount of time, we think of a schedule S as consisting of a sequence of job "slots" $1, 2, 3, \ldots$, where $S(t)$ is the job scheduled in slot t.

Formally, the input is a sequence of pairs $(d_1, g_1), (d_2, g_2), \ldots, (d_n, g_n)$ where $g_i \in \mathbb{R}^+$ is the profit (gain) obtainable from job i, and $d_i \in \mathbb{N}$ is the deadline for job i. In section 4.5 we are going to consider the case where jobs have arbitrary durations—given by a positive integer. However, when durations are arbitrary, rather than of the same unit value, a greedy approach does not "seem"[1] to work.

A *schedule* is an array $S(1), S(2), \ldots, S(d)$ where $d = \max d_i$, that is, d is the latest deadline, beyond which no jobs can be scheduled. If $S(t) = i$, then job i is scheduled at time t, $1 \le t \le d$. If $S(t) = 0$, then no job is scheduled at time t. A schedule S is *feasible* if it satisfies two conditions:

Condition 1: If $S(t) = i > 0$, then $t \le d_i$, i.e., every scheduled job meets its deadline.

Condition 2: If $t_1 \ne t_2$ and also $S(t_1) \ne 0$, then $S(t_1) \ne S(t_2)$, i.e., each job is scheduled at most once.

Problem 2.16. *Write a program that takes as input a schedule S, and a sequence of jobs, and checks whether S is feasible.*

Let the total profit of schedule S be $P(S) = \sum_{t=1}^{d} g_{S(t)}$, where $g_0 = 0$. We want to find a feasible schedule S whose profit $P(S)$ is as large as possible; this can be accomplished with the greedy algorithm 2.3, which orders jobs in non-increasing order of profits and places them as late as possible within their deadline. It is surprising that this algorithm works, and it seems to be a scientific confirmation of the benefits of procrastination.

Line 7 in algorithm 2.3 finds the latest possible free slot that meets the deadline; if no such free slot exists, then job i cannot be scheduled. That is, if there is no t satisfying both $S(t) = 0$ and $t \le d_i$, then the last command on line 7, $S(t) \longleftarrow i$, is *not* executed, and the for-loop considers the next i.

---

[1] We say "seem" in quotes because there is no known proof that a greedy algorithm will not do; such a proof would require a precise definition of what it means for a solution to be given by a greedy algorithm—a difficult task in itself (see [Allan Borodin (2003)]).

Algorithm 2.3 Job scheduling

1: Sort the jobs in non-increasing order of profits: $g_1 \geq g_2 \geq \ldots \geq g_n$
2: $d \longleftarrow \max_i d_i$
3: **for** $t : 1..d$ **do**
4:　　　$S(t) \longleftarrow 0$
5: **end for**
6: **for** $i : 1..n$ **do**
7:　　　Find the largest t such that $S(t) = 0$ and $t \leq d_i$, $S(t) \longleftarrow i$
8: **end for**

Problem 2.17. *Implement algorithm 2.3 for job scheduling.*

Theorem 2.18. *The greedy solution to job scheduling is optimal. That is, the profit $P(S)$ of the schedule S computed by algorithm 2.3 is as large as possible.*

A schedule is *promising* if it can be extended to an optimal schedule. Schedule S' *extends* schedule S if for all $1 \leq t \leq d$, if $S(t) \neq 0$, then $S(t) = S'(t)$. For example, $S' = (2, 0, 1, 0, 3)$ extends $S = (2, 0, 0, 0, 3)$.

Lemma 2.19. *"S is promising" is an invariant for the (second) for-loop in algorithm 2.3.*

In fact, just as in the case of Kruskal's algorithm in the previous section, we must make the definition of "promising" in lemma 2.19 more precise: we say that "S is promising *after* the i-th iteration of the loop in algorithm 2.3" if S can be extended to an optimal schedule using jobs from those among $\{i + 1, i + 2, \ldots, n\}$, i.e., using a subset of those jobs that have not been considered yet.

Problem 2.20. *Consider the following input*

$$\{\underbrace{(1, 10)}_{1}, \underbrace{(1, 10)}_{2}, \underbrace{(2, 8)}_{3}, \underbrace{(2, 8)}_{4}, \underbrace{(4, 6)}_{5}, \underbrace{(4, 6)}_{6}, \underbrace{(4, 6)}_{7}, \underbrace{(4, 6)}_{8}\},$$

where the jobs have been numbered underneath for convenience. Trace the workings of algorithm 2.3 on this input. On the left place the job numbers in the appropriate slots; on the right, show how the optimal solution is adjusted to keep the "promising" property. Start in the following configuration:

$$S^0 = \boxed{\begin{array}{c|c|c|c} 0 & 0 & 0 & 0 \end{array}} \text{ and } S^0_{\text{opt}} = \boxed{\begin{array}{c|c|c|c} 2 & 4 & 5 & 8 \end{array}}$$

Problem 2.21. *Why does lemma 2.19 imply theorem 2.18? (Hint: this is a simple observation).*

We now prove lemma 2.19.

Proof. The proof is by induction. Basis case: after the 0-th iteration of the loop, $S = (0, 0, \ldots, 0)$ and we may extend it with jobs $\{1, 2, \ldots, n\}$, i.e., we have all the jobs at our disposal; so S is promising, as we can take *any* optimal schedule, and it will be an extension of S.

Induction step: Suppose that S is promising, and let S_{opt} be *some* optimal schedule that extends S. Let S' be the result of one more iteration through the loop where job i is considered. We must prove that S' continues being promising, so the goal is to show that there is an optimal schedule S'_{opt} that extends S'. We consider two cases:

$$S = \boxed{\ \ |\ 0\ |\ \ |\ 0\ |\ j\ |\ \ |\ \ }$$

$$S_{\text{opt}} = \boxed{\ \ |\ 0\ |\ \ |\ i\ |\ \ |\ j\ |\ \ }$$

Fig. 2.6 If S has job j in a position, then S_{opt} has also job j in *the same* position. If S has a zero in a given position (no job is scheduled there) then S_{opt} may have zero or a different job in the same position.

Case 1: job i cannot be scheduled. Then $S' = S$, so we let $S'_{\text{opt}} = S_{\text{opt}}$, and we are done. The only subtle thing is that S was extendable into S_{opt} with jobs in $\{i, i + 1, \ldots, n\}$, but after the i-th iteration we no longer have job i at our disposal.

Problem 2.22. *Show that this "subtle thing" mentioned in the paragraph above is not a problem.*

Case 2: job i is scheduled at time t_0, so $S'(t_0) = i$ (whereas $S(t_0) = 0$) and t_0 is the latest possible time for job i in the schedule S. We have two subcases.

Subcase a: job i is scheduled in S_{opt} at time t_1:

If $t_1 = t_0$, then, as in case 1, just let $S'_{\text{opt}} = S_{\text{opt}}$.

If $t_1 < t_0$, then let S'_{opt} be S_{opt} except that we interchange t_0 and t_1, that is we let $S'_{\text{opt}}(t_0) = S_{\text{opt}}(t_1) = i$ and $S'_{\text{opt}}(t_1) = S_{\text{opt}}(t_0)$. Then S'_{opt} is feasible (why 1?), it extends S' (why 2?), and $P(S'_{\text{opt}}) = P(S_{\text{opt}})$ (why 3?).

The case $t_1 > t_0$ is not possible (why 4?).

Subcase b: job i is not scheduled in S_{opt}. Then we simply define S'_{opt} to be the same as S_{opt}, except $S'_{\text{opt}}(t_0) = i$. Since S_{opt} is feasible, so is S'_{opt}, and since S'_{opt} extends S', we only have to show that $P(S'_{\text{opt}}) = P(S_{\text{opt}})$.

This follows from the following claim:

Claim 2.23. *Let* $S_{\text{opt}}(t_0) = j$. *Then* $g_j \leq g_i$.

Proof. We prove the claim by contradiction: assume that $g_j > g_i$ (note that in this case $j \neq 0$). Then job j was considered before job i. Since job i was scheduled at time t_0, job j must have been scheduled at time $t_2 \neq t_0$ (we know that job j was scheduled in S since $S(t_0) = 0$, and $t_0 \leq d_j$, so there was a slot for job j, and therefore it was scheduled). But S_{opt} extends S, and $S(t_2) = j \neq S_{\text{opt}}(t_2)$—contradiction. □

This finishes the proof of the induction step. □

Problem 2.24. *Make sure you can answer all the "why's" in the above proof. Also, where in the proof of the claim we use the fact that $j \neq 0$?*

Problem 2.25. *Under what condition on the inputs is there a unique optimal schedule? If there is more than one optimal schedule, and given one such optimal schedule, is there always an arrangement of the jobs, still in a non-increasing order of profits, that results in the algorithm outputting this particular optimal schedule?*

2.3 Further examples and problems

2.3.1 *Make-change*

The make-change problem, briefly described in the introduction to this chapter, consists in paying a given amount using the least number of coins, using some fixed denomination, and an unlimited supply of coins of each denomination.

Consider the following greedy algorithm to solve the make-change problem, where the denominations are $C = \{1, 10, 25, 100\}$. On input $n \in \mathbb{N}$, the algorithm outputs the smallest list L of coins (from among C) whose sum equals n.

Note that s equals the sum of the values of the coins in L, and that strictly speaking L is a *multiset* (the same element may appear more than once in a multiset).

Problem 2.26. *Implement algorithm 2.4 for making change.*

Problem 2.27. *Show that algorithm 2.4 (with the given denominations) does* not *necessarily produce an optimal solution. That is, present an n for which the output L contains more coins than the optimal solution.*

Algorithm 2.4 Make-change

1: $C \longleftarrow \{1, 10, 25, 100\}$; $L \longleftarrow \emptyset$; $s \longleftarrow 0$
2: **while** $(s < n)$ **do**
3:         find the largest x in C such that $s + x \leq n$
4:         $L \longleftarrow L \cup \{x\}$; $s \longleftarrow s + x$
5: **end while**
6: **return** L

Problem 2.28. *Suppose that* $C = \{1, p, p^2, \ldots, p^n\}$, *where* $p > 1$ *and* $n \geq 0$ *are integers. That is, "$C \longleftarrow \{1, 10, 25, 100\}$" in line 1 of algorithm 2.4 is replaced by "$C \longleftarrow \{1, p, p^2, \ldots, p^n\}$." Show that with this series of denominations (for some fixed p, n) the greedy algorithm above always finds an optimal solution. (Hint: Start with a suitable definition of a promising list.)*

2.3.2 *Maximum weight matching*

Let $G = (V_1 \cup V_2, E)$ be a bipartite graph, i.e, a graph with edge set $E \subseteq V_1 \times V_2$ with disjoint sets V_1 and V_2. $w : E \longrightarrow \mathbb{N}$ assigns a weight $w(e) \in \mathbb{N}$ to each edge $e \in E = \{e_1, \ldots, e_m\}$. A *matching* for G is a subset $M \subseteq E$ such that no two edges in M share a common vertex. The weight of M is $w(M) = \sum_{e \in M} w(e)$.

Problem 2.29. *Give a simple greedy algorithm which, given a bipartite graph with edge weights, attempts to find a matching with the largest possible weight.*

Problem 2.30. *Give an example of a bipartite graph with edge weights for which your algorithm in problem 2.29 fails to find a matching with the largest possible weight.*

Problem 2.31. *Suppose all edge weights in the bipartite graph are distinct, and each is a power of 2. Prove that your greedy algorithm always succeeds in finding a maximum weight matching in this case. (Assume for this question that all the edges are there, i.e., that $E = V \times V$.)*

2.3.3 *Shortest path*

The following example of a greedy algorithm is very beautiful. It reminds one of the cartographers of old, who produced maps of the world with white spots—the unknown and unexplored places.

Suppose that we are given a graph $G = (V, E)$, a designated start node s, and a cost function for each edge $e \in E$, denoted $c(e)$. We are asked to compute the cheapest paths from s to every other node in G, where the cost of a path is the sum of the costs of its edges.

Consider the following greedy algorithm: the algorithm maintains a set S of explored nodes, and for each $u \in S$ it stores a value $d(u)$, which is the cheapest path inside S, starting at s and ending at u.

Initially, $S = \{s\}$ and $d(s) = 0$. Now, for each $v \in V - S$ we find the shortest path to v by traveling inside the explored part S to some $u \in S$, followed by a single edge (u, v). See figure 2.7.

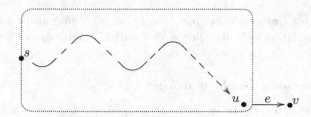

Fig. 2.7 Computing the rank of page A.

That is, we compute:

$$d'(v) = \min_{u \in S, e=(u,v)} d(u) + c(e). \tag{2.3}$$

We choose the node $v \in V - S$ for which (2.3) is minimized, add v to S, and set $d(v) = d'(v)$, and repeat. Thus we add one node at a time to the explored part, and we stop when $S = V$.

This greedy algorithm for computing the shortest path is due to Edsger Dijkstra. It is not difficult to see that its running time is $O(n^2)$.

Problem 2.32. *Design the algorithm in pseudo-code, and show that at the end, for each $u \in V$, $d(u)$ is the cost of the cheapest path from s to u.*

Problem 2.33. *The* Open Shortest Path First *(OSPF) is a routing protocol for IP, described in detail in* RFC 2328 *(where* RFC *stands for "Request for Comment," which is a series of memoranda published by the Internet Engineering Task Force describing the working of the Internet). The commonly used routing protocol OSPF uses Dijkstra's greedy algorithm for computing the so called "shortest paths tree," which for a particular node x on the Internet, lists the best connections to all other nodes on x's subnetwork.*

Write a program that implements a simplified dynamic routing policy mechanism. *More precisely, you are to implement a routing table management daemon, which maintains a link-state database as in the OSPF interior routing protocol. We assume that all nodes are either routers or networks (i.e., there are no "bridges," "hubs," etc.).*

Call your program routed *(as in* routing daemon*). Once started in command line, it awaits instructions and performs actions:*

(1) add rt ⟨routers⟩
This command adds routers to the routing table, where ⟨routers⟩ *is a comma separated list of (positive) integers and integer ranges. That is,* ⟨routers⟩ *can be* 6,9,10-13,4,8 *which would include routers*

rt4,rt6,rt8,rt9,rt10,rt11,rt12,rt13

Your program should be robust enough to accept any such legal sequence (including a single router), and to return an error message if the command attempts to add a router that already exists (but other valid routers in the list ⟨routers⟩ *should be added regardless).*

(2) del rt ⟨routers⟩
Deletes routers given in ⟨routers⟩. *If the command attempts to delete a router that does not exist, an error message should be returned; we want robustness: routers that exist should be deleted, while attempting to delete non-existent routers should return an error message (specifying the "offending" routers). The program should not stop after displaying an error message.*

(3) add nt ⟨networks⟩
Add networks as specified in ⟨networks⟩; *same format as for adding routers. So for example "*add nt 89*" would result in the addition of* nt89. *The handling of errors should be done analogously to the case of adding routers.*

(4) del nt ⟨networks⟩
Deletes networks given in ⟨networks⟩.

(5) con *x y z*
Connect node x and node y, where x, y are existing routers and networks (for example, x = rt8 *and y =* rt90, *or x =* nt76 *and y =* rt1*) and z is the cost of the connection. If x or y does not exist an error message should be returned. Note that the network is directed; that is, the following two commands are not equivalent: "*con rt3 rt5 1*" and "*con rt5 rt3 1.*"*

It is important to note that two networks cannot be connected directly; an attempt to do so should generate an error message. If *a connection between x and y already exists, it is updated with the new cost z.*

(6) `display`

This command displays the routing table, i.e., the link-state database. For example, the result of adding `rt3`, `rt5`, `nt8`, `nt9` *and giving the commands* "`con rt5 rt3 1`" *and* "`con rt3 nt8 6`" *would display the following routing table:*

```
     rt3  rt5  nt8  nt9
rt3        1
rt5
nt8   6
nt9
```

Note that (according to the RFC 2338, *describing OSPF Version 2) we read the table as follows:* "*column first, then row.*" *Thus, the table says that there is a connection from* `rt5` *to* `rt3`, *with cost 1, and another connection from* `rt3` *to* `nt8`, *with cost 6.*

(7) `tree x`

This commands computes the tree of shortest paths, with x as the root, from the link-state database. Note that x must be a router in this case. The output should be given as follows:

$$w_1 : x, v_1, v_2, \ldots, v_n, y_1$$
$$: \text{no path to } y_2$$
$$w_3 : x, u_1, u_2, \ldots, u_m, y_3$$
$$\vdots$$

where w_1 is the cost of the path (the sum of the costs of the edges), from x to y_1, with v_i's the intermediate nodes (i.e., the "hops") to get from x to y_1. Every node y_j in the database should be listed; if there is no path from x to y_j it should say so, as in the above example output.

Following the example link-state database in the explanation of the `display` *command, the output of executing the command* "`tree rt5`" *would be:*

```
1 : rt5,rt3
7 : rt5,rt3,nt8
  : no path to nt9
```

> *Just as it is done in the OSPF standard, the path-tree should be computed with Dijkstra's greedy algorithm.*
>
> *Finally, there may be several paths of the same value between two nodes; in that case, explain in the comments in your program how does your scheme select one of them.*

(8) `quit`

Kills the daemon.

2.3.4 *Huffman codes*

One more important instance of a greedy solution is given by the Huffman algorithm, which is a widely used and effective technique for loss-less data compression. Huffman's algorithm uses a table of the frequencies of occurrences of the characters to build an optimal way of representing each character as a binary string. See §16.3 in [Cormen *et al.* (2009)] for details, but the following example illustrates the key idea.

Suppose that we have a string s over the alphabet $\{a, b, c, d, e, f\}$, and $|s| = 100$. Suppose also that the characters in s occur with the frequencies $44, 14, 11, 17, 8, 6$, respectively. As there are six characters, if we were using fixed-length binary codewords to represent them we would require three bits, and so 300 characters to represent the string.

Instead of a fixed-length encoding we want to give frequent characters a short codeword and infrequent characters a long codeword. We consider only codes in which no codeword is also a prefix of some other codeword. Such codes are called *prefix codes*; there is no loss of generality in restricting attention to prefix codes, as it is possible to show that any code can always be replaced with a prefix code that is at least as good.

Encoding and decoding is simple with a prefix code; to encode we just concatenate the codewords representing each character of the file. Since no codeword is a prefix of any other, the codeword that begins an encoded string is unambiguous, and so decoding is easy.

A prefix code can be given with a binary tree where the leaves are labeled with a character and its frequency, and each internal node is labeled with the sum of the frequencies of the leaves in its subtree. See figure 2.8. We construct the code of a character by traversing the tree starting at the root, and writing a 0 for a left-child and a 1 for a right-child.

Let Σ be an alphabet of n characters and let $f : \Sigma \longrightarrow \mathbb{N}$ be the frequencies function. The Huffman algorithm builds a tree T corresponding to the optimal code in a bottom-up manner. It begins with a set of $|\Sigma|$ leaves

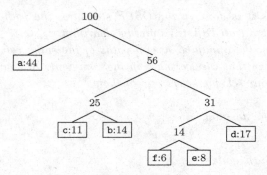

Fig. 2.8   Binary tree for the variable-length prefix code.

and performs a sequence of $|\Sigma| - 1$ "merging" operations to create the final tree. At each step, the two least-frequent objects are merged together; the result of a merge of two objects is a new object whose frequency is the sum of the frequencies of the two objects that were merged.

Algorithm 2.5 Huffman

  $n \leftarrow |\Sigma|$; $Q \leftarrow \Sigma$
  for $i = 1..n - 1$ **do**
       allocate a new node z
       left$[z] \leftarrow x = $ extract-min(Q)
       right$[z] \leftarrow y = $ extract-min(Q)
       $f(z) \leftarrow f(x) + f(y)$
       insert z in Q
  end for

Problem 2.34. *Consider a file consisting of ASCII 100 characters, with the following frequencies:*

character	a	b	c	d	e	f	g	h
frequency	40	15	12	10	8	6	5	4

Using the standard ASCII encoding this file requires 800 bits. Compute a variable length prefix encoding for this file, and compute the total number of bits when using that encoding.

Problem 2.35. *Write a program that takes as input a text file, over, say, the ASCII alphabet, and uses Huffman's algorithm to compress it into a binary string. The compressed file should include a header containing the mapping of characters to bit strings, so that a properly compressed file can* *be decompressed. Your program should be able to do both: compress and decompress. Compare your solution to standard compression tools such as* gzip[2].

2.4 Answers to selected problems

Problem 2.2. A leaf is a vertex with one outgoing edge; suppose there is no leaf. Pick a vertex, take one of its outgoing edges. As each vertex has at least two adjacent edges, we keep going arriving at one edge, and leaving by the other. As there are finitely many edges we must eventually form a cycle. Contradiction.

We now show by induction on n that a tree with n nodes must have exactly $n - 1$ edges. Basis case: $n = 1$, so the tree consists of a single node, and hence it has no edges; $n - 1 = 1 - 1 = 0$ edges. Induction step: suppose that we have a tree with $n + 1$ nodes. Pick a leaf and the edge that connects it to the rest of the tree. Removing this leaf and its edge results in a tree with n nodes, and hence—by induction hypothesis—with $n - 1$ edges. Thus, the entire tree has $(n - 1) + 1 = n$ edges, as required.

Problem 2.4. We prove this by induction, with the basis case $n = 3$ (since a graph—without multiple edges between the same pair of nodes—cannot have a cycle with less than 3 nodes). If $n = 3$, and there are more than $n - 1 = 2$ edges, there must be exactly 3 edges. So the graph is a cycle (a "triangle"). Induction step: consider a graph with $n + 1$ many nodes ($n \geq 3$), and at least $n + 1$ many edges. If the graph has a node with zero or one edges adjacent to it, then by removing that node (and its edge, if there is one), we obtain a graph with n nodes and at least n edges, and so—by induction hypothesis—the resulting graph has a cycle, and so the original graph also has a cycle. Otherwise, all nodes have at least two adjacent edges. Suppose v_0 is such a node, and $(v_0, x), (v_0, y)$ are two edges. Remove v_0 from the graph, and remove the edges $(v_0, x), (v_0, y)$ and replace them by the single edge (x, y). Again—by induction hypothesis—there must be a cycle in the resulting graph. But then there must be a cycle in the original graph as well. (Note that there are $n + 1$ nodes, so after removing v_0 there are n nodes, and $n \geq 3$.)

---

[2]gzip implements the Lempel-Ziv-Welch (LZW) algorithm, which is a loss-less data compression algorithm, available on UNIX platforms. It takes as input any file, and outputs a compressed version with the .gz extension. It is described in RFCs 1951 and 1952.

Problem 2.5. We know that lines 1-2 of algorithm 2.1 require at most $m^2 + 1$ steps. We must also create the array D, which requires n more steps (where n is the number of vertices).

The for loop on line 3 will go through exactly m iterations. "$T \cup \{e_i\}$ has no cycle" (where $e_i = (r, s)$) is equivalent to "$D[r] \neq D[s]$", so the check on line 4 only requires one step. For the purpose of establishing an upper bound it is safe to assume that every check returns "true", so we must go through the entirety of algorithm 2.2 in every iteration of the for loop.

Algorithm 2.2 requires 2 assignments, followed by a loop which runs n times and has at most 2 steps; algorithm 2.2 is $O(2n + 2) = O(n)$.

So the composite algorithm, where algorithm 2.2 is used to accomplish line 4 of algorithm 2.1 and insertion sort is used for line 1, is clearly $O(m^2 + n + 1 + m(2n + 2))$. Identically, if $p = \max(n, m)$, the algorithm is $O(p^2)$.

In other words, if the number of edges is greater than the number of vertices the bottleneck is the sorting algorithm. Moreover, under the assumption that the graph in question is connected, the number of vertices is at least $n - 1$; any graph with $n - 1$ edges is either already a spanning tree or is not connected, so it is safe to assume $m \geq n$. Using merge sort, heap sort or quick sort would improve the complexity to $O(m \log(m))$.

Problem 2.8. We start from the basis case: before the first iteration, T_0 is the empty set ($i = 0$). Since G is connected, obviously $\{e_1, e_2, \ldots, e_m\} = E$ connects all nodes in V.

Next we prove induction. Assume that, after $i - 1$ iterations, $T_{i-1} \cup \{e_i, \ldots, e_m\}$ connects all nodes in V. On iteration i, we have two cases:
Case 1: $T_{i-1} \cup \{e_i\}$ has no cycle, so $T_i = T_{i-1} \cup \{e_i\}$. $T_i \cup \{e_{i+1}, \ldots, e_m\}$ and $T_{i-1} \cup \{e_i, \ldots, e_m\}$ are the same set, e_i has just moved from the "remaining" edges to T. By the hypothesis, the latter edge set connects all nodes in V, so the prior must as well.
Case 2: $T_{i-1} \cup \{e_i\}$ contains a cycle, so $T_i = T_{i-1}$. Consider any two nodes $u, v \in V$. By the hypothesis, there is a path from u to v consisting of edges in $T_{i-1} \cup \{e_i, \ldots, e_m\}$. If e_i is not in this path, then we're done; there is still a path between u and v, as we've only lost access to e_i. If $e_i = (a, b)$ is in this path, we can replace it with another path from a to b; e_i was in a cycle, so another such path necessarily exists.

We have found a path connecting arbitrary u and v in $T_i \cup \{e_i, \ldots, e_m\}$ given that one existed in $T_{i-1} \cup \{e_i, \ldots, e_m\}$, thereby completing the induction step and proving that (2.4) is a loop invariant.

Clearly, after all $i = m$ iterations, this loop invariant reads "$T_i \cup \{e_{i+1}, \ldots\}$ connects all nodes in V." But e_m was the last edge, so $\{e_{i+1}, \ldots\}$ is the empty set. Therefore, T_m connects all nodes in V. By construction, T_m cannot contain any cycles; any edge which would have completed a cycle was simply not included. So, after m iterations, T connects all nodes in V and is acyclic — T is a spanning tree of G.

Problem 2.9. Given an undirected graph $G = (V, E)$, a connected component $C = (V_c, E_c)$ of G is a nonempty subset V' of V (along with its included edges) such that for all pairs of vertices $u, v \in V'$, there is a path from u to v (which we will state as "u and v are connected"), and moreover for all pairs of vertices x, y such that $x \in V'$ and $y \in V - V'$, x and y are *not* connected (i.e. there is no path from x to y). We can make a few quick observations about connected components:

(1) The connected components of any graph comprise a partition of its edge and vertex sets, as connectedness is an equivalence relation.

(2) Given any edge, both of its endpoints are in the same component, as it defines a path connecting them.

(3) Given any two vertices in a connected component, there is a path connecting them. Similarly, any two vertices in different components are necessarily not connected.

(4) Given any path, every contained edge is in the same component.

A spanning forest is a collection of spanning trees — one for each connected component. That is, an edge set $F \subseteq E$ is a spanning forest of $G = (V, E)$ if and only if:

(1) F contains no cycles.

(2) $(\forall u, v \in V)$, F connects u and v if and only if u and v are connected in G.

Let $G = (V, E)$ be a graph that is not connected. That is, G has more than one component. Let T_i denote the state of T, in Kruskal's, after i iterations. Let $C = (V_c, E_c)$ be a component of G. We will use the following loop invariant as proof that Kruskal's Algorithm results in a spanning forest for G:

$$\text{The edge set } T_i \cup \{e_{i+1}, \ldots, e_m\} \text{ connects all nodes in } V_c. \quad (2.4)$$

The basis case clearly works; $T_0 \cup \{e_1, \ldots, e_m\} = E$. Every vertex in V_c is connected in G, and we have every edge in G at our disposal.

Assume that $T_{i-1} \cup \{e_i, \ldots, e_m\}$ connects all nodes in V_c.

Case 1: e_i is not in E_c. Clearly e_i has no effect on the connectedness of V_c, as any path in C must be a subset of E_c.

Case 2: $e_i \in E_c$ and $T_{i-1} \cup \{e_i\}$ contains a cycle. Let u, v be nodes adjacent to e_i. T_{i-1} does not contain a cycle by construction, so e_i completes a cycle in $T_{i-1} \cup \{e_i\}$. Thus, there is already a path (u, v) in T_{i-1}, which can be used to replace e_i in any other path. Therefore, $T_{i-1} \cup \{e_{i+1}, \ldots, e_m\}$ connects everything that was connected by $T_{i-1} \cup \{e_i, \ldots, e_m\}$, so the assignment of $T_i = T_{i-1}$, with the "loss of access" to e_i, preserves the loop invariant.

Case 3: $e_i \in E_c$ and $T_{i-1} \cup \{e_i\}$ does not contain a cycle. Then $T_i = T_{i-1} \cup \{e_i\}$, so $T_i \cup \{e_{i+1}, \ldots, e_m\} = T_{i-1} \cup \{e_i, \ldots, e_m\}$, so the loop invariant holds.

We have shown through induction that the loop invariant (2.4) holds. Note that C was an arbitrary connected component, so T_m for each component $C = (V_c, E_c)$ in G, T_m connects every node in V_c. Obviously, if any two nodes in V are not connected in G, T does not connect them; doing so would require edges not in E. Therefore, T_m meets both conditions imposed on a spanning forest above.

Problem 2.12. Let e be any edge in $T_2 - T_1$. We must prove the existence of $e' \in T_1 - T_2$ such that $(T_1 \cup \{e\}) - \{e'\}$ is a spanning tree. Since $e \notin T_1$, by adding e to T_1 we obtain a cycle (by lemma 2.3, which is proved in problem 2.4). A cycle has at least 3 edges (the graph G has at least 3 nodes, since otherwise it could not have two distinct spanning trees!). So in this cycle, there is an edge e' not in T_2. The reason is that if every edge e' in the cycle did belong to T_2, then T_2 itself would have a cycle. By removing e', we break the cycle but the resulting graph, $(T_1 \cup \{e\}) - \{e'\}$, is still connected and of size $|T_1| = |T_2|$, i.e., the right size for a tree, so it must be acyclic (for otherwise, we could get rid of some edge, and have a spanning tree of size smaller than T_1 and T_2—but all spanning trees have the same size), and therefore $(T_1 \cup \{e\}) - \{e'\}$ is a spanning tree.

Problem 2.13. First, note that if we give G to Kruskal's algorithm, with the edges in the order of their indices as (i.e., skip the sorting step), the resulting tree will include e_1 - a cycle cannot be formed with the first (or second) edge, so e_1 will be added to T in the first iteration. Therefore, there is necessarily a spanning tree T_1 of G such that $e_1 \in T_1$.

For contradiction, assume that there is a MCST T_2 such that $e_1 \notin T_2$. By the Exchange Lemma, there is an e_j in T_2 such that $T_3 = T_2 \cup \{e_1\} - \{e_j\}$ is a spanning tree. But $c(e_1) < c(e_j)$, so $c(T_3) < c(T_2)$; that is, T_2 is not a minimum cost spanning tree. We've found our contradiction; there cannot be a MCST that does not contain e_1. Therefore, any MCST includes e_1.

Problem 2.14. Let T be any MCST for a graph G. Reorder the edges of G by costs, just as in Kruskal's algorithm. For any block of edges of the same cost, put those edges which appear in T before all the other edges in that block. Now prove the following loop invariant: the set of edges S selected by the algorithm with the initial ordering as described is always a subset of T. Initially $S = \emptyset \subseteq T$. In the induction step, $S \subseteq T$, and S' is the result of adding one more edge to S. If $S' = S$ there is nothing to do, and if $S' = S \cup \{e\}$, then we need to show that $e \in T$. Suppose that it isn't. Let T' be the result of Kruskal's algorithm, which we know to be a MCST. By the exchange lemma, we know that there exists an $e' \notin T'$ such that $T \cup \{e\} - \{e'\}$ is a ST, and since T was a MCST, we know $c(e') \leq c(e)$, and hence e' was considered *before* e. Since e' is not in T', it was rejected, so it must have created a cycle in S, and hence in T—contradiction. Thus $S \cup \{e\} \subseteq T$.

Problem 2.20. Here is the trace of the algorithm; note that we modify the optimal solution only as far as it is necessary to preserve the extension property.

$$S^1 = \boxed{1 \mid 0 \mid 0 \mid 0} \qquad S^1_{\text{opt}} = \boxed{1 \mid 4 \mid 5 \mid 8}$$

$$S^2 = \boxed{1 \mid 3 \mid 0 \mid 0} \qquad S^2_{\text{opt}} = \boxed{1 \mid 3 \mid 5 \mid 8}$$

$$S^3 = \boxed{1 \mid 3 \mid 0 \mid 5} \qquad S^3_{\text{opt}} = \boxed{1 \mid 3 \mid 8 \mid 5}$$

$$S^4 = \boxed{1 \mid 3 \mid 6 \mid 5} \qquad S^4_{\text{opt}} = \boxed{1 \mid 3 \mid 6 \mid 5}$$

Problem 2.21. Assume that after every iteration, S is promising. After the final iteration, S is still promising, but the only unscheduled tasks are those that cannot extend S at any time. In other words, S cannot be extended outside of the vacuous re-assignment of "no task" to unoccupied times; such extensions do not change the cost of S, so it must be optimal.

Identically, assume the last addition made to the schedule is on iteration i. Before the last task was scheduled, S_{i-1} was promising. Moreover, this last task was the only remaining task which could feasibly extend S, as none of those after it was scheduled. Clearly the profit gained from scheduling this task is the same regardless of when it is scheduled, so every extension of S_{i-1} has the same profit, equal to that of S_i.

Problem 2.22. Since $S' = S$ and $S'_{\text{opt}} = S_{\text{opt}}$ we must show that S is extendable into S_{opt} with jobs in $\{i+1, i+2, \ldots, n\}$. Since job i could not be scheduled in S, and S_{opt} extends S (i.e., S_{opt} has all the jobs that S

had, and perhaps more), it follows that i could not be in S_{opt} either, and so i was not necessary in extending S into S_{opt}.

Problem 2.24. why 1. To show that S'_{opt} is feasible, we have to show that no job is scheduled twice, and no job is scheduled after its deadline. The first is easy, because S_{opt} was feasible. For the second we argue like this: the job that was at time t_0 is now moved to $t_1 < t_0$, so certainly if t_0 was before its deadline, so is t_1. The job that was at time t_1 (job i) has now been moved forward to time t_0, but we are working under the assumption that job i was scheduled (at this point) in slot t_0, so $t_0 \leq d_i$, and we are done. **why 2.** S'_{opt} extends S' because S_{opt} extended S, and the only difference is positions t_1 and t_0. They coincide in position t_0 (both have i), so we only have to examine position t_1. But $S(t_1) = 0$ since $S_{opt}(t_1) = i$, and S does not schedule job i at all. Since the only difference between S and S' is in position t_0, it follows that $S'(t_1) = 0$, so it does not matter what $S'_{opt}(t_1)$ is, it will extend S'. **why 3.** They schedule the same set of jobs, so they must have the same profit. **why 4.** Suppose $t_1 > t_0$. Since S_{opt} extends S, it follows that $S(t_1) = 0$. Since $S_{opt}(t_1) = i$, it follows that $t_1 \leq d_i$. But then, the algorithm would have scheduled i in t_1, not in t_0.

The fact that $j \neq 0$ is used in the last sentence of the proof of claim 2.23, where we conclude a contradiction from $S(t_2) = j \neq S_{opt}(t_2)$. If j were 0 then it could very well be that $S(t_2) = j = 0$ but $S_{opt}(t_2) \neq 0$.

Problem 2.27. With the denominations $\{1, 10, 25, 100\}$, there are many values for which algorithm 2.4 does not produce an optimal solution. Consider, for example, the case $n = 33$. Algorithm 2.4 grants the solution $\{25, 1, 1, 1, 1, 1, 1, 1, 1\}$ (which contains 9 "coins") whereas the optimal solution is $\{10, 10, 10, 1, 1, 1\}$, with cardinality 6.

Problem 2.28. Define a *promising list* to be one that can be extended to an optimal list of coins. Now show that L is promising is a loop invariant. Basis case: Initially, L is empty, so any optimal solution extends L. Hence L is promising. Induction step: Assume that L is promising, and show that L continues being promising after one more execution of the loop: Suppose L is promising, and $s < N$. Let L' be the list that extends L to the optimal solution, i.e., $L, L' = L_{opt}$. Let x be the largest item in C such that $s + x \leq N$. **Case (a):** $x \in L'$. Then $L' = x, L''$, so that L, x can be extended to the optimal solution L_{opt} by L''. **Case (b):** $x \notin L'$. We show that this case is not possible. To this end we prove the following claim:

Claim: If $x \notin L'$, then there is a sub-list L_0 of L' such that $x = $ sum of elements in L_0.

Proof of claim: Let B be the smallest number such that $B \geq x$, and some sub-list of L' sums to B. Let this sub-list be $\{e_1, e_2, \ldots, e_l\}$, where $e_i \leq e_{i+1}$ (i.e., the elements are in non-decreasing order). Since x is the largest coin that fits in $N - s$, and the sum of the coins in L' is $N - s$, it follows that every coin in L' is $\leq x$. Since $e_l \neq x$ (as $x \notin L'$), it follows that $l > 1$. Let $D = x - (e_2 + \ldots + e_l)$. By definition of B we know that $D > 0$. Each of the numbers $x, e_2, \ldots, e_l$ is divisible by e_1 (to see this note that all the coins are powers of p, i.e. in the set $\{1, p, p^2, \ldots, p^n\}$, and $e_l < x$ so $e_1 < x$). Thus $D \geq e_1$. On the other hand $x \leq e_1 + e_2 + \ldots + e_l$, so we also know that $D \leq e_1$, so in fact $D = e_1$. Therefore $x = e_1 + e_2 + \ldots + e_l$, and we are done. (end proof of claim)

Thus $\{e_1, e_2, \ldots, e_l\}$ can be replaced by the single coin x. If $l = 1$, then $x = e_1 \in L'$, which is a contradiction. If $l > 1$, then

$$L, x, L' - \{e_1, e_2, \ldots, e_l\}$$

sums up to N, but it has less coins than $L, L' = L_{\text{opt}}$ which is a contradiction. Thus case (b) is not possible.

Problem 2.29. See algorithm 2.6

Algorithm 2.6 Solution to problem 2.29

$w(e_1) \geq w(e_2) \geq \ldots \geq w(e_m)$
$M \leftarrow \emptyset$
for $i : 1..m$ **do**
    if $M \cup \{e_i\}$ does *not* contain two edges with a common vertex
    then
        $M \leftarrow M \cup \{e_i\}$
    end if
end for

Problem 2.31. Let M_{opt} be an optimal matching. Define "M is promising" to mean that M can be extended to M_{opt} with edges that have not been considered yet. We show that "M is promising" is a loop invariant of our algorithm. The result will follow from this (it will also follows that there is a *unique* max matching). Basis case: $M = \emptyset$, so it is certainly promising. Induction step: Assume M is promising, and let M' be M after considering edge e_i. We show that: $e_i \in M' \iff e_i \in M_{\text{opt}}$.

$[\Longrightarrow]$ Assume that $e_i \in M'$, since the weights are distinct, and powers of 2, $w(e_i) > \sum_{j=i+1}^{m} w(e_j)$ (to see why this holds, see problem 9.1), so unless $e_i \in M_{\text{opt}}$, $w(M_{\text{opt}}) < w$ where w is the result of algorithm.

[$\Longleftarrow$] Assume that $e_i \in M_{\text{opt}}$, so $M \cup \{e_i\}$ has no conflict, so the algorithm would add it.

Problem 2.32. This problem refers to Dijkstra's algorithm for the shortest path; for more background see §24.3, page 658, in [Cormen *et al.* (2009)] and §4.4, page 137, in [Kleinberg and Tardos (2006)]. The proof is simple: define S to be promising if for all the nodes v in S, $d(v)$ is indeed the shortest distance from s to v. We now need to show by induction on the number of iterations of the algorithm that "S is promising" is a loop invariant. The basis case is $S = \{s\}$ and $d(s) = 0$, so it obviously holds. For the induction step, suppose that v is the node just added, so $S' = S \cup \{v\}$. Suppose that there is a shorter path in G from s to v; call this path p (so p is just a sequence of nodes, starting at s and finishing at v). Since p starts inside S (at s) and finishes outside S (at v), it follows that there is an edge (a, b) such that a, b are consecutive nodes on p, where a is in S and b is in $V - S$. Let $c(p)$ be the cost of path p, and let $d'(v)$ be the value the algorithm found; we have $c(p) < d'(v)$. We now consider two cases: $b = v$ and $b \neq v$, and see that both yield a contradiction. If $b = v$, then the algorithm would have used a instead of u. If $b \neq v$, then the cost of the path from s to b is even smaller than $c(p)$, so the algorithm would have added b instead of v. Thus, no such path p exists.

2.5   Notes

Any book on algorithms has a chapter on greedy algorithms. For example, chapter 16 in [Cormen *et al.* (2009)] or chapter 4 in [Kleinberg and Tardos (2006)].

In Problem 2.5 we discuss the complexity of Kruskal's algorithm, which depends on which sorting algorithm is used to put the edges in order of costs. Insertion sort is mentioned (each item on the list is inserted in its proper position), but there are many sorting algorithms. There is also selection sort (find the minimum value, swaps it with the value in the first position, and repeat), mergesort (discussed in Section 3.1), heapsort (like selection sort, but using a heap for efficiency), quicksort (pick an item, put all smaller items before it, all larger items after it, and repeat on those two parts — thus, like mergesort, it is a divide and conquer algorithm), bubble sort (start at the beginning, and compare the first two elements, and if the first is greater than the second, swaps them, and continue for each pair of adjacent elements to the end, and start again with the first two elements, repeating until no swaps have occurred on the last pass). There are many others.

We also point out that there is a profound connection between a mathematical structure called *matroids* and greedy algorithms. A matroid, also known as an *independence structure*, captures the notion of "independence," just like the notion of independence in linear algebra.

A matroid M is a pair (E, I), where E is a finite set and I is a collection of subsets of E (called the *independent sets*) with the following three properties:

(i) The empty set is in I, i.e., $\emptyset \in I$.

(ii) Every subset of an independent set is also independent, i.e., if $x \subseteq y$, then $y \in I \Rightarrow x \in I$.

(iii) If x and y are two independent sets, and x has more elements than y, then there exists an element in x which is not in y that when added to y still gives an independent set. This is called the *independent set exchange property*.

The last property is of course reminiscent of our exchange lemma, lemma 2.11.

A good way to understand the meaning of this definition is to think of E as a set of vectors (in $\mathbb{R}^n$) and I all the subsets of E consisting of linearly independent vectors; check that all three properties hold.

For a review of the connection between matroids and greedy algorithms see [Papadimitriou and Steiglitz (1998)], chapter 12, "Spanning Trees and Matroids."

For a study of which optimization problems can be optimally or approximately solved by "greedy-like" algorithms see [Allan Borodin (2003)].

A well known algorithm for computing a maximum matching in a bipartite graph is the Hopcroft-Karp algorithm; see, for example, [Cormen *et al.* (2009)]. This algorithm runs in polynomial time (i.e., efficiently), but it is not greedy—the greedy approach seems to fail as section 2.3.2 insinuates.

Chapter 3

Divide and Conquer

> Si vis pacem, para bellum
>
> ─────────────────────────
>
> De Re Militari, [Renatus (4th
> or 5th century AD)]

Divide et impera—divide and conquer—was a Roman military strategy that consisted in securing command by breaking a large concentration of power into portions that alone were weaker, and methodically dispatching those portions one by one. This is the idea behind divide and conquer algorithms: take a large problem, divide it into smaller parts, solve those parts *recursively*, and combine the solutions into a solution to the whole.

The paradigmatic example of a divide and conquer algorithm is merge sort, where we have a large list of items to be sorted; we break it up into two smaller lists (divide), sort those recursively (conquer), and then combine those two sorted lists into one large sorted list. We present this algorithm in section 3.1. We also present a divide and conquer algorithm for binary integer multiplication—section 3.2, and graph reachability—section 3.3.

The divide and conquer approach is often used in situations where there is a brute force/exhaustive search algorithm that solves the problem, but the divide and conquer algorithm improves the running time. This is, for example, the case of binary integer multiplication. The last example in this chapter is a divide and conquer algorithm for reachability (Savitch's algorithm) that minimizes the use of memory, rather than the running time.

In order to analyze the use of resources (whether time or space) of a recursive procedure we must solve recurrences; see, for example, [Rosen (2007)] or [Cormen *et al.* (2009)] for the necessary background—"the master method" for solving recurrences. We provide a short discussion in the Notes section at the end of this chapter.

3.1   Mergesort

Suppose that we have two lists of numbers that are already sorted. That is, we have a list $a_1 \leq a_2 \leq \cdots \leq a_n$ and $b_1 \leq b_2 \leq \cdots \leq b_m$. We want to combine those two lists into one long sorted list $c_1 \leq c_2 \leq \cdots \leq c_{n+m}$. Algorithm 3.1 does the job.

Algorithm 3.1 Merge two lists

Pre-condition: $a_1 \leq a_2 \leq \cdots \leq a_n$ and $b_1 \leq b_2 \leq \cdots \leq b_m$

$\quad p_1 \longleftarrow 1; \ p_2 \longleftarrow 1; \ i \longleftarrow 1$

$\quad$ **while** $i \leq n + m$ **do**

$\quad\quad$ **if** $a_{p_1} \leq b_{p_2}$ **then**

$\quad\quad\quad c_i \longleftarrow a_{p_1}$

$\quad\quad\quad p_1 \longleftarrow p_1 + 1$

$\quad\quad$ **else**

$\quad\quad\quad c_i \longleftarrow b_{p_1}$

$\quad\quad\quad p_2 \longleftarrow p_2 + 1$

$\quad\quad$ **end if**

$\quad\quad i \longleftarrow i + 1$

$\quad$ **end while**

Post-condition: $c_1 \leq c_2 \leq \cdots \leq c_{n+m}$

Problem 3.1. *Note that algorithm 3.1 is incomplete as stated; for example, suppose that $n < m$ and all the elements of the a_i list are smaller than b_1. In this case, after the n-th iteration of the while-loop $p_1 = n + 1$, and one more iteration checks for $a_{p_1} \leq b_{p_2}$ resulting in an "out of bounds index." Modify the algorithm to fix this.*

The mergesort algorithm sorts a given list of numbers by first dividing them into two lists of length $\lceil n/2 \rceil$ and $\lfloor n/2 \rfloor$, respectively, then sorting each list recursively, and finally combining the results using algorithm 3.1.

In algorithm 3.2, line 1 sets L to be the list of the input numbers $a_1, a_2, \ldots, a_n$. These are integers, not necessarily ordered. Line 2 checks if L is not empty or consists of a single element; if that is the case, then the list is already sorted—this is where the recursion "bottoms out," by returning the same list. Otherwise, in line 5 we let L_1 consist of the first $\lceil n/2 \rceil$ elements of L and L_2 consist of the last $\lfloor n/2 \rfloor$ elements of L.

Problem 3.2. *Show that $L = L_1 \cup L_2$.*

Algorithm 3.2 Mergesort

Pre-condition: A list of integers $a_1, a_2, \ldots, a_n$
1:   $L \longleftarrow a_1, a_2, \ldots, a_n$
2:   **if** $|L| \leq 1$ **then**
3:       **return** L
4:   **else**
5:       $L_1 \longleftarrow$ first $\lceil n/2 \rceil$ elements of L
6:       $L_2 \longleftarrow$ last $\lfloor n/2 \rfloor$ elements of L
7:       **return** Merge(Mergesort(L_1), Mergesort(L_2))
8:   **end if**
Post-condition: $a_{i_1} \leq a_{i_2} \leq \cdots \leq a_{i_n}$

In section 9.3.6 we show how to use the theory of fixed points to prove the correctness of recursive algorithms. For us this will remain a theoretical demonstration, as it is not easy to come up with the least fixed point that interprets a recursion. We are going to give natural proofs of correctness using induction.

Problem 3.3. *Prove the correctness of the Mergesort algorithm, taking into account your solution to problem 3.1.*

Let $T(n)$ bound the running time of the mergesort algorithm on lists of length n. Clearly,

$$T(n) \leq T(\lceil n/2 \rceil) + T(\lfloor n/2 \rfloor) + cn,$$

where cn, for some constant c, is the cost of the merging of the two lists (algorithm 3.1). Furthermore, the asymptotic bounds are not affected by the floors and the ceils, and so we can simply say that $T(n) \leq 2T(n/2) + cn$. Thus, $T(n)$ is bounded by $O(n \log n)$.

Problem 3.4. *Implement mergesort for sorting a list of words into lexicographic order.*

3.2   Multiplying numbers in binary

Consider the example of multiplication of two binary numbers, using the junior school algorithm, given in figure 3.1.

This school multiplication algorithm is very simple. To multiply x times y, where x, y are two numbers in binary, we go through y from right to left;

	1	2	3	4	5	6	7	8
x					1	1	1	0
y					1	1	0	1
s_1					1	1	1	0
s_2				0	0	0	0	
s_3			1	1	1	0		
s_4		1	1	1	0			
$x \times y$	1	0	1	1	0	1	1	0

Fig. 3.1   Multiply 1110 times 1101, i.e., 14 times 13.

when we encounter a 0 we write a row of as many zeros as $|x|$, the length of x. When we encounter a 1 we copy x. When we move to the next bit of y we shift by one space to the left. At the end we produce the familiar "stairs" shape—see s_1, s_2, s_3, s_4 in figure 3.1 (henceforth, figure 3.1 is our running example of binary multiplication).

Once we obtain the "stairs," we go back to the top step (line s_1) and to its right-most bit (column 8). To obtain the product we add all the entries in each column with the usual carry operation. For example, column 5 contains two ones, so we write a 0 in the last row (row $x \times y$) and carry over 1 to column 4. It is not hard to see that multiplying two n-bit integers takes $O(n^2)$ primitive bit operations.

We now present a divide and conquer algorithm that takes only $O(n^{\log 3}) \approx O(n^{1.59})$ operations. The speed-up obtained from the divide and conquer procedure appears slight—but the improvement does become substantial as n grows very large.

Let x and y be two n-bit integers. We break them up into two smaller $n/2$-bit integers as follows:

$$x = (x_1 \cdot 2^{n/2} + x_0),$$
$$y = (y_1 \cdot 2^{n/2} + y_0).$$

Thus x_1 and y_1 correspond to the high-order bits of x and y, respectively, and x_0 and y_0 to the low-order bits of x and y, respectively. The product of x and y appears as follows in terms of those parts:

$$xy = (x_1 \cdot 2^{n/2} + x_0)(y_1 \cdot 2^{n/2} + y_0)$$
$$= x_1 y_1 \cdot 2^n + (x_1 y_0 + x_0 y_1) \cdot 2^{n/2} + x_0 y_0. \qquad (3.1)$$

A divide and conquer procedure appears surreptitiously. To compute the product of x and y we compute the four products $x_1 y_1, x_1 y_0, x_0 y_1, x_0 y_0$, *recursively*, and then we combine them as in (3.1) to obtain xy.

Let $T(n)$ be the number of operations that are required to compute the product of two n-bit integers using the divide and conquer procedure that arises from (3.1). Then

$$T(n) \le 4T(n/2) + cn, \tag{3.2}$$

since we have to compute the four products $x_1y_1, x_1y_0, x_0y_1, x_0y_0$ (this is where the $4T(n/2)$ factor comes from), and then we have to perform three additions of n-bit integers (that is where the factor cn, where c is some constant, comes from). Notice that we do not take into account the product by 2^n and $2^{n/2}$ (in (3.1)) as they simply consist in shifting the binary string by an appropriate number of bits to the left (n for 2^n and $n/2$ for $2^{n/2}$). These shift operations are inexpensive, and can be ignored in the complexity analysis.

When we solve the standard recurrence given by (3.2), we can see that $T(n) \le O(n^{\log 4}) = O(n^2)$, so it seems that we have gained nothing over the brute force procedure.

It appears from (3.1) that we have to make four recursive calls; that is, we need to compute the four multiplications $x_1y_1, x_1y_0, x_0y_1, x_0y_0$. But we can get away with only three multiplications, and hence three recursive calls: x_1y_1, x_0y_0 and $(x_1 + x_0)(y_1 + y_0)$; the reason being that

$$(x_1y_0 + x_0y_1) = (x_1 + x_0)(y_1 + y_0) - (x_1y_1 + x_0y_0). \tag{3.3}$$

See figure 3.2 for a comparison of the cost of operations.

	multiplications	additions	shifts
Method (3.1)	4	3	2
Method (3.3)	3	4	2

Fig. 3.2   Reducing the number of multiplications by one increase the number of additions and subtractions by one—something has to give. But, as multiplications are more expensive, the trade is worth it.

Algorithm 3.3 implements the idea given by (3.3).

Note that in lines 1 and 2 of the algorithm, we break up x and y into two parts x_1, x_0 and y_1, y_0, respectively, where x_1, y_1 consist of the $\lfloor n/2 \rfloor$ high order bits, and x_0, y_0 consist of the $\lceil n/2 \rceil$ low order bits.

Problem 3.5. *Prove the correctness of algorithm 3.3.*

Algorithm 3.3 clearly takes $T(n) \le 3T(n/2) + dn$ operations. Thus, the running time is $O(n^{\log 3}) \approx O(n^{1.59})$—to see this read the discussion on solving recurrences in the Notes section of this chapter.

Algorithm 3.3 Recursive binary multiplication

Pre-condition: Two n-bit integers x and y

1: **if** $n = 1$ **then**
2:        **if** $x = 1 \wedge y = 1$ **then**
3:             **return** 1
4:        **else**
5:             **return** 0
6:        **end if**
7: **end if**
8: $(x_1, x_0) \longleftarrow$ (first $\lfloor n/2 \rfloor$ bits, last $\lceil n/2 \rceil$ bits) of x
9: $(y_1, y_0) \longleftarrow$ (first $\lfloor n/2 \rfloor$ bits, last $\lceil n/2 \rceil$ bits) of y
10: $z_1 \longleftarrow \text{Multiply}(x_1 + x_0, y_1 + y_0)$
11: $z_2 \longleftarrow \text{Multiply}(x_1, y_1)$
12: $z_3 \longleftarrow \text{Multiply}(x_0, y_0)$
13: **return** $z_2 \cdot 2^n + (z_1 - z_2 - z_3) \cdot 2^{\lceil n/2 \rceil} + z_3$

Problem 3.6. *Implement the binary multiplication algorithm. Assume that the input is given in the command line as two strings of zeros and ones.*

3.3   Savitch's algorithm

In this section we are going to give a divide and conquer solution to the graph reachability problem. Recall the graph-theoretic definitions that were given at the beginning of section 2.1. Here we assume that we have a (directed) graph G, and we want to establish whether there is a path from some node s to some node t; note that we are not even searching for a shortest path (as in section 2.3.3 or in section 4.2); we just want to know if node t is reachable from node s.

As a twist on minimizing the running time of algorithms, we are going to present a very clever divide and conquer solution that reduces drastically the amount of space, i.e., memory. Savitch's algorithm solves directed reachability in space $O(\log^2 n)$, where n is the number of vertices in the graph. This is remarkable, as $O(\log^2 n)$ bits of memory is very little space indeed, for a graph with n vertices! We assume that the graph is presented as an $n \times n$ adjacency matrix (see page 29), and so it takes exactly n^2 bits of memory—that is, "work memory," which we use to implement the stack.

It might seem futile to commend an algorithm that takes $O(\log^2 n)$ bits of space when the input itself requires n^2 bits. If the input already takes so much space, what benefit is there to requiring small space for the computations? The point is that the input does not have to be presented in its entirety. The graph may be given *implicitly*, rather than *explicitly*. For example, the "graph" $G = (V, E)$ may be the entire World Wide Web, where V is the set of all web pages (at a given moment in time) and there is an edge from page x to page y if there is hyperlink in x pointing to y. We may be interested in the existence of a path in the WWW, and we can query the pages and their links piecemeal without maintaining the representation of the entire WWW in memory. The sheer size of the WWW is such that it may be beneficial to know that we only require as much space as the square of the logarithm of the number of web pages.

Incidentally, we are not saying that Savitch's algorithm is the ideal solution to the "WWW hyperlink connectivity problem"; we are simply giving an example of an enormous graph, and an algorithm that uses very little working space with respect to the size of the input.

Define the Boolean predicate $R(G, u, v, i)$ to be true iff there is a path in G from u to v of length at most 2^i. The key idea is that if a path exists from u to v, then any such path must have a mid-point w; a seemingly trivial observation that nevertheless inspires a very clever recursive procedure. In other words there exist paths of distance at most 2^{i-1} from u to w and from w to v, i.e.,

$$R(G, u, v, i) \iff (\exists w)[R(G, u, w, i-1) \land R(G, w, v, i-1)]. \qquad (3.4)$$

Algorithm 3.4 computes the predicate $R(G, u, v, i)$ based on the recurrence given in (3.4). Note that in algorithm 3.4 we are computing $R(G, u, v, i)$; the recursive calls come in line 9 where we compute $R(G, u, w, i-1)$ and $R(G, w, v, i-1)$.

Problem 3.7. *Show that algorithm 3.4 is correct (i.e., it computes $R(G, u, v, i)$ correctly) and it requires at most $i \cdot s$ space, where s is the number of bits required to keep record of a single node. Conclude that it requires $O(\log^2 n)$ space on a graph G with n nodes.*

Problem 3.8. *Algorithm 3.4 truly uses very little space to establish connectivity in a graph. But what is the time complexity of this algorithm?*

Problem 3.9. *Your task is to write a program which implements Savitch's algorithm, in a way that at each step outputs the contents of the recursion stack. Suppose, for example, that the input is the following graph:*

Algorithm 3.4 Savitch

1: **if** $i = 0$ **then**
2:         **if** $u = v$ **then**
3:                 **return** T
4:         **else if** (u, v) is an edge **then**
5:                 **return** T
6:         **end if**
7: **else**
8:         **for** every vertex w **do**
9:                 **if** $\mathrm{R}(G, u, w, i - 1)$ and $\mathrm{R}(G, w, v, i - 1)$ **then**
10:                        **return** T
11:                 **end if**
12:         **end for**
13: **end if**
14: **return** F

$\bullet^1$ ——— $\bullet^2$ ——— $\bullet^3$ ——— $\bullet^4$. *Then the recursion stack would look as follows for the first 6 steps:*

		$R(1,4,0)$	F	$R(2,4,0)$	F
		$R(1,1,0)$	T	$R(1,2,0)$	T
	$R(1,4,1)$	$R(1,4,1)$	$R(1,4,1)$	$R(1,4,1)$	$R(1,4,1)$
	$R(1,1,1)$	$R(1,1,1)$	$R(1,1,1)$	$R(1,1,1)$	$R(1,1,1)$
$R(1,4,2)$	$R(1,4,2)$	$R(1,4,2)$	$R(1,4,2)$	$R(1,4,2)$	$R(1,4,2)$
Step 1	Step 2	Step 3	Step 4	Step 5	Step 6

3.4   Further examples and problems

3.4.1   *Extended Euclid's algorithm*

We revisit an old friend from section 1.1, namely the extended Euclid's algorithm—see problem 1.9, and the corresponding solution on page 21 containing algorithm 1.8. We present a recursive version, as algorithm 3.5, where the algorithm returns three values, and hence we use the notation $(x, y, z) \longleftarrow (x', y', z')$ as a convenient shorthand for $x \longleftarrow x'$, $y \longleftarrow y'$ and $z \longleftarrow z'$. Note the interesting similarity between algorithm 1.8 and the Gaussian lattice reduction—algorithm 7.3.

Problem 3.10. *Show that algorithm 3.5 works correctly.*

Algorithm 3.5 Extended Euclid's algorithm (recursive)

Pre-condition: $m > 0, n \geq 0$

1: $a \longleftarrow m; \ b \longleftarrow n$
2: **if** $b = 0$ **then**
3:        **return** $(a, 1, 0)$
4: **else**
5:        $(d, x, y) \longleftarrow$ Euclid$(b, \text{rem}(a, b))$
6:        **return** $(d, y, x - \text{div}(a, b) \cdot y)$
7: **end if**

Post-condition: $mx + ny = d = \gcd(m, n)$

Problem 3.11. *Implement the extended Euclid's algorithm (algorithm 3.5). Assume that the input is given in the command line, as two integers.*

3.4.2 *Quicksort*

Quicksort is a commonly used algorithm for sorting. It was designed in the late 1950s by T. Hoare[1]. Quicksort is easy to define: in order to sort a list I of items, pick one item x from I (call this item the *pivot*), and create two new lists, S and L: all those items less than or equal to the pivot, S, and all those items greater than the pivot, L. Now recursively sort S and L, to create S' and L' and the new sorted list I' is given by S', x, L'.

It is interesting to note that Quicksort can be easily implemented in a functional language, as it operates on lists and it is naturally a recursive function. For example, it can be implemented in Haskell with a few lines of code as follows:

```
qsort [] = []
qsort (x:xs) = qsort smaller ++ [x] ++ qsort larger
  where
    smaller = [a | a <- xs, a <= x]
    larger = [b | b <- xs, b > x]
```

Note that in this implementation (see pg. 10 of [Hutton (2007)]) we picked the first element of the list as the pivot; there are randomized version of Quicksort where the pivot is picked at random from the list.

---

[1]The same Hoare who was already quoted on page vii; recall also that we introduced Hoare's logic as a mechanism for proving algorithm and program correctness on page 1.

Problem 3.12. *Implement Quicksort, and analyze its complexity. For the complexity, provide both worst-case run time and average running time.*

3.4.3 *Git bisect*

Git is a widely used program for version control of computer files, and for coordinating the collaboration of multiple people on a large programming project[2]. In fact, the solutions to the programming problems contained in this book, as well as the implementations of all the algorithms, are maintained in a publicly viewable Git repository on GitHub (a web-based Git repository): `https://github.com/michaelsoltys/IAA-Code` .

As explained in the Git documentation, `git bisect` uses a binary search algorithm to find which commit in a project's history introduced a bug. In order to deploy it, the user specifies a "bad" commit that is known to contain the bug, and a "good" commit that is known to be before the bug was introduced. Then `git bisect` picks a commit between those two endpoints and asks whether the selected commit is "good" or "bad." It continues narrowing down the range until it finds the exact commit that introduced the change.

In fact, `git bisect` can be used to find the commit that changed any property of a project; for example, the commit that fixed a bug, or the commit that caused a benchmarks performance to improve. To support this more general usage, the terms "old" and "new" can be used in place of "good" and "bad," or any other terms can be used.

3.5   Answers to selected problems

Problem 3.1. The problem only arises when $p_1 > n$ or $p_2 > m$. We can change the condition of the while-loop to $p_1 \leq n \wedge p_2 \leq m$. Of course, this means that the while-loop will terminate early, when one input list has not been completely accounted for in $C = \{c_1, c_2, \dots\}$. As such, another loop needs to be added after the first. If $p_1 \leq n$ it should assign the remaining elements from $a_{p_1}, \dots, a_n$ to the remaining variables in C; otherwise $p_2 \leq m$, so $b_{p_2}, \dots, b_m$ should be given to the rest of C.

---

[2] "Programming" is understood here in a wide sense, as it can mean anything from working on the Linux kernel, to website development, to a LaTeX collaboration. See `https://git-scm.com` for more information.

A more elegant solution becomes available if we require that the elements of each list are finite. We can simply add an infinitely large element to the end of each list before starting the while-loop; clearly it will never be evaluated as less than or equal to a finite value in the opposing list, so it will never be assigned to an element of C.

Problem 3.2. It is enough to show that $\lceil n/2 \rceil + \lfloor n/2 \rfloor = n$. If n is even, then $\lceil n/2 \rceil = \lfloor n/2 \rfloor = n/2$, and $n/2 + n/2 = n$. If n is odd, then $n = 2k+1$, and so $\lceil n/2 \rceil = k+1$ while $\lfloor n/2 \rfloor = k$ and $(k+1)+k = 2k+1 = n$.

Problem 3.3. We must show that given a list of integers $L = a_1, a_2, \ldots, a_n$, the algorithm returns a list L', which consists of the numbers in L in non-decreasing order. The recursion itself suggest the right induction; we use the CIP (see page 233). If $|L| = 1$ then $L' = L$ and we are done. Otherwise, $|L| = n > 1$, and we obtain two lists L_1 and L_2 (of lengths $\lceil n/2 \rceil$ and $n - \lceil n/2 \rceil$), which, by induction hypothesis, are returned ordered. Now it remains to prove the correctness of the merging procedure, algorithm 3.1, which can also be done by induction.

Problem 3.5. Clearly, the base case is correct; given two 1-bit integers, if both integers are not 1, then at least one of them is 0, so the product is 0.

Assume that the algorithm is correct for all $n < n'$. Then the multiplications to find z_1, z_2, and z_3 are correct. Therefore, equations (3.1) and (3.3) provide proof of induction.

Problem 3.8. $O(2^{\log^2 n}) = O(n^{\log n})$, so the time complexity of Savitch's algorithm is super-polynomial, and so not very good.

Problem 3.10. First note that the second argument decreases at each recursive call, but by definition of remainder, it is non-negative. Thus, by the LNP, the algorithm terminates. We prove partial correctness by induction on the value of the second argument. In the basis case $n = 0$, so in line 1 $b \longleftarrow n = 0$, so in line 2 $b = 0$ and the algorithm terminates in line 3 and returns $(a, 1, 0) = (m, 1, 0)$, so $mx + ny = m \cdot 1 + n \cdot 0 = m$ while $d = m$, and so we are done.

In the induction step we assume that the recursive procedure returns correct values for all pairs of arguments where the second argument is $< n$ (thus, we are doing complete induction). We have that

$$(d, x, y) \longleftarrow \text{Extended-Euclid}(b, \text{rem}(a, b))$$
$$= \text{Extended-Euclid}(n, \text{rem}(m, n)),$$

from lines 1 and 5. Note that $0 \leq \text{rem}(m, n) < n$, and so we can apply the induction hypothesis and we have that:

$$n \cdot x + \text{rem}(m, n) \cdot y = d = \gcd(n, \text{rem}(m, n)).$$

First note that by problem 1.6 we have that $d = \gcd(m, n)$. Now we work on the left-hand side of the equation. We have:

$$n \cdot x + \text{rem}(m, n) \cdot y$$
$$= n \cdot x + (m - \text{div}(m, n) \cdot n) \cdot y$$
$$= m \cdot y + n \cdot (x - \text{div}(m, n) \cdot y)$$
$$= m \cdot y + n \cdot (x - \text{div}(a, b) \cdot y)$$

and we are done as this is what is returned in line 6.

3.6 Notes

For a full discussion of Mergesort and binary multiplication, see §5.1 and §5.5, respectively, in [Kleinberg and Tardos (2006)]. Mergesort has an interesting history (for details see the Chapter 3, "Sorting," in [Christian and Griffiths (2016)]): in 1945 John von Neumann wrote a program to demonstrate the power of the stored-program computer; as he was a genius, the program did not merely illustrate the stored-program paradigm, but also introduced a new way of sorting: Mergesort. See [Katajainen and Träff (1997)] for a meticulous study of this algorithm.

For a discussion of the analysis of recursive algorithms see section 9.3.6.

For more background on Savitch's algorithm (section 3.3) see theorem 7.5 in [Papadimitriou (1994)], §8.1 in [Sipser (2006)] or theorem 2.7 in [Kozen (2006)].

The reachability problem is ubiquitous in computer science. Suppose that we have a graph G with n nodes. In section 2.3.3 we presented a $O(n^2)$ time greedy algorithm for reachability, due to Dijkstra. In this chapter, in section 3.3, we presented a divide and conquer algorithm that requires $O(\log^2 n)$ space, due to Savitch . In section 4.2 we will present a dynamic programming algorithm that computes the shortest paths for all the pairs of nodes in the graph—it is due to Floyd and takes time $O(n^3)$. In subsection 4.2.1 we present another dynamic algorithm due to Bellman and Ford (which can cope with edges of negative weight). In 2005, Reingold showed that undirected reachability can be computed in space $O(\log n)$; see [Reingold (2005)] for this remarkable, but difficult, result. Note that Reingold's algorithm works for undirected graphs only.

See chapter 7 in [Rosen (2007)] for an introduction to solving recurrence relations, and §4.5, pages 93–103, in [Cormen *et al.* (2009)] for a very thorough discussion of the "master method" for solving recurrences. Here we include a very short discussion; we want to solve recurrences of the following form:

$$T(n) = aT(n/b) + f(n), \tag{3.5}$$

where $a \geq 1$ and $b > 1$ are constants and $f(n)$ is an asymptotically positive function—meaning that there exists an n_0 such that $f(n) > 0$ for all $n \geq n_0$. There are three cases for solving such a recurrence.

Case 1 is $f(n) = O(n^{\log_b a - \varepsilon})$ for some constant $\varepsilon > 0$; in this case we have that $T(n) = \Theta(n^{\log_b a})$. Case 2 is $f(n) = \Theta(n^{\log_b a} \log^k n)$ with $k \geq 0$; in this case we have that $T(n) = \Theta(n^{\log_b a} \log^{k+1} n)$. Finally, Case 3 is $f(n) = \Omega(n^{\log_b a + \varepsilon})$ with $\varepsilon > 0$, and $f(n)$ satisfies the *regularity condition*, namely $af(n/b) \leq cf(n)$ for some constant $c < 1$ and all sufficiently large n; in this case $T(n) = \Theta(f(n))$.

For example, the recurrence that appears in the analysis of mergesort is $T(n) = 2T(n/2) + cn$, so $a = 2$ and $b = 2$, and so $\log_b a = \log_2 2 = 1$, and so we can say that $f(n) = \Theta(n^{\log_b a} \log^k n) = \Theta(n \log n)$, i.e., $k = 1$ in Case 2, and so $T(n) = \Theta(n \log n)$ as was pointed out in the analysis.

Chapter 4

Dynamic Programming

> Those who cannot remember
> the past are condemned to
> repeat it.
> _____
> George Santayana

Dynamic programming is an algorithmic technique that is closely related to the divide and conquer approach we saw in the previous chapter. However, while the divide and conquer approach is essentially recursive, and so "top down," dynamic programming works "bottom up."

A dynamic programming algorithm creates an array of related but simpler subproblems, and then, it computes the solution to the big complicated problem by using the solutions to the easier subproblems which are stored in the array. We usually want to maximize profit or minimize cost.

There are three steps in finding a dynamic programming solution to a problem: (i) Define a class of subproblems, (ii) give a recurrence based on solving each subproblem in terms of simpler subproblems, and (iii) give an algorithm for computing the recurrence.

4.1 Longest monotone subsequence problem

Input: $d, a_1, a_2, \ldots, a_d \in \mathbb{N}$.
Output: L = length of the longest monotone non-decreasing subsequence.

Note that a subsequence need not be consecutive, that is $a_{i_1}, a_{i_2}, \ldots, a_{i_k}$ is a monotone subsequence provided that

$$1 \leq i_1 < i_2 < \ldots < i_k \leq d,$$
$$a_{i_1} \leq a_{i_2} \leq \ldots \leq a_{i_k}.$$

71

For example, the length of the longest monotone subsequence (henceforth LMS) of $\{4, 6, 5, 9, 1\}$ is 3.

We first define an array of subproblems: $R(j)$ = length of the longest monotone subsequence which ends in a_j. The answer can be extracted from array R by computing $L = \max_{1 \leq j \leq n} R(j)$.

The next step is to find a recurrence. Let $R(1) = 1$, and for $j > 1$,

$$R(j) = \begin{cases} 1 & \text{if } a_i > a_j \text{ for all } 1 \leq i < j \\ 1 + \max_{1 \leq i < j}\{R(i)|a_i \leq a_j\} & \text{otherwise} \end{cases}.$$

We finish by writing an algorithm that computes R; see algorithm 4.1.

Algorithm 4.1 Longest monotone subsequence (LMS)

$R(1) \leftarrow 1$
for $j : 2..d$ **do**
    max $\leftarrow 0$
    for $i : 1..j - 1$ **do**
        if $R(i) >$ max and $a_i \leq a_j$ **then**
            max $\leftarrow R(i)$
        end if
    end for
    $R(j) \leftarrow$ max $+1$
end for

Problem 4.1. *Once we have computed all the values of the array R, how could we build an actual monotone non-decreasing subsequence of length L?*

Problem 4.2. *What would be the appropriate pre/post-conditions of the above algorithms? Prove correctness with an appropriate loop invariant.*

Problem 4.3. *Consider the following variant of the Longest Monotone Subsequence problem. The input is $d, a_1, a_2, \ldots, a_d \in \mathbb{N}$, but the output is the length of the longest subsequence of $a_1, a_2, \ldots, a_d$, where any two consecutive members of the subsequence differ by at most 1. For example, the longest such subsequence of $\{7, 6, 1, 4, 7, 8, 20\}$ is $\{7, 6, 7, 8\}$, so in this case the answer would be 4. Give a dynamic programming solution.*

Problem 4.4. *Implement algorithm 4.1; your program should take an extra step parameter, call it s, where, just as in problem 4.3, any two consecutive members of the subsequence differ by at most s, that is, $|a_{i_j} - a_{i_{j+1}}| \leq s$, for any $1 \leq j < k$.*

4.2 All pairs shortest path problem

Input: Directed graph $G = (V, E)$, $V = \{1, 2, \ldots, n\}$, and a cost function
$C(i, j) \in \mathbb{N}^+ \cup \{\infty\}$, $1 \leq i, j \leq n$, $C(i, j) = \infty$ if (i, j) is not an edge.
Output: An array D, where $D(i, j)$ the length of the shortest directed path
from i to j.

Recall that we have defined undirected graphs in section 2.1; a *directed
graph* (or *digraph*) is a graph where the edges have a direction, i.e., the
edges are arrows. Also recall that in section 2.3.3 we have given a greedy
algorithm for computing the shortest paths from a designated node s to all
the nodes in an (undirected) graph.

Problem 4.5. *Construct a family of graphs $\{G_n\}$, where G_n has $O(n)$
many nodes, and exponentially many paths, that is $\Omega(2^n)$ paths. Conclude,
therefore, that an exhaustive search is not a feasible solutions to the "all
pairs shortest path problem."*

Define an array of subproblems: let $A(k, i, j)$ be the length of the shortest path from i to j such that all *intermediate* nodes on the path are in
$\{1, 2, \ldots, k\}$. Then $A(n, i, j) = D(i, j)$ will be the solution. The convention
is that if $k = 0$ then $[k] = \{1, 2, \ldots, k\} = \emptyset$.

Define a recurrence: first initialize the array for $k = 0$, $A(0, i, j) =
C(i, j)$. Now we want to compute $A(k, i, j)$ for $k > 0$. To design the
recurrence, notice that the shortest path between i and j either includes
k or does not. Assume we know $A(k - 1, r, s)$ for all r, s. Suppose node
k is not included. Then, obviously, $A(k, i, j) = A(k - 1, i, j)$. If, on the
other hand, node k occurs on a shortest path, then it occurs exactly once,
so $A(k, i, j) = A(k - 1, i, k) + A(k - 1, k, j)$. Therefore, the shortest path
length is obtained by taking the minimum of these two cases:

$$A(k, i, j) = \min\{A(k - 1, i, j), A(k - 1, i, k) + A(k - 1, k, j)\}.$$

Write an algorithm: it turns out that we only need space for a two-
dimensional array $B(i, j) = A(k, i, j)$, because to compute $A(k, *, *)$ from
$A(k - 1, *, *)$ we can overwrite $A(k - 1, *, *)$.

Our solution is algorithm 4.2, known as Floyd's algorithm (or the Floyd-
Warshall algorithm). It is remarkable as it runs in time $O(n^3)$, where n
is the number of vertices, while there may be up to $O(n^2)$ edges in such a
graph. In lines 1–5 we initialize the array B, i.e., we set it equal to C. Note
that before line 6 is executed, it is the case that $B(i, j) = A(k - 1, i, j)$ for
all i, j.

Algorithm 4.2 Floyd

1: **for** $i : 1..n$ **do**
2:          **for** $j : 1..n$ **do**
3:                    $B(i,j) \longleftarrow C(i,j)$
4:          **end for**
5: **end for**
6: **for** $k : 1..n$ **do**
7:          **for** $i : 1..n$ **do**
8:                    **for** $j : 1..n$ **do**
9:                              $B(i,j) \longleftarrow \min\{B(i,j), B(i,k) + B(k,j)\}$
10:                   **end for**
11:          **end for**
12: **end for**
13: **return** $D \longleftarrow B$

Problem 4.6. *Why does the overwriting method in algorithm 4.2 work? The worry is that $B(i,k)$ or $B(k,j)$ may have already been updated (if $k < j$ or $k < i$). However, the overwriting does work; explain why. We could have avoided a 3-dimensional array by keeping two 2-dimensional arrays instead, and then overwriting would not be an issue at all; how would that work?*

Problem 4.7. *In algorithm 4.2, what are appropriate pre and post-conditions? What is an appropriate loop invariant?*

Problem 4.8. *Implement Floyd's algorithm using the two dimensional array and the overwriting method.*

4.2.1   *Bellman-Ford algorithm*

Suppose that we want to find the shortest path from s to t, in a directed graph $G = (V, E)$, where edges have non-negative costs. Let $\text{OPT}(i, v)$ denote the minimal cost of an i-path from v to t, where an i-path is a path that uses at most i edges. Let p be an optimal i-path with cost $\text{OPT}(i, v)$; if no such p exists we adopt the convention that $\text{OPT}(i, v) = \infty$.

If p uses $i-1$ edges, then $\text{OPT}(i, v) = \text{OPT}(i-1, v)$, and if p uses i edges, and the first edge is $(v, w) \in E$, then $\text{OPT}(i, v) = c(v, w) + \text{OPT}(i - 1, w)$, where $c(v, w)$ is the cost of edge (v, w). This gives us the recursive formula, for $i > 0$: $\text{OPT}(i, v) = \min\{\text{OPT}(i-1, v), \min_{w \in V}\{c(v, w) + \text{OPT}(i-1, w)\}\}$.

Problem 4.9. *Implement Bellman-Ford's algorithm.*

4.3 Simple knapsack problem

Input: $w_1, w_2, \ldots, w_d, C \in \mathbb{N}$, where C is the knapsack's capacity.

Output: $\max_S\{K(S)|K(S) \leq C\}$, where $S \subseteq [d]$ and $K(S) = \sum_{i \in S} w_i$.

This is an NP-hard[1] problem, which means that we cannot expect to find a polynomial time algorithm that works in general. We give a dynamic programming solution that works for relatively small C; note that for our method to work the inputs $w_1, \ldots, w_d, C$ must be (non-negative) integers. We often abbreviate the name "simple knapsack problem" with SKS.

Define an array of subproblems: we consider the first i weights (i.e., $[i]$) summing up to an *intermediate* weight limit j. We define a Boolean array R as follows:

$$R(i,j) = \begin{cases} \mathsf{T} & \text{if } \exists S \subseteq [i] \text{ such that } K(S) = j \\ \mathsf{F} & \text{otherwise} \end{cases},$$

for $0 \leq i \leq d$ and $0 \leq j \leq C$. Once we have computed all the values of R we can obtain the solution M as follows: $M = \max_{j \leq C}\{j | R(d, j) = \mathsf{T}\}$.

Define a recurrence: we initialize $R(0, j) = \mathsf{F}$ for $j = 1, 2, \ldots, C$, and $R(i, 0) = \mathsf{T}$ for $i = 0, 1, \ldots, d$.

We now define the recurrence for computing R, for $i, j > 0$, in a way that hinges on whether we include object i in the knapsack. Suppose that we do *not* include object i. Then, obviously, $R(i, j) = \mathsf{T}$ iff $R(i-1, j) = \mathsf{T}$. Suppose, on the other hand, that object i *is* included. Then it must be the case that $R(i, j) = \mathsf{T}$ iff $R(i-1, j-w_i) = \mathsf{T}$ and $j - w_i \geq 0$, i.e., there is a subset $S \subseteq [i-1]$ such that $K(S)$ is exactly $j - w_i$ (in which case $j \geq w_i$). Putting it all together we obtain the following recurrence for $i, j > 0$:

$$R(i,j) = \mathsf{T} \iff R(i-1, j) = \mathsf{T} \vee (j \geq w_i \wedge R(i-1, j-w_i) = \mathsf{T}). \quad (4.1)$$

Figure 4.1 summarizes the computation of the recurrence.

We finally design algorithm 4.3 that uses the same space saving trick as algorithm 4.2; it employs a one-dimensional array $S(j)$ for keeping track of a two-dimensional array $R(i, j)$. This is done by overwriting $R(i, j)$ with $R(i+1, j)$.

In algorithm 4.3, in line 1 we initialize the array for $i = j = 0$. In lines 2–4 we initialize the array for $i = 0$ and $j \in \{1, 2, \ldots, C\}$. Note that

---

[1]NP is the class of problems solvable in polynomial time on a *nondeterministic* Turing machine. A problem P is NP-hard if every problem in NP is reducible to P in polynomial time, that is, every problem in NP can be efficiently restated in terms of P. When a problem is NP-hard this is an indication that it is probably *intractable*, i.e., it cannot be solved efficiently in general. For more information on this see any book on complexity, for example [Papadimitriou (1994); Sipser (2006); Soltys (2009)].

R	0	$\cdots$	$j-w_i$	$\cdots$	j	$\cdots$	C
0	T	F$\cdots$F	F	F$\cdots$F	F	F$\cdots$F	F
	T						
$\vdots$							
	T						
$i-1$	T		**c**		**b**		
i	T				**a**		
	T						
$\vdots$							
	T						
d	T						

Fig. 4.1 The recurrence given by the equivalence (4.1) can be interpreted as follows: we place a T in the square labeled with **a** if and only if at least one of the following two conditions is satisfied: there is a T in the position right above it, i.e., in the square labeled with **b** (if we can construct j with the first $i-1$ weights, surely we can construct j with he first i weights), or there is a T in the square labeled with **c** (if we can construct $j-w_i$ with the first $i-1$ weights, surely we can construct j with the first i weights). Also note that to fill the square labeled with **a** we only need to look at two squares, and neither of those two squares is to the right; this will be important in the design of the algorithm (algorithm 4.3).

after each execution of the i-loop (line 5) it is the case that $S(j) = R(i,j)$ for all j.

Problem 4.10. *We are using a one dimensional array to keep track of a two dimensional array, but the overwriting is not a problem; explain why.*

Problem 4.11. *The assertion $S(j) = R(i,j)$ can be proved by induction on the number of times the i-loop in algorithm 4.3 is executed. This assertion implies that upon termination of the algorithm, $S(j) = R(d,j)$ for all j. Prove this formally, by giving pre/post-conditions, a loop invariant, and a standard proof of correctness.*

Problem 4.12. *Construct an input for which algorithm 4.3 would make an error if the inner loop "for decreasing $j : C..1$" (line 6) were changed to "for $j : 1..C$."*

Problem 4.13. *Implement algorithm 4.3.*

Algorithm 4.3 is a nice illustration of the powerful idea of *program refinement*. We start with the idea of computing $R(i,j)$ for all i,j. We then

---

Algorithm 4.3 Simple knapsack (SKS)

1: $S(0) \longleftarrow$ T
2: **for** $j : 1..C$ **do**
3:      $S(j) \longleftarrow$ F
4: **end for**
5: **for** $i : 1..d$ **do**
6:      **for** *decreasing* $j : C..1$ **do**
7:          **if** $(j \geq w_i$ and $S(j - w_i) =$ T$)$ **then**
8:              $S(j) \longleftarrow$ T
9:          **end if**
10:     **end for**
11: **end for**

---

realize that we only really need two rows in memory; to compute row i we only need to look up row $i - 1$. We then take it further and see that by updating row i from right to left we do not require row $i - 1$ at all—we can do it *mise en place*. By starting with a robust idea, and by successively trimming it, we obtain a slick solution.

But how good is our dynamic programming solution in terms of the complexity of the problem? That is, how many steps does it take to compute the solution *proportionally* to the size of the input? We must construct a $d \times C$ table and fill it in, so the time complexity of our solution is $O(d \cdot C)$. This seems acceptable at first glance, but we were saying in the introduction to this section that SKS is an NP-hard problem; what gives?

The point is that the input is assumed to be given in binary, and to encode C in binary we require only $\log C$ bits, and so the number of columns (C) is in fact exponential in the size of the input ($C = 2^{\log C}$). On the other hand, d is the number of weights, and since those weights must be listed somehow, the size of the list of weights is certainly bigger than d (i.e., this list cannot be encoded—in general—with $\log d$ bits; it requires at least d bits).

All we can say is that if C is of size $O(d^k)$, for some constant k, then our dynamic programming solution works in polynomial time in the size of the input. In other words, we have an efficient solution for "small" values of C. Another way of saying this is that as long as $|C|$ (the size of the binary encoding of C) is $O(\log d)$ our solution works in polynomial time.

Problem 4.14. *Show how to construct the actual optimal set of weights once R has been computed.*

Problem 4.15. *Define a "natural" greedy algorithm for solving SKS; let* $\overline{M}$ *be the output of this algorithm, and let* M *be the output of the dynamic programming solution given in this section. Show that either* $\overline{M} = M$ *or* $\overline{M} > \frac{1}{2}C$.

Problem 4.15 introduces surreptitiously the concept of *approximation algorithms*. As was mentioned at the beginning of this section (see footnote on page 75), SKS is an example of an NP-hard problem, a problem for which we suspect there may be no efficient solution in the general case. That is, the majority of experts believe that any algorithm—attempting to solve SKS in the general case—on infinitely many inputs will take an inordinate number of steps (i.e., time) to produce a solution.

One possible compromise is to design an efficient algorithm that does not give an *optimal* solution—which may not even be required—but only a solution with some guarantees as to its closeness to an optimal solution. Thus, we merely *approximate* the optimal solution but at least our algorithm runs quickly. The study of such compromises is undertaken by the field of approximation algorithms.

Finally, in the section below we give a greedy solution to SKS in the particular case where the weights have a certain "increasing property." This is an example of a *promise* problem, where we can expect some convenient condition on the inputs; a condition that we need not check for, but assume that we have. Note that we have been using the term "promising" to prove the correctness of greedy algorithms—this is a different notion from that of a "promise problem."

4.3.1 *Dispersed knapsack problem*

Input: $w_1, \ldots, w_d, C \in \mathbb{N}$, such that $w_i \geq \sum_{j=i+1}^{d} w_j$ for $i = 1, \ldots, d-1$.
Output: $S_{\max} \subseteq [d]$ where $K(S_{\max}) = \max_{S \subseteq [d]} \{K(S) | K(S) \leq C\}$.

Problem 4.16. *Give a "natural" greedy algorithm which solves Dispersed Knapsack by filling in the blanks in algorithm 4.4.*

Problem 4.17. *Give a definition of what it means for an intermediate solution* S *in algorithm 4.4 to be "promising." Show that the loop invariant "S is promising" implies that the greedy algorithm gives the optimal solution. Finally, show that "S is promising" is a loop invariant.*

Algorithm 4.4 Dispersed knapsack

   $S \longleftarrow \emptyset$
   for $i : 1..d$ **do**
        if _____ **then**

           _____

        end if
   end for

4.3.2 *General knapsack problem*

Input: $w_1, w_2, \ldots, w_d, v_1, \ldots, v_d, C \in \mathbb{N}$
Output: $\max_{S \subseteq [d]}\{V(S)|K(S) \le C\}$, $K(S) = \sum_{i \in S} w_i$, $V(S) = \sum_{i \in S} v_i$.

Thus, the general knapsack problem (which we abbreviate as GKS) has a positive integer value v_i besides each weight w_i, and the goal is to have as valuable a knapsack as possible, without exceeding C, i.e., the weight capacity of the knapsack.

More precisely, $V(S) = \sum_{i \in S} v_i$ is the total value of the set S of weights. The goal is to maximize $V(S)$, subject to the constraint that $K(S)$, which is the sum of the weights in S, is at most C. Note that SKS is a special case of GKS where $v_i = w_i$, for all $1 \le i \le d$.

To solve GKS, we start by computing the same Boolean array $R(i,j)$ that was used to solve SKS. Thus $R(i,j)$ ignores the values v_i, and only depends on the weights w_i. Next we define another array $V(i,j)$ that depends on the values v_i as follows:

$$V(i,j) = \max\{V(S)|S \subseteq [i] \text{ and } K(S) = j\}, \qquad (4.2)$$

for $0 \le i \le d$ and $0 \le j \le C$.

Problem 4.18. *Give a recurrence for computing the array $V(i,j)$, using the Boolean array $R(i,j)$—assume that the array $R(i,j)$ has already been computed. Also, give an algorithm for computing $V(i,j)$.*

Problem 4.19. *If the definition of $V(i,j)$ given in (4.2) is changed so that we only require $K(S) \le j$ instead of $K(S) = j$, then the Boolean array $R(i,j)$ is not needed in the recurrence. Give the recurrence in this case.*

4.4   Activity selection problem

Input: A list of activities $(s_1, f_1, p_1), \ldots, (s_n, f_n, p_n)$, where $p_i > 0$, $s_i < f_i$ and s_i, f_i, p_i are non-negative real numbers.

Output: A set $S \subseteq [n]$ of selected activities such that no two selected activities overlap, and the profit $P(S) = \sum_{i \in S} p_i$ is as large as possible.

An *activity i* has a fixed start time s_i, finish time f_i and profit p_i. Given a set of activities, we want to select a subset of non-overlapping activities with maximum total profit. A typical example of the activity selection problem is a set of lectures with fixed start and finish times that need to be scheduled in a single class room.

Define an array of subproblems: sort the activities by their finish times, $f_1 \leq f_2 \leq \ldots \leq f_n$. As it is possible that activities finish at the same time, we select the *distinct* finish times, and denote them $u_1 < u_2 < \ldots < u_k$, where, clearly, $k \leq n$. For instance, if we have activities finishing at times 1.24, 4, 3.77, 1.24, 5 and 3.77, then we partition them into four groups: activities finishing at times $u_1 = 1.24$, $u_2 = 3.77$, $u_3 = 4$, $u_4 = 5$.

Let u_0 be $\min_{1 \leq i \leq n} s_i$, i.e., the earliest start time. Thus,

$$u_0 < u_1 < u_2 < \ldots < u_k,$$

as it is understood that $s_i < f_i$. Define an array $A(0..k)$ as follows:

$$A(j) = \max_{S \subseteq [n]} \{ P(S) \mid S \text{ is feasible and } f_i \leq u_j \text{ for each } i \in S \},$$

where S is *feasible* if no two activities in S overlap. Note that $A(k)$ is the maximum possible profit for all feasible schedules S.

Problem 4.20. *Give a formal definition of what it means for a schedule of activities to be feasible, i.e., express precisely that the activities in a set S "do not overlap."*

Define a recurrence for $A(0..k)$. In order to give such a recurrence we first define an auxiliary array $H(1..n)$ such that $H(i)$ is the index of the largest distinct finish time no greater than the start time of activity i. Formally, $H(i) = l$ if l is the largest number such that $u_l \leq s_i$. To compute $H(i)$, we need to search the list of distinct finish times. To do it efficiently, for each i, apply the binary search procedure that runs in logarithmic time in the length of the list of distinct finish times (try $l = \lfloor \frac{k}{2} \rfloor$ first). Since the length k of the list of distinct finish times is at most n, and we need to apply binary search for each element of the array $H(1..n)$, the time required to compute all entries of the array is $O(n \log n)$.

We initialize $A(0) = 0$, and we want to compute $A(j)$ given that we already have $A(0), \ldots, A(j-1)$. Consider $u_0 < u_1 < u_2 < \ldots < u_{j-1} < u_j$. Can we beat profit $A(j - 1)$ by scheduling some activity that finishes at time u_j? Try all activities that finish at this time and compute maximum profit in each case. We obtain the following recurrence:

$$A(j) = \max\{A(j-1), \max_{1 \le i \le n} \{p_i + A(H(i)) \mid f_i = u_j\}\}, \qquad (4.3)$$

where $H(i)$ is the greatest l such that $u_l \le s_i$. Consider the example given in figure 4.2.

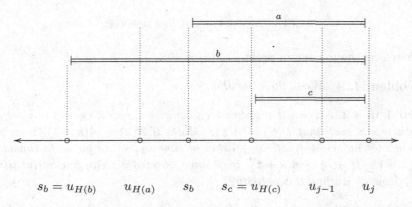

Fig. 4.2 In this example we want to compute $A(j)$. Suppose that some activity finishing at time u_j must be scheduled in order to obtain the maximum possible profit. In this figure there are three activities that end at time u_j: a, b, c, given by $(s_a, f_a, p_a), (s_b, f_b, p_b), (s_c, f_c, p_c)$, respectively, where of course the assumption is that $u_j = f_a = f_b = f_c$. The question is which of these three activities must be selected. In order to establish this, we must look at each activity a, b, c in turn, and see what is the most profitable schedule that we can get if we *insist* that the given activity is scheduled. For example, if we insist that activity a be scheduled, we must see what is the most profitable schedule we can get where all other activities must finish by s_a, which effectively means that all other activities must finish by $u_{H(a)}$. Note that in this example we have that $u_{H(a)} < s_a$, but $u_{H(b)} = s_b$ and $u_{H(c)} = s_c$. When all is said, we must find which of the three values $p_a + A(H(a)), p_b + A(H(b)), p_c + A(H(c))$ is maximal.

Consider the éxample in figure 4.3. To see how the bottom row of the right-hand table in figure 4.3 was computed, note that according to the recurrence (4.3), we have:

$$A(2) = \max\{20, 30 + A(0), 20 + A(1)\} = 40,$$
$$A(3) = \max\{40, 30 + A(0)\} = 40.$$

Activity i:	1	2	3	4
Start s_i:	0	2	3	2
Finish f_i:	3	6	6	10
Profit p_i:	20	30	20	30
$H(i)$:	0	0	1	0

j:	0	1	2	3
u_j:	0	3	6	10
$A(j)$:	0	20	40	40

Fig. 4.3   An example with four activities.

Therefore, the maximum profit is $A(3) = 40$.

Problem 4.21. *Write the algorithm.*

Problem 4.22. *Given that A has been computed, how do you find a set of activities S such that $P(S) = A(k)$? Hint: If $A(k) = A(k-1)$, then we know that no selected activity finishes at time u_k, so we go on to consider $A(k-1)$. If $A(k) > A(k-1)$, then some selected activity finishes at time u_k. How do we find this activity?*

Problem 4.23. *Implement the dynamic programming solution to the "activity selection with profits problem." Your algorithm should compute the value of the most profitable set of activities, as well as output an explicit list of those activities.*

4.5   Jobs with deadlines, durations and profits

Input: A list of jobs $(d_1, t_1, p_1), \ldots, (d_n, t_n, p_n)$.
Output: A feasible schedule $C(1..n)$ such that the profit of C, denoted $P(C)$, is the maximum possible among feasible schedules.

In section 2.2 we considered the job scheduling problems for the case where each job takes unit time, i.e., each duration $d_i = 1$. We now generalize this to the case in which each job i has an arbitrary duration d_i, deadline t_i and profit p_i. We assume that d_i and t_i are positive integers, but the profit p_i can be a positive real number. We say that the schedule $C(1..n)$ is *feasible* if the following two conditions hold (let $C(i) = -1$ denote that job i is *not* scheduled, and so $C(i) \geq 0$ indicates that it *is* scheduled, and note that we do allow jobs to be scheduled at time 0):

(1) if $C(i) \geq 0$, then $C(i) + d_i \leq t_i$; and,
(2) if $i \neq j$ and $C(i), C(j) \geq 0$, then

    (a) $C(i) + d_i \leq C(j)$; or,
    (b) $C(j) + d_j \leq C(i)$.

The first condition is akin to saying that each scheduled job finishes by its deadline and the second condition is akin to saying that no two scheduled jobs overlap. The goal is to find a feasible schedule $C(1..n)$ for the n jobs for which the profit $P(C) = \sum_{C(i) \geq 0} p_i$, the sum of the profits of the scheduled jobs, is maximized.

A job differs from an activity in that a job can be scheduled any time as long as it finishes by its deadline; an activity has a fixed start time and finish time. Because of the flexibility in scheduling jobs, it is "harder" to find an optimal schedule for jobs than to select an optimal subset of activities.

Note that job scheduling is "at least as hard as SKS." In fact an SKS instance $w_1, \ldots, w_n, C$ can be viewed as a job scheduling problem in which each duration $d_i = w_i$, each deadline $t_i = C$, and each profit $p_i = w_i$. Then the maximum profit of any schedule is the same as the maximum weight that can be put into the knapsack. This seemingly innocent idea of "at least as hard as" is in fact a powerful tool widely used in the field of computational complexity to compare the relative difficulty of problems. By restating a general instance of job scheduling as an instance of SKS we provided a *reduction* of job scheduling to SKS, and shown thereby that if one were able to solve job scheduling efficiently, one would automatically have an efficient solution to SKS.

To give a dynamic programming solution to the job scheduling problem, we start by sorting the jobs according to deadlines. Thus, we assume that $t_1 \leq t_2 \leq \ldots \leq t_n$.

It turns out that to define a suitable array A for solving the problem, we must consider all possible integer times t, $0 \leq t \leq t_n$ as a deadline for the first i jobs. It is not enough to only consider the specified deadline t_i given in the problem input. Thus define the array $A(i, t)$ as follows:

$$A(i,t) = \max \left\{ P(C) : \begin{array}{l} C \text{ is a feasible schedule} \\ \text{only jobs in } [i] \text{ are scheduled} \\ \text{all scheduled jobs finish by time } t \end{array} \right\}.$$

We now want to design a recurrence for computing $A(i, t)$. In the usual style, consider the two cases that either job i occurs or does not occur in the optimal schedule (and note that job i will not occur in the optimal schedule if $d_i > \min\{t_i, t\}$). If job i does not occur, we already know the optimal profit.

If, on the other hand, job i does occur in an optimal schedule, then we may as well assume that it is the last job (among jobs $\{1, \ldots, i\}$) to be scheduled, because it has the latest deadline. Hence we assume that job i is scheduled as late as possible, so that it finishes either at time t, or at time t_i, whichever is smaller, i.e., it finishes at time $t_{\min} = \min\{t_i, t\}$.

Problem 4.24. *In light of the discussion in the above two paragraphs, find a recurrence for $A(i, t)$.*

Problem 4.25. *Implement your solution.*

4.6   Further examples and problems

4.6.1   *Consecutive subsequence sum problem*

Input: Real numbers $r_1, \ldots, r_n$
Output: For each consecutive subsequence of the form $r_i, r_{i+1}, \ldots, r_j$ let

$$S_{ij} = r_i + r_{i+1} + \cdots + r_j$$

where $S_{ii} = r_i$. Find $M = \max_{1 \le i \le j \le n} S_{ij}$.

For example, in figure 4.4 we have a sample consecutive subsequence sum problem. There, the solution is $M = S_{35} = 3 + (-1) + 2 = 4$.

This problem can be solved in time $O(n^2)$ by systematically computing all of the sums S_{ij} and finding the maximum (there are $\binom{n}{2}$ pairs $i, j \le n$ such that $i < j$). However, there is a more efficient dynamic programming solution which runs in time $O(n)$.

Define the array $M(1..n)$ by:

$$M(j) = \max\{S_{1j}, S_{2j}, \ldots, S_{jj}\}.$$

See figure 4.4 for an example.

Problem 4.26. *Explain how to find the solution M from the array $M(1..n)$.*

Problem 4.27. *Complete the four lines indicated in algorithm 4.5 for computing the values of the array $M(1..n)$, given $r_1, r_2, \ldots, r_n$.*

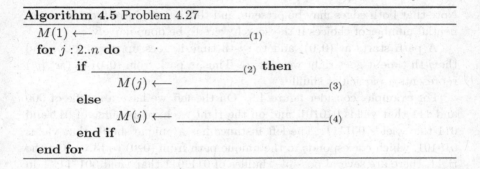

j	1	2	3	4	5	6	7
r_j	1	−5	3	−1	2	−8	3
$M(j)$	1	−4	3	2	4	−4	3

Fig. 4.4   An example of computing $M(j)$.

Algorithm 4.5 Problem 4.27

$M(1) \longleftarrow$ _____(1)
for $j : 2..n$ **do**
    if _____(2) **then**
        $M(j) \longleftarrow$ _____(3)
    else
        $M(j) \longleftarrow$ _____(4)
    end if
end for

4.6.2   *Shuffle*

In this section we are going to study an algorithm that works on strings; see Section 8.2 for the background on strings, alphabets and languages.

If u, v, and w are strings over an alphabet Σ, then w is a *shuffle* of u and v provided there are (possibly empty) strings x_i and y_i such that $u = x_1 x_2 \cdots x_k$ and $v = y_1 y_2 \cdots y_k$ and $w = x_1 y_1 x_2 y_2 \cdots x_k y_k$. A shuffle is sometimes instead called a "merge" or an "interleaving." The intuition for the definition is that w can be obtained from u and v by an operation similar to shuffling two decks of cards. We use $w = u \odot v$ to denote that w is a shuffle of u and v; note, however, that in spite of the notation there can be many different shuffles w of u and v. The string w is called a *square* provided it is equal to a shuffle of a string u with itself, namely provided $w = u \odot u$ for some string u. [Buss and Soltys (2013)] showed that the set of squares is NP-complete; this is true even for (sufficiently large) finite alphabets. See Section 4.3 for NP-completeness.

In the early 1980's, Mansfield [Mansfield (1982, 1983)] and Warmuth and Haussler [Warmuth and Haussler (1984)] studied the computational complexity of the shuffle operation. The paper [Mansfield (1982)] gave a polynomial time dynamic programming algorithm for deciding the following shuffle problem: Given inputs u, v, w, can w be expressed as a shuffle of u and v, that is, does $w = u \odot v$?

The idea behind the algorithm of [Mansfield (1982)] is to construct a grid graph, with $(|x|+1) \times (|y|+1)$ nodes; the lower-left node is represented with $(0,0)$ and the upper-right node is represented with $(|x|,|y|)$. For any $i < |x|$ and $j < |y|$, we have the edges:

$$\begin{cases} ((i,j),(i+1,j)) & \text{if } x_{i+1} = w_{i+j+1} \\ ((i,j),(i,j+1)) & \text{if } y_{j+1} = w_{i+j+1}. \end{cases} \tag{4.4}$$

Note that both edges may be present, and this in turn introduces an exponential number of choices if the search were to be done naïvely.

A path starts at $(0,0)$, and the i-th time it goes up we pick x_i, and the j-th time it goes right we pick y_j. Thus, a path from $(0,0)$ to $(|x|,|y|)$ represents a particular shuffle.

For example, consider figure 4.5. On the left we have a shuffle of 000 and 111 that yields 010101, and on the right we have a shuffle of 011 and 011 that yields 001111. The left instance has a unique shuffle that yields 010101, which corresponds to the unique path from $(0,0)$ to $(3,3)$. On the right, there are several possible shuffles of $011, 011$ that yield 001111 — in fact, eight of them, each corresponding to a distinct path from $(0,0)$ to $(3,3)$.

The dynamic programming algorithm in [Mansfield (1982)] computes partial solutions along the top-left to bottom-right diagonal lines in the grid graph.

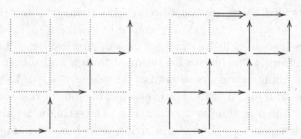

Fig. 4.5 On the left we have a shuffle of 000 and 111 that yields 010101, and on the right we have a shuffle of 011 and 011 that yields 001111. The double arrow in the right diagram is there to show that there may be other arrows beside the solid arrows; the double arrow is $((1,3),(2,3))$ and it is there because $x_{1+1} = x_2 = 1 = w_5 = w_{1+3+1}$. The edges are placed according to (4.4).

The number of paths is always bounded by:

$$\binom{|x|+|y|}{|x|}$$

and this bound is achieved for $\langle 1^n, 1^n, 1^{2n} \rangle$. Thus, the number of paths can be exponential in the size of the input, and so an exhaustive search is not feasible in general.

Problem 4.28. *Given the discussion in this section, propose a dynamic programming algorithm that on input w, u, v checks whether $w = u \odot v$.*

4.7 Answers to selected problems

Problem 4.1. Once we've computed the values of R, we can follow it backward from the end of a longest non-decreasing subsequence. Such a sequence must end on an index j such that $R(j)$ is maximal. If $R(j) = 1$, we're done. Otherwise, to find the index preceding j, find any index $i < j$ such that $R(i) = R(j) - 1$ and $a_i \leq a_j$; one necessarily exists, or $R(j)$ would be smaller. Continue backtracking as such until arriving at the beginning of the subsequence, where R is 1.

Problem 4.2. Algorithm 4.1 requires only that its input is a finite sequence of ordered objects (i.e., objects for which the "$\leq$" makes sense). Its post-condition, which we aim to prove, is that for all j in $\{1, 2, \ldots, d\}$, $R(j)$ is the length of the longest non-decreasing subsequence ending with a_j.

We claim that after j iterations of the outer "for" loop, $R(j)$ is the length of the longest subsequence ending with a_j, and moreover, that the same is true for all $i < j$. The prior implies the latter, as once a value is assigned to $R(i)$ the algorithm never reassigns it.

The proof will be by complete induction over j. Let S_j denote any longest non-decreasing subsequence ending in a_j for any index j. For the base case, clearly $R(1) = 1$ is the correct assignment; the empty subsequence has length less than 1, and the only other subsequence, $\{a_1\}$, is trivially non-decreasing with cardinality 1. Assume, then, that for all $i < j$, $R(i)$ has been assigned the correct value. If $S_j = \{a_j\}$, then there is no $i < j$ such that $a_i \leq a_j$, so the value of max will never be changed after its initial assignment of 0. As such, $R(j)$ is given the correct value, 1. If, on the other hand, $|S_j| > 1$, then there is an element a_i directly preceding a_j in S_j, where $a_i \leq a_j$ and $i < j$. Clearly there is an S_i such that $S_j = S_i \cup \{a_j\}$, so $|S_j| = |S_i| + 1 = R(i) + 1$.

Assume that max $\neq R(i)$ after iteration i of the inner for loop. $a_i \leq a_j$, so $R(i) < $ max. Thus there is an $i' < i$ such that $a_{i'} \leq a_j$ and $R(i') > R(i)$. But $S_{i'} \cup \{a_j\}$ is non-decreasing, ends on a_j, and has cardinality greater than S_j — a contradiction. Similarly, max cannot be reassigned afterward, as this leads the same contradiction. Thus, at the end of iteration j, $R(j)$ is assigned the correct value, $R(i) + 1$. So, after iteration d, $R(j)$ is correct for all j.

Problem 4.3. In order to find the length of the longest subsequence over which any two consecutive members differ by at most 1, we can simply edit the "if" condition in algorithm 4.1. Specifically, "$a_i \le a_j$" can be replaced with "$|a_i - a_j| \le 1$".

Problem 4.5. Consider the graph G_n in figure 4.6. It contains $2 + n + n = 2n + 2$ nodes, and 2^n paths from s to t; starting at s we have a choice to go to node 1 or node 1', and then we always have a choice to go up or down, so $2 \times 2^{n-1}$ paths that land us at n or n'. Finally, we just go to t. Note that we have given an undirected graph; but simply giving all the edges a "left-to-right" direction gives us an example for directed graphs.

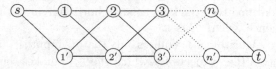

Fig. 4.6   Exponentially many paths (problem 4.5).

Problems 4.6 and 4.7. The pre-condition is that $\forall i, j \in [n]$ we have that $B(i, j) = A(0, i, j)$. The post-condition is that $\forall i, j \in [n]$ we have that $B(i, j) = A(n, i, j)$. The loop invariant is that after the k-th iteration of the main loop, $B(i, j) = A(k, i, j)$. To prove the loop invariant note that $B(i, j)$ is given by $\min\{B(i, j), B(i, k) + B(k, j)\}$, so the only worry is that $B(i, k)$ or $B(k, j)$ was *already* updated, so we are not getting $A(k - 1, i, k)$ or $A(k - 1, k, j)$ as we should, but rather $A(k, i, k)$ or $A(k, k, j)$. But, it turns out that $A(k, i, k) = A(k - 1, i, k)$ and $A(k, k, j) = A(k - 1, k, j)$, because the shortest path from i to k (or k to j) does *not* contain k as an intermediate node.

Problem 4.10. Overwriting does not create a problem, because the values of j are considered in decreasing order $C, C - 1, \ldots, 1$. Thus the array position $S(j - w_i)$ has not yet been updated when the reference is made.

Problem 4.11. The pre-condition is that for all j, $S(j) = R(0, j)$. The post-condition is that for all j, $S(j) = R(d, j)$. Let the loop invariant be the assertion that after the i-th step, $S(j) = R(i, j)$. This loop invariant holds since we start "filling" S in from the right, and we only change false to true (never true to false—the reason is that if we could build an intermediate value j with the first $(i-1)$ weights, we can certainly still construct it with the first i weights).

Problem 4.12. Consider $w_1 = w_2 = 1$, $w_3 = 2$ and $C = 3$, so the table on this input would look as follows:

	0	1	2	3
	T	F	F	F
$w_1 = 1$	T	T	F	F
$w_2 = 1$	T	T	T	F
$w_3 = 2$	T	T	T	T

Now consider the row for $w_1 = 1$, and the entry for the column labeled with 2. That entry is an F, as it should be, but if the for-loop in algorithm 4.3 were not a decreasing loop, then we would update that entry to a T since for $j = 2$, we have that $2 \geq w_1$ and $S(2 - w_1) = $ T.

Problem 4.14. First, we need to find the solution; so we look in the last row (i.e., row d) for the largest non-zero j. That is, the solution is given by $M = \max_{0 \leq j \leq C}[R(d, j) = $ T$]$. Now we check if $R(d-1, M) = $ T. If yes, then we know that weight w_d is not necessary, so we do not include it, and continue looking at $R(d-2, M)$. If no, then because $R(d, M) = $ T, we know that $M - w_d \geq 0 \wedge R(d-1, M - w_d) = $ T. So we include w_d, and continue looking at $R(d-1, M - w_d)$. We stop when we reach the first column of the array.

Problem 4.15. The natural greedy algorithm that attempts to solve SKS is the following: order the weights from the heaviest to the lightest, and add them in that order for as long as possible. Assume that $\overline{M} \neq M$, and let S_0 be the result of this greedy procedure, i.e., a subset of $\{1, \ldots, d\}$ such that $K(S_0) = \overline{M}$. First show that there is at least one weight in S_0: If $S_0 = \emptyset$, then $\overline{M} = 0$, and all weights must be larger than C, but then $M = 0$, so $\overline{M} = M$ which is not the case by assumption. Now show that there is at least one weight not in S_0: if all the weights are in S, then again $\overline{M} = \sum_{i=1}^{d} w_i = M$. Finally, show now that $\overline{M} > \frac{1}{2}C$ by considering the first weight, call it w_j, which has been rejected after at least one weight has been added (note that such a weight must exist; we may assume that there are no weights larger than the capacity C, and if there are we can just not consider them; therefore, the first weight on the list is added, and then we know that some weight will come along which won't be added; we consider the first such weight): If $w_j \leq \frac{1}{2}C$, then the sum of the weights which are already in is $> \frac{1}{2}C$, so $\overline{M} > \frac{1}{2}C$. If $w_j > \frac{1}{2}C$, then, since the objects are ordered by greedy in non-increasing order of weights, the weights that are already in are $> \frac{1}{2}C$, so again $\overline{M} > \frac{1}{2}C$.

Problem 4.16. In the first space put $w_i + \sum_{j \in S} w_j \leq C$ and in the second space put $S \longleftarrow S \cup \{i\}$.

Problem 4.17. Define "S is promising" to mean that S can be extended, using weights which have *not* been considered yet, to an optimal solution $S_{\max}$. At the end, when no more weights have been left to consider, the loop invariant still holds true, so S itself must be optimal.

We show that "S is promising" is a loop invariant by induction on the number of iterations. Basis case: $S = \emptyset$, so S is clearly promising. Induction step: Suppose that S is promising (so S can be extended, using weights which have not been considered yet, to $S_{\max}$). Let S' be S after one more iteration. Suppose $i \in S'$. Since $w_i \geq \sum_{j=i+1}^{d} w_j$, it follows that:

$$K(S') \geq K(S) + \sum_{j=i+1}^{d} w_j$$

so S' already contains at least as much weight as any extension of S not including w_i. If S' is optimal, we are done. Otherwise, $S_{\max}$ has more weight than S', so it must contain w_i. Suppose $i \notin S'$; then we have that $w_i + \sum_{j \in S} w_j > C$, so $i \notin S_{\max}$. As such, S' can be extended (using weights which have not been considered yet!) to $S_{\max}$. In either case, S' is promising.

Problem 4.18. $V(i, j) = 0$ if $i = 0$ or $j = 0$. And for $i, j > 0$, $V(i, j)$ is

$$\begin{cases} V(i-1, j) & \text{if } j < w_i \text{ or } R(i-1, j-w_i) = \mathsf{F} \\ \max\{v_i + V(i-1, j-w_i), V(i-1, j)\} & \text{otherwise} \end{cases}$$

To see that this works, suppose that $j < w_i$. Then weight i cannot be included, so $V(i, j) = V(i-1, j)$. If $R(i-1, j-w_i) = \mathsf{F}$, then there is no subset $S \subseteq \{1, \ldots, i\}$ such that $i \in S$ and $K(S) = j$, so again weight i is not included, and $V(i, j) = V(i-1, j)$.

Otherwise, if $j \geq w_i$ and $R(i-1, j-w_i) = \mathsf{T}$, then weight i may or may not be included in S. We take the case which offers more value: $\max\{v_i + V(i-1, j-w_i), V(i-1, j)\}$.

Problem 4.19. By changing the definition of $V(i, j)$ given in (4.2) to have $K(S) \leq j$ (instead of $K(S) = j$), we can take the recurrence given for V in the solution to problem 4.18 and simply get rid of the part "or $R(i-1, j-w_i) = \mathsf{F}$" to obtain a recurrence for V that does not require computing R.

Problem 4.20. Suppose a schedule S contains activities $\{a_1, a_2, \dots\}$, where $a_n = (s_n, f_n, p_n)$ is the start time, finish time and profit of a_n for all n. S is feasible if, for all $a_i, a_j \in S$, either $f_i \leq s_j$ or $f_j \leq s_i$; that is, the first of the two must be finished before the second is started, as they clearly overlap otherwise.

Problem 4.21. The algorithm must include a computation of the distinct finish times, i.e., the u_i's, as well as a computation of the array H. Here we just give the algorithm for computing A based on the recurrence (4.3). The assumption is that there are n activities and k distinct finish times.

Algorithm 4.6 Activity selection

$A(0) \longleftarrow 0$
for $j : 1..k$ **do**
    max $\longleftarrow 0$
    for $i = 1..n$ **do**
        if $f_i = u_j$ **then**
            if $p_i + A(H(i)) >$ max **then**
                max $\longleftarrow p_i + A(H(i))$
            end if
        end if
    end for
    if $A(j-1) >$ max **then**
        max $\longleftarrow A(j-1)$
    end if
    $A(j) \longleftarrow$ max
end for

Problem 4.22. We show how to find the actual set of activities: Suppose $k > 0$. If $A(k) = A(k-1)$, then no activity has been scheduled to end at time u_k, so we proceed recursively to examine $A(k-1)$. If, on the other hand, $A(k) \neq A(k-1)$, then we know that some activity has been scheduled to end at time u_k. We have to find out which one it is. We know that in this case $A(k) = \max_{1 \leq i \leq n} \{p_i + A(H(i)) | f_i = u_k\}$, so we examine all activities i, $1 \leq i \leq n$, and output the (first) activity i_0 such that $A(k) = p_{i_0} + A(H(i_0))$ and $f_{i_0} \leq u_k$. Now we repeat the procedure with $A(H(i_0))$. We end when $k = 0$.

Problem 4.24. Initialization: $A(0, t) = 0$, $0 \leq t \leq t_n$. To compute $A(i, t)$

for $i > 0$ first define $t_{\min} = \min\{t, t_i\}$. Now

$$A(i, t) = \begin{cases} A(i-1, t) & \text{if } t_{\min} < d_i \\ \max\{A(i-1, t), p_i + A(i-1, t_{\min} - d_i)\} & \text{otherwise} \end{cases}$$

Justification: If job i is scheduled in the optimal schedule, it finishes at time $t_{\min}$, and starts at time $t_{\min} - d_i$. If it is scheduled, the maximum possible profit is $A(i-1, t_{\min} - d_i) + p_i$. Otherwise, the maximum profit is $A(i-1, t)$.

Problem 4.26. $M = \max_{1 \le j \le n} M(j)$

Problem 4.27.

(1) $r_1 (= S_{11})$
(2) $M(j-1) > 0$
(3) $M(j-1) + r_j$
(4) r_j

4.8 Notes

Any algorithms textbook will have a section on dynamic programming; see for example chapter 15 in [Cormen *et al.* (2009)] and chapter 6 in [Kleinberg and Tardos (2006)].

While matroids serve as a good abstract model for greedy algorithms, a general model for dynamic programming is being currently developed. See [Aleknovich *et al.* (2005)].

The material on the shuffle operation, Section 4.6.2, comes from [Buss and Soltys (2013)] and from [Mhaskar and Soltys (2015)]. The initial work on shuffles arose out of abstract formal languages, and shuffles were motivated later by applications to modeling sequential execution of concurrent processes. To the best of the author's knowledge, the shuffle operation was first used in formal languages by Ginsburg and Spanier [Ginsburg and Spanier (1965)]. Early research with applications to concurrent processes can be found in Riddle [Riddle (1973, 1979)] and Shaw [Shaw (1978)]. A number of authors, including [Gischer (1981); Gruber and Holzer (2009); Jantzen (1981, 1985); Jedrzejowicz (1999); Jedrzejowicz and Szepietowski (2001, 2005); Mayer and Stockmeyer (1994); Ogden *et al.* (1978); Shoudai (1992)] have subsequently studied various aspects of the complexity of the shuffle and iterated shuffle operations in conjunction with regular expression operations and other constructions from the theory of programming languages.

In [Mansfield (1983)], gave a polynomial time algorithms for deciding whether a string w can be written as the shuffle of k strings $u_1, \ldots, u_k$, so that $w = u_1 \odot u_2 \odot \cdots \odot u_k$, for a *constant* integer k. The paper [Mansfield (1983)] further proved that if k is allowed to vary, then the problem becomes NP-complete (via a reduction from EXACT COVER WITH 3-SETS). Warmuth and Haussler [Warmuth and Haussler (1984)] gave an independent proof of this last result and went on to give a rather striking improvement by showing that this problem remains NP-complete even if the k strings $u_1, \ldots, u_k$ are equal. That is to say, the question of, given strings u and w, whether w is equal to an *iterated shuffle* $u \odot u \odot \cdots \odot u$ of u is NP-complete. Their proof used a reduction from 3-PARTITION. [Soltys (2013)] shows that the problem of whether $w = u \odot v$ can be solved with circuits of logarithmic depth, but not with circuits of bounded depth.

As mentioned in Section 4.6.2, a string w is defined to be a *square* if it can be written $w = u \odot u$ for some u. Erickson [Erickson (2010)] in 2010, asked on the *Stack Exchange* discussion board about the computational complexity of recognizing squares, and in particular whether this is polynomial time decidable. This problem was repeated as an open question in [Henshall *et al.* (2012)]. An online reply to [Erickson (2010)] by Austrin [Austrin (2010)] showed that the problem of recognizing squares is polynomial time decidable provided that each alphabet symbol occurs at most four times in w (by a reduction from 2-SAT); however, the general question has remained open. The present paper resolves this by proving that the problem of recognizing squares is NP-complete, even over a sufficiently large fixed alphabet.

Chapter 5

Online Algorithms

Never-ending *Walpurgisnacht*

Sir Roger Scruton [Scruton (2015)]

The algorithms presented thus far were *offline* algorithms, in the sense that the entire input was given at the beginning. In this chapter we change our paradigm and consider *online* algorithms, where the input is never-ending, presented piecemeal, and the algorithm has to make decisions based on incomplete information, without knowledge of future events.

A typical example of an application is a caching discipline; consider a hard disk from which data is read into a random access memory. Typically, the random access memory is much smaller, and so it must be decided which data has to be overwritten with new data. New requests for data from the hard disk arrive continuously, and it is hard to predict future requests.

Thus we must overwrite parts of the random access memory with new requests, but we must do the overwriting judiciously, so that we minimize future *misses*: data that is required but not present in the random access memory, and so it has to be brought in from the hard disk. Minimizing the number of misses is difficult when the future requests are unknown.

Correctness in the context of online algorithm has a different nuance; it means that the algorithm minimizes strategic errors. That is, an online algorithm will typically do worse than a corresponding offline algorithm that sees the entire input, but we want it to be as competitive as possible, given its intrinsic limitations. Thus, in the context of online algorithms, we are concerned with performance evaluation.

We introduce the subject of online algorithms with the list accessing problem in section 5.1, and then present paging algorithms in section 5.2.

5.1   List accessing problem

We are in charge of a filing cabinet containing l labeled but unsorted files. We receive a sequence of requests to access files; each request is a file label. After receiving a request for a file we must locate it, process it, and return it to the cabinet.

Since the files are unordered we must flip through the files starting at the beginning, until the requested file is located. If a file is in position i, we incur a search cost of i in locating it. If the file is not in the cabinet, the cost is l, which is the total number of files. After taking out the file, we must return it to the cabinet, but we may choose to reorganize the cabinet; for instance, we might put it closer to the front. The incentive for such a reorganization is that it may save us some search time in the future: if a certain file is requested frequently, it is wise to insert it closer to the front. Our goal is to find a reorganization rule that minimizes the search time.

Let $\sigma = \sigma_1, \sigma_2, \ldots, \sigma_n$ be a finite sequence of n requests. To service request σ_i, a list accessing algorithm ALG must search for the item labeled σ_i by traversing the list from the beginning, until it finds it. The cost of retrieving this item is the index of its position on the list. Thus, if item σ_i is in position j, the cost of retrieving it is j. Furthermore, the algorithm may reorganize the list at any time.

The work associated with a reorganization is the minimum number of transpositions of consecutive items needed to carry it out. Each transposition has a cost of 1, however, immediately after accessing an item, we allow it to be moved free of charge to any location closer to the front of this list. These are *free* transpositions, while all other transpositions are *paid*. Let ALG(σ) be the sum of the costs of servicing all the items on the list σ, i.e., the sum of the costs of all the searches plus the sum of the costs of all paid transpositions.

Problem 5.1. *What is the justification for this "free move"? In other words, why does it make sense to allow placing an item "for free" right after accessing it? Finally, show that given a list of l items, we can always reorder it in any way we please by doing only transpositions of consecutive items.*

We consider the *static list accessing model*, where we have a list of l items, and the only requests are to access an item on the list, i.e., there are no insertions or deletions. Many algorithms have been proposed for managing lists; we are going to examine *Move To Front (MTF)*, where after accessing an item, we move it to the front of the list, without changing the relative order of the other items.

Further, we assume that σ consists of *only* those items which appear on the list of MTF—this is not a crucial simplification; see problem 5.7. Notice that $\text{MTF}(\sigma)$ is simply the sum of the costs of all the searches, since we only change the position of an item when we retrieve it, in which case we move it for free to the front.

Theorem 5.2. *Let* OPT *be an optimal (offline) algorithm for the static list accessing model. Suppose that* OPT *and* MTF *both start with the same list configuration. Then, for any sequence of requests* σ, *where* $|\sigma| = n$, *we have that*

$$\text{MTF}(\sigma) \leq 2 \cdot \text{OPT}_S(\sigma) + \text{OPT}_P(\sigma) - \text{OPT}_F(\sigma) - n, \qquad (5.1)$$

where $\text{OPT}_S(\sigma), \text{OPT}_P(\sigma), \text{OPT}_F(\sigma)$ *are the total cost of searches, the total number of paid transpositions and the total number of free transpositions, of* OPT *on* σ, *respectively.*

Proof. Imagine that both MTF and OPT process the requests in σ, while each algorithm works on its own list, starting from the same initial configuration. You may think of MTF and OPT as working in parallel, starting from the same list, and neither starts to process σ_i until the other is ready to do so.

Let

$$a_i = t_i + (\Phi_i - \Phi_{i-1}) \qquad (5.2)$$

where t_i is the actual cost that MTF incurs for processing this request (so t_i is in effect the position of item σ_i on the list of MTF *after* the first $i - 1$ requests have been serviced). Φ_i is a *potential function*, and here it is defined as the number of *inversions* in MTF's list with respect to OPT's list. An inversion is defined to be an ordered pair of items x_j and x_k, where x_j precedes x_k in MTF's list, but x_k precedes x_j in OPT's list.

Problem 5.3. *Suppose that* $l = 3$, *and the list of* MTF *is* x_1, x_2, x_3, *and the list of* OPT *is* x_3, x_2, x_1. *What is* Φ *in this case? In fact, how can we compute* $\text{OPT}(\sigma)$, *where* σ *is an arbitrary sequence of requests, without knowing how* OPT *works?*

Note that Φ_0 depends only on the initial configurations of MTF and OPT, and since we assume that the lists are initially identical, $\Phi_0 = 0$. Finally, the value a_i in (5.2) is called the *amortized cost*, and its intended meaning is the cost of accessing σ_i, i.e., t_i, plus a measure of the increase of the "distance" between MTF's list and OPT's list after processing σ_i, i.e., $\Phi_i - \Phi_{i-1}$.

It is obvious that the cost incurred by MTF in servicing σ, denoted $\text{MTF}(\sigma)$, is $\sum_{i=1}^{n} t_i$. But instead of computing $\sum_{i=1}^{n} t_i$, which is difficult, we compute $\sum_{i=1}^{n} a_i$ which is much easier. The relationship between the two summations is,

$$\text{MTF}(\sigma) = \sum_{i=1}^{n} t_i = \Phi_0 - \Phi_n + \sum_{i=1}^{n} a_i, \tag{5.3}$$

and since we agreed that $\Phi_0 = 0$, and Φ_i is always positive, we have that,

$$\text{MTF}(\sigma) \le \sum_{i=1}^{n} a_i. \tag{5.4}$$

So now it remains to compute an upper bound for a_i.

Problem 5.4. *Show the second equality of equation (5.3).*

Assume that the i-th request, σ_i, is in position j of OPT, and in position k of MTF (i.e., this is the position of this item *after* the first $(i-1)$ requests have been completed). Let x denote this item—see figure 5.1.

We are going to show that

$$a_i \le (2s_i - 1) + p_i - f_i, \tag{5.5}$$

where s_i is the search cost incurred by OPT for accessing request σ_i, and p_i and f_i are the paid and free transpositions, respectively, incurred by OPT when servicing σ_i. This shows that

$$\sum_{i=1}^{n} a_i \le \sum_{i=1}^{n} ((2s_i - 1) + p_i - f_i)$$

$$= 2(\sum_{i=1}^{n} s_i) + (\sum_{i=1}^{n} p_i) - (\sum_{i=1}^{n} f_i) - n$$

$$= 2\text{OPT}_S(\sigma) + \text{OPT}_P(\sigma) - \text{OPT}_F(\sigma) - n,$$

which, together with the inequality (5.4), will show (5.1).

We prove (5.5) in two steps: in the first step MTF makes its move, i.e., moves x from the k-th slot to the beginning of its list, and we measure the change in the potential function *with respect to* the configuration of the list of OPT *before* OPT makes its own moves to deal with the request for x.

In the second step, OPT makes its move and now we measure the change in the potential function *with respect to* the configuration of the list of MTF

Fig. 5.1 x is in position k in MTF, and in position j in OPT. Note that in the figure it appears that $j < k$, but we make no such assumption in the analysis. Let $*$ denote items located before x in MTF but after x in OPT, i.e., the $*$ indicate inversions with respect to x. There may be other inversions involving x, namely items which are after x in MTF but before x in OPT, but we are not concerned with them.

after MTF has completed its handling of the request (i.e., with x at the beginning of the list of MTF).

See figure 5.1: suppose that there are v such $*$, i.e., v inversions of the type represented in the figure. Then, there are at least $(k - 1 - v)$ items that precede x in both list.

Problem 5.5. *Explain why at least $(k-1-v)$ items precede x in both lists.*

But this implies that $(k-1-v) \leq (j-1)$, since x is in the j-th position in OPT. Thus, $(k-v) \leq j$. So what happens when MTF moves x to the front of the list? In terms of inversions two things happen: (i) $(k-1-v)$ new inversions are created, with respect to OPT's list, before OPT itself deals with the request for x. (ii) v inversions are eliminated, again with respect to OPT's list, before OPT itself deals with the request for x.

Therefore, the contribution to the amortized cost is:

$$k + ((k-1-v) - v) = 2(k-v) - 1 \overset{(1)}{\leq} 2j - 1 \overset{(2)}{=} 2s - 1 \qquad (5.6)$$

where (1) follows from $(k-v) \leq j$ shown above, and (2) follows from the fact that the search cost incurred by OPT when looking for x is exactly j. Note that (5.6) looks similar to (5.5), but we are missing $+p_i - f_i$. These terms will come from considering the second step of the analysis: OPT makes its move and we measure the change of potential with respect to MTF with x at the beginning of the list. This is dealt with in the next problem.

Problem 5.6. *In the second step of the analysis, MTF has made its move and OPT, after retrieving x, rearranges its list. Show that each paid transposition contributes 1 to the amortized cost and each free transposition contributes -1 to the amortized cost.*

This finishes the proof. □

In the *dynamic list accessing model* we also have *insertions*, where the cost of an insertion is $l + 1$—here l is the length of the list—, and *deletions*, where the cost of a deletion is the same as the cost of an access, i.e., the position of the item on the list. MTF always deletes the item at position l.

Problem 5.7. *Show that theorem 5.2 still holds in the dynamic case.*

The *infimum* of a subset $S \subseteq \mathbb{R}$ is the largest element r, not necessarily in S, such that for all all $s \in S$, $r \leq s$. We say that an online algorithm is *c-competitive* if there is a constant α such that for all finite input sequences $\text{ALG}(\sigma) \leq c \cdot \text{OPT}(\sigma) + \alpha$. The infimum over the set of all values c such that ALG is c-competitive is called the *competitive ratio* of ALG and is denoted $\mathcal{R}(\text{ALG})$.

Problem 5.8. *Observe that* $\text{OPT}(\sigma) \leq n \cdot l$, *where l is the length of the list and n is $|\sigma|$.*

Problem 5.9. *Show that* MTF *is a 2-competitive algorithm, and that* $\mathcal{R}(\text{MTF}) \leq 2 - \frac{1}{l}$.

Problem 5.10. *In the chapters on online and randomized algorithms (this chapter and the next) we need to generate random values. Use the Python* **random** *library to generate those random values; implement* OPT *and* MTF *and compare them on a random sequence of requests. You may want to plot the competitiveness of* MTF *with respect to* OPT *using* **gnuplot***.*

The traditional approach to studying online algorithms falls within the framework of *distributional*, also known as *average-case*, complexity: a distribution on event sequences is hypothesized, and the expected payoff per event is analyzed. However, in this chapter we present a more recent approach to *competitive analysis*, whereby the payoff of an online algorithm is measured by comparing its performance to that of an *optimal offline algorithm*. Competitive analysis thus falls within the framework of *worst case* complexity.

5.2 Paging

Consider a two-level *virtual memory system*: each level, slow and fast, can store a number of fixed-size memory units called *pages*. The slow memory stores N pages, and the fast memory stores k pages, where $k < N$. The k is usually much smaller than N.

Given a request for page p_i, the system must make page p_i available in the fast memory. If p_i is already in the fast memory, called a *hit*, the system need not do anything. Otherwise, on a *miss*, the system incurs a *page fault*, and must copy the page p_i from the slow memory to the fast memory. In doing so, the system is faced with the following problem: which page to evict from the fast memory to make space for p_i. In order to *minimize* the number of page faults, the choice of which page to evict must be made wisely.

Typical examples of fast and slow memory pair are a RAM and hard disk, respectively, or a processor-cache and RAM, respectively. In general, we shall refer to the fast memory as "the cache." Because of its important role in the performance of almost every computer system, paging has been extensively studied since the 1960s, and the common paging schemes are listed in figure 5.2.

LRU	*Least Recently Used*
CLOCK	*Clock Replacement*
FIFO	*First-In/First-Out*
LIFO	*Last-In/First-Out*
LFU	*Least Frequently Used*
LFD	*Longest Forward Distance*

Fig. 5.2 Paging disciplines: the top five are online algorithms; the last one, LFD, is an offline algorithm. We shall see in section 5.2.6 that LFD is in fact the optimal algorithm for paging.

All the caching disciplines in figure 5.2, except for the last one, are online algorithms; that is, they are algorithms that make decisions based on past events, rather than the future. The last algorithm, LFD, replaces the page whose next request is the latest, which requires knowledge of future requests, and hence it is an offline algorithm.

5.2.1 *Demand paging*

Demand paging algorithms never evict a page from the cache unless there is a page fault, that is, they never evict preemptively. All the paging disciplines in figure 5.2 are demand paging. We consider the *page fault model*, where we charge 1 for bringing a page into the fast memory, and we charge nothing for accessing a page which is already there. As the next theorem shows this is a very general model.

Theorem 5.11. *Any page replacement algorithm, online or offline, can be modified to be demand paging without increasing the overall cost on any request sequence.*

Proof. In a demand paging algorithm a page fault causes exactly one eviction (once the cache is full, that is), and there are no evictions between misses. So let ALG be any paging algorithm. We show how to modify it to make it a demand paging algorithm ALG′, in such a way that on any input sequence ALG′ incurs at most the cost (makes at most as many page moves from slow to fast memory) as ALG, i.e., $\forall \sigma$, $\mathrm{ALG}'(\sigma) \leq \mathrm{ALG}(\sigma)$.

Suppose that ALG has a cache of size k. Define ALG′ as follows: ALG′ also has a cache of size k, plus k registers. ALG′ runs a simulation of ALG, keeping in its k registers the page numbers of the pages that ALG would have had in its cache. Based on the behavior of ALG, ALG′ makes decisions to evict pages[1].

Suppose page p is requested. If p is in the cache of ALG′, then just service the request. Otherwise, if a page fault occurs, ALG′ behaves according to the following two cases:

Case 1: If ALG also has a page fault (that is, the number of p is *not* in the registers), and ALG evicts a page from register i to make room for p, then ALG′ evicts a page from slot i in its cache, to make room for p.

Case 2: If ALG does not have a page fault, then the number of p must be in, say, register i. In that case, ALG′ evicts the contents of slot i in its cache, and moves p in there.

Thus ALG′ is a demand paging algorithm.

We now show that ALG′ incurs at most the cost of ALG on any input sequence; that is, ALG′ has at most as many page faults as ALG. To do this, we pair each page move of ALG′ with a page move of ALG in a unique manner as follows: If ALG′ and ALG both incur a page fault, then match the corresponding page moves. Otherwise, if ALG already had the page in its cache, it must have moved it there before, so match that move with the current move of ALG′.

It is never the case that two different moves of ALG′ are matched with a single move of ALG. To see this, suppose that on some input sequence, we encounter for the first time the situation where two moves of ALG′ are matched with the same move of ALG. This can only happen in the following situation: page p is requested, ALG′ incurs a page fault, it moves p into

---

[1]The assumption in this proof is that ALG does not re-arrange its slots—i.e., it never permutes the contents of its cache.

its cache, and we match this move with a past move of ALG, which has been matched already! But this means that page p was already requested, and after it has been requested, it has been evicted from the cache of ALG$'$ (otherwise, ALG$'$ would not have had a page fault).

ALG$'$ evicted page p while ALG did not, so they were not in the same slot. But ALG$'$ put (the first time) p in the same slot as ALG, contradiction. Therefore, we could not have matched a move twice. Thus, we can match each move of ALG$'$ with a move of ALG, in a one-to-one manner, and hence ALG$'$ makes at most as many moves as ALG. See figure 5.3.

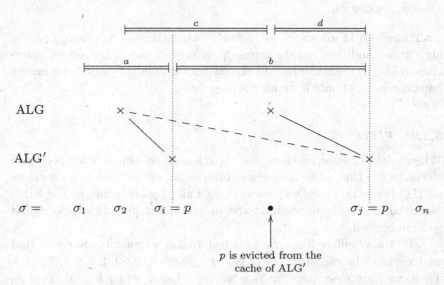

Fig. 5.3 Suppose that i, j is the smallest pair such that there exists a page p with the property that $\sigma_i = \sigma_j = p$. ALG$'$ incurs a page fault at σ_i and σ_j, and the two corresponding page moves of ALG$'$ are both matched with the same page move of p by ALG somewhere in the stretch a. We show that this is not possible: if ALG$'$ incurs a page fault at $\sigma_i = \sigma_j = p$ it means that somewhere in b the page p is evicted—this point is denoted with '•'. If ALG did not evict p in the stretch c, then ALG also evicts page p at '•' and so it must then bring it back to the cache in stretch d—we would match the × at σ_j with that move. If ALG did evict p in the stretch c, then again it would have to bring it back in before σ_j. In any case, there is a later move of p that would be matched with the page fault of ALG$'$ at σ_j.

Problem 5.12. *In figure 5.3 we postulate the existence of a "smallest" pair i, j with the given properties. Show that if such a pair exists then there exists a "smallest" such pair; what does "smallest" mean in this case?*

The idea is that ALG does not gain anything by moving a page into its cache preemptively (before the page is actually needed). ALG' waits for the request before taking the same action.

In the meantime (between the time that ALG moves in the page and the time that it is requested and ALG' brings it in), ALG' can only gain, because there are no requests for that page during that time, but there might be a request for the page that ALG evicted preemptively.

Note that in the simulation, ALG' only needs k extra registers, to keep track of the page numbers of the pages in the cache of ALG, so it is an *efficient* simulation. □

Theorem 5.11 allows for us to restrict our attention to demand paging algorithms, and thus use the terms "page faults" and "page moves" interchangeably, in the sense that in the context of demand paging, we have a page move if and only if we have a page fault.

5.2.2 *FIFO*

When a page must be replaced, the *oldest* page is chosen. It is not necessary to record the time when a page was brought in; all we need to do is create a FIFO (First-In/First-Out) queue to hold all pages in memory. The FIFO algorithm is easy to understand and program, but its performance is not good in general.

FIFO also suffers from the so called *Belady's anomaly*. Suppose that we have the following sequence of page requests: $1, 2, 3, 4, 1, 2, 5, 1, 2, 3, 4, 5$. Then, we have more page faults when $k = 4$ than when $k = 3$. That is, FIFO has more page faults with a bigger cache!

Problem 5.13. *For a general i, provide a sequence of page requests that illustrates Belady's anomaly incurred by FIFO on cache sizes i and $i + 1$. In your analysis, assume that the cache is initially empty.*

5.2.3 *LRU*

The optimal algorithm for page replacement, OPT, evicts the page whose next request is the latest, and if some pages are never requested again, then anyone of them is evicted. This is an impractical algorithm from the point of view of online algorithms as we do not know the future.

However, if we use the recent past as an approximation of the near future, then we will replace the page that *has not been used for the longest period of time*. This approach is the *Least Recently Used (LRU)* algorithm.

LRU replacement associates with each page the time of that page's last use. When a page must be replaced, LRU chooses that page that has not been used for the longest period of time. The LRU algorithm is considered to be good, and is often implemented—the major problem is *how* to implement it; two typical solutions are counters and stacks.

Counters: Keep track of the time when a given page was last referenced, updating the counter every time we request it. This scheme requires a search of the page table to find the LRU page, and a write to memory for each request; an obvious problem might be clock overflow.

Stack: Keep a stack of page numbers. Whenever a page is referenced, it is removed from the stack and put on the top. In this way, the top of the stack is always the most recently used page, and the bottom is the LRU page. Because entries are removed from the middle of the stack, it is best implemented by a doubly-linked list.

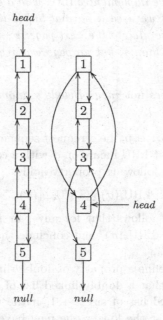

Fig. 5.4 LRU stack implementation with a doubly-linked list. The requested page is page 4; the left list shows the state *before* page 4 is requested, and the right list shows the state *after* the request has been serviced.

How many pointer operations need to be performed in the example in figure 5.4? Six, if we count as follows: remove old head and add new head (2 operations), connect 4 with 1 (2 operations), connect 3 with 5 (2 operations). However, we could have also counted disconnecting 3 with 4 and 4 with 5, giving 4 more pointer operations, giving us a total of 10. A third strategy would be not to count disconnecting pointers, in which case we would get half of these operations, 5. It does not really matter how we count, because the point is that in order to move a requested page (after a hit) to the top, we require a small *constant* number of pointer operations, regardless of how we count them.

Problem 5.14. *List the pointer operations that have to be performed if the requested page is* not *in the cache. Note that you should list the pointer operations (not just give a "magic number"), since we just showed that there are three different (all reasonable) ways to count them. Again, the point is, that if a page has to be brought in from the slow memory to the cache, a small constant number of pointer operations have to be performed.*

Problem 5.15. *We have implemented* LRU *with a doubly-linked list. What would be the problem if we used a normal linked list instead? That is, if every page had only a pointer to the next page: $i \rightsquigarrow j$, meaning that i was requested more recently than j, but no page was requested later than i and sooner than j.*

Lemma 5.16. LRU *does* not *incur Belady's anomaly (on any cache size and any request sequence).*

Proof. Let $\sigma = p_1, p_2, \ldots, p_n$ be a request sequence, and let $\mathrm{LRU}_i(\sigma)$ be the number of faults that LRU incurs on σ with a cache of size i. We show that for all i and σ, the following property holds:

$$\mathrm{LRU}_i(\sigma) \geq \mathrm{LRU}_{i+1}(\sigma). \qquad (5.7)$$

Once we show (5.7), it follows that for any pair $i < j$ and any request sequence σ, $\mathrm{LRU}_i(\sigma) \geq \mathrm{LRU}_j(\sigma)$, and conclude that LRU does not incur Belady's anomaly.

To show (5.7), we define a property of doubly-linked lists which we call "embedding." We say that a doubly-linked list of size i can be *embedded* in another doubly-linked list of size $i + 1$, if the two doubly-linked lists are identical, except that the longer one may have one more item at the "end." See figure 5.5, where the doubly-linked list of size 3 on the left can be embedded in the doubly-linked list of size 4 on the right.

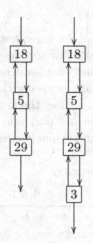

Fig. 5.5 The list on the left can be *embedded* into the list on the right.

At the beginning of processing the request sequence, when the caches are getting filled up, the two lists are identical, but once the caches are full, the LRU_{i+1} cache will have one more item.

Claim 5.17. *After processing each request, the doubly-linked list of LRU_i can be embedded into the doubly-linked list of LRU_{i+1}.*

Proof. We prove this claim by induction on the number of steps. Basis case: if $n = 1$, then both LRU_i and LRU_{i+1} incur a fault and bring in p_1. Induction step: suppose that the claim holds after step n; we show that it also holds after step $n + 1$. Consider the following cases: (1) LRU_i has a hit on p_{n+1}, (2) LRU_i has a fault on p_{n+1}, (2a) LRU_{i+1} also has a fault, (2b) LRU_{i+1} does not have a fault.

Problem 5.18. *Show that in each case the embedding property is being preserved.*

This finishes the proof of the claim.   □

Problem 5.19. *Use the claim to prove (5.7).*

This finishes the proof of the lemma.   □

5.2.4   *Marking algorithms*

Consider a cache of size k and fix a request sequence σ. We divide the request sequence into *phases* as follows: phase 0 is the empty sequence. For every $i \geq 1$, phase i is the maximal sequence following phase $i - 1$ that contains at most k distinct page requests; that is, if it exists, phase $i + 1$ begins on the request that constitutes the $k + 1$ distinct page request since the start of the i-th phase. Such a partition is called a k-*phase partition*. This partition is well defined and is independent of any particular algorithm processing σ.

For example, a 3-phase partition:

$$\underbrace{1, 2, 1, 2, 1, 2, 3,}_{\text{3-phase \#1}} \underbrace{4, 5, 6, 6, 6, 6, 6, 6, 6, 4, 5, 4,}_{\text{3-phase \#2}} \underbrace{7, 7, 7, 7, 1, 2}_{\text{3-phase \#3}}.$$

Let σ be any request sequence and consider its k-phase partition. Associate with each page a bit called the *mark*. The marking is done for the sake of analysis (this is not implemented by the algorithm, but "by us" to keep track of the doings of the algorithm). For each page, when its mark bit is set we say that the page is *marked*, and otherwise, *unmarked*.

Suppose that at the beginning of each k-phase we unmark all the pages, and we mark a page when it is first requested during the k-phase. A *marking algorithm* never evicts a marked page from its fast memory.

For example, suppose that $k = 2$, and σ is a request sequence. We show the 2-phases of σ:

$$\sigma = \underbrace{1, 1, 3, 1}_{\text{2-phase \#1}}, \underbrace{5, 1, 5, 1, 5, 1}_{\text{2-phase \#2}}, \underbrace{3, 4, 4, 4}_{\text{2-phase \#3}}, \underbrace{2, 2, 2, 2}_{\text{2-phase \#4}}. \tag{5.8}$$

See figure 5.6 to examine the marking in this example. Note that after each phase, every page is unmarked and we begin marking afresh, and except for the last phase, all phases are always complete (they have exactly k distinct requests, 2 in this case).

With a marking algorithm, once a request for page p in phase i is made, p stays in the cache until the end of phase i—the first time p is requested, it is marked, and it stays marked for the entire phase, and a marking algorithm never evicts a marked page.

The intuition is that marking algorithms are good schemes for page replacement because, in any given phase, there are at most k distinct pages, so they all fit in a cache of size k; it does not make sense to evict them in that phase, as we can only lose by evicting—the evicted page might be requested again.

step	1	2	3	4	5	step	1	2	3	4	5
1	×					10	×				×
2	×					11			×		
3	×		×			12			×	×	
4	×		×			13			×	×	
5					×	14			×	×	
6	×				×	15		×			
7	×				×	16		×			
8	×				×	17		×			
9	×				×	18		×			

Fig. 5.6 Marking in example (5.8).

Theorem 5.20. LRU *is a marking algorithm*

Proof. We argue by contradiction; suppose that LRU on a cache of size k is not a marking algorithm. Let σ be a request sequence where there exists a k-phase partition, during which some marked page p is evicted. Consider the first request for p during this k-phase:

$$\sigma = p_1, p_2, p_3, \ldots, \ldots, \underbrace{\ldots, p, \ldots, \ldots, \ldots,}_{k\text{-phase}} \ldots, \ldots$$

Immediately after p is serviced, it is marked as the most recently used page in the cache (i.e., it is put at the top of the doubly-linked list).

In order for p to leave the cache, LRU must incur a page fault while p is the least recently used page. It follows that during the k-phase in question, $k+1$ distinct pages were requested: there are the $k-1$ pages that pushed p to the end of the list, there is p, and the page that got p evicted. Contradiction; a k-phase has at most k distinct pages. □

5.2.5 FWF

Flush When Full (FWF) is a very naïve page replacement algorithm that works as follows: whenever there is a page fault and there is no space left in the cache, evict all pages currently in the cache—call this action a "flush."

More precisely, we consider the following version of the FWF algorithm: each slot in the cache has a single bit associated with it. At the beginning, all these bits are set to zero. When a page p is requested, FWF checks only the slots with a marked bit. If p is found, it is serviced. If p is not found, then it has to be brought in from the slow memory (even if it actually is in the cache, in an unmarked slot). FWF looks for a slot with a zero bit, and one of the following happens: (1) a slot with a zero bit (an unmarked page) is found, in which case FWF replaces that page with p. (2) a slot with a zero bit is not found (all pages are marked), in which case FWF unmarks all the slots, and replaces any page with p, and it marks p's bit.

Problem 5.21. *Show that* FWF *is a marking algorithm. Show that* FIFO *is not a marking algorithm.*

Problem 5.22. *A page replacement algorithm* ALG *is* conservative *if, on any consecutive input subsequence containing k or fewer distinct page requests,* ALG *will incur k or fewer page faults. Prove that* LRU *and* FIFO *are conservative, but* FWF *is not.*

5.2.6   LFD

The optimal page replacement algorithm turns out to be LFD (*Longest Forward Distance*—see figure 5.2). LFD evicts the page that will not be used for the longest period of time, and as such, it cannot be implemented in practice because it requires knowledge of the future. However, it is very useful for comparison studies, i.e., competitive analysis.

Theorem 5.23. LFD *is the optimal (offline) page replacement algorithm, i.e.,* OPT = LFD.

Proof.   We will show that if ALG is any paging algorithm (online or offline), then on any sequence of requests σ, $\text{ALG}(\sigma) \geq \text{LFD}(\sigma)$. As usual, $\text{ALG}(\sigma)$ denotes the number of page faults of ALG on the sequence of requests σ. We assume throughout that all algorithms are working with a cache of a fixed size k. We need to prove the following claim.

Claim 5.24. *Let* ALG *be any paging algorithm. Let $\sigma = p_1, p_2, \ldots, p_n$ be any request sequence. Then, it is possible to construct an offline algorithm* ALG_i *that satisfies the following three properties:*

(1) ALG_i *processes the first $i-1$ requests of σ exactly as* ALG *does,*
(2) *if the i-th request results in a page fault,* ALG_i *evicts from the cache the page with the "longest forward distance,"*
(3) $\text{ALG}_i(\sigma) \leq \text{ALG}(\sigma)$

Proof. Divide σ into three segments as follows:

$$\sigma = \sigma_1, p_i, \sigma_2,$$

where σ_1 and σ_2 each denote a block of requests.

Recall the proof of theorem 5.11 where we simulated ALG with ALG′ by running a "ghost simulation" of the contents of the cache of ALG on a set of registers, so ALG′ would know what to do with its cache based on the contents of those registers. We do the same thing here: ALG_i runs a simulation of ALG on a set of registers.

As on σ_1, ALG_i is just ALG, it follows that $\text{ALG}_i(\sigma_1) = \text{ALG}(\sigma_1)$, and also, they both do or do not incur a page fault on p_i. If they do not, then let ALG_i continue behaving just like ALG on σ_2, so that $\text{ALG}_i(\sigma) = \text{ALG}(\sigma)$.

However, if they do incur a page fault on p_i, ALG_i evicts the page with the longest forward distance from its cache, and replaces it with p_i. If ALG also evicts the same page, then again, let ALG_i behave just like ALG for the rest of σ, so that $\text{ALG}_i(\sigma) = \text{ALG}(\sigma)$.

Finally, suppose that they both incur a fault at p_i, but ALG evicts some page q and ALG_i evicts some page p, and $p \neq q$; see figure 5.7. If both $p, q \notin \sigma_2$, then let ALG_i behave just like ALG, except the slots with p and q are interchanged (that is, when ALG evicts from the q-slot, ALG_i evicts from the p-slot, and when ALG evicts from the p-slot, ALG_i evicts from the q-slot).

ALG:		✗			p	
ALG_i:		q			✗	

Fig. 5.7   ALG evicts q and ALG_i evicts p, denoted with ✗ and ✗ respectively, and they both replace their evicted page with p_i.

If $q \in \sigma_2$ but $p \notin \sigma_2$, then again let ALG_i, when forced with an eviction, act just like ALG with the two slots interchanged. Note that in this case it may happen that $\text{ALG}_i(\sigma_2) < \text{ALG}(\sigma_2)$, since ALG evicted q, which is going to be requested again, but ALG_i evicted p which will never be requested.

Problem 5.25. *Explain why the case $q \notin \sigma_2$ and $p \in \sigma_2$ is not possible.*

Otherwise, we can assume that ALG_i evicts page p and ALG evicts page q, $p \neq q$, and:

$$\sigma_2 = p_{i+1}, \ldots, q, \ldots, p, \ldots, p_n. \tag{5.9}$$

Assume that the q shown in (5.9) is the earliest instance of q in σ_2. As before, let ALG_i act just like ALG with the q-slot and p-slot interchanged. We know for sure that ALG will have a fault at q. Suppose ALG does not have a fault at p; then, ALG never evicted p, so ALG_i never evicted q, so ALG_i did not have a fault at q. Therefore, $\text{ALG}_i(\sigma_2) \leq \text{ALG}(\sigma_2)$.   □

We now show how to use claim 5.24 to prove that LFD is in fact the optimal algorithm. Let $\sigma = p_1, p_2, \ldots, p_n$ be any sequence of requests. By the claim, we know that: $\text{ALG}_1(\sigma) \leq \text{ALG}(\sigma)$. Applying the claim again, we get $(\text{ALG}_1)_2(\sigma) \leq \text{ALG}_1(\sigma)$. Define $\overline{\text{ALG}}_j$ to be $(\cdots((\text{ALG}_1)_2)\cdots)_j$. Then, we obtain that $\overline{\text{ALG}}_j(\sigma) \leq \overline{\text{ALG}}_{j-1}(\sigma)$.

Note that $\overline{\text{ALG}}_n$ acts just like LFD on σ, and therefore we have that $\text{LFD}(\sigma) = \overline{\text{ALG}}_n(\sigma) \leq \text{ALG}(\sigma)$, and we are done.   □

Henceforth, OPT can be taken to be synonymous with LFD.

Theorem 5.26. *Any marking algorithm* ALG *is* $\left(\frac{k}{k-h+1}\right)$*-competitive, where k is the size of its cache, and h is the size of the cache of* OPT.

Proof. Fix any request sequence σ and consider its k-phase partition. Assume, for now, that the last phase of σ is complete (in general, the last phase may be incomplete).

Claim 5.27. *For any phase $i \geq 1$, a marking algorithm* ALG *incurs at most k page faults.*

Proof. This follows because there are k distinct page references in each phase. Once a page is requested, it is marked and therefore cannot be evicted until the phase has been completed. Consequently, ALG cannot fault twice on the same page.   □

If we denote the i-th k-phase of σ by σ_i, we can express the above claim as $\text{ALG}(\sigma_i) \leq k$. Thus, if there are s phases, $\text{ALG}(\sigma) \leq s \cdot k$.

Claim 5.28. $\text{OPT}(\sigma) \geq s \cdot (k - h + 1)$, *where again we assume that the requests are $\sigma = \sigma_1, \sigma_2, \ldots, \sigma_s$, where σ_s is complete.*

Proof. Let p_a be the first request of phase i, and p_b the last request of phase i. Suppose first that phase $i + 1$ exists (that is, i is *not* the last phase). Then, we partition σ into k-phases (even though the cache of OPT is of size k, we still partition σ into k-phases):

$$\sigma = \ldots, p_{a-1}, \underbrace{p_a, p_{a+1}, \ldots, p_b}_{k\text{-phase }\#i}, \underbrace{p_{b+1}, \ldots,}_{k\text{-phase }\#i+1} \ldots$$

After processing request p_a, OPT has at most $h - 1$ pages in its cache, not including p_a. From (and including) p_{a+1} until (and including) p_{b+1}, there are at least k distinct requests. Therefore, OPT must incur at least $k - (h - 1) = k - h + 1$ faults on this segment. To see this, note that there are two cases.

Case 1: p_a appears again in $p_{a+1}, \ldots, p_{b+1}$; then there are at least $(k + 1)$ distinct requests in the segment $p_{a+1}, \ldots, p_{b+1}$, and since OPT has a cache of size h, regardless of the contents of the cache, there will be at least $(k + 1) - h = k - h + 1$ page faults.

Case 2: Suppose that p_a does *not* appear again in $p_{a+1}, \ldots, p_{b+1}$, then since p_a is requested at the beginning of phase i, it is for sure in the cache by the time we start servicing $p_{a+1}, \ldots, p_{b+1}$. Since it is not requested again, it is taking up a spot in the cache, so at most $(h - 1)$ slots in the cache can be taken up by some of the elements requested in $p_{a+1}, \ldots, p_{b+1}$; so again, we have at least $k - (h - 1) = k - h + 1$ many faults.

If i is the last phase (so $i = s$), we do not have p_{b+1}, so we can only say that we have at least $k - h$ faults, but we make it up with p_1 which has not been counted. □

It follows from claims 5.27 and 5.28 that:

$$\mathrm{ALG}(\sigma) \leq s \cdot k \quad \text{and} \quad \mathrm{OPT}(\sigma) \geq s \cdot (k - h + 1),$$

so that:

$$\frac{\mathrm{ALG}(\sigma)}{s \cdot k} \leq 1 \leq \frac{\mathrm{OPT}(\sigma)}{s \cdot (k - h + 1)},$$

so finally:

$$\mathrm{ALG}(\sigma) \leq \left(\frac{k}{k - h + 1} \right) \cdot \mathrm{OPT}(\sigma).$$

In the case that σ can be divided into s complete phases.

As was mentioned above, in general, the last phase may not be complete. Then, we repeat this analysis with $\sigma = \sigma_1, \sigma_2, \ldots, \sigma_{s-1}$, and for σ_s we use α at the end, so we get:

$$\mathrm{ALG}(\sigma) \leq \left(\frac{k}{k - h + 1} \right) \cdot \mathrm{OPT}(\sigma) + \alpha.$$

Problem 5.29. *Work this out.*

Therefore, in either case we obtain that any marking algorithm ALG is $\left(\frac{k}{k-h+1} \right)$-competitive. □

Problem 5.30. *Implement all the disciplines in figure 5.2. Judge them experimentally, by running them on a string of random requests, and plotting their costs—compared to* LFD.

5.3   Answers to selected problems

Problem 5.1. Think of the filing cabinet mentioned at the beginning of this chapter. As we scan the filing cabinet while searching for a particular file, we keep a pointer at a given location along the way (i.e., we "place a finger" as a bookmark in that location) and then insert the accessed file in that location almost free of additional search or reorganization costs. We also assume that it would not make sense to move the file to a later location. Finally, any permutation can be written out as a product of transpositions (check any abstract algebra textbook).

Problem 5.3. The answer is 3. Note that in a list of n items there are $\binom{n}{2} = \frac{n \cdot (n-1)}{2}$ *unordered* pairs (and $n \cdot (n-1)$ ordered pairs), so to compute Φ, we enumerate all those pairs, and increase a counter by 1 (starting from 0) each time we encounter an inversion. For the second question, note that while we do not know how OPT works exactly, we know that it services σ with the optimal cost, i.e., it services σ in the cheapest way possible. Thus, we can find $\text{OPT}(\sigma)$ by an exhaustive enumeration: given our list $x_1, x_2, \ldots, x_l$ and a sequence of requests $\sigma = \sigma_1, \sigma_2, \ldots, \sigma_n$, we build a tree where the root is labeled with $x_1, x_2, \ldots, x_l$, and the children of the root are all the $l!$ permutations of the list. Then each node in turn has $l!$ many children; the depth of the tree is n. We calculate the cost of each branch and label the leaves with those costs. The cost of each branch is the sum of the costs of all the transpositions required to produce each consecutive node, and the costs of the searches associated with the corresponding list configurations. The cheapest branch (and there may be several) is precisely $\text{OPT}(\sigma)$.

Problem 5.4.

$$\sum_{i=1}^{n} t_i = \sum_{i=1}^{n} (a_i - \Phi_i + \Phi_{i-1}) = \sum_{i=1}^{n} a_i + \sum_{i=1}^{n} \Phi_{i-1} - \sum_{i=1}^{n} \Phi_i$$

$$= \sum_{i=1}^{n} a_i + \sum_{i=0}^{n-1} \Phi_i - \sum_{i=1}^{n} \Phi_i = \sum_{i=1}^{n} a_i + \left(\Phi_0 + \sum_{i=1}^{n-1} \Phi_i\right) - \left(\Phi_n + \sum_{i=1}^{n-1} \Phi_i\right)$$

and canceling in the last term gives us $\Phi_0 - \Phi_n + \sum_{i=1}^{n} a_i$.

Problem 5.5. The number of elements before x in MTF is $(k-1)$, since x is in the k-th position. Of these $(k-1)$ elements, v are $*$. Both lists contain exactly the same elements, and the $(k-1-v)$ non-$*$ before x in MTF must all be before x in OPT (if an element is before x in MTF and after x in OPT, then by definition it would be a $*$).

Problem 5.6. In the case of a paid transposition, the only change in the number of inversions can come from the two transposed items, as the relative order with respect to all the other items remains the same. In the case of a free transposition, we know that MTF already put the transposed item x at the front of its list, and we know that free transpositions can only move x forward, so the number of items before x in OPT decreases by 1.

Problem 5.8. OPT is the optimal offline algorithm, and hence it must do at least as well as any algorithm ALG. Suppose we service all requests one-by-one in the naïve way, without making any rearrangements. The cost of this scheme is bounded about by $n \cdot l$, the number of requests times the length of the list. Hence, $\text{OPT}(\sigma) \leq n \cdot l$.

Problem 5.9. By theorem 5.2 we know that

$$\text{MTF}(\sigma) \leq 2 \cdot \text{OPT}_S(\sigma) + \text{OPT}_P(\sigma) - \text{OPT}_F(\sigma) - n$$

and the RHS is

$$\leq 2 \cdot \text{OPT}_S(\sigma) + \text{OPT}_P(\sigma) \leq 2 \cdot (\text{OPT}_S(\sigma) + \text{OPT}_P(\sigma)) = 2 \cdot \text{OPT}(\sigma).$$

This shows that MTF is 2-competitive (with $\alpha = 0$). For the second part, we repeat the above argument, but without "losing" the n factor, so we have $\text{MTF}(\sigma) \leq 2 \cdot \text{OPT}(\sigma) - n$. On the other hand, $\text{OPT}(\sigma) \leq n \cdot l$ (by problem 5.8), so

$$2 \cdot \text{OPT}(\sigma) - n \leq \left(2 - \frac{1}{l}\right) \cdot \text{OPT}(\sigma)$$

Problem 5.12. In the proof of theorem 5.11 we define a matching between the page moves (from slow memory into the cache) of ALG and ALG'. In order to show that the matching is one-to-one we postulate the existence of a pair i, j, $i \neq j$, with the following properties: (i) there exists a page p such that $\sigma_i = \sigma_j = p$, (ii) ALG' incurs a page fault at σ_i and σ_j, and (iii) ALG' has to move p into the cache to service σ_i and σ_j and those two moves are matched with the same move of p by ALG. For the sake of the argument in the proof of theorem 5.11 we want the "smallest" such pair—so we use the Least Number Principle (see page 233) to show that if such pairs exist at all, there must exist pairs where $i + j$ is minimal; we take any such pair.

Problem 5.13. Consider the following list:

$$\underbrace{1,2,3\ldots,i,i+1}_{1},\underbrace{1,2,3,\ldots,i-1}_{2},\underbrace{i+2}_{3},\underbrace{1,2,3,\ldots,i,i+1,i+2}_{4}.$$

If we have a cache of size $i+1$, then we incur $i+1$ faults in segment 1 (because the cache is initially empty), then we have $i-1$ hits in segment 2, then we have another page fault in segment 3 so we evict 1, and in segment 4 we lag behind by 1 all the way, so we incur $i+2$ page faults. Hence, we incur $i+1+1+i+2 = 2i+4$ page faults in total.

Suppose now that we have a cache of size i. Then we incur $i+1$ page faults in segment 1, then we have $i-1$ page faults in segment 2, and one page fault in segment 3, hence $2i+1$ page faults before starting segment 4. When segment 4 starts, we already have pages 1 through $i-1$ in the cache, so we have hits, and then when $i+1$ is requested, we have a fault, and when $i+2$ is requested we have a hit, and hence only one fault in segment 4. Therefore, we have $2i+2$ page faults with a cache of size i. To understand this solution, make sure that you keep track of the contents of the cache after each of the four segments has been processed. Note that i has to be at least 3 for this example to work.

Problem 5.14. If the requested page is not in the cache, we must:

(1) Remove the null pointer $(+1)$
(2) Disconnect the last from 2nd to last item $(+2)$
(3) Add null pointer from new last item $(+1)$
(4) Remove head $(+1)$
(5) Connect new first item (requested page) to old first item $(+2)$
(6) Add new head $(+1)$

for a total of 8 pointer operations.

Problem 5.15. The problem with a singly-linked list is that to find the predecessor of a page we need to start the search always at the beginning of the list, increasing the overhead of maintaining the stack.

Problem 5.18. Case 1. If LRU_i has a hit on p_{n+1}, then so does LRU_{i+1}, as LRU_i could be embedded in LRU_{i+1} after step n. Therefore, neither of the linked lists changes on step $n+1$, so LRU_i can still be embedded in LRU_{i+1} after step $n+1$.

Case 2a. If LRU_i and LRU_{i+1} both have faults on p_{n+1}, then each list will undergo two changes: the last (i.e. least recently used) page will be removed from the "end", and p_{i+1} will be added as the head. Removing the last page from each list does not stop LRU_i from being embedded in

LRU_{i+1}; it simply causes each list to end one page "sooner", so the page at the end of LRU_i after step n is now the "extra" page at the end of LRU_{i+1}. Clearly adding the same new head to each list does not inhibit embedding either, so after $n+1$ steps LRU_i can still be embedded in LRU_{i+1}.

Case 2b. Assume LRU_i has a fault on p_{n+1} and LRU_{i+1} does not. Both lists must contain i pages, after step n, and moreover these must be the same pages in the same order for LRU_i to be embedded in LRU_{i+1}. So the least recently used page in LRU_i will be removed in step $n+1$, but this will not stop LRU_i from being embedded, as the removed page is now the extra page at the end of LRU_{i+1}. Again, clearly the addition of the same page, p_{n+1}, to the start of both lists does not affect embedding, so induction is complete.

Problem 5.19. After $n-1$ steps, the linked list of LRU_i can be embedded in that of LRU_{i+1}. Consider any $p_n \in \sigma$. If p_n is in LRU_i's list, then it is in the same index in LRU_{i+1}, so the cost of accessing p_n is identical. If p_n is not in LRU_i's list, it may be the last element of LRU_{i+1}'s list, in which case LRU_{i+1} accesses p_n with smaller cost than that of LRU_i. Otherwise, it is not in either list, so again the cost is the same. Since this is true for every $p \in \sigma$, we can conclude that $LRU_i(\sigma) \leq LRU_{i+1}(\sigma)$.

Problem 5.21. FWF really implements the marking bit, so it is almost a marking algorithm by definition. FIFO is not a marking algorithm because with $k = 3$, and the request sequence $1, 2, 3, 4, 2, 1$ it will evict 2 in the second phase even though it is marked.

Problem 5.22. We must assume that the cache is of size k. Otherwise the claim is not true: for example, suppose that we have a cache of size 1, and the following sequences: $1, 2, 1, 2$. Then, in that sequence of 4 requests there are only 2 distinct requests, yet with a cache of size 1, there would be 4 faults, for *any* page-replacement algorithm. With a cache of size k, LRU is never going to evict a page during this consecutive subsequence, once the page has been requested. Thus, each distinct page request can only cause one fault. Same goes for FIFO. Thus, they are both conservative algorithms. However, it is possible that half-way through the consecutive subsequence, the cache of FWF is going to get full, and FWF is going to evict everybody. Hence, FWF may have more than one page fault on the same page during this consecutive subsequence.

Problem 5.25. If $p \in \sigma_2$ and $q \notin \sigma_2$, then q would have a "longer forward distance" than p, and so p would not have been evicted by ALG. Rather, ALG would have evicted q or some other page that was not to be requested again.

Problem 5.29. Let Σ_{s-1} denote the first $s-1$ complete phases of σ. We know that

$$\text{ALG}(\Sigma_{s-1}) \leq \left(\frac{k}{k-h+1}\right) \cdot \text{OPT}(\Sigma_{s-1})$$

Clearly, at most $k-1$ faults can occur in phase σ_s in either algorithm, as it is not a complete k-phase. Therefore,

$$\text{ALG}(\sigma) \leq \text{ALG}(\Sigma_{s-1}) + k - 1$$
$$\leq \left(\frac{k}{k-h+1}\right) \cdot \text{OPT}(\Sigma_{s-1}) + k - 1$$
$$\leq \left(\frac{k}{k-h+1}\right) \cdot \text{OPT}(\sigma) + k - 1$$

5.4   Notes

A very complete text book on online algorithms is [Borodin and El-Yaniv (1998)]. See also [Dorrigiv and López-Ortiz (2009)] from the SIGACT news online algorithms column.

Chapter 6

Randomized Algorithms

> Even a message enciphered on a
> three-rotor Enigma might take
> twenty-four hours to decode, as
> the bombes clattered their way
> through the billions of
> permutations. A four-rotor
> Enigma, multiplying the
> numbers by a factor of
> twenty-six, would theoretically
> take the best part of a month.
>
> Enigma, pg 27 [Harris (1996)]

It is very interesting that we can design procedures which, when confronted with a profusion of choices, instead of laboriously examining all the possible answers to those choices, they flip a coin to decide which way to go, and still "tend to" obtain the right output.

Obviously we save time when we resort to randomness, but what is very surprising is that the output of such procedures can be meaningful. That is, there are problems that computationally appear very difficult to solve, but when allowed the use of randomness it is possible to design procedures that solve those hard problems in a satisfactory manner: the output of the procedure is correct with a small probability of error. In fact this error can be made so small that it becomes negligible (say 1 in 2^{100}—the estimated number of atoms in the observable universe). Thus, many experts believe that the definition of "feasibly computable" ought to be "computable in polynomial time *with randomness*", rather than just "in polynomial time."

The advent of randomized algorithms came with the problem of primality testing, which in turn was spurred by the then burgeoning field of cryptography. Historically the first such algorithm was due to [Solovay and Strassen (1977)]. Primality testing remains one of the best problems to showcase the power of randomized algorithms; in this chapter we present the Rabin-Miller algorithm that came after the Solovay-Strassen algorithm, but it is somewhat simpler. Interestingly enough, there is now known a polynomial time algorithm for primality testing (due to [Agrawal *et al.* (2004)]), but the Rabin-Miller algorithm is still used in practice as it is more efficient (and its probability of error is negligible).

In this chapter we present three examples of randomized algorithms: an algorithm for perfect matching, for string pattern matching and finally the Rabin-Miller algorithm. We close with a discussion of cryptography.

6.1 Perfect matching

Consider a bipartite graph $G = (V \cup V', E)$, where $E \subseteq V \times V'$, and its adjacency matrix is defined as follows: $(A_G)_{ij} = x_{ij}$ if $(i, j') \in E_G$, and $(A_G)_{ij} = 0$ otherwise. See the example given in figure 6.1.

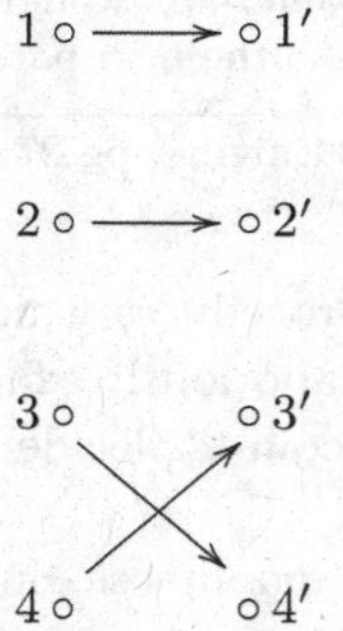

$$\begin{pmatrix} x_{11} & 0 & 0 & 0 \\ 0 & x_{22} & 0 & 0 \\ 0 & 0 & 0 & x_{34} \\ 0 & 0 & x_{43} & 0 \end{pmatrix}$$

Fig. 6.1 On the left we have a bipartite graph $G = (V \cup V', E)$ where $V = \{1, 2, 3, 4\}$, $V' = \{1', 2', 3', 4'\}$ and $E \subseteq V \times V'$, $E = \{(1, 1'), (2, 2'), (3, 4'), (4, 3')\}$. On the right we have the corresponding adjacency matrix A_G.

Let S_n be the set of all the permutations of n elements. More precisely, S_n is the set of bijections $\sigma : [n] \longrightarrow [n]$. Clearly, $|S_n| = n!$, and it is a well known result from algebra that any permutation $\sigma \in S_n$ can be written as a product of transpositions (that is, permutations that simply exchange two elements in $[n]$ and leave every other element fixed). Any permutation in S_n may be written as a product of transpositions, and although there are many ways to do this (i.e., a representation by transpositions is not unique), the parity of the number of transpositions is constant for any given permutation σ. Let $\text{sgn}(\sigma)$ be 1 or -1, depending on whether the parity of σ is even or odd, respectively.

Recall the Lagrange formula for the determinant:

$$\det(A) = \sum_{\sigma \in S_n} \text{sgn}(\sigma) \prod_{i=1}^{n} A_{i\sigma(i)}. \tag{6.1}$$

Lemma 6.1. *Let $G = (V \cup V', E)$ be a graph where $n = |V| = |V'|$ and $E \subseteq V \times V'$. Then, the graph G has a perfect matching (i.e., each vertex in V can be paired with a unique vertex in V') iff it is the case that $\det(A_G) = \sum_{\sigma \in S_n} \text{sgn}(\sigma) \prod_{i=1}^{n} (A_G)_{i\sigma(i)} \neq 0$.*

Problem 6.2. *Prove lemma 6.1*

Since $|S_n| = n!$, computing the summation over all the σ in S_n, as in (6.1), is computationally very expensive, so we randomly assign values to the x_{ij}'s. The integer determinant, unlike the symbolic determinant, can be computed very efficiently—for example with Berkowitz's algorithm. Let $A_G(x_1, \ldots, x_m)$, $m = |E_G|$, be A_G with its variables renamed to $x_1, \ldots, x_m$. Note that $m \leq n^2$ and each x_l represents some x_{ij}. We obtain a randomized algorithm for the perfect matching problem—see algorithm 6.1.

Algorithm 6.1 Perfect matching

Choose m random integers $i_1, \ldots, i_m$ in $\{1, \ldots, M\}$ where $M = 2m$
compute the integer determinant of $A_G(i_1, \ldots, i_m)$
if $\det(A_G(i_1, \ldots, i_m)) \neq 0$ **then**
       return yes, G has a perfect matching
else
       return no, G *probably* has no perfect matching
end if

Algorithm 6.1 is a polynomial time *Monte Carlo algorithm*: "yes" answers are reliable and final, while "no" answers are in danger of a *false negative*. The false negative can arise as follows: G may have a perfect matching, but $(i_1, \ldots, i_m)$ may happen to be a root of the polynomial $\det(A_G(x_1, \ldots, x_m))$. However, the probability of a false negative (i.e., the probability of error) can be made negligibly small, as we shall see shortly.

In line 1 of algorithm 6.1 we say, somewhat enigmatically, "choose m random numbers." How do we "choose" these random numbers? It turns out that the answer to this question is not easy, and obtaining a source of randomness is the Achilles heel of randomized algorithms. We have the science of *pseudo-random number generators* at our disposal, and other approaches, but this formidable topic lies outside the scope of this book, and so we shall naïvely assume that we have "some source of randomness."

We want to show the correctness of our randomized algorithm, so we need to show that the probability of error is negligible. We start with the Schwarz-Zipper lemma.

Lemma 6.3 (Schwarz-Zippel). *Consider polynomials over $\mathbb{Z}$, and let $p(x_1, \ldots, x_m) \neq 0$ be a polynomial, where the degree of each variable is $\leq d$ (when the polynomial is written out as a sum of monomials), and let $M > 0$. Then the number of m-tuples $(i_1, \ldots, i_m) \in \{1, 2, \ldots, M\}^m$ such that $p(i_1, \ldots, i_m) = 0$ is $\leq mdM^{m-1}$.*

Proof. Induction on m (the number of variables). If $m = 1$, $p(x_1)$ can have at most $d = 1 \cdot d \cdot M^{1-1}$ many roots, by the Fundamental Theorem of Algebra.

Suppose the lemma holds for $(m - 1)$, and now we want to give an upper bound of mdM^{m-1} on the number of tuples $(i_1, \ldots, i_m)$ such that $p(i_1, \ldots, i_m) = 0$. First we write $p(x_1, \ldots, x_m)$ as $y_d x_m^d + \cdots + y_0 x_m^0$, where each coefficient $y_i = y_i(x_1, \ldots, x_{m-1}) \in \mathbb{Z}[x_1, \ldots, x_{m-1}]$.

So how many tuples $(i_1, \ldots, i_m)$ such that $p(i_1, \ldots, i_m) = 0$ are there? We partition such tuples into two sets: those that set $y_d = 0$ and those that do not. The result is bounded above by the sum of the upper bounds of the two sets; we now give those upper bounds.

Set 1. By the induction hypothesis, y_d is zero for at most $(m - 1)dM^{m-2}$ many $(i_1, \ldots, i_{m-1})$ tuples, and x_m can take M values, and so $p(x_1, \ldots, x_m)$ is zero for at most $(m - 1)dM^{m-1}$ tuples. Note that we are over-counting here; we are taking *all* tuples that set $y_d = 0$.

Set 2. For each combination of M^{m-1} values for $x_1, \ldots, x_{m-1}$, there are at most d roots of the resulting polynomial (again by the Fundamental Theorem of Algebra), i.e., dM^{m-1}. Note that again we are over-counting as some of those settings to the $x_1, \ldots, x_m$ will result in $y_d = 0$.

Adding the two upper bounds gives us mdM^{m-1}. □

Lemma 6.4. *Algorithm 6.1 is correct.*

Proof. We want to show that algorithm 6.1 for perfect matching is a reliable Monte Carlo algorithm, which means that "yes" answers are 100% correct, while "no" answers admit a negligible probability of error.

If the algorithm answers "yes," then $\det(A_G(i_1, \ldots, i_m)) \neq 0$ for some randomly selected $i_1, \ldots, i_m$, but then the symbolic determinant $\det(A_G(x_1, \ldots, x_m)) \neq 0$, and so, by lemma 6.1, G has a perfect matching. So "yes" answers indicate with absolute certainty that there is a perfect matching.

Suppose that the answer is "no." Then we apply lemma 6.3 to $\det(A_G(x_1, \ldots, x_m))$, with $M = 2m$, and obtain that the probability of a false negative is

$$\leq \frac{m \cdot d \cdot M^{m-1}}{M^m} = \frac{m \cdot 1 \cdot (2m)^{m-1}}{(2m)^m} = \frac{m}{2m} = \frac{1}{2}.$$

Now suppose we perform "many independent experiments," meaning that we run algorithm 6.1 k many times, each time choosing a random set $i_1, \ldots, i_m$. Then, if the answer *always* comes zero we know that the probability of error is $\leq \left(\frac{1}{2}\right)^k = \frac{1}{2^k}$. For $k = 100$, the error becomes *negligible*.
$\square$

In the last paragraph of the proof of lemma 6.4 we say that we run algorithm 6.1 k many times, and so bring down the probability of error to being less than $\frac{1}{2^k}$, which for $k = 100$ is truly negligible. Running the algorithm k times to get the answer is called *amplification* (because we decrease drastically the probability of error, and so amplify the certainty of having a correct answer); note that the beauty of this approach is that while we run the algorithm only k times, the probability of error goes down exponentially quickly to $\frac{1}{2^k}$. Just to put things in perspective, if $k = 100$, then $\frac{1}{2^{100}}$ is so minuscule that by comparison the probability of earth being hit by a large meteor—while running the algorithm—is a virtual certainty (and being hit by a large meteor would spare anyone the necessity to run algorithms in the first place).

Problem 6.5. *Show how to use algorithm 6.1 to find a perfect matching.*

Perfect matching can be easily reduced[1] to a "max flow problem": as an example, consider the perfect matching problem given in figure 6.1; add two new nodes s, t, and connect s to all the nodes in the left-column of the matching problem, and connect t to all the nodes in the right-column of the matching problem, and give each edge a capacity of 1, and ask if there is a flow $\geq n$ (where n is the number of nodes in each of the two components of the given bipartite graph) from s to t; see figure 6.2.

---

[1] Recall that we have examined briefly the idea of *reductions* on page 83.

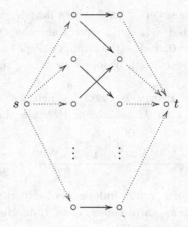

Fig. 6.2   Reduction of perfect matching to max flow.

As the max flow problem can be solved in polynomial time without using randomness, it follows that perfect matching can also be solved in polynomial time without randomness. Still, the point of this section was to exhibit a simple randomized algorithm, and that we have accomplished.

6.2   Pattern matching

In this section we design a randomized algorithm for pattern matching. Consider the set of strings over $\{0,1\}$, and let $M : \{0,1\} \longrightarrow M_{2\times 2}(\mathbb{Z})$, that is, M is a map from strings to 2×2 matrices over the integers $(\mathbb{Z})$ defined as follows:

$$M(\varepsilon) = \begin{bmatrix} 1 & 0 \\ 0 & 1 \end{bmatrix}; \quad M(0) = \begin{bmatrix} 1 & 0 \\ 1 & 1 \end{bmatrix}; \quad M(1) = \begin{bmatrix} 1 & 1 \\ 0 & 1 \end{bmatrix},$$

and for strings $x, y \in \{0,1\}^*$, $M(xy) = M(x)M(y)$, where the operation on the left-hand side is concatenation of strings, and the operation on the right-hand side is multiplication of matrices.

Problem 6.6. *Show that $M(x)$ is well defined, that is, no matter how we evaluate M on x we always get the same result. Also show that M is one-to-one.*

Problem 6.7. *Show that for $x \in \{0,1\}^n$, the entries of $M(x)$ are bounded by the n-th Fibonacci number. For a formal definition of Fibonacci numbers, see problem 9.5 on page 233.*

By considering the matrices $M(x)$ modulo a suitable prime p, i.e., by taking all the entries of $M(x)$ modulo a prime p, we perform efficient randomized pattern matching. We wish to determine whether x is a substring of y, where $|x| = n$, $|y| = m$, $n \leq m$. Define

$$y(i) = y_i y_{i+1} \cdots y_{n+i-1},$$

for appropriate $i \in \{1, \ldots, m - n + 1\}$. Select a prime $p \in \{1, \ldots, nm^2\}$, and let $A = M(x) \pmod{p}$ and $A(i) = M(y(i)) \pmod{p}$. Note that

$$A(i + 1) = M^{-1}(y_i) A(i) M(y_{n+i}) \pmod{p},$$

which makes the computation of subsequent $A(i)$'s efficient.

Algorithm 6.2 Pattern matching

Pre-condition: $x, y \in \{0, 1\}^*$, $|x| = n$, $|y| = m$ and $n \leq m$
1: select a random prime $p \leq nm^2$
2: $A \longleftarrow M(x) \pmod{p}$
3: $B \longleftarrow M(y(1)) \pmod{p}$
4: **for** $i = 1, \ldots, m - n + 1$ **do**
5:       **if** $A = B$ **then**
6:            **if** $x = y(i)$ **then**
7:                **return** found a match at position i
8:            **end if**
9:       **end if**
10:       $B \longleftarrow M^{-1}(y_i) \cdot B \cdot M(y_{n+i})$
11: **end for**

What is the probability of getting a false positive? It is the probability that $A(i) = M(y(i)) \pmod{p}$ even though $A(i) \neq M(y(i))$. This is less than the probability that $p \in \{1, \ldots, nm^2\}$ divides a (non-zero) entry in $A(i) - M(y(i))$. Since these entries are bounded by $F_n < 2^n$, less than n distinct primes can divide any of them. On the other hand, there are $\pi(nm^2) \approx (nm^2)/(\log(nm^2))$ primes in $\{1, \ldots, nm^2\}$ (by the Prime Number Theorem). So the probability of a false positive is $O(1/m)$.

Note that algorithm 6.2 has no error; it is randomized, but all potential answers are checked for a *false positive* (in line 6). Checking for these potential candidates is called *fingerprinting*. The idea of fingerprinting is to check only those substrings that "look" like good candidates, making sure that when we "sniff" for a candidate we never miss the solution (in this case, if $x = y(i)$, for some i, then $y(i)$ will always be a candidate).

On the other hand, there may be j's such that $x \neq y(j)$ and yet they are candidates; but the probability of that is small. The use of randomness in algorithm 6.2 just lowers the average time complexity of the procedure; such algorithms are called *Las Vegas algorithms*.

6.3   Primality testing

One way to determine whether a number p is prime, is to try all possible numbers $n < p$, and check if any are divisors[2]. Obviously, this brute force procedure has exponential time complexity in the length of p, and so it has a prohibitive time cost. Although a polytime (deterministic) algorithm for primality is now known (see [Agrawal *et al.* (2004)]), the Rabin-Miller randomized algorithm for primality testing is simpler and more efficient, and therefore still used in practice.

Fermat's Little theorem (see theorem 9.22) provides a "test" of sorts for primality, called the Fermat test; the Rabin-Miller algorithm (algorithm 6.3) is based on this test. When we say that p passes the Fermat test at a, what we mean is that $a^{(p-1)} \equiv 1 \pmod{p}$. Thus, all primes pass the Fermat test for all $a \in \mathbb{Z}_p - \{0\}$.

Unfortunately, there are also composite numbers n that pass the Fermat tests for every $a \in \mathbb{Z}_n^*$; these are the so called *Carmichael numbers*, for example, 561, 1105, 1729, etc.

Lemma 6.8. *If p is a composite non-Carmichael number, then it passes at most half of the tests in $\mathbb{Z}_p^*$. That is, if p is a composite non-Carmichael number, then for at most half of the a's in the set $\mathbb{Z}_p^*$ it is the case that $a^{(p-1)} \equiv 1 \pmod{p}$.*

Proof.   We say that a is a *witness* for p if a fails the Fermat test for p. That is, a is a witness if $a^{(p-1)} \not\equiv 1 \pmod{p}$. Let $S \subseteq \mathbb{Z}_p^*$ consist of those elements $a \in \mathbb{Z}_p^*$ for which $a^{p-1} \equiv 1 \pmod{p}$. It is easy to check that S is in fact a subgroup of $\mathbb{Z}_p^*$. Therefore, by Lagrange's theorem (theorem 9.2.3), $|S|$ must divide $|\mathbb{Z}_p^*|$. Suppose now that there exists an element $a \in \mathbb{Z}_p^*$ for which $a^{p-1} \not\equiv 1 \pmod{p}$. Then, $S \neq \mathbb{Z}_p^*$, so the next best thing it can be is "half" of $\mathbb{Z}_p^*$, so $|S|$ must be at most half of $|\mathbb{Z}_p^*|$. $\square$

Problem 6.9. *Give an alternative proof of lemma 6.8 sans groups.*

---

[2]This section requires a little bit of number theory; see Section 9.2 for all the necessary background.

A number is *pseudoprime* if it is either prime or Carmichael. The last lemma suggests an algorithm for pseudoprimeness: on input p, check whether $a^{(p-1)} \equiv 1 \pmod{p}$ for some random $a \in \mathbb{Z}_p - \{0\}$. If p fails this test (i.e., $a^{(p-1)} \not\equiv 1 \pmod{p}$), then p is composite for sure. If p passes the test, then p is probably pseudoprime. We show that the probability of error in this case is $\leq \frac{1}{2}$. Suppose p is not pseudoprime. If $\gcd(a, p) \neq 1$, then $a^{(p-1)} \not\equiv 1 \pmod{p}$ (by proposition 9.20), so assuming that p passed the test, it must be the case that $\gcd(a, p) = 1$, and so $a \in \mathbb{Z}_p^*$. But then, by lemma 6.8, at least half of the elements of $\mathbb{Z}_p^*$ are witnesses of non-pseudoprimeness.

Problem 6.10. *Show that if* $\gcd(a, p) \neq 1$ *then* $a^{(p-1)} \not\equiv 1 \pmod{p}$.

The informal algorithm for pseudoprimeness described in the paragraph above is the basis for the Rabin-Miller algorithm which we discuss next. The Rabin-Miller algorithm extends the pseudoprimeness test to deal with Carmichael numbers.

Algorithm 6.3 Rabin-Miller

1: If $n = 2$, accept; if n is even and $n > 2$, reject.
2: Choose at random a positive a in $\mathbb{Z}_n$.
3: **if** $a^{(n-1)} \not\equiv 1 \pmod{n}$ **then**
4:       reject
5: **else**
6:       Find s, h such that s is odd and $n - 1 = s2^h$
7:       Compute the sequence $a^{s \cdot 2^0}, a^{s \cdot 2^1}, a^{s \cdot 2^2}, \ldots, a^{s \cdot 2^h} \pmod{n}$
8:       **if** all elements in the sequence are 1 **then**
9:             accept
10:       **else if** the last element different from 1 is -1 **then**
11:             accept
12:       **else**
13:             reject
14:       **end if**
15: **end if**

Note that this is a polytime (randomized) algorithm: computing powers $\pmod{n}$ can be done efficiently with *repeated squaring*—for example, if $(n - 1)_b = c_r \ldots c_1 c_0$, then compute

$$a_0 = a, a_1 = a_0^2, a_2 = a_1^2, \ldots, a_r = a_{r-1}^2 \pmod{n},$$

and so $a^{n-1} = a_0^{c_0} a_1^{c_1} \cdots a_r^{c_r}$ (mod n). Thus obtaining the powers in lines 6 and 7 is not a problem.

Problem 6.11. *Implement the Rabin-Miller algorithm. In the first naïve version, the algorithm should run on integer inputs (the built in* `int` *type). In the second, more sophisticated version, the algorithm should run on inputs which are numbers encoded as binary strings, with the trick of repeated squaring in order to cope with large numbers.*

Theorem 6.12. *If n is a prime then the Rabin-Miller algorithm accepts it; if n is composite, then the algorithm rejects it with probability $\geq \frac{1}{2}$.*

Proof. If n is prime, then by Fermat's Little theorem $a^{(n-1)} \equiv 1$ (mod n), so line 4 cannot reject n. Suppose that line 13 rejects n; then there exists a b in $\mathbb{Z}_n$ such that $b \not\equiv \pm 1$ (mod n) and $b^2 \equiv 1$ (mod n). Therefore, $b^2 - 1 \equiv 0$ (mod n), and hence

$$(b-1)(b+1) \equiv 0 \quad (\text{mod } n).$$

Since $b \not\equiv \pm 1$ (mod n), both $(b-1)$ and $(b+1)$ are strictly between 0 and n, and so a prime n cannot divide their product. This gives a contradiction, and therefore no such b exists, and so line 13 cannot reject n.

If n is an odd composite number, then we say that a is a *witness* (of compositness) for n if the algorithm rejects on a. We show that if n is an odd composite number, then at least half of the a's in $\mathbb{Z}_n$ are witnesses. The distribution of those witnesses in $\mathbb{Z}_n$ appears to be very irregular, but if we choose our a at random, we hit a witness with probability $\geq \frac{1}{2}$.

Because n is composite, either n is the power of an odd prime, or n is the product of two odd co-prime numbers. This yields two cases.

Case 1: Suppose that $n = q^e$ where q is an odd prime and $e > 1$. Set $t := 1 + q^{e-1}$. From the binomial expansion of t^n we obtain:

$$t^n = (1 + q^{e-1})^n = 1 + nq^{e-1} + \sum_{l=2}^{n} \binom{n}{l} (q^{e-1})^l, \qquad (6.2)$$

and therefore $t^n \equiv 1$ (mod n). If $t^{n-1} \equiv 1$ (mod n), then $t^n \equiv t$ (mod n), which from the observation about t and t^n is not possible, hence t is a line 4 witness. But the set of line 4 non-witnesses, $S_1 := \{a \in \mathbb{Z}_n | a^{(n-1)} \equiv 1$ (mod n)$\}$, is a subgroup of $\mathbb{Z}_n^*$, and since it is not equal to $\mathbb{Z}_n^*$ (t is not in it), by Lagrange's theorem S_1 is at most half of $\mathbb{Z}_n^*$, and so it is at most half of $\mathbb{Z}_n$.

Case 2: Suppose that $n = qr$, where q, r are co-prime. Among all line 13 non-witnesses, find a non-witness for which the -1 appears in the largest position in the sequence in line 7 of the algorithm (note that -1 is a line 13 non-witness, so the set of these non-witnesses is not empty). Let x be such a non-witness and let j be the position of -1 in its sequence, where the positions are numbered starting at 0; $x^{s \cdot 2^j} \equiv -1 \pmod{n}$ and $x^{s \cdot 2^{j+1}} \equiv 1 \pmod{n}$. The line 13 non-witnesses are a subset of $S_2 := \{a \in \mathbb{Z}_n^* | a^{s \cdot 2^j} \equiv \pm 1 \pmod{n}\}$, and S_2 is a subgroup of $\mathbb{Z}_n^*$.

By the CRT there exists $t \in \mathbb{Z}_n$ such that

$$\begin{array}{ll} t \equiv x \pmod{q} \\ t \equiv 1 \pmod{r} \end{array} \quad \Rightarrow \quad \begin{array}{ll} t^{s \cdot 2^j} \equiv -1 \pmod{q} \\ t^{s \cdot 2^j} \equiv 1 \pmod{r} \end{array}$$

Hence t is a witness because $t^{s \cdot 2^j} \not\equiv \pm 1 \pmod{n}$ but on the other hand $t^{s \cdot 2^{j+1}} \equiv 1 \pmod{n}$.

Problem 6.13. *Show that $t^{s \cdot 2^j} \not\equiv \pm 1 \pmod{n}$.*

Therefore, just as in case 1, we have constructed a $t \in \mathbb{Z}_n^*$ which is not in S_2, and so S_2 can be at most half of $\mathbb{Z}_n^*$, and so at least half of the elements in $\mathbb{Z}_n$ are witnesses. □

Problem 6.14. *First show that the sets S_1 and S_2 (in the proof of theorem 6.12) are indeed subgroups of $\mathbb{Z}_n^*$, and that in case 2 all non-witnesses are contained in S_2. Then show that at least half of the elements of $\mathbb{Z}_n$ are witnesses when n is composite, without using group theory.*

Note that by running the algorithm k times on independently chosen a, we can make sure that it rejects a composite with probability $\geq 1 - \frac{1}{2^k}$ (it will always accept a prime with probability 1). Thus, for $k = 100$ the probability of error, i.e., of a false positive, is negligible.

6.4 Public key cryptography

Cryptography has well known applications to security; for example, we can use our credit cards when purchasing online because, when we send our credit card numbers, they are encrypted, and even though they travel through a public channel, no one but the intended recipient can read them. Cryptography has also a fascinating history: from the first uses recorded by Herodotus during the Persian wars five centuries BC, to the exploits at Bletchley Park during WWII—the reader interested in the history of cryptography should read the fascinating book [Singh (1999)].

A *Public Key Cryptosystem (PKC)* consists of three sets: K, the set of (pairs of) *keys*, M, the set of *plaintext* messages, and C, the set of *ciphertext* messages. A pair of keys in K is $k = (k_{priv}, k_{pub})$; the *private* (or *secret*) key and the *public* key, respectively. For each k_{pub} there is a corresponding *encryption* function $e_{k_{pub}} : M \longrightarrow C$ and for each k_{priv} there is a corresponding *decryption* function $d_{k_{priv}} : C \longrightarrow M$.

The property that the encryption and decryption functions must satisfy is that if $k = (k_{priv}, k_{pub}) \in K$, then $d_{k_{priv}}(e_{k_{pub}}(m)) = m$ for all $m \in M$. The necessary assumption is that it must be difficult to compute $d_{k_{priv}}(c)$ just from knowing k_{pub} and c. But, with the additional *trapdoor* information k_{priv}, it becomes easy to compute $d_{k_{priv}}(c)$.

In the following sections we present three different encryption schemes: Diffie-Hellman, which is not really a PKC but rather a way of agreeing on a secret key over an insecure channel, as well as ElGamal and RSA. All three require large primes (in practice about 2,000 bit long); a single prime for Diffie-Hellman and ElGamal, and a pair of primes for RSA. But how does one find large primes? The answer will of course involve the Rabin-Miller algorithm from the previous section.

Here is how we go about it: we know by the Prime Number Theorem that there are about $\pi(n) = n/\log n$ many primes $\leq n$. This means that there are $2^n/n$ primes among n-bit integers, roughly 1 in n, and these primes are fairly uniformly distributed. So we pick an integer at random, in a given range, and apply the Rabin-Miller algorithm to it.

6.4.1 *Diffie-Hellman key exchange*

If p is prime, then one can show—though the proof is difficult and we omit it here—that there exists a $g \in \mathbb{Z}_p^*$ such that $\langle g \rangle = \{g^1, g^2, \ldots, g^{p-1}\} = \mathbb{Z}_p^*$. This g is called a *primitive root* for $\mathbb{Z}_p^*$. Given an $h \in \mathbb{Z}_p^*$, the *Discrete Log Problem (DLP)* is the problem of finding an $x \in \{1, \ldots, p-1\}$ such that $g^x \equiv h \pmod{p}$. That is, $x = \log_g(h)$.

For example, $p = 56609$ is a prime number and $g = 2$ is a generator for $\mathbb{Z}_{56609}^*$, that is $\mathbb{Z}_{56609}^* = \{2^1, 2^2, 2^3, \ldots, 2^{56608}\}$, and $\log_2(38679) = 11235$.

Problem 6.15. *If $p = 7$, explain why $g = 3$ would work as a generator for $\mathbb{Z}_p^*$. Is every number in $\mathbb{Z}_7^*$ a generator for $\mathbb{Z}_7^*$?*

The DLP is assumed to be a difficult problem. We are going to use it to set up a way for Alice and Bob to agree on a secret key over an insecure channel. First Alice and Bob agree on a large prime p and an integer $g \in \mathbb{Z}_p^*$. In fact, g does not have to be a primitive root for p; it is sufficient, and much easier, to pick a number g of order roughly $p/2$. See, for example, exercise 1.31 in [Hoffstein *et al.* (2008)]. The numbers p, g are public knowledge, that is, $k_{\text{pub}} = \langle p, g \rangle$.

Then Alice picks a secret a and Bob picks a secret b. Alice computes $A := g^a \pmod{p}$ and Bob computes $B := g^b \pmod{p}$. Then Alice and Bob exchange A and B over an insecure link. On her end, Alice computes $A' := B^a \pmod{p}$ and Bob, on his end, computes $B' := A^b \pmod{p}$. Clearly,

$$A' \equiv_p B^a \equiv_p (g^b)^a \equiv_p g^{ab} \equiv_p (g^a)^b \equiv_p A^b \equiv_p B'.$$

This common value $A' = B'$ is their secret key. Thus, Diffie-Hellman is not really a fully-fledged PKC; it is just a way for two parties to agree on a secret value over an insecure channel. Also note that computing A and B involves computing large powers of g modulo the prime p; if this is done naïvely by multiplying g times itself a many times, then this procedure is impractical for large a. We use repeated squaring instead; see page 127 where we discuss this procedure.

Problem 6.16. *Suppose that Alice and Bob agree on $p = 23$ and $g = 5$, and that Alice's secret is $a = 8$ and Bob's secret is $b = 15$. Show how the Diffie-Hellman exchange works in this case. What is the resulting secret key?*

Suppose that Eve is eavesdropping on this exchange. She is capable of gleaning the following information from it: $\langle p, g, g^a \pmod{p}, g^b \pmod{p} \rangle$. Computing $g^{ab} \pmod{p}$ (i.e., $A' = B'$) from this information is known as the *Diffie-Hellman Problem* (DHP), and it is assumed to be difficult when p is a large prime number.

But suppose that Eve has an efficient way of solving the DLP. Then, from $g^a \pmod{p}$ she computes a, and from $g^b \pmod{p}$ she computes b, and now she can easily compute $g^{ab} \pmod{p}$. On the other hand, it is not known if solving DHP efficiently yields an efficient solution for the DLP.

Problem 6.17. *Consider Shank's algorithm—algorithm 6.4. Show that Shank's algorithm computes x, such that $g^x \equiv_p h$, in time $O(n \log n)$ that is, in time $O(\sqrt{p} \log(\sqrt{p}))$.*

Problem 6.18. *Implement algorithm 6.4.*

Algorithm 6.4 Shank's babystep-giantstep

Pre-condition: p prime, $\langle g \rangle = \mathbb{Z}_p^*$, $h \in \mathbb{Z}_p^*$

1: $n \longleftarrow 1 + \lfloor \sqrt{p} \rfloor$
2: $L_1 \longleftarrow \{g^0, g^1, g^2, \ldots, g^n\} \pmod{p}$
3: $L_2 \longleftarrow \{hg^0, hg^{-n}, hg^{-2n}, \ldots, hg^{-n^2}\} \pmod{p}$
4: Find $g^i \equiv_p hg^{-jn} \in L_1 \cap L_2$
5: $x \longleftarrow jn + i$
6: **return** x

Post-condition: $g^x \equiv_p h$

While it seems to be difficult to mount a direct attack on Diffie-Hellman, that is, to attack it by solving the related discrete logarithm problem, there is a rather insidious way of breaking it, called "the man-in-the-middle" attack. It consists in Eve taking advantage of the lack of authentication for the parties; that is, how does Bob know that he is receiving a message from Alice, and how does Alice know that she is receiving a message from Bob? Eve can take advantage of that, and intercept a message A from Alice intended for Bob and replace it with $E = g^e \pmod{p}$, and intercept the message B from Bob intended for Alice and also replace it with $E = g^e \pmod{p}$, and from then on read all the correspondence by pretending to be Bob to Alice, and Alice to Bob, translating message encoded with $g^{ae} \pmod{p}$ to message encoded with $g^{be} \pmod{p}$, and vice versa.

Problem 6.19. *Suppose that $f : \mathbb{N} \times \mathbb{N} \longrightarrow \mathbb{N}$ is a function with the following properties:*

- *for all $a, b, g \in \mathbb{N}$, $f(g, ab) = f(f(g, a), b) = f(f(g, b), a)$,*
- *for any g, $h_g(c) = f(g, c)$ is a one-way function, that is, a function that is easy to compute, but whose inverse is difficult to compute[3].*

Explain how f could be used for public key crypto in the style of Diffie-Hellman.

---

[3]The existence of such functions is one of the underlying assumptions of cryptography; the discrete logarithm is an example of such a function, but there is no proof of existence, only a well-founded supposition.

6.4.2 *ElGamal*

This is a true PKC, where Alice and Bob agree on public p, g, such that p is a prime and $\mathbb{Z}_p^* = \langle g \rangle$. Alice also has a private a and publishes a public $A := g^a \pmod{p}$. Bob wants to send a message m to Alice, so he creates an *ephemeral* key b, and sends the pair c_1, c_2 to Alice where:

$$c_1 := g^b \pmod{p}; \qquad c_2 := mA^b \pmod{p}.$$

Then, in order to read the message, Alice computes:

$$c_1^{-a} c_2 \equiv_p g^{-ab} m g^{ab} \equiv_p m.$$

Note that to compute c_1^{-a} Alice first computes the inverse of c_1 in $\mathbb{Z}_p^*$, which she can do efficiently using the extended Euclid's algorithm (see algorithm 1.8 or algorithm 3.5), and then computes the a-th power of the result.

More precisely, here is how we compute the inverse of a k in $\mathbb{Z}_n^*$. Observe that if $k \in \mathbb{Z}_n^*$, then $\gcd(k, n) = 1$, so using algorithm 1.8 we obtain s, t such that $sk + tn = 1$, and further s, t can be chosen so that s is in $\mathbb{Z}_n^*$. To see that, first obtain any s, t, and then just add to s the appropriate number of positive or negative multiples of n to place it in the set $\mathbb{Z}_n^*$, and adjust t by the same number of multiples of opposite sign.

Problem 6.20. *Let $p = 7$ and $g = 3$.*

(1) Let $a = 4$ be Alice's secret key, so

$$A = g^a \pmod{p} = 3^4 \pmod{7} = 4.$$

Let $p = 7, g = 3, A = 4$ be public values.
Suppose that Bob wants to send the message $m = 2$ to Alice, with ephemeral key $b = 5$. What is the corresponding pair $\langle c_1, c_2 \rangle$ that he sends to Alice? Show what are the actual values and how are they computed.

(2) What does Alice do in order to read the message $\langle 5, 4 \rangle$? That is, how does Alice extract m out of $\langle c_1, c_2 \rangle = \langle 5, 4 \rangle$?

Problem 6.21. *We say that we can break ElGamal, if we have an efficient way for computing m from $\langle p, g, A, c_1, c_2 \rangle$. Show that we can break ElGamal if and only if we can solve the DHP efficiently.*

Problem 6.22. *Write an application which implements the ElGamal digital signature scheme. Your command-line program ought to be invoked as follows:* `sign 11 6 3 7` *and then accept a single line of* ASCII *text until* *the new-line character appears (i.e., until you press enter). That is, once you type* **sign** 11 6 3 7 *at the command line, and press return, you type a message: 'A message' and after you have pressed return again, the digital signature, which is going to be a pair of positive integers, will appear below.*

We now explain how to obtain this digital signature: first convert the characters in the string 'A message' into the corresponding ASCII codes, and then obtain a hash of those codes by multiplying them all modulo 11; the result should be the single number 5.

To see this observe the table:

A	65	10
	32	1
m	109	10
e	101	9
s	115	1
s	115	5
a	97	1
g	103	4
e	101	8
.	46	5

The first column contains the characters, the second the corresponding ASCII codes, and the i-th entry in the third column contains the product of the first i codes modulo 11. The last entry in the third column is the hash value 5.

We sign the hash value, i.e., if the message is $m =$ A message., then we sign $hash(m) = 5$. Note that we invoke **sign** with four arguments, i.e., we invoke it with p, g, x, k (in our running example, $11, 6, 3, 7$ respectively).

Here p must be a prime, $1 < g, x, k < p - 1$, and $\gcd(k, p - 1) = 1$. This is a condition of the input; you don't have to test in your program whether the condition is met—we may assume that it is.

Now the algorithm signs $h(m)$ as follows: it computes

$$r = g^k \pmod{p}$$
$$s = k^{-1}(h(m) - xr) \pmod{(p - 1)}$$

If s is zero, start over again, by selecting a different k (meeting the required conditions). The signature of m is precisely the pair of numbers (r, s). In our running example we have the following values:

$$m = \text{A message}; \quad h(m) = 5; \quad p = 11; \quad g = 6; \quad x = 3; \quad k = 7$$

and so the signature of 'A message' *with the given parameters will be:*

$$r = 6^7 \pmod{11} = 8$$
$$s = 7^{-1}(5 - 3 \cdot 8) \pmod{(11-1)}$$
$$= 3 \cdot (-19) \pmod{10}$$
$$= 3 \cdot 1 \pmod{10}$$
$$= 3$$

i.e., the signature of 'A message' *would be* $(r,s) = (8,3)$.

Problem 6.23. *In problem 6.22:*

(1) *Can you identify the (possible) weaknesses of this digital signature scheme? Can you compose a different message* m' *such that* $h(m) = h(m')$?

(2) *If you receive a message* m, *and a signature pair* (r,s), *and you only know* p, g *and* $y = g^x \pmod{p}$, *i.e.,* p, g, y *are the public information, how can you "verify" the signature—and what does it mean to verify the signature?*

(3) *Research on the web a better suggestion for a hash function* h.

(4) *Show that when used without a (good) hash function, ElGamal's signature scheme is existentially forgeable; i.e., an adversary Eve can construct a message* m *and a valid signature* (r,s) *for* m.

(5) *In practice* k *is a random number; show that it is absolutely necessary to choose a new random number for each message.*

(6) *Show that in the verification of the signature it is essential to check whether* $1 \leq r \leq p - 1$, *because otherwise Eve would be able to sign message of her choice, provided she knows one valid signature* (r,s) *for some message* m, *where* m *is such that* $1 \leq m \leq p - 1$ *and* $\gcd(m, p-1) = 1$.

6.4.3 *RSA*

Choose two odd primes p, q, and set $n = pq$. Choose $k \in \mathbb{Z}^*_{\phi(n)}$, $k > 1$. Advertise f, where $f(m) \equiv m^k \pmod{n}$. Compute l, the inverse of k in $\mathbb{Z}^*_{\phi(n)}$. Now $\langle n, k \rangle$ are public, and the key l is secret, and so is the function g, where $g(C) \equiv C^l \pmod{n}$. Note that $g(f(m)) \equiv_n m^{kl} \equiv_n m$.

Problem 6.24. *Show that* $m^{kl} \equiv m \pmod{n}$. *In fact there is an implicit assumption about* m *in order for this to hold; what is this assumption?*

Problem 6.25. *Observe that we could break RSA if factoring were easy.*

We now make two observations about the security of RSA. The first one is that the primes p, q cannot be chosen "close" to each other. To see what we mean, note that:

$$n = \left(\frac{p+q}{2}\right)^2 - \left(\frac{p-q}{2}\right)^2.$$

Since p, q are close, we know that $s := (p-q)/2$ is small, and $t := (p+q)/2$ is only slightly larger than $\sqrt{n}$, and $t^2 - n = s^2$ is a perfect square. So we try the following candidate values for t:

$$\lceil\sqrt{n}\rceil + 0, \quad \lceil\sqrt{n}\rceil + 1, \quad \lceil\sqrt{n}\rceil + 2, \ldots$$

until $t^2 - n$ is a perfect square s^2. Clearly, if s is small, we will quickly find such a t, and then $p = t + s$ and $q = t - s$.

The second observation is that if were to break RSA by computing l efficiently from n and k, then we would be able to factor n in randomized polynomial time. Since $\phi(n) = \phi(pq) = (p-1)(q-1)$, it follows that:

$$p + q = n - \phi(n) + 1$$
$$pq = n, \tag{6.3}$$

and from these two equations we obtain:

$$(x - p)(x - q) = x^2 - (p+q)x + pq = x^2 - (n - \phi(n) + 1)x + n.$$

Thus, we can compute p, q by computing the roots of this last polynomial. Using the classical quadratic formula $x = (-b \pm \sqrt{b^2 - 4ac})/2a$, we obtain that p, q are:

$$\frac{(n - \phi(n) + 1) \pm \sqrt{(n - \phi(n) + 1)^2 - 4n}}{2}.$$

Suppose that Eve is able to compute l from n and k. If Eve knows l, then she knows that whatever $\phi(n)$ is, it divides $kl - 1$, and so she has equations (6.3) but with $\phi(n)$ replaced with $(kl - 1)/a$, for some a. This a can be computed in randomized polynomial time, but we do not present the method here. Thus, the claim follows.

If Eve is able to factor she can obviously break RSA; on the other hand, if Eve can break RSA—by computing l from n, k—, then she would be able to factor in randomized polytime.

On the other hand, Eve may be able to break RSA *without* computing l, so the preceding observations do not imply that breaking RSA is as hard as factoring.

6.5 Further problems

There is a certain reversal of priorities in cryptography, in that difficult problem become allies, rather than obstacles. On page 75 we mentioned NP-hard problems, which are problems for which there are no feasible solutions when the instances are "big enough."

The Simple Knapsack Problem (SKS) (see section 4.3) is one such problem, and we can use it to define a cryptosystem. The *Merkle-Hellman subset-sum cryptosystem* is based on SKS, and it works as follows. First, Alice creates a secret key consisting of the following elements:

- A *super-increasing sequence*: $\mathbf{r} = (r_1, r_2, \ldots, r_n)$ where $r_i \in \mathbb{N}$, and the property of being "super-increasing" refers to $2r_i \leq r_{i+1}$, for all $1 \leq i < n$.
- A pair of positive integers A, B with two conditions: $2r_n < B$ and $\gcd(A, B) = 1$.

The public key consists of $\mathbf{M} = (M_1, M_2, \ldots, M_n)$ where $M_i = Ar_i$ (mod B).

Suppose that Bob wants to send a plain-text message $x \in \{0, 1\}^n$, i.e., x is a binary string of length n. Then he uses Alice's public key to compute $S = \sum_{i=1}^{n} x_i M_i$, where x_i is the i-th bit of x, interpreted as integer 0 or 1. Bob now sends S to Alice.

For Alice to read the message she computes $S' = A^{-1}S$ (mod B), and she solves the subset-sum problem S' using the super-increasing $\mathbf{r}$. The subset-sum problem, for a general sequence $\mathbf{r}$, is very difficult, but when $\mathbf{r}$ is super-increasing (note that $\mathbf{M}$ is assumed not to be super-increasing!) the problem can be solved with a simple greedy algorithm.

More precisely, Alice finds a subset of $\mathbf{r}$ whose sum is precisely S'. Any subset of $\mathbf{r}$ can be identified with a binary string of length n, by assuming that x_i is 1 iff r_i is in this subset. Hence Alice "extracts" x out of S'.

For example, let $\mathbf{r} = (3, 11, 24, 50, 115)$, and $A = 113, B = 250$. Check that all conditions are met, and verify that $\mathbf{M} = (89, 243, 212, 150, 245)$. To send the secret message $x = 10101$, we compute

$$S = 1 \cdot 89 + 0 \cdot 243 + 1 \cdot 212 + 0 \cdot 150 + 1 \cdot 245 = 546.$$

Upon receiving S, we multiply it times 177, the inverse of 113 in mod 250, and obtain 142. Now x may be extracted out of 142 with a simple greedy algorithm.

Problem 6.26. *Two parts:*

(1) Show that if $\mathbf{r} = (r_1, r_2, \ldots, r_n)$ is a super-increasing sequence then $r_{i+1} > \sum_{j=1}^{i} r_j$, for all $1 \le i < n$.

(2) Suppose that $\mathbf{r} = (r_1, r_2, \ldots, r_n)$ is a super-increasing sequence, and suppose that there is a subset of $\mathbf{r}$ whose sum is S. Provide a (natural) greedy algorithm for computing this subset, and show that your algorithm is correct.

Problem 6.27. *Implement the Merkle-Hellman subset-sum cryptosystem. Call the program* `sscrypt`, *and it should work with three switches:* `-e` `-d` `-v`, *for encrypt, decrypt and verify. That is,*

   `sscrypt -e` $M_1 \, M_2 \ldots M_n \, x$

encrypts the string $x = x_1 x_2 \ldots x_n \in \{0,1\}^n$ *with the public key given by* $\mathbf{M} = (M_1, M_2, \ldots, M_n)$, *and outputs* S. *On the other hand,*

   `sscrypt -d` $r_1 \, r_2 \ldots r_n \, A \, B \, S$

decrypts the string $x = x_1 x_2 \ldots x_n \in \{0,1\}^n$ *from* S *using the secret key given by* $\mathbf{r} = (r_1, r_2, \ldots, r_n)$ *and* A, B; *that is, it outputs* x *on input* $\mathbf{r}, A, B, S$. *Finally,*

   `sscrypt -v` $r_1 \, r_2 \ldots r_n \, A \, B$

checks that $\mathbf{r} = (r_1, r_2, \ldots, r_n)$ *is super-increasing, it checks that* $2r_n < B$ *and that* $\gcd(A, B) = 1$, *and outputs the corresponding public key given by* $\mathbf{M} = (M_1, M_2, \ldots, M_n)$.

6.6 Answers to selected problems

Problem 6.5. We use algorithm 6.1 to find perfect matching (if one exists) as follows: pick $1 \in V$, and consider each $(1, i') \in E$ in turn, remove it from G to obtain $G_{1,i'} = ((V - \{1\}) \cup (V' - \{i'\}), E_{1,i'})$, where $E_{1,i'}$ consists of all the edges of E except those adjacent on 1 or i', until for some $i' \in V'$ we obtain a $G_{1,i'}$ for which the algorithm answers "yes." Then we know that there is a perfect matching that matches 1 and i'. Continue with $G_{1,i'}$.

Problem 6.6. $M(x)$ is well defined because matrix multiplication is associative. We now show that $M(x) = M(y)$ implies that $x = y$ (i.e., the map M is one-to-one). Given $M = M(x)$ we can "decode" x uniquely as follows: if the first column of M is greater than the second (where the comparison is made component-wise), then the last bit of x is zero, and otherwise it is 1. Let M' be M where we subtract the smaller column from the larger, and repeat.

Problem 6.7. For a given string x, $M(x_1x_2\ldots x_n)$ is such that the "smaller" column is bounded by f_{n-1} and the "larger" column is bounded by f_n. We can show this inductively: the basis case, $x = x_1$, is obvious. For the inductive step, assume it holds for $x \in \{0,1\}^n$, and show it still holds for $x \in \{0,1\}^{n+1}$: this is clear as whether x_{n+1} is 0 or 1, one column is added to the other, and the other column remains unchanged.

Problem 6.9. Given that p is composite and non-Carmichael, there is at least one $a \in \mathbb{Z}_p^*$ such that $a^{(p-1)} \not\equiv 1 \pmod{p}$ and $\gcd(p,a) = 1$. Let $B = \{b_1, b_2, \ldots\}$ be the set of non-witnesses. Multiply each element of B by a to get witnesses $\{a_1, a_2, \ldots\}$. Each of these witnesses is unique, as $a \in \mathbb{Z}_p^*$, so there are at least as many witnesses as non-witnesses.

Let b be a potential non-witness; that is, b is any element of $\mathbb{Z}_p^*$ such that $\gcd(p,b) = 1$. if we multiply a by any *Fermat Liar* (i.e., non-witness), we get a witness. If there is only one non-witness, we're done. Otherwise, let b_1, b_2 be two non-witnesses. We know $\gcd(p,b_1) = \gcd(p,b_2) = 1$, as otherwise b_1 and b_2 would be witnesses. Assume $ab_1 = ab_2 + kp$, and let $g = \gcd(a,p)$.

Problem 6.10. Suppose that $\gcd(a,p) \neq 1$. By proposition 9.20 we know that if $\gcd(a,p) \neq 1$, then a does not have a (multiplicative) inverse in $\mathbb{Z}_p$. Thus, it is not possible for $a^{(p-1)} \equiv 1 \pmod{p}$ to be true, since then it would follow that $a \cdot a^{(p-2)} \equiv 1 \pmod{p}$, and hence a would have a (multiplicative) inverse.

Problem 6.13. To see why $t^{s\cdot 2^j} \not\equiv \pm 1 \pmod{n}$ observe the following: suppose that $a \equiv -1 \pmod{q}$ and $a \equiv 1 \pmod{r}$, where $\gcd(q,r) = 1$. Suppose that $n = qr|(a+1)$, then $q|(a+1)$ and $r|(a+1)$, and since $r|(a-1)$ as well, it follows that $r|[(a+1) - (a-1)]$, so $r|2$, so $r = 2$, so n must be even, which is not possible since we deal with even n's in line 1 of the algorithm.

Problem 6.14. Showing that S_1, S_2 are subgroups of $\mathbb{Z}_n^*$ is easy; it is obvious in both cases that 1 is there, and closure and existence of inverse can be readily checked.

To give the same proof without group theory, we follow the cases in the proof of theorem 6.12. Let t be the witness constructed in case 1. If d is a (stage 3) non-witness, we have $d^{p-1} \equiv 1 \pmod{p}$, but then $dt \pmod{p}$ is a witness. Moreover, if d_1, d_2 are distinct (stage 3) non-witnesses, then $d_1t \not\equiv d_2t \pmod{p}$. Otherwise, $d_1 \equiv_p d_1 \cdot t \cdot t^{p-1} \equiv_p d_2 \cdot t \cdot t^{p-1} \equiv_p d_2$. Thus the number of (stage 3) witnesses must be at least as large as the number of non-witnesses.

We do the same for case 2; let d be a non-witness. First, $d^{s \cdot 2^j} \equiv \pm 1$ (mod p) and $d^{s \cdot 2^{j+1}} \equiv 1$ (mod p) owing to the way that j was chosen. Therefore dt (mod p) is a witness because $(dt)^{s \cdot 2^j} \not\equiv \pm 1$ (mod p) and $(dt)^{s \cdot 2^{j+1}} \equiv 1$ (mod p).

Second, if d_1 and d_2 are distinct non-witnesses, $d_1 t \not\equiv d_2 t$ (mod p). The reason is that $t^{s \cdot 2^{j+1}} \equiv 1$ (mod p). Hence $t \cdot t^{s \cdot 2^{j+1}-1} \equiv 1$ (mod p). Therefore, if $d_1 t \equiv d_2 t$ (mod p), then $d_1 \equiv_p d_1 t \cdot t^{s \cdot 2^{j+1}-1} \equiv_p d_2 t \cdot t^{s \cdot 2^{j+1}-1} \equiv_p d_2$. Thus in case 2, as well, the number of witnesses must be at least as large as the number of non-witnesses.

Problem 6.15. $3^1 = 3, 3^2 = 9 = 2, 3^3 = 2 \cdot 3 = 6, 3^4 = 6 \cdot 3 = 4, 3^5 = 4 \cdot 3 = 5, 3^6 = 5 \cdot 3 = 1$, all computations (mod 7), and thus $g = 3$ generates all numbers in $\mathbb{Z}_7^*$. Not every number is a generator: for example, 4 is not.

Problem 6.16. Alice and Bob agree to use a prime $p = 23$ and base $g = 5$. Alice chooses secret $a = 8$; sends Bob $A = g^a$ (mod p)

$$A = 5^8 \pmod{23} = 16$$

Bob chooses secret $b = 15$; sends Alice $B = g^b$ (mod p)

$$B = 5^{15} \pmod{23} = 19$$

Alice computes $s = B^a$ (mod p)

$$s = 19^8 \pmod{23} = 9$$

Bob computes $s = A^b$ (mod p)

$$s = 16^{15} \pmod{23} = 9$$

As can be seen, both end up having $s = 9$, their shared secret key.

Problem 6.19. Suppose that we have a one-way function as in the question. First Alice and Bob agree on a public g and exchange it (the eavesdropper knows g therefore). Then, let Alice generate a secret a and let Bob generate a secret b. Alice sends $f(g, a)$ to Bob and Bob sends $f(g, b)$ to Alice. Notice that because h_g is one-way, an eavesdropper cannot get a or b from $h_g(a) = f(g, a)$ and $h_g(b) = f(g, b)$. Finally, Alice computes $f(f(g, b), a)$ and Bob computes $f(f(g, a), b)$, and by the properties of the function both are equal to $f(g, ab)$ which is their secret shared key. The eavesdropper cannot compute $f(g, ab)$ feasibly.

Problem 6.20. For the first part,

$$c_1 = g^b \pmod{p} = 3^5 \pmod{7} = 5$$
$$c_2 = mA^b \pmod{p} = 2 \cdot 4^5 \pmod{7} = 2 \cdot 2 = 4$$

For the second part,

$$
\begin{aligned}
m &= c_1^{-a} c_2 \quad (\text{mod } p) \\
&= 5^{-4} 4 \quad (\text{mod } 7) \\
&= (5^{-1})^4 4 \quad (\text{mod } 7) \\
&= 3^4 4 \quad (\text{mod } 7) \\
&= 4 \cdot 4 \quad (\text{mod } 7) \\
&= 2
\end{aligned}
$$

Problem 6.21. The DHP on input $\langle p, g, A \equiv_p g^a, B \equiv_p g^b \rangle$ outputs g^{ab} (mod p), and the ElGamal problem, call it ELGP, on input

$$
\langle p, g, A \equiv_p g^a, c_1 \equiv_p g^b, c_2 \equiv_p m A^b \rangle \tag{6.4}
$$

outputs m. We want to show that we can break Diffie-Hellman, i.e., solve DHP efficiently, if and only if we can break ElGamal, i.e., solve ELGP efficiently. The key-word here is *efficiently*, meaning in polynomial time.

($\Rightarrow$) Suppose we can solve DHP efficiently; we give an efficient procedure for solving ELGP: given the input (6.4) to ELGP, we obtain g^{ab} (mod p) from $A \equiv_p g^a$ and $c_1 \equiv g^b$ using the efficient solver for DHP. We then use the extended Euclidean algorithm, see problem 1.9—and note that the extended Euclid's algorithm runs in polynomial time, to obtain $(g^{ab})^{-1}$ (mod p). Now,

$$
c_2 \cdot (g^{ab})^{-1} \equiv_p m g^{ab} (g^{ab})^{-1} \equiv_p m = m
$$

where the last equality follows from $m \in \mathbb{Z}_p$.

($\Leftarrow$) Suppose we have an efficient solver for the ELGP. To solve the DHP, we construct the following input to ELGP:

$$
\langle p, g, A \equiv_p g^a, c_1 \equiv_p g^b, c_2 = 1 \rangle.
$$

Note that $c_2 = 1 \equiv_p \underbrace{(g^{ab})^{-1}}_{=m} A^b$, so using the efficient solver for ELGP we obtain $m \equiv_p (g^{ab})^{-1}$, and now using the extended Euclid's algorithm we obtain the inverse of $(g^{ab})^{-1}$ (mod p), which is just g^{ab} (mod p), so we output that.

Problem 6.23.

(1) The weakness of our scheme lies in the hash function, which computes the same hash values for different messages, and in fact it is easy to find messages with the same hash value—for example, by

adding pairs of letters (anywhere in the message) such that their corresponding ASCII values are inverses modulo p.

Examples (from the assignments) of messages with the same hash value are: "A mess" and "L message." In general, by its nature, any hash function is going to have such *collisions*, i.e., messages such that:

$$h(\text{A message.}) = h(\text{A mess}) = h(\text{L message}) = 5,$$

but there are hash functions which are *collision-resistant* in the sense that it is computationally hard to find two messages m, m' such that $h(m) = h(m')$. A good hash function is also a *one-way function* in the sense that given a value y it is computationally hard to find an m such that $h(m) = y$.

(2) Verifying the signature means checking that it was the person in possession of x that signed the document m. Two subtle things: first we say "in possession of x" rather than the "legitimate owner of x," simply because x may have been compromised (for example stolen). Second, and this is why this scheme is so brilliant, we can check that "someone in possession of x" signed the message, even *without knowing what x is*! We know y, where $y = g^x \pmod p$, but for large p, it is difficult to compute x from y (this is called the Discrete Log Problem, DLP).

Here is how we verify that "someone in possession of x" signed the message m. We check $0 < r < p$ and $0 < s < p - 1$ (see Q6), and we compute $v := g^{h(m)} \pmod p$ and $w := y^r r^s \pmod p$; g, p are public, m is known, and the function $h : \mathbb{N} \longrightarrow [p-1]$ is also known, and r, s is the given signature. If v and w match, then the signature is valid.

To see that this works note that we defined $s := k^{-1}(h(m) - xr) \pmod{p-1}$. Thus, $h(m) = xr + sk \pmod{p-1}$. Now, Fermat's Little Theorem (FLT—see page 114 in the textbook), says that $g^{p-1} = 1 \pmod p$, and therefore

$$g^{h(m)} \overset{(*)}{=} g^{xr+sh} = (g^x)^r (g^k)^s = y^r r^s \pmod p.$$

The FLT is applied in the $(*)$ equality: since $h(m) = xr + sk \pmod{p-1}$ it follows that $(p-1)|(h(m) - (xr+sk))$, which means that $(p-1)z = h(m) - (xr + sk)$ for some z, and since $g^{(p-1)z} = (g^{(p-1)})^z = 1^z = 1 \pmod p$, it follows that $g^{h(m)-(xr+sk)} = 1 \pmod p$, and so $g^{h(m)} = g^{xr+sk} \pmod p$.

(3) Here are the hash functions implemented by GPG, version 2.0.30: MD5, SHA1, RIPEMD160, SHA256, SHA384, SHA512, SHA224.

(4) To see this, let b, c be numbers such that $\gcd(c, p - 1) = 1$. Set $r = g^b y^c$, $s = -rc^{-1} \pmod{p - 1}$ and $m = -rbc^{-1} \pmod{p - 1}$. Then (m, r, s) satisfies $g^m = y^r r^s$. Since in practice a hash function h is applied to the message, and it is the hash value that is really signed, to forge a signature for a meaningful message is not so easy. An adversary has to find a meaningful message $\tilde{m}$ such that $h(\tilde{m}) = h(m)$, and when h is collision-resistant this is hard.

(5) If the same random number k is used in two different messages $m \neq m'$, then it is possible to compute k as follows: $s - s' = (m - m')k^{-1} \pmod{p - 1}$, and hence $k = (s - s')^{-1}(m - m') \pmod{p - 1}$.

(6) Let m' be a message of Eve's choice, $u = m'm^{-1} \pmod{p - 1}$, $s' = su \pmod{p - 1}$, r' and integer such that $r' = r \pmod{p}$ and $r' = ru \pmod{p - 1}$. This r' can be obtained by the so called Chinese Reminder Theorem (see theorem 9.30). Then (m', r', s') is accepted by the verification procedure.

Problem 6.24. Why $m^{kl} \equiv_n m$? Observe that $kl = 1 + (-t)\phi(n)$, where $(-t) > 0$, and so $m^{kl} \equiv_n m^{1+(-t)\phi(n)} \equiv_n m \cdot (m^{\phi(n)})^{(-t)} \equiv_n m$, because $m^{\phi(n)} \equiv_n 1$. Note that this last statement does not follow directly from Euler's theorem (theorem 9.29), because $m \in \mathbb{Z}_n$, and not necessarily in $\mathbb{Z}_n^*$. Note that to make sure that $m \in \mathbb{Z}_n^*$ it is enough to insist that we have $0 < m < \min\{p, q\}$; so we break a large message into small pieces.

It is interesting to note that we can bypass Euler's theorem, and just use Fermat's Little theorem: we know that $m^{(p-1)} \equiv_p 1$ and $m^{(q-1)} \equiv_q 1$, so $m^{(p-1)(q-1)} \equiv_p 1$ and $m^{(q-1)(p-1)} \equiv_q 1$, thus $m^{\phi(n)} \equiv_p 1$ and $m^{\phi(n)} \equiv_q 1$. This means that $p | (m^{\phi(n)} - 1)$ and $q | (m^{\phi(n)} - 1)$, so, since p, q are distinct primes, it follows that $(pq) | (m^{\phi(n)} - 1)$, and so $m^{\phi(n)} \equiv_n 1$.

Problem 6.25. If factoring integers were easy, RSA would be easily broken: if we were able to factor n, we would obtain the primes p, q, and hence it would be easy to compute $\phi(n) = \phi(pq) = (p - 1)(q - 1)$, and from this we obtain l, the inverse of k.

Problem 6.26. We show that $\forall i \in [n - 1]$ it is the case that $r_{i+1} \sum_{j=1}^{i} r_j$ by induction on i. The basis case is $i - 1$, so

$$r_2 \geq 2r_1 > r_1 = \sum_{j=1}^{i} r_j,$$

where $r_2 \geq 2r_1$ by the property of being super-increasing. For the induction step we have

$$r_{i+1} \geq 2r_i = r_i + r_i > r_i + \sum_{j=1}^{i-1} r_j = \sum_{j=1}^{i} r_j,$$

where we used the property of being super-increasing and the induction hypothesis.

Here is the algorithm for the second question:

$X \longleftarrow S$
$Y \longleftarrow \emptyset$
for $i = n \ldots 1$ **do**
　　　if $(r_i \leq X)$ **then**
　　　　　$X \longleftarrow X - r_i$
　　　　　$Y \longleftarrow Y \cup \{i\}$
　　end if
end for

---

and let the pre-condition state that $\{r_i\}_{i=1}^{n}$ is super-increasing and that there exists an $S \subseteq \{r_i\}_{i=1}^{n}$ such that $\sum_{i \in S} r_i = S$. Let the post-condition state that $\sum_{i \in Y} r_i = S$.

Define the following loop invariant: "Y is promising" in the sense that it can be extended, with indices of weights not considered yet, into a solution. That is, after considering i, there exists a subset E of $\{i - 1, \ldots, 1\}$ such that $\sum_{j \in X \cup E} r_j = S$.

The basis case is trivial since initially $X = \emptyset$, and since the pre-condition guarantees the existence of a solution, X can be extended into that solution.

For the induction step, consider two cases. If $r_i > X$ then i is not added, but Y can be extended with $E' \subseteq \{i - 1, i - 2, \ldots, 1\}$. The reason is that by induction hypothesis X was extended into a solution by some $E \subseteq \{i, i - 1, \ldots, 1\}$ and i was not part of the extension as r_i was too big to fit with what was already in Y, i.e., $E' = E$.

If $r_i \leq X$ then $i \in E$ since by previous part the remaining weights would not be able to close the gap between S and $\sum_{j \in Y} r_j$.

6.7　Notes

Regarding the epigraph at the beginning of the chapter, the novel Enigma [Harris (1996)] is a great introduction to the early days of crypto-analysis; also, there is a great 2001 movie adaptation.

Although we have not discussed the *Min-Cut Max-Flow* problem in this book, most introductions to algorithms do. See for example chapter 7 in [Kleinberg and Tardos (2006)]. Also, [Fernández and Soltys (2013)] discusses the Min-Max principle, and relates it to several other fundamental principles of combinatorics.

It is difficult to generate random numbers; see, for example, chapter 7 in [Press *et al.* (2007)].

Algorithm 6.3, the Rabin-Miller algorithm, abbreviated here as RM, is implemented in OpenSSL, which is a toolkit for the Transport Layer Security (TLS) and Secure Sockets Layer (SSL) protocols. It is also a general-purpose cryptography library.

One can test huge numbers for primality with the command:

```
openssl prime <number>
```

Newer versions of OpenSSL can also generate a prime number of a given number of bits:

```
openssl prime -generate -bits 2048
```

Also note that one can easily compute large powers of a number modulo a prime with Python, just give the command:

```
>>> pow(x,y,z)
```

which returns $x^y \pmod{z}$.

Section 6.3 on the Rabin-Miller algorithm was written while the author was spending a sabbatical year at the University of Colorado in Boulder, 2007-08, and this section was much improved from the discussions with Jan Mycielski.

Credit for inventing the Monte Carlo method often goes to Stanisław Ulam, a Polish born mathematician who worked with John von Neumann on the United States Manhattan Project during World War II. Ulam is also known for designing the hydrogen bomb with Edward Teller in 1951. He invented the Monte Carlo method in 1946 while pondering the probabilities of winning a card game of solitaire.

Section 6.2 is based on [Karp and Rabin (1987)].

The first polytime algorithm for primality testing was devised by [Agrawal *et al.* (2004)]. This algorithm is known as the "AKS Primality Test" (following the last names of the inventors: Agrawal-Kayal-Saxena). However, AKS is not feasible; RM is still the standard for primality testing.

In fact, it was the randomized test for primality that stirred interest in randomized computation in the late 1970's. Historically, the first randomized algorithm for primality was given by [Solovay and Strassen (1977)]; a good exposition of this algorithm, with all the necessary background, can be found in §11.1 in [Papadimitriou (1994)], and another in §18.5 in [von zur Gathen and Gerhard (1999)].

R. D. Carmichael first noted the existence of the Carmichael numbers in 1910, computed fifteen examples, and conjectured that though they are infrequent there were infinitely many. In 1956, Erdös sketched a technique for constructing large Carmichael numbers ([Hoffman (1998)]), and a proof was given by [Alford *et al.* (1994)] in 1994.

The first three Carmichael numbers are 561, 1105, 1729, where the last number shown on this list is called the Hardy-Ramanujan number, after a famous anecdote of the British mathematician G. H. Hardy regarding a hospital visit to the Indian mathematician Srinivasa Ramanujan. Hardy wrote: *I remember once going to see him when he was ill at Putney. I had ridden in taxi cab number 1729 and remarked that the number seemed to me rather a dull one, and that I hoped it was not an unfavorable omen. "No," he replied, "it is a very interesting number; it is the smallest number expressible as the sum of two cubes in two different ways.".* The reader is encouraged to see the movie *The Man Who Knew Infinity*, a 2015 film about Srinivasa Ramanujan.

Section 6.4 is based on material from [Hoffstein *et al.* (2008)] and [Delfs and Knebl (2007)].

RSA is named following the last names of its inventors: Rivest-Shamir-Adleman.

GnuPG, or GPG, is a free implementation of the OpenPGP standard as defined by RFC4880 (also known as PGP). GPG allows to encrypt and sign data and communication, and it features a complete key management system. Here are some more examples of usage of GPG:

```
gpg --gen-keys
gpg --list-keys
gpg --armor -r 9B070A58 -e example.txt
gpg --armor --clearsign example.txt
gpg --verify example.txt.asc
```

The first command generates a new public and secret key pair. The second lists all the keys in the key-ring, and displays a summary about each. The third line encrypts the text file `example.txt` with the public key with id

9B070A58, which is the key of the author[4]. The fourth line produces a signature of `example.txt` which ensures that the file has not been modified; the signature is attached as text to the file. The last command verifies the signature resulting from the previous command.

Public keys can be advertised on personal homepages, or uploaded to the Public Key Infrastructure (PKI). An example of PKI is the MIT PGP Public Key Server, `https://pgp.mit.edu`, which can be searched for keys (by ids, names, emails, etc.):

```
gpg --keyserver hkp://pgp.mit.edu --search-keys 0x9B070A58
```

Note that the URL of the keyserver is given with the HKP protocol, where HKP stands for "OpenPGP HTTP Keyserver Protocol."

Similar operations can be performed with OpenSSL; for example, we can generate RSA secret keys as follows:

```
openssl genrsa -out mysecretrsakey.pem 512
openssl genrsa -out mysecretrsakey.pem 4096
```

The two parameters 512 and 4096 give the size of the primes; note that with 4096 the generation is a bit longer; this is where the Rabin Miller algorithm is employed. The following option generates the corresponding public key:

```
openssl rsa -in mysecretrsakey.pem -pubout
```

We can generating an elliptic curve key:

```
openssl ecparam -out myeckey.pem -name prime256v1 -genkey
```

and a complete list of types of elliptic curves:

```
openssl ecparam -list_curves
```

As was already discussed, we can use OpenSSL to test directly for primality:

```
openssl prime 32948230523084029834023
```

note that the number returned is always hexadecimal; it is amazing that such large numbers can be tested for primality; it is because of the RM theorem that this can be done so quickly.

---

[4]The author's GPG public key with id 9B070A58: `http://www.msoltys.com/gpgkey`

Chapter 7

Algorithms in Linear Algebra

Kraj bez matematyki nie wytrzyma współzawodnictwa z tymi, którzy uprawiają matematykę. *A country without mathematics cannot compete with those who pursue it.*

Hugo Steinhaus quoted on page 147 of [Duda (1977)]

7.1 Introduction

This chapter requires basic linear algebra, but not much beyond linear independence, determinants, and the characteristic polynomial. We are going to focus on matrices, in some case on matrices over finite fields. For the reader who is unfamiliar with the foundations of Linear Algebra we recommend [Halmos (1995)].

We say that a set of vectors $\{v_1, v_2, \ldots, v_n\}$ is *linearly independent* if $\sum_{i=1}^{n} c_i v_i = 0$ implies that $c_i = 0$ for all i, and that they *span* a vector space $V \subseteq \mathbb{R}^n$ if whenever $v \in V$, then there exist $c_i \in \mathbb{R}$ such that $v = \sum_{i=1}^{n} c_i v_i$. We denote this as $V = \text{span—textbf}\{v_1, v_2, \ldots, v_n\}$. A set of vectors $\{v_1, v_2, \ldots, v_n\}$ in $\mathbb{R}^n$ is a *basis* for a vector space $V \subseteq \mathbb{R}^n$ if they are linearly independent and span V. Let $x \cdot y$ denote the *dot-product* of two vectors, defined as $x \cdot y = (x_1, x_2, \ldots, x_n) \cdot (y_1, y_2, \ldots, y_n) = \sum_{i=1}^{n} x_i y_i$, and the *norm* of a vector x is defined as $\|x\| = \sqrt{x \cdot x}$. Two vectors x, y are *orthogonal* if $x \cdot y = 0$.

7.2   Gaussian Elimination

We say that a matrix is in *row-echelon form* if it satisfies the following two conditions: (i) if there are non-zero rows, the first non-zero entry of such rows is 1, (the *pivot*), and (ii) the first non-zero entry of row $i+1$ is to the right of the first non-zero entry of row i. In short, a matrix is in row-echelon form if it looks as follows:

$$\begin{bmatrix} 1 * \ldots * * * \ldots * * * \ldots * * \\ 1 * \ldots * * * \ldots * * \\ \ddots \qquad 1 * \ldots * * \\ 0 \qquad\qquad 1 \ldots \\ \ddots \qquad\qquad \vdots \ddots \end{bmatrix} \qquad (7.1)$$

where the *'s indicate arbitrary entries.

We define the function Gaussian Elimination, $GE : M_{n \times m} \longrightarrow M_{n \times n}$, to be the function which when given an $n \times m$ matrix A as input, it outputs an $n \times n$ matrix $GE(A)$, with the property that $GE(A)A$ is in row-echelon form. We call this property the *correctness condition* of GE.

We show how to compute $GE(A)$, given A. The idea is, of course, that $GE(A)$ is equal to a product of elementary matrices which bring A to row-echelon form. We start by defining elementary matrices. Let T_{ij} be a matrix with zeros everywhere except in the (i,j)-th position, where it has a 1. A matrix E is an *elementary matrix* if E has one of the following three forms:

$$I + aT_{ij} \quad i \neq j \qquad\qquad \text{(elementary of type 1)}$$
$$I + T_{ij} + T_{ji} - T_{ii} - T_{jj} \qquad\qquad \text{(elementary of type 2)}$$
$$I + (c-1)T_{ii} \quad c \neq 0 \qquad\qquad \text{(elementary of type 3)}$$

Let A be any matrix. If E is an elementary matrix of type 1, then EA is A with the i-th row replaced by the sum of the i-th row and a times the j-th row. If E is an elementary matrix of type 2, then EA is A with the i-th and j-th rows interchanged. If E is an elementary matrix of type 3, then EA is A with the i-th row multiplied by $c \neq 0$.

The Gaussian Elimination algorithm is a divide and conquer type of algorithm, with a recursive call to smaller matrices. That is, we compute GE recursively, on the number of rows of A. If A is a $1 \times m$ matrix, $A = [a_{11} a_{12} \ldots a_{1m}]$, then:

$$GE(A) = \begin{cases} [1/a_{1i}] & \text{where } i = \min\{1, 2, \ldots, m\} \text{ such that } a_{i1} \neq 0 \\ [1] & \text{if } a_{11} = a_{12} = \cdots = a_{1m} = 0 \end{cases} \qquad (7.2)$$

In the first case, $GE(A) = [1/a_{1i}]$, $GE(A)$ is just an elementary matrix of size 1×1, and type 3, $c = a_{i1}$. In the second case, $GE(A)$ is a 1×1 identity, so an elementary matrix of type 1 with $a = 0$. Also note that in the first case we divide by a_{1i}. This is not needed when the underlying field is $\mathbb{Z}_2$, since a non-zero entry is necessarily 1. However, our arguments hold regardless of the underlying field, so we want to make the function GE field independent.

Suppose now that $n > 1$. If $A = 0$, let $GE(A) = I$. Otherwise, let:

$$GE(A) = \begin{bmatrix} 1 & 0 \\ 0 & GE((EA)[1|1]) \end{bmatrix} E \qquad (7.3)$$

where E is a product of at most $n + 1$ elementary matrices, defined below. Note that $C[i|j]$ denotes the matrix C with row i and j deleted, so $(EA)[1|1]$ is the matrix A multiplied by E on the left, and then the first row and column are deleted from the result. Also note that we make sure that $GE(A)$ is of the appropriate size (i.e., it is an $n \times n$ matrix), by placing $GE((EA)[1|1])$ inside a matrix padded with a 1 in the upper-left corner, and zeros in the remaining of the first row and column.

We now define the matrix E, given an A as input. There are two cases: the first column of A is zero or it is not.

Case 1: If the first column of A is zero, let j be the first non-zero column of A (such a column exists by the assumption $A \neq 0$). Let i be the index of the first row of A such that $A_{ij} \neq 0$. If $i > 1$, let $E = I_{1i}$ (E interchanges row 1 and row i). If $i = 1$, but $A_{lj} = 0$ for $1 < l \leq n$, then $E = I$ (do nothing). If $i = 1$, and $1 < i'_1 < i'_2 < \cdots < i'_k$ are the indices of the other rows with $A_{i'_l j} \neq 0$, let $E = E_{i'_1} E_{i'_2} \cdots E_{i'_k}$, where $E_{i'_l}$ is the elementary matrix that adds the first row of A to the i'_l-th row, of A so that it clears the j-th entry of the i'_l-th row (this is over $\mathbb{Z}_2$; over a bigger field, we might need *a multiple* of the first row to clear the i'_l-th row).

Case 2: If the first column of A is not zero, then let a_{i1} be its first non-zero entry (i.e., $a_{j1} = 0$ if $j < i$). We want to compute a sequence of elementary matrices, whose product will be denoted by E, which accomplish the following sequence of steps:

(1) they interchange the first and i-th row,
(2) they divide the first row by a_{i1},
(3) and they use the first row to clear all the other entries in the first column.

Let $a_{i_1 1}, a_{i_2 1}, \ldots, a_{i_k 1}$ be the list of all the non-zero entries in the first column of A, not including a_{i1}, ordered so that:
$$i < i_1 < i_2 < \cdots < i_k$$
Let the convention be that if a_{i1} is the *only* non-zero entry in the first row, then $k = 0$. Define E to be:
$$E = E_{i_1} E_{i_2} \cdots E_{i_k} E' E''$$
where $E_{i_j} = I - a_{i_j 1} T_{i_j 1}$, so E_{i_j} clears the first entry from the i_j-th row of A. Note that if $k = 0$ (if a_{i1} is the only non-zero entry in the first column of A), then $E = E'' E'$. Let
$$E'' = I + \left(\frac{1}{a_{i1}} - 1 \right) T_{11} \quad \text{and} \quad E' = I + T_{i1} + T_{1i} - T_{ii} - T_{11}$$
Thus, E'' divides the first row by a_{i1}, and E' interchanges the first row and the i-th row.

Algorithm 7.1 Gaussian Elimination

Pre-condition: An $n \times m$ matrix $A = [a_{ij}]$ over some field $\mathbb{F}$

1: **if** $n = 1$ **then**
2:     **if** $a_{11} = a_{12} = \cdots = a_{1m} = 0$ **then**
3:         **return** $[1]$
4:     **else**
5:         **return** $[1/a_{1\ell}]$ where $\ell = \min_{i \in [n]} \{ a_{1i} \neq 0 \}$
6:     **end if**
7: **else**
8:     **if** $A = 0$ **then**
9:         **return** I
10:     **else**
11:         **if** first column of A is zero **then**
12:             Compute E as in Case 1.
13:         **else**
14:             Compute E as in Case 2.
15:         **end if**
16:         **return** $\begin{bmatrix} 1 & 0 \\ 0 & GE((EA)[1|1]) \end{bmatrix} E$
17:     **end if**
18: **end if**

Post-condition: $GE(A)$ is in row-echelon form

Problem 7.1. *Implement algorithm 7.1 over $\mathbb{F} = \mathbb{R}$ using floating point arithmetic.*

7.2.1 Formal proofs of correctness over $\mathbb{Z}_2$

This section contains advanced material related to the field of proof complexity. The interested reader is encouraged to first review Section 9.4, and in particular 9.4.1.1, which present the background related to the propositional proof systems PK and EPK.

In order to simplify the presentation, we limit ourselves to the field of two elements $\mathbb{Z}_2 = \{0, 1\}$, but these results holds over more general fields. However, over bigger fields one has to contend with the encoding of the field elements with Boolean variables; this is trivial in the case of the two element field $\mathbb{Z}_2$.

We define the Boolean formula $RowEchelon(C_{11}, C_{12}, \ldots, C_{nm})$ to be the disjunction of (7.4) and (7.5) below:

$$\bigwedge_{1 \leq i \leq n, 1 \leq j \leq m} \neg C_{ij} \tag{7.4}$$

$$\bigwedge_{1 \leq i < n, 1 < j \leq m} \left((\neg C_{(i+1)1} \wedge \ldots \wedge \neg C_{(i+1)(j-1)} \wedge C_{(i+1)j}) \supset \bigvee_{1 \leq k \leq j-1} C_{ik} \right) \tag{7.5}$$

Note that (7.4) states that C is the zero matrix, and (7.5) states that the first non-zero entry of row $i + 1$ is to the right of the first non-zero entry of row i. Moreover, if the $(i + 1)$-st row has a non-zero entry, then the i-th row *must* also have a non-zero entry. Note that we do not need to state the condition that the first non-zero entry of each row is 1, since the field is $\mathbb{Z}_2$; over more general fields, we would have to state this condition as well.

We will abuse notation slightly, and sometimes write $RowEchelon(C)$ in place of $RowEchelon(C_{11}, C_{12}, \ldots, C_{nm})$.

Theorem 7.2. *EPK proves the correctness of GE with proofs of size polynomial in the given matrix. More precisely, the family of tautologies given by:*

$$\{\bigwedge \|C = GE(A)A\|_{n,m} \supset RowEchelon(C)\} \tag{7.6}$$

has short EPK proofs.

Proof. We prove that (7.6) has short EPK proofs. More precisely, from the constructions of the derivations given below, it is possible to come up with a constant d, so that the size of these derivations (measured in the number of symbols) is bounded by $(n + m)^d$, $n, m \geq 1$. We do not give d explicitly.

We build the proof of (7.6) inductively on n. Suppose first that A is a $1 \times m$ matrix. Let $G = GE(A)$, then from (7.2) we see that $G = [1]$, so it is represented by the single extension definition $G_{11} \leftrightarrow 1$. Now, define $C = GA$ with m extension definitions, and show that $\bigwedge \|C = A\|_{1,m}$. Since A has only one row, and it is a matrix over $\mathbb{Z}_2$, it follows that A is in row-echelon form, and hence $RowEchelon(C)$ follows.

Now suppose that A is a $(n+1) \times m$ matrix. Let $G' = GE((EA)[1|1])$, and we already have the set of extension definitions for G' by induction. Thus, from:

$$G = \begin{bmatrix} 1 & 0 \\ 0 & G' \end{bmatrix} E$$

we obtain the set of extension definitions for $G = GE(A)$. This set is short because the definition of E is short, and because the definition of G' is short, by induction. More precisely, E is given by at most $n + 2$ elementary matrices of size $(n + 1) \times (n + 1)$ each; thus, it involves $n + 1$ new matrix definitions, each definition of size bounded by $O((n+1)^3)$ (just recall the definition of $\|C = AB\|_{n+1}$). Each of the elementary matrices that make up E (see the definition of E above), over $\mathbb{Z}_2$, has a definition of constant size (in terms of the entries of A). Thus, the extension definitions of E are of size bounded by $O((n + 1)^4)$. Therefore, G can be defined with $O((n+1)^4) + ($nr. of extension definitions for $G')$ extension definitions, which is $O(\sum_{k=1}^{n+1} k^4) \leq O((n+1)^5)$ many extension definitions in total for G.

Let $C' = G'((EA)[1|1])$, and $C = GA$. By induction,

$$\bigwedge \|C' = G'((EA)[1|1])\|_n \supset RowEchelon(C')$$

has an EPK proof of size bounded by $(n + m)^d$. We now want to show that given the extension definitions for G' and G, $RowEchelon(C') \supset RowEchelon(C)$ has short EPK proofs. Since

$$C = GA = \begin{bmatrix} 1 & 0 \\ 0 & G' \end{bmatrix} EA = \begin{bmatrix} \text{first row of } EA \\ 0 \quad G'((EA)[1|1]) \end{bmatrix} = \begin{bmatrix} \text{first row of } EA \\ 0 \quad C' \end{bmatrix}$$

To see this, note that the first column of EA is zero, except possibly for the first entry. By the choice of E, either $(EA)_{11} \neq 0$, in which case we have $RowEchelon(C)$, or the first non-zero entry of the first row of EA is to the left of the first non-zero column of C', in which case we also have $RowEchelon(C)$. Also note that we use associativity of iterated matrix products in the above reasoning. That is, we assume that the way we parenthesize an iterated matrix product is not important, since by associativity we always get the same result. This can be shown with short EPK proofs as well. □

Theorem 7.3. *The existence of the inverse of $GE(A)$ can be shown with short EPK proofs.*

Proof. We have to show that given $\|G = GE(A)\|_n$, the Boolean variables $G_{11}^{-1}, G_{12}^{-1}, \ldots, G_{nn}^{-1}$, corresponding to G^{-1}, can be constructed with short extension definitions, and that EPK proves $\|GG^{-1} = I\|_n$ with short proofs.

Just as we defined G inductively with extension definitions, we define G^{-1} inductively. Given $E = E_{i_1} E_{i_2} \cdots E_{i_k} E' E''$, we can compute E^{-1} immediately by letting it be $E''^{-1} E'^{-1} E_{i_k}^{-1} \cdots E_{i_2}^{-1} E_{i_1}^{-1}$. Each of these inverses can be computed very easily, because they are elementary matrices. So, since we are dealing with $\mathbb{Z}_2$, $E'' = E''$, and E' is also its own inverse, and E_{i_j} is a matrix with 1s on the diagonal, and 1 in the position (p, q), so $E_{i_j}^{-1}$ is a matrix with 1s on the diagonal, and a 1 in position (q, p).

Thus, we showed how to compute G^{-1}. We still need to show that the family of tautologies $\{\|GG^{-1} = I\|_{n,m}\}$ has short EPK proofs, for any $n \times m$ matrix A. We can prove this inductively on the number of rows of A, just as in the proof of Theorem 7.2, so we do not repeat it here. □

Corollary 7.4. *It can be shown with short EPK proofs that $GE(A)A$ has 1s on the main diagonal, or its last row is zero.*

Proof. The truth of this assertion is obvious from (7.1). Let $C = GA$, and suppose that there is a zero entry on the diagonal, i.e., $\neg \bigwedge_{1 \le i \le n} C_{ii} \leftrightarrow 1$. We want to show that the last row is zero, $\bigwedge_{1 \le i \le n} C_{ni} \leftrightarrow 0$. We know that $RowEchelon(C)$ is valid, and provable in polysize EPK (by Theorem (7.2)). From (7.5) we can conclude with short EPK proofs that:

$$\bigwedge_{1 \le j \le k} \neg C_{ij} \supset \bigwedge_{1 \le j \le k+1} \neg C_{(i+1)j} \tag{7.7}$$

That is, if the first k entries of row i are zero, then the first $(k + 1)$ entries of row $(i + 1)$ are zero. Let C_{ii} be the zero, with the smallest i. Now, from (7.7) we prove that:

$$\bigwedge_{1 \le j \le i} C_{ij} \leftrightarrow 0 \tag{7.8}$$

Using (7.7) repeatedly, for $0 \le k \le n - i$, we show that the first $(i + k)$ entries of row $(i + k)$ are zero. Thus, we can conclude that the first n

entries of the n-th row are zero, and, therefore, the n-th (last) row is zero altogether.

In fact, note that given $RowEchelon(C)$, all we needed was polysize PK to prove that if some C_{ii} is zero, then the last row of C is zero. $\square$

7.3 Gram-Schmidt

Problem 7.5. *Let $V \subseteq \mathbb{R}^n$ be a vector space, and $\{v_1, v_2, \ldots, v_n\}$ its basis. Consider algorithm 7.2 and show that it produces an orthogonal basis $\{v_1^*, v_2^*, \ldots, v_n^*\}$ for the vector space V. In other words, show that $v_i^* \cdot v_j^* = 0$ when $i \neq j$, and that $span\{v_1, v_2, \ldots, v_n\} = span\{v_1^*, v_2^*, \ldots, v_n^*\}$. Line 4 has a division by the square of the norm of v_j^*; show that this will never result in an attempted division by zero.*

Algorithm 7.2 Gram-Schmidt

Pre-condition: $\{v_1, \ldots, v_n\}$ a basis for $\mathbb{R}^n$

1: $v_1^* \longleftarrow v_1$
2: **for** $i = 2, 3, \ldots, n$ **do**
3:     **for** $j = 1, 2, \ldots, (i-1)$ **do**
4:         $\mu_{ij} \longleftarrow (v_i \cdot v_j^*)/\|v_j^*\|^2$
5:     **end for**
6:     $v_i^* \longleftarrow v_i - \sum_{j=1}^{i-1} \mu_{ij} v_j^*$
7: **end for**

Post-condition: $\{v_1^*, \ldots, v_n^*\}$ an orthogonal basis for $\mathbb{R}^n$

Problem 7.6. *Implement the Gram-Schmidt algorithm (algorithm 7.2), but with the following twist: instead of computing over $\mathbb{R}$, the real numbers, compute over $\mathbb{Z}_2$, the field of two elements, where addition and multiplication are defined as follows:*

+	0	1		$\cdot$	0	1
0	0	1		0	0	0
1	1	0		1	0	1

In fact, this "twist" makes the implementation much easier, as you do not have to deal with the precision issues involved in implementing division operations over the field of real numbers.

7.4 Gaussian lattice reduction

Suppose that $\{v_1, v_2, \ldots, v_n\}$ are linearly independent vectors in $\mathbb{R}^n$. The *lattice L* spanned by these vectors is the set $\{\sum_{i=1}^{n} c_i v_i : c_i \in \mathbb{Z}\}$, i.e., L consists of linear combinations of the vectors $\{v_1, v_2, \ldots, v_n\}$ where the coefficients are limited to be integers.

Problem 7.7. *Suppose that $\{v_1, v_2\}$ span a lattice in $\mathbb{R}^2$. Consider algorithm 7.3 and show that it terminates and outputs a new basis $\{v_1, v_2\}$ for L where v_1 is the shortest vector in the lattice L, i.e., $\|v_1\|$ is as small as possible among all the vectors of L.*

Algorithm 7.3 Gauss lattice reduction in dimension 2

Pre-condition: $\{v_1, v_2\}$ are linearly independent in $\mathbb{R}^2$

1: **loop**
2:      **if** $\|v_2\| < \|v_1\|$ **then**
3:          swap v_1 and v_2
4:      **end if**
5:      $m \longleftarrow \lfloor v_1 \cdot v_2 / \|v_1\|^2 \rceil$
6:      **if** $m = 0$ **then**
7:          **return** v_1, v_2
8:      **else**
9:          $v_2 \longleftarrow v_2 - m v_1$
10:     **end if**
11: **end loop**

7.5 Computing the characteristic polynomial

There are two fast algorithms that compute the characteristic polynomial of a matrix: Csanky's algorithm and Berkowitz's algorithm. The characteristic polynomial of a matrix is usually defined as $p_A(x) = \det(xI - A)$, for a given matrix A. Let p_A^{CSANKY} and p_A^{BERK} denote the coefficients of the characteristic polynomial of A given as column vectors, respectively. Let $p_A^{\text{CSANKY}}(x)$ and $p_A^{\text{BERK}}(x)$ denote the actual characteristic polynomials, with coefficients computed by the respective algorithms.

7.5.1 Csanky's algorithm

Newton's symmetric polynomials are defined as follows: $s_0 = 1$, and for $1 \leq k \leq n$, by:

$$s_k = \frac{1}{k} \sum_{i=1}^{k} (-1)^{i-1} s_{k-i} \mathrm{tr}(A^i) \tag{7.9}$$

Then, $p_A^{\mathrm{CSANKY}}(x) = s_0 x^n - s_1 x^{n-1} + s_2 x^{n-2} - \cdots \pm s_n x^0$.

Problem 7.8. *Write an algorithm that implements Csanky's algorithm with Newton's symmetric polynomials.*

We now present Csanky's algorithm with matrix operations, following the ideas in §13.4 of [von zur Gathen (1993)]. We restate (7.9) in matrix form: $s = Ts - b$ where s, T, b are given, respectively, as follows:

$$\begin{pmatrix} s_1 \\ s_2 \\ \vdots \\ s_n \end{pmatrix}, \quad \begin{pmatrix} 0 & 0 & 0 & \cdots \\ \frac{1}{2}\mathrm{tr}(A) & 0 & 0 & \cdots \\ \frac{1}{3}\mathrm{tr}(A^2) & \frac{1}{3}\mathrm{tr}(A) & 0 & \cdots \\ \frac{1}{4}\mathrm{tr}(A^3) & \frac{1}{4}\mathrm{tr}(A^2) & \frac{1}{4}\mathrm{tr}(A) & \cdots \\ \vdots & \vdots & \vdots & \ddots \end{pmatrix}, \quad \begin{pmatrix} \mathrm{tr}(A) \\ \frac{1}{2}\mathrm{tr}(A^2) \\ \vdots \\ \frac{1}{n}\mathrm{tr}(A^n) \end{pmatrix}$$

Then $s = -b(I - T)^{-1}$. Note that $(I - T)$ is an invertible matrix as it is lower triangular, with 1s on the main diagonal. The inverse of $(I - T)$ can be computed recursively using the following idea: if C is lower-triangular, with no zeros on the main diagonal, then

$$C = \begin{pmatrix} C_1 & 0 \\ E & C_2 \end{pmatrix} \quad \Rightarrow \quad C^{-1} = \begin{pmatrix} C_1^{-1} & 0 \\ -C_2^{-1}EC_1^{-1} & C_2^{-1} \end{pmatrix}$$

There are $O(\log(n))$ many steps and the whole procedure can be simulated in $O(\log^2(n))$ parallel steps.

Problem 7.9. *Implement Csanky's algorithm with matrix operations.*

7.5.2 Berkowitz's algorithm

Berkowitz's algorithm, just as Csanky's algorithm, allows us to reduce the computation of the characteristic polynomial to matrix powering. Its advantage is that it works over any field.

Berkowitz's algorithm computes the characteristic polynomial of a matrix in terms of the characteristic polynomial of its principal minor:

$$A = \begin{pmatrix} a_{11} & R \\ S & M \end{pmatrix} \tag{7.10}$$

where R is an $1 \times (n-1)$ row matrix and S is a $(n-1) \times 1$ column matrix and M is $(n-1) \times (n-1)$. Let $p(x)$ and $q(x)$ be the characteristic polynomials of A and M respectively. Suppose that the coefficients of p form the column vector

$$p = \begin{pmatrix} p_n \ p_{n-1} \ \cdots \ p_0 \end{pmatrix}^t \tag{7.11}$$

where p_i is the coefficient of x^i in $\det(xI - A)$, and similarly for q. Then:

$$p = C_1 q \tag{7.12}$$

where C_1 is an $(n+1) \times n$ *Toeplitz* lower triangular matrix (Toeplitz means that the values on each diagonal are constant) and where the entries in the first column are defined as follows: $c_{i1} = 1$ if $i = 1$, $c_{i1} = -a_{11}$ if $i = 2$, and $c_{i1} = -(RM^{i-3}S)$ if $i \geq 3$. Berkowitz's algorithm consists in repeating this for q, and continuing so that p is expressed as a product of matrices. Thus:

$$p_A^{\text{BERK}} = C_1 C_2 \cdots C_n \tag{7.13}$$

where C_i is an $(n+2-i) \times (n+1-i)$ Toeplitz matrix defined as above except A is replaced by its i-th principal sub-matrix. Note that $C_n = (1 \quad -a_{nn})^t$.

Since each element of C_i can be explicitly defined in terms of A using matrix powering, and since the iterated matrix product can be reduced to matrix powering by a standard method, the entire product (7.13) can be expressed in terms of A using matrix powering.

Problem 7.10. *Write a program implementing Berkowitz's algorithm.*

7.5.3 *Proving properties of the characteristic polynomial*

Lemma 7.11. *Similar matrices have the same characteristic polynomial; that is, if P is any invertible matrix, then $p_A = p_{PAP^{-1}}$.*

Proof. Observe that $\text{tr}(AB) = \sum_i \sum_j a_{ij} b_{ji} = \sum_j \sum_i b_{ji} a_{ij} = \text{tr}(BA)$, so using the associativity of matrix multiplication, $\text{tr}(PA^iP^{-1}) = \text{tr}(A^iPP^{-1}) = \text{tr}(A^i)$. Inspecting (7.9), we see that a proof by induction on the s_i proves this lemma. $\qquad\square$

Lemma 7.12. *If A is a matrix of the form:*

$$\begin{pmatrix} B & 0 \\ C & D \end{pmatrix} \tag{7.14}$$

where B and D are square matrices (not necessarily of the same size), and the upper-right corner is zero, then $p_A(x) = p_B(x) \cdot p_D(x)$.

Proof.   Let s_i^A, s_i^B, s_i^D be the coefficients of the characteristic polynomials (as given by (7.9)) of A, B, D, respectively. We want to show by induction on i that

$$s_i^A = \sum_{j+k=i} s_j^B s_k^D,$$

from which the claim of the lemma follows. The Basis Case: $s_0^A = s_0^B = s_0^D = 1$. For the Induction Step, by definition and by the induction hypothesis, we have that s_{i+1}^A equals

$$= \sum_{j=0}^{i} (-1)^j s_{i-j}^A \operatorname{tr}(A^{j+1}) = \sum_{j=0}^{i} (-1)^j \left[\sum_{p+q=i-j} s_p^B s_q^D \right] \operatorname{tr}(A^{j+1})$$

and by the form of A (i.e., (7.14)):

$$= \sum_{j=0}^{i} (-1)^j \left[\sum_{p+q=i-j} s_p^B s_q^D \right] (\operatorname{tr}(B^{j+1}) + \operatorname{tr}(D^{j+1}))$$

to see how this formula simplifies, we divide it into two parts:

$$= \sum_{j=0}^{i} (-1)^j \left[\sum_{p+q=i-j} s_p^B s_q^D \right] \operatorname{tr}(B^{j+1}) + \sum_{j=0}^{i} (-1)^j \left[\sum_{p+q=i-j} s_p^B s_q^D \right] \operatorname{tr}(D^{j+1}).$$

Consider first the left-hand side. When $q = 0$, p ranges over $\{i, i-1, \ldots, 0\}$, and $j+1$ ranges over $\{1, 2, \ldots, i+1\}$, and therefore, by definition, we obtain s_{i+1}^B. Similarly, when $q = 1$, we obtain s_i^B, and so on, until we obtain s_1^B. Hence we have:

$$= \sum_{j=0}^{i+1} s_{i-j}^B s_j^D + \sum_{j=0}^{i} (-1)^j \left[\sum_{p+q=i-j} s_p^B s_q^D \right] \operatorname{tr}(D^{j+1}).$$

The same reasoning, but fixing p instead of q on the right-hand side, gives us:

$$= \sum_{j=0}^{i+1} s_{i-j}^B s_j^D + \sum_{j=0}^{i+1} s_j^B s_{i-j}^D = \sum_{j+k=i+1} s_j^B s_k^D$$

which gives us the induction step and the proof of the lemma. $\square$

To show that $p_A(A) = 0$ it is sufficient to show that $p_A(A)e_i = 0$ for all vectors e_i in the standard basis $\{e_1, e_2, \ldots, e_n\}$. Let k be the largest integer such that

$$\{e_i, Ae_i, \ldots, A^{k-1}e_i\} \tag{7.15}$$

is linearly independent; we know that $k - 1 < n$, by the principle of linear independence (this is the first place where we use linear independence). Then, (7.15) is a basis for a subspace W of $\mathbb{F}^n$, and W is invariant under A, i.e., given any $w \in W$, $Aw \in W$.

Using Gaussian Elimination we write $A^k e_i$ as a linear combination of the vectors in (7.15). Using the coefficients of this linear combination we write a monic polynomial

$$g(x) = x^k + c_1 x^{k-1} + \cdots + c_k x^0 \tag{7.16}$$

such that $g(A)e_i = 0$.

Let A_W be A restricted to the basis (7.15), that is, A_W is a matrix representing the linear transformation $T_A : \mathbb{F}^n \longrightarrow \mathbb{F}^n$ induced by A, restricted to the subspace W. The matrix A_W^t has the following simple form:

$$\begin{pmatrix} 0 & 0 \; 0 \ldots 0 & -c_k \\ \hline 1 & 0 \; 0 \ldots 0 & -c_{k-1} \\ 0 & 1 \; 0 \ldots 0 & -c_{k-2} \\ \vdots & \ddots & \vdots \\ 0 & 0 \; 0 \ldots 1 & -c_1 \end{pmatrix} \tag{7.17}$$

i.e., it is the *companion matrix* of the polynomial $g(x)$. Since $p_A = p_{A^t}$, we consider the transpose of A_W, since A_W^t has the property that its principal submatrix is also a companion matrix, and that will be used in a proof by induction in the next lemma.

Lemma 7.13. *The polynomial $g(x)$ is the characteristic polynomial of A_W, in other words, $g(x) = p_{A_W}(x)$.*

Proof. We will drop the W from A_W as there is no danger of confusion (the original matrix A does not appear in the proof); thus, A is a $k \times k$ matrix, with 1s below the main diagonal, and zeros everywhere else except (possibly) in the last column where it has the negations of the coefficients of $g(x)$.

As was noted above, A is divided into four quadrants, with the upper-left containing just 0. Let $R = (0 \ldots 0 \; -c_k)$ be the row vector in the upper-right quadrant. Let $S = e_1$ be the column vector in the lower-left quadrant, i.e., the first column of A without the top entry. Finally, let M be the principal submatrix of A, $M = A[1|1]$; the lower-right quadrant.

Let $s_0, s_1, \ldots, s_k$ be the Newton's symmetric polynomials of A.

To prove that $g(x) = p_{A_{T_W}}(x)$ we prove something stronger: we show that (i) for all $0 \le i \le k$ $(-1)^i s_i = c_i$, and (ii) $p_A(A) = 0$.

We show this by induction on the size of the matrix A. Since the principal submatrix of A (i.e., M) is *also* a companion matrix, we assume that for $i < k$, the coefficients of the symmetric polynomial of M are equal to the c_i's, and that $p_M(M) = 0$. (Note that the Basis Case of the induction is a 1×1 matrix, and it is trivial to prove.)

Since for $i < k$, $\text{tr}(A^i) = \text{tr}(M^i)$, it follows from (7.9) and the induction hypothesis that for $i < k$, $(-1)^i s_i = c_i$ (note that $s_0 = c_0 = 1$).

Next we show that $(-1)^k s_k = c_k$. By definition (i.e., by (7.9)) we have that s_k is equal to:

$$\frac{1}{k}(s_{k-1}\text{tr}(A) - s_{k-2}\text{tr}(A^2) + \cdots + (-1)^{k-2}s_1\text{tr}(A^{k-1}) + (-1)^{k-1}s_0\text{tr}(A^k))$$

and by the induction hypothesis and the fact that for $i < k$ $\text{tr}(A^i) = \text{tr}(M^i)$ we have:

$$=\frac{1}{k}(-1)^{k-1}(c_{k-1}\text{tr}(M) + c_{k-2}\text{tr}(M^2) + \cdots + c_1\text{tr}(M^{k-1}) + c_0\text{tr}(A^k)).$$

Note that $\text{tr}(A^k) = -kc_k + \text{tr}(M^k)$, so:

$$=\frac{1}{k}(-1)^{k-1}\left[c_{k-1}\text{tr}(M) + c_{k-2}\text{tr}(M^2) + \cdots + c_1\text{tr}(M^{k-1}) + c_0\text{tr}(M^k)\right]$$
$$+ (-1)^k c_k$$

Observe that

$$\text{tr}(c_{k-1}M + c_{k-2}M^2 + \cdots + c_1 M^{k-1} + c_0 M^k) = \text{tr}(p_M(M)M) = \text{tr}(0) = 0$$

since $p_M(M) = 0$ by the induction hypothesis. Therefore, $s_k = (-1)^k c_k$.

It remains to prove that $p_A(A) = \sum_{i=0}^{k} c_i A^{k-i} = 0$. First, show that for $1 \le i \le (k-1)$:

$$A^{i+1} = \left(\begin{array}{c|c} 0 & RM^i \\ \hline M^i S & \sum_{j=0}^{i-1} M^j SRM^{(i-1)-j} + M^{i+1} \end{array} \right) \qquad (7.18)$$

(For A of the form given by (7.17), and R, S, M defined as in the first paragraph of the proof.) Define w_i, X_i, Y_i, Z_i as follows:

$$
\begin{aligned}
A^{i+1} &= \begin{pmatrix} w_{i+1} & X_{i+1} \\ Y_{i+1} & Z_{i+1} \end{pmatrix} = \begin{pmatrix} w_i & X_i \\ Y_i & Z_i \end{pmatrix} \begin{pmatrix} 0 & R \\ S & M \end{pmatrix} \\
&= \begin{pmatrix} X_i S & w_i R + X_i M \\ Z_i S & Y_i R + Z_i M \end{pmatrix}
\end{aligned}
\tag{7.19}
$$

We want to show that the right-most matrix of (7.19) is equal to the right-hand side of (7.18). First note that:

$$
X_{i+1} = \sum_{j=0}^{i} w_{i-j} R M^j \qquad w_{i+1} = \sum_{j=0}^{i-1} (R M^j S) w_{i-1-j}
\tag{7.20}
$$

With the convention that $w_0 = 1$. Since $w_1 = 0$, a straight-forward induction shows that $w_{i+1} = 0$. Therefore, at this point the right-most matrix of (7.19) can be simplified to:

$$
\begin{pmatrix} 0 & R M^i \\ Z_i S & Y_i R + Z_i M \end{pmatrix}
$$

Again by Lemma 5.1 in [Soltys and Cook (2004)] we have:

$$
Y_{i+1} = M^i S + \sum_{j=0}^{i-2} (R M^j S) Y_{i-1-j} \qquad Z_{i+1} = M^{i+1} + \sum_{j=0}^{i-1} Y_{i-1-j} R M^j
$$

By the same reasoning as above, $\sum_{j=0}^{i-2} (R M^j S) Y_{i-1-j} = 0$, so putting it all together we obtain the right-hand side of (7.18).

Using the induction hypothesis $(p_M(M) = 0)$ it is easy to show that the first row and column of $p_A(A)$ are zero. Also, by the induction hypothesis, the term M^{i+1} in the principal submatrix of $p_A(A)$ disappears but leaves $c_k I$. Therefore, it will follow that $p_A(A) = 0$ if we show that

$$
\sum_{i=2}^{k} c_{k-i} \sum_{j=0}^{i-2} M^j S R M^{(i-2)-j}
\tag{7.21}
$$

is equal to $-c_k I$.

Some observations about (7.21): for $0 \le j \le i - 2 \le k - 2$, the first column of M^j is just e_{j+1}. And SR is a matrix of zeros, with $-c_k$ in the upper-right corner. Thus $M^j SR$ is a matrix of zeros except for the last column which is $-c_k e_{j+1}$. Thus, $M^j SR M^{(i-2)-j}$ is a matrix with zeros everywhere, except in row $(j+1)$ where it has the bottom row of $M^{(i-2)-j}$

multiplied by $-c_k$. Let $\mathbf{m}^{(i-2)-j}$ denote the $1 \times (k-1)$ row vector consisting of the bottom row of $M^{(i-2)-j}$. Therefore, (7.21) is equal to:

$$-c_k \cdot \left(\begin{array}{c} \sum_{i=2}^{k} c_{k-i} \mathbf{m}^{(i-2)} \\ \hline \sum_{i=3}^{k} c_{k-i} \mathbf{m}^{(i-3)} \\ \hline \vdots \\ \hline \sum_{i=k}^{k} c_{k-i} \mathbf{m}^{(i-k)} \end{array} \right) \tag{7.22}$$

We want to show that (7.22) is equal to $-c_k I$ to finish the proof of $p_A(A) = 0$. To accomplish this, let l denote the l-th row of the matrix in (7.22) starting with the bottom row. We want to show, by induction on l, that the l-th row is equal to e_{k-l}.

The Basis Case is $l = 0$:

$$\sum_{i=k}^{k} c_{k-i} \mathbf{m}^{(i-k)} = c_0 \mathbf{m}^0 = e_k,$$

and we are done.

For the induction step, note that $\mathbf{m}^{l+1}$ is equal to $\mathbf{m}^l$ shifted to the left by one position, and with

$$\mathbf{m}^l \cdot (-c_{k-1} \ -c_{k-2} \ldots -c_1)^t \tag{7.23}$$

in the last position. We introduce some more notation: let r_l denote the $k - l$ row of (7.22). Thus r_l is $1 \times (k-1)$ row vector. Let $\overleftarrow{r}_l$ denote r_l shifted by one position to the left, and with a zero in the last position. This can be stated succinctly as follows:

$$\overleftarrow{r}_l \overset{\text{def}}{=} \lambda i j \langle 1, (k-1), e(r_l, 1, i+1) \rangle.$$

Based on (7.22) and (7.23) we can see that:

$$r_{l+1} = \overleftarrow{r}_l + [r_l \cdot (-c_{k-1} \ -c_{k-2} \ldots -c_1)^t] e_k + c_l \mathbf{m}^0.$$

(Here the "·" in the square brackets denotes the dot product of the two vectors.) Using the induction hypothesis: $\overleftarrow{r}_l = e_{k-(l+1)}$, and

$$r_l \cdot (-c_{k-1} \ -c_{k-2} \ldots -c_1)^t = e_{k-l} \cdot (-c_{k-1} \ -c_{k-2} \ldots -c_1)^t = -c_l$$

so $r_{l+1} = e_{k-l} - c_l e_k + c_l e_k = e_{k-(l+1)}$ as desired. This finishes the proof of the fact that the matrix in (7.22) is the identity matrix, which in turn proves that (7.21) is equal to $-c_k I$, and this ends the proof of $p_A(A) = 0$, which finally finishes the main induction argument, and proves the lemma.

$$\square$$

It is interesting to note that lemma 7.13 can also be proved (feasibly) for Berkowitz's algorithm instead, and the proof is in fact much simpler: consider again the matrix given by (7.17). We assume inductively that p_M^{BERK} (the characteristic polynomial of the principal submatrix of (7.17)) is given by $(1\ c_1\ c_2\ \dots\ c_{k-1})^t$. Since $R = (0\ \dots\ 0\ -c_k)$ and $S = e_1$, $p_A^{\text{BERK}} = B \cdot p_M^{\text{BERK}}$, where B (the matrix given by Berkowitz's algorithm) is an $(n+1) \times n$ matrix with 1s on the main diagonal, 0s everywhere else, except for $+c_k$ in position $(n+1, 1)$. From this, it is easy to see that p_A^{BERK} is given by $(1\ c_1\ c_2\ \dots\ c_k)^t$.

Lemma 7.14. *The polynomial $g(x)$ divides $p_A(x)$.*

Proof. Extend (7.15) to a full basis of $\mathbb{F}^n$:

$$B = \{e_i, Ae_i, \dots, A^{k-1}e_i, e_{j_1}, e_{j_2}, \dots, e_{j_{n-k}}\}.$$

This extension can be carried out easily with Gaussian Elimination, by checking which vectors from the standard basis ($\{e_1, e_2, \dots, e_n\}$) are in the span consisting of (7.15) and those vectors that have already been added, and adding only those that are not. This is the only other place (besides the paragraph following the proof of lemma 7.12) where we need to use the principle of linear independence.

Let P be the change of basis for A from the standard basis to B. Then,

$$PAP^{-1} = \begin{pmatrix} A_W & 0 \\ * & E \end{pmatrix}$$

where A_W is a $k \times k$ block, and E is a $(n-k) \times (k-n)$ block (corresponding to the extension), and we have a block of zeros above E since W is invariant under A. By lemma 7.12 it follows that $p_A(x) = p_{PAP^{-1}}(x) = p_{A_W}(x) \cdot p_E(x)$. By lemma 7.13, $p_{A_W} = g(x)$, and so $g(x)$ divides $p_A(x)$. $\square$

Theorem 7.15. *We can prove the Cayley-Hamilton Theorem (CHT) from the principle of linear independence, when the characteristic polynomial is computed by Csanky's algorithm.*

Proof. By lemma 7.14,

$$p_A(A)e_i = (p_{A_W}(A) \cdot p_E(A))e_i = (g(A) \cdot p_E(A))e_i = p_E(A) \cdot (g(A)e_i) = 0.$$

Since this is true for any e_i in the standard basis, it follows that $p_A(A) = 0$. $\square$

7.6   Answers to selected problems

Problem 7.5. We are going to prove a loop invariant on the outer loop of algorithm 7.2, that is, we are going to prove a loop invariant on the for-loop (indexed on i) that starts on line 2 and ends on line 7. Our invariant consists of two parts: after the k-th iteration of the loop, the following two statements hold true:

(1) the set $\{v_1^*, \ldots, v_{k+1}^*\}$ is orthogonal, and
(2) $\mathrm{span}\{v_1, \ldots, v_{k+1}\} = \mathrm{span}\{v_1^*, \ldots, v_{k+1}^*\}$.

Basis case: after zero iterations of the for-loop, that is, before the for-loop is ever executed, we have, from line 1 of the algorithm, that $v_1^* \longleftarrow v_1$, and so the first statement is true because $\{v_1^*\}$ is orthogonal (a set consisting of a single non-zero vector is always orthogonal—and $v_1^* = v_1 \neq 0$ because the assumption (i.e., pre-condition) is that $\{v_1, \ldots, v_n\}$ is linearly independent, and so none of these vectors can be zero), and the second statement also holds trivially since if $v_1^* = v_1$ then $\mathrm{span}\{v_1\} = \mathrm{span}\{v_1^*\}$.

Induction Step: Suppose that the two conditions hold after the first k iterations of the loop; we are going to show that they continue to hold after the $k + 1$ iteration. Consider:

$$v_{k+2}^* = v_{k+2} - \sum_{j=1}^{k+1} \mu_{(k+1)j} v_j^*,$$

which we obtain directly from line 6 of the algorithm; note that the outer for-loop is indexed on i which goes from 2 to n, so after the k-th execution of line 2, for $k \geq 1$, the value of the index i is $k + 1$. We show the first statement, i.e., that $\{v_1^*, \ldots, v_{k+2}^*\}$ are orthogonal. Since, by induction hypothesis, we know that $\{v_1^*, \ldots, v_{k+1}^*\}$ are already orthogonal, it is enough to show that for $1 \leq l \leq k + 1$, $v_l^* \cdot v_{k+2}^* = 0$, which we do next:

$$v_l^* \cdot v_{k+2}^* = v_l^* \cdot \left(v_{k+2} - \sum_{j=1}^{k+1} \mu_{(k+2)j} v_j^* \right)$$

$$= (v_l^* \cdot v_{k+2}) - \sum_{j=1}^{k+1} \mu_{(k+2)j}(v_l^* \cdot v_j^*)$$

and since $v_l^* \cdot v_j^* = 0$ unless $l = j$, we have:

$$= (v_l^* \cdot v_{k+2}) - \mu_{(k+2)l}(v_l^* \cdot v_l^*)$$

and using line 4 of the algorithm we write:

$$= (v_l^* \cdot v_{k+2}) - \frac{v_{k+2} \cdot v_l^*}{\|v_l^*\|^2}(v_l^* \cdot v_l^*) = 0$$

where we have used the fact that $v_l \cdot v_l = \|v_l\|^2$ and that $v_l^* \cdot v_{k+2} = v_{k+2} \cdot v_l^*$.

For the second statement of the loop invariant we need to show that

$$\text{span}\{v_1, \ldots, v_{k+2}\} = \text{span}\{v_1^*, \ldots, v_{k+2}^*\}, \tag{7.24}$$

assuming, by the induction hypothesis, that $\text{span}\{v_1, \ldots, v_{k+1}\} = \text{span}\{v_1^*, \ldots, v_{k+1}^*\}$. The argument will be based on line 6 of the algorithm, which provides us with the following equality:

$$v_{k+2}^* = v_{k+2} - \sum_{j=1}^{k+1} \mu_{(k+2)j} v_j^*. \tag{7.25}$$

Given the induction hypothesis, to show (7.24) we need only show the following two things:

(1) $v_{k+2} \in \text{span}\{v_1^*, \ldots, v_{k+2}^*\}$, and
(2) $v_{k+2}^* \in \text{span}\{v_1, \ldots, v_{k+2}\}$.

Using (7.25) we obtain immediately that $v_{k+2} = v_{k+2}^* + \sum_{j=1}^{k+1} \mu_{(k+2)j} v_j^*$ and so we have (1). To show (2) we note that

$$\text{span}\{v_1, \ldots, v_{k+2}\} = \text{span}\{v_1^*, \ldots, v_{k+1}^*, v_{k+2}\}$$

by the induction hypothesis, and so we have what we need directly from (7.25).

Finally, note that we never divide by zero in line 4 of the algorithm because we always divide by $\|v_j^*\|$, and the only way for the norm to be zero is if the vector itself, v_j^*, is zero. But we know from the post-condition that $\{v_1^*, \ldots, v_n^*\}$ is a basis, and so these vectors must be linearly independent, and so none of them can be zero.

Problem 7.7. A reference for this algorithm can be found in [Hoffstein *et al.* (2008)] in §6.12.1. Also [von zur Gathen and Gerhard (1999)], §16.2, gives a treatment of the algorithm in higher dimensions.

Let $p = v_1 \cdot v_2 / \|v_1\|^2$, and keep the following relationship in mind:

$$\lfloor p \rceil = \lfloor p + \frac{1}{2} \rfloor = m \in \mathbb{Z} \iff p \in [m - \frac{1}{2}, m + \frac{1}{2}) \subseteq \mathbb{R},$$

where, following standard calculus terminology, the set $[a, b)$, for $a, b \in \mathbb{R}$, denotes the set of all $x \in \mathbb{R}$ such that $a \leq x < b$.

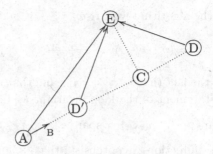

Fig. 7.1   The projection of v_2, given as $\vec{AE}$, onto v_1, given as $\vec{AB}$. The resulting vector is $\vec{AC} = v_2 - pv_1$, where $p = v_1 \cdot v_2 / \|v_1\|^2$. Letting $m = \lfloor p \rceil$, the vector $v_2 - mv_1$, is given by $\vec{D'E}$ or $\vec{DE}$, depending on whether $m < p$ or not, respectively. Of course, $D' = C = D$ when $p = m$.

We now give a proof of termination. Suppose first that $|p| = \frac{1}{2}$. If $p = -\frac{1}{2}$, then $m = 0$ and the algorithm stops. If $p = \frac{1}{2}$, then $m = 1$, which means that we go through the loop one more time with $v'_1 = v_1$ and $\|v'_2\| = \|v_2 - v_1\| = \|v_2\|$, and, more importantly, in the next round $p = -\frac{1}{2}$, and again the algorithm terminates.

If $p = m$, i.e., p was an integer to begin with (giving $\vec{CE} = \vec{D'E} = \vec{DE}$ in figure 7.1), then simply by the Pythagorean theorem $\|\vec{CE}\|$ has to be shorter than $\|\vec{AE}\|$ (as v_1, v_2 are non-zero, as $m \neq 0$).

So we may assume that $|p| \neq \frac{1}{2}$ and $p \neq m$. The two cases where $m < p$, giving D', or $m > p$, giving D, are symmetric, and so we treat only the latter case. It must be that $|p| > \frac{1}{2}$ for otherwise m would have been zero, resulting in termination. Note that $\|\vec{CD}\| \leq \frac{1}{2}\|\vec{AB}\|$, because $\vec{AD} = m\vec{AB}$. From this and the Pythagorean theorem we know that:

$$\|\vec{AE}\|^2 = \|\vec{AC}\|^2 + \|\vec{CE}\|^2 = p^2\|\vec{AB}\|^2 + \|\vec{CE}\|^2$$
$$\|\vec{DE}\|^2 = \|\vec{CD}\|^2 + \|\vec{CE}\|^2 \leq p^2\|\vec{AB}\|^2 + \|\vec{CE}\|^2$$

and so $\|\vec{AE}\|^2 - \|\vec{DE}\|^2 \geq (p^2 - \frac{1}{4})\|\vec{AB}\|^2$, and, as we already noted, if the algorithm does not end in line 6 that means that $|p| > \frac{1}{2}$, and so it follows that $\|\vec{AE}\| > \|\vec{DE}\|$, that is, v_2 is longer than $v_2 - mv_1$, and so the new v_2 (line 9) is shorter than the old one.

Let v'_1, v'_2 be the two vectors resulting in one iteration of the loop from v_1, v_2. As we noted above, when $|p| = \frac{1}{2}$ termination comes in one or two steps. Otherwise, $\|v'_1\| + \|v'_2\| < \|v_1\| + \|v_2\|$, and as there are finitely many pairs of points in a lattice bounded by the sum of the two norms of the original vectors, and the algorithm ends when one of the vectors becomes zero, this procedure must end in finitely many steps.

7.7 Notes

This chapter is based on several articles of the author. Sections 7.2 and 7.2.1, Gaussian Elimination and its proof of correctness, are base on Section 3.1 in [Soltys (2002b)]. Section 7.5 is based on a sequence of papers where the author was looking for feasible proofs of the main properties of the characteristic polynomial (properties such as the fact that the characteristic polynomial of a matrix is also its annihilator and that the constant term is the determinant of the matrix). Several algorithms were studies in this line of research: Csanky's algorithm, Section 7.5.1, is based on [Soltys (2005)], and Berkowitz's algorithm, Section 7.5.2, is based on [Soltys (2002a)]. The original presentation of Berkowitz's algorithm can be found here [Berkowitz (1984)].

Chapter 8

Computational Foundations

> Technology is the making of
> metaphors from the natural
> world. Flight is the metaphor of
> air, wheels are the metaphor of
> water, food is the metaphor of
> earth. The metaphor of fire is
> electricity.
>
> E. L. Doctorow [Doctorow
> (1971)], pg. 224

8.1 Introduction

The first serious attempt to build a computer was undertaken in the 1820s
by Charles Babbage. The machine was called a *Difference Engine* and it
computed with the decimal number system and was powered by cranking
a handle. Alas, Babbage never managed to build a finished product, as
the manufacturing of precision parts was a prodigious engineering problem
given the technology of his time.

Computer programs are nothing but implementations of algorithms in
a chosen programming language. Programs run on hardware, and just
like programs are instantiations of algorithms, hardware is the material
incarnation of a particular computing model. In this chapter we will explore
different models of computation, which are then instantiated in a machine
running on electricity. We will introduce several types of finite automata,
and conclude with the presentation of a Turing machine.

8.2 Alphabets, strings and languages

An *alphabet* is a finite, non-empty set of distinct symbols, denoted usually by Σ. For example, $\Sigma = \{0, 1\}$, the usual binary alphabet, or $\Sigma = \{a, b, c, \ldots, z\}$, the usual lower-case letters of the English alphabet. A *string*, also called *word*, is a finite ordered sequence of symbols chosen from some alphabet. For example, 010011101011 is a string over the binary alphabet. The notation $|w|$ denotes the *length* of the string w, e.g., $|010011101011| = 12$. The *empty string*, ε, is the unique string such that $|\varepsilon| = 0$. We sometimes write Σ_ε to emphasize that $\varepsilon \in \Sigma$. Σ^k is the set of strings over Σ of length exactly k, for example, if $\Sigma = \{0, 1\}$, then:

$$\Sigma^0 = \{\varepsilon\},$$
$$\Sigma^1 = \Sigma,$$
$$\Sigma^2 = \{00, 01, 10, 11\}.$$

The set Σ^* is called *Kleene's star* of Σ, and it is the set of all strings over Σ. Note that $\Sigma^* = \Sigma^0 \cup \Sigma^1 \cup \Sigma^2 \cup \ldots$, while $\Sigma^+ = \Sigma^1 \cup \Sigma^2 \cup \ldots$. If x, y are strings, and $x = a_1 a_2 \ldots a_m$ and $y = b_1 b_2 \ldots b_n$ then their *concatenation* is just their juxtaposition, i.e., $x \cdot y = a_1 a_2 \ldots a_m b_1 b_2 \ldots b_n$. We often write xy, instead of $x \cdot y$, and $w\varepsilon = \varepsilon w = w$. A *language* L is a collection of strings over some alphabet Σ, i.e., $L \subseteq \Sigma^*$. For example,

$$L = \{\varepsilon, 01, 0011, 000111, \ldots\} = \{0^n 1^n | n \geq 0\} \tag{8.1}$$

Note that $\{\varepsilon\} \neq \emptyset$; one is the language consisting of the single string ε, and the other is the empty language.

We let Σ_ℓ denote a generic alphabet of size ℓ. For example, we can let $\Sigma_1 = \{1\}, \Sigma_2 = \{0, 1\}$, etc.

Problem 8.1. *What is the size of Σ_2^k? What is the size of Σ_ℓ^k? Let L be the set of strings over Σ_ℓ where no symbol can occur more than once; what is $|L|$?*

Let $w = w_1 w_2 \ldots w_n$, where for each i, $w_i \in \Sigma$. In order to emphasize the array structure of w, we sometimes represent it as $w[1..n]$. We say that v is a *subword* of w if $v = w_i w_{i+1} \ldots w_j$, where $i \leq j$. If $i = j$, then v is a single symbol in w; if $i = 1$ and $j = n$, then $v = w$; if $i = 1$, then v is a *prefix* of w (sometimes denoted $v \sqsubseteq w$) and if $j = n$, then v is a *suffix* of w (sometimes denoted $w \sqsupseteq v$). We can express that v is a subword more succinctly as follows: $v = w[i..j]$, and when the delimiters do not have to be expressed explicitly, we use the notation $v \leq w$. We say that v is a *subsequence* of w if $v = w_{i_1} w_{i_2} \ldots w_{i_k}$, for $i_1 < i_2 < \ldots < i_k$.

8.3 Regular languages

In this chapter we examine different types of languages, i.e., different types of sets of strings. We classify them according to the computational models that describe them. Regular languages are in some sense the simplest languages, in that they are described by computers without memory, also known as Finite Automata. Not surprisingly, only certain languages are regular, and we require stronger models of computation, such as Push-Down Automata (Section 8.4.2) or Turing Machines (Section 8.5) to describe more complicated languages.

8.3.1 *Deterministic Finite Automaton*

A *Deterministic Finite Automaton (DFA)* is a model of computation given by a tuple $A = (Q, \Sigma, \delta, q_0, F)$ where:

i Q is a finite set of *states.*
ii Σ is an *alphabet*, i.e., a finite set of input symbols.
iii $\delta : Q \times \Sigma \longrightarrow Q$ is a *transition function* i.e., the "program" that runs the DFA. Given $q \in Q, a \in \Sigma$, δ computes the next state $\delta(q, a) = p \in Q$.
iv q_0 is the *start state*, also called an *initial state (q_0).*
v F is a set of *final* or *accepting* states.

To see whether A accepts a string w, we "run" A on $w = a_1 a_2 \ldots a_n$ as follows: $\delta(q_0, a_1) = q_1$, $\delta(q_1, a_2) = q_2$, until $\delta(q_{n-1}, a_n) = q_n$. We say that A *accepts* w iff $q_n \in F$, i.e., if q_n is one of the final (accepting) states. More precisely: A accepts w if there exists a sequence of states $r_0, r_1, \ldots, r_n$, where $n = |w|$, such that $r_0 = q_0$, $\delta(r_i, w_{i+1}) = r_{i+1}$ where $i = 0, 1, \ldots, n-1$ and w_j is the j-th symbol of w, and $r_n \in F$. Otherewise, we say that A *rejects* w.

For example, consider the language

$$L_{01} = \{w|\ w \text{ is of the form } x01y \in \Sigma^* \},$$

which is the set of strings that have 01 as a substring. So, $111 \notin L_{01}$, but $001 \in L_{01}$.

Suppose that we want to design a DFA $A = (Q, \Sigma, \delta, q_0, F)$ for L_{01}. That is, A accepts the strings in L_{01}, and rejects the strings not in L_{01}. Let $\Sigma = \{0, 1\}$, $Q = \{q_0, q_1, q_2\}$, and $F = \{q_1\}$. There are two ways to present δ: as a *transition diagram* or as a *transition table*; see figure 8.1.

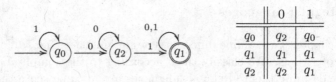

	0	1
q_0	q_2	q_0
q_1	q_1	q_1
q_2	q_2	q_1

Fig. 8.1   DFA accepting $L = \{w \mid w$ is of the form $x01y \in \Sigma^*\}$. On the left given as a transition diagram, and on the right as a transition table.

At this point we know that simply presenting A as a candidate DFA for L_{01} is not sufficient. We must also prove that A is correct. This will be easier once we define an *extended transition function* later in this section, but for now a simple argument by induction on the length of $w \in \Sigma^*$ will do.

Problem 8.2. *Prove that A is a correct DFA for L_{01}.*

Problem 8.3. *Design a DFA for $\{w : |w| \geq 3$ and its third symbol is $0\}$.*

Problem 8.4. *Design a DFA for $\{w : $ every odd position of w is a $1\}$.*

Problem 8.5. *Consider the following two languages:*

$$B_n = \{a^k = \underbrace{aa \cdots a}_{k} : k \text{ is a multiple of } n \} \subseteq \{a\}^*$$

$$C_n = \{(w)_b \in \{0,1\}^* : w \text{ is divisible by } n \}$$

Note that $(w)_b$ is the binary representation of the number $w \in \mathbb{N}$. What are their DFAs?

Problem 8.6. *Consider a vending machine which takes coins as input, where the allowed coins constitute the following alphabet of symbols:*

$$①, ⑤, ⑩, ㉕.$$

Naturally, a string is just an ordered sequence of coins. Design a transition function for the vending machine which accepts any sequence of coins where the total value of the coins sums up to a multiple of 25.

Given a transition function δ, its *extended transition function* (ETF), denoted $\hat{\delta}$, is defined inductively. The basis case: $\hat{\delta}(q, \varepsilon) = q$, and the induction step: if $w = xa$, $w, x \in \Sigma^*$ and $a \in \Sigma$, then

$$\hat{\delta}(q, w) = \hat{\delta}(q, xa) = \delta(\hat{\delta}(q, x), a).$$

Thus $\hat{\delta} : Q \times \Sigma^* \longrightarrow Q$, and $w \in L(A) \iff \hat{\delta}(q_0, w) \in F$. Here $L(A)$ is the set of all those strings (and only those) which are accepted by A, called the *language of A*.

We can now define the *language* of a DFA A to be

$$L(A) = \{w | \hat{\delta}(q_0, w) \in F\},$$

and we can say that a language L is *regular* iff there exists a DFA A such that $L = L(A)$. The next natural question to ask is what operations on languages preserve their regularity. Regular languages are well behaved, and many natural operations preserve their regularity; we start with the three basic ones, which are called *regular operations*:

  i *Union*: $L \cup M = \{w | w \in L \text{ or } w \in M\}$
  ii *Concatenation*: $LM = \{xy | x \in L \text{ and } y \in M\}$
  iii *Kleene's Star* (or *Kleene's closure*):

$$L^* = \{w | w = x_1 x_2 \ldots x_n \text{ and } x_i \in L\}.$$

We have already introduced Kleene's Star in the context of alphabets (section 8.2), where alphabets can be seen as a particular language (of strings of length one). But there is an important difference in how Kleene's Star acts on the two: note that $\Sigma^+ = \Sigma^* - \{\varepsilon\}$, but it is not true in general for languages that $L^+ = L^* - \{\varepsilon\}$.

Problem 8.7. *Why is $L^+ = L^* - \{\varepsilon\}$ not necessarily true?*

Theorem 8.8. *Regular languages are closed under regular operations (union, concatenation and Kleene's Star).*

Proof. Suppose we have two regular languages, A, B, and so they have their corresponding DFAs, M_1, M_2. Consider the union $A \cup B$: take the corresponding DFAs M_1 and M_2; let M be such that $Q_M = Q_{M_1} \times Q_{M_2}$, i.e., the Cartesian product of the two state sets. Let:

$$\delta_M((r_1, r_2), a) = (\delta_{M_1}(r_1, a), \delta_{M_2}(r_2, a))$$

For concatenation and star we need the notion of "nondeterminism," which we introduce in the next section—see Problem 8.13. $\square$

The key idea in the proof of Theorem 8.8 is to expand the notion of a state. A set of states is really a finite set of "descriptors" of different situations. These descriptors can be literally anything, such as sets of states from another machines—as we shall see when we introduce nondeterministic finite automata next.

8.3.2   *Nondeterministic Finite Automata*

A *Nondeterministic Finite Automaton (NFA)* is defined similarly to a DFA, except that the the transition function δ becomes a *transition relation*. Thus, $\delta \subseteq Q \times \Sigma \times Q$, i.e., on the same pair (q, a) there may be more than one possible new state (or none). Equivalently, we can look at δ as $\delta : Q \times \Sigma \longrightarrow \mathcal{P}(Q)$, where $\mathcal{P}(Q)$ is the power set of Q.

NFAs are similar to DFAs, but they allow "branching." What this means is that in a particular configuration, where a DFA is in one state, an NFA can be in several (or one, or none). A good analogy is the forking mechanism in the C programming language. Since an NFA can be in several states simultaneously, it allows for a certain degree of parallelism.

For example, we consider $L_n = \{w|\ n$-th symbol from the end is 1 $\}$. An NFA for L_n is given in figure 8.2.

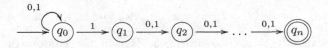

Fig. 8.2   NFA for $L_n = \{w|\ n$-th symbol from the end is 1 $\}$.

Problem 8.9. *At least how many states does any DFA recognizing L_n require?*

The definition of acceptance changes slightly: N accepts w if $w = y_1 y_2 \ldots y_m$ where $y_i \in \Sigma_\varepsilon$, so that there exists a sequence of states $r_0, r_1, \ldots, r_m$ such that $r_0 = q_0$, and $r_{i+1} \in \delta(r_i, y_{i+1})$ for $i = 0, 1, \ldots, m-1$ and $r_m \in F$. That is, w is accepted if there exists a *padding* of w with ε's for which there exists an accepting sequence of states.

Problem 8.10. *When padding a string with ε's we never need a contiguous stretch of ε's longer than the number of states. In other words, if a padding exists, it can be found in a finite number of steps. Explain why, and bound the time of the search for a working padding.*

The ε transitions are very handy in designing NFAs, as is illustrated in figure 8.3.

In the NFA in figure 8.3 we do not want a period by itself, i.e., '.' is not a properly formed number in decimal notation; we want digits to be either a prefix or a suffix; we could refine it further by disallowing a segment of zeros to be a prefix, etc. In the end, the NFA describes exactly what we

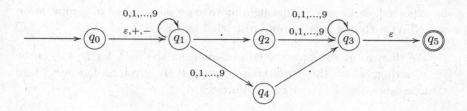

Fig. 8.3   NFA for the set of decimal numbers.

mean by a number in a given context, and then this definition becomes the way in which a given parser gives meaning to code.

To define the concept of the extended transition function for NFAs, i.e., $\hat{\delta}$, we need the concept of ε-closure. Given q, ε-close(q) is the set of all states p which are reachable from q by following arrows labeled by ε. Formally, $q \in \varepsilon$-close(q), and if $p \in \varepsilon$-close(q), and $p \xrightarrow{\varepsilon} r$, then $r \in \varepsilon$-close(q).

We can now define the *extended transition relation* for NFAs as follows: $\hat{\delta}(q, \varepsilon) = \varepsilon$-close($q$); suppose $w = xa$ and $\hat{\delta}(q, x) = \{p_1, p_2, \ldots, p_n\}$, and furthermore $\cup_{i=1}^{n} \delta(p_i, a) = \{r_1, r_2, \ldots, r_m\}$. Then,

$$\hat{\delta}(q, w) = \bigcup_{i=1}^{m} \varepsilon\text{-close}(r_i).$$

Theorem 8.11. *DFAs and NFAs are equivalent.*

Proof.   Clearly, DFAs are a special case of NFAs. Thus, we must show that every NFA can be re-designed as a DFA. To this end we use a technique known as *subset construction*.

First, we assume that an NFA N has no ε-transitions. Let M be the corresponding DFA, and $Q_M = \mathcal{P}(Q_N)$, where $\mathcal{P}(Q_N)$ is the power-set of Q_N, meaning that it consists of all the possible subsets of sets of Q_N, and

$$\delta_M(Q, a) := \bigcup_{q \in Q} \delta_N(q, a),$$

where $Q \in \mathcal{P}(Q_N)$, and let

$$F_M = \{Q \in \mathcal{P}(Q_N) : Q \cap F_N \neq \emptyset\}.$$

Finally, we let $(q_M)_0 := \{(q_N)_0\}$. If N has ε-transitions, then

$$\delta_M(Q, a) := \bigcup_{q \in Q} \varepsilon\text{-closure}(\delta_N(q, a)).$$

Note that the construction has a cost: since $|\mathcal{P}(Q_N)| = 2^{|Q_N|}$, we can see that there is an exponential increase of states. Something like this was to be expected, as we are simulating a more expressive model of computation (an NFA) with one that is more restricted (a DFA). □

We show as an example the conversion from the NFA for L_2 (L_2 is the set of strings where the penultimate symbol is 0), given on figure 8.4 into the corresponding DFA, given in figure 8.5.

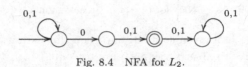

Fig. 8.4   NFA for L_2.

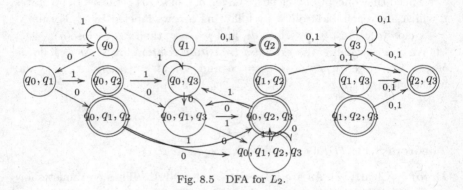

Fig. 8.5   DFA for L_2.

In the diagram of conversion of NFA into DFA (figures 8.4 and 8.5), there is one thing to notice: a whole batch of states have been generated, together with the corresponding arrows—but they are not necessary! Those are the states on the right side of the diagram. This is wasteful. Instead, start generating states and connections from $\{q_0\}$. Connect and generate only those states that are needed for transitions; ignore the rest. Sometimes this does not help, and all the states are needed.

Corollary 8.12. *A language is regular $\Longleftrightarrow$ it is recognized by some DFA $\Longleftrightarrow$ it is recognized by some NFA.*

Problem 8.13. *Finish the proof of Theorem 8.8, that is, show that the operations of concatenation and star preserve regularity.*

8.3.3 *Regular Expressions*

Regular Expressions are familiar to anyone using a computer. They are the means of finding patterns in text. This author is an avid user of the text editor VIM[1], and it is hard to find an editor with a more versatile pattern matching and replacement feature. For example, the command

```
:23,43s/\(.*\n\)\{3\}/&\r/
```

inserts a blank line every third line, between lines 23 and 43 (inclusive). In fact, VIM, like most text processors, implements a set of commands that are well beyond the scope of using just regular expressions.

A *Regular Expression*, abbreviated as *RE*, is a syntactic object meant to express a set of strings, i.e., a language. In this sense, REs are a model of computation, just like DFAs or NFAs. They are defined formally by structural induction. In the Basis Case: $a \in \Sigma, \varepsilon, \emptyset$. In the Induction Step: If E, F are regular expressions, then so are $E + F, EF, (E)^*, (E)$.

Using your intuition about RE, you should be able to do Problem 8.14.

Problem 8.14. *What are $L(a), L(\varepsilon), L(\emptyset), L(E + F), L(EF), L(E^*)$? This problem is asking you to define the semantics of RE.*

Problem 8.15. *Give a RE for the set of strings of 0s and 1s **not** containing 101 as a substring.*

Theorem 8.16. *A language is regular if and only if it is given by some regular expression.*

We are going to prove Theorem 8.16 in two parts. First, suppose we wish to convert a Regular Expression R to an NFA A. To this end we use structural induction, and at each step of the construction we ensure that the NFA A has the following three properties (i.e., invariants of the construction): (i) exactly one accepting state; (ii) no arrow into the initial state; (iii) no arrow out of the accepting state.

We follow the convention that if there is no arrow out of a state on a particular symbol, then the computation *rejects*. Formally, we can institute a "trash state," T, which is a rejecting state with a self-loop on all symbols in Σ, and imagine that there is an arrow on $\sigma \in \Sigma$ from state q to T if there was no arrow on σ out of q. Basis Case: the regular expression R is of the form: $\varepsilon, \emptyset, a \in \Sigma$. In this case, the NFA has one of three corresponding forms depicted in figure 8.6.

---
[1] http://www.vim.org

Fig. 8.6 $\varepsilon, \emptyset, a$ NFAs.

For the induction step, we construct bigger Regular Expressions from smaller ones in three possible ways: $R + S$, RS, R^*. The corresponding NFAs are constructed, respectively, as follows:

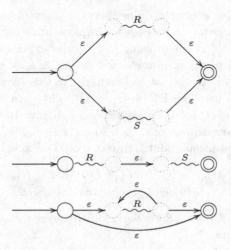

Fig. 8.7 $R + S$, RS, R^* NFAs. We use dotted circles to denote the initial and final states of the previous NFA, and the wiggly line denotes all of its other states.

As an example, we convert the Regular Expression $(0 + 01)^*$ to an NFA using this procedure.

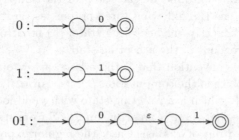

We are now going to prove the other direction of Theorem 8.16: given an NFA, we will construct a corresponding regular expression. We present two ways to accomplish this construction.

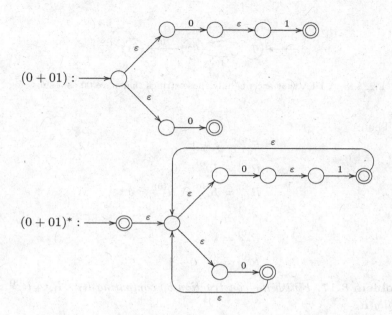

8.3.3.1 *Method 1*

This method is a great example of Dynamic Programming, which we covered in Chapter 4. Suppose A has n states, and let $R_{ij}^{(k)}$ denote the RE whose language is the set of strings w such that: w takes A from state q_i to state q_j with all intermediate states with their index $\leq k$. Then, the R such that $L(R) = L(A)$ is given by the following expression:

$$R := R_{1j_1}^{(n)} + R_{1j_2}^{(n)} + \cdots + R_{1j_k}^{(n)},$$

where $F = \{j_1, j_2, \ldots, j_k\}$. So now we build $R_{ij}^{(k)}$ by induction on k. For the basis case, let $k = 0$, and $R_{ij}^{(0)} = x + a_1 + a_2 + \cdots + a_k$ where $i \xrightarrow{a_l} j$ and $x = \emptyset$ if $i \neq j$ and $x = \varepsilon$ if $i = j$. In the induction step $k > 0$, and

$$R_{ij}^{(k)} = \underbrace{R_{ij}^{(k-1)}}_{\text{path does not visit } k} + \underbrace{R_{ik}^{(k-1)} \left(R_{kk}^{(k-1)}\right)^* R_{kj}^{(k-1)}}_{\text{visits } k \text{ at least once}}.$$

Clearly, this process builds the appropriate R from the ground up.

As an example we convert a DFA that accepts only those strings that have 00 as a substring. The DFA is given in figure 8.8.

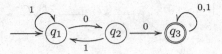

Fig. 8.8   A DFA that accepts only those strings that have 00 as a substring.

Then:

$$R_{11}^{(0)} = \varepsilon + 1$$
$$R_{12}^{(0)} = R_{23}^{(0)} = 0$$
$$R_{13}^{(0)} = R_{31}^{(0)} = R_{32}^{(0)} = \emptyset$$
$$R_{21}^{(0)} = 1$$
$$R_{22}^{(0)} = \varepsilon$$
$$R_{33}^{(0)} = \varepsilon + 0 + 1$$

Problem 8.17. *Finish the construction by computing $R^{(1)}, R^{(2)}, R^{(3)}$, and finally R.*

8.3.3.2   *Method 2*

We convert a DFA into a RE by first converting it into a Generalized NFA, which is a NFA that allows regular expressions as labels of its arrows. We define a *Generalized NFA (GNFA)* formally as follows:

$$\delta : (Q - \{q_{\text{accept}}\}) \times (Q - \{q_{\text{start}}\}) \longrightarrow \mathcal{R}$$

where the start and accept states are unique.

We say that G accepts $w = w_1 w_2 \ldots w_n$, $w_i \in \Sigma^*$, if there exists a sequence of states $q_0 = q_{\text{start}}, q_1, \ldots, q_n = q_{\text{accept}}$ such that for all i, $w_i \in L(R_i)$ where $R_i = \delta(q_{i-1}, q_i)$.

When translating from a DFA into a GNFA, if there is no arrow $i \longrightarrow j$, we label it with $\emptyset$. For each i, we label the self-loop with ε. We now eliminate states from G until left with just $q_{\text{start}} \xrightarrow{R} q_{\text{accept}}$. The elimination of states is accomplished as shown in figure 8.9.

This ends the proof of Theorem 8.16.

8.3.4   *Algebraic laws for Regular Expressions*

Regular Expressions obey a number of algebraic laws; these laws can be used to simplify RE, or to restate RE in a different way.

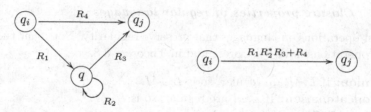

Fig. 8.9 A step in reduction of states.

Law	Description
$R + P = P + R$	commutativity of $+$
$(R + P) + Q = R + (P + Q)$	associativity of $+$
$(RP)Q = R(PQ)$	associativity of concatenation
$\emptyset + R = R + \emptyset = R$	$\emptyset$ identity for $+$
$\varepsilon R = R\varepsilon = R$	ε identity for concatenation
$\emptyset R = R\emptyset = \emptyset$	$\emptyset$ annihilator for concatenation
$R(P + Q) = RP + RQ$	left-distributivity
$(P + Q)R = PR + QR$	right-distributivity
$R + R = R$	idempotent law for union

Note that commutativity of concatenation, $RP = PR$, is conspicuously missing, as it is not true in general for RE; indeed, $ab \neq ba$ as strings. Here are six more laws associated with Kleene's star:

$$(R^*)^* = R^* \qquad \emptyset^* = \varepsilon \qquad \varepsilon^* = \varepsilon$$
$$R^+ = RR^* = R^*R \quad R^* = R^+ + \varepsilon \quad (R + P)^* = (R^*P^*)^*$$

Note that $R^* = R^+ + \varepsilon$ does *not* mean that $L(R^+) = L(R^*) - \{\varepsilon\}$.

The question now is how can we check if a given statement is a valid algebraic law? The answer is fascinating because it contradicts everything that we learned in mathematics: we can check that an alleged law is valid by testing it on a particular instance. Thus, we can verify a universal statement with a single instance. In other words, to test whether $E = F$, where E, F are RE with variables $(R, P, Q, \ldots)$, convert E, F to concrete RE C, D by replacing variables by symbols. Then check if $L(C) = L(D)$, and if so, we can conclude that $E = F$. For example, to show that $(R + P)^* = (R^*P^*)^*$, we replace R, P by $a, b \in \Sigma$, to obtain $(a + b)^* = (a^*b^*)^*$, and we check whether this particular instance is true. It is, so we can conclude that $(R + P)^* = (R^*P^*)^*$ is true. This property is often referred to as the "Test for RE Algebraic Laws."

8.3.5   *Closure properties of regular languages*

We list operations on languages that preserve regularity. Note that the first three operations have been presented in Theorem 8.8.

  i **Union:** If L, M are regular, so is $L \cup M$.
 ii **Concatenation:** If L, M are regular, so is $L \cdot M$.
iii **Kleene's Star:** If L is regular, so is L^*.
 iv **Complementation:** If L is regular, so is $L^c = \Sigma^* - L$.
  v **Intersection:** If L, M are regular, so is $L \cap M$.
 vi **Reversal:** If L is regular, so is $L^R = \{w^R | w \in L\}$, where $(w_1 w_2 \ldots w_n)^R = w_n w_{n-1} \ldots w_1$.
vii **Homomorphism:** $h : \Sigma^* \longrightarrow \Sigma^*$, where

$$h(w) = h(w_1 w_2 \ldots w_n) = h(w_1) h(w_2) \ldots h(w_n).$$

  For example, $h(0) = ab, h(1) = \varepsilon$, then $h(0011) = abab$. $h(L) = \{h(w) | w \in L\}$. If L is regular, then so is $h(L)$.
viii **Inverse Homomorphism:** $h^{-1}(L) = \{w | h(w) \in L\}$. Let A be the DFA for L; construct a DFA for $h^{-1}(L)$ as follows: $\delta(q, a) = \hat{\delta}_A(q, h(a))$.
 ix **Not proper prefix:** If A is regular, so is the language

$$\text{NOPREFIX}(A) = \{w \in A : \text{ no proper prefix of } w \text{ is in } A \}.$$

  x **Does not extend:** If A is regular, so is the language

$$\text{NOEXTEND}(A) = \{w \in A : w \text{ is not a proper prefix of any string in } A \}.$$

Problem 8.18. *Show that the above operations preserve regularity.*

8.3.6   *Complexity of transformations and decisions*

In this section we summarize the complexity, i.e., best known algorithm, for transformations between various formalizations of regular languages. We are going to use the notation A $\hookrightarrow$ B to denote the transformation from formalism A to formalism B.

  i NFA $\hookrightarrow$ DFA: $O(n^3 2^n)$
 ii DFA $\hookrightarrow$ NFA: $O(n)$
iii DFA $\hookrightarrow$ RE: $O(n^3 4^n)$
 iv RE $\hookrightarrow$ NFA: $O(n)$

Problem 8.19. *Justify the complexities for each transformation above.*

Now consider the following decision properties for regular languages:

i Is a given language empty?
ii Is a given string in a given language?
iii Are two given languages actually the same language?

Problem 8.20. *What is the complexity of the above three decision problems? Note that in each case it must be clarified what "given" means; that is, how a given language is "given."*

8.3.7 *Equivalence and minimization of automata*

We are often interested in finding a minimal DFA for a given language. We say that two states are *equivalent* if for all strings w, $\hat{\delta}(p, w)$ is accepting $\iff \hat{\delta}(q, w)$ is accepting. If two states are not equivalent, they are *distinguishable*.

We have a recursive (divide-and-conquer) procedure for finding pairs of distinguishable states. First, if p is accepting and q is not, then $\{p, q\}$ is a pair of distinguishable states. This is the "bottom" case of the recursion. If $r = \delta(p, a)$ and $s = \delta(q, a)$, where $a \in \Sigma$ and $\{r, s\}$ are already found to be distinguishable, then $\{p, q\}$ are distinguishable; this is the recursive case. We want to formalize this with the so called *table filling algorithm*, which is a recursive algorithm for finding distinguishable pairs of states.

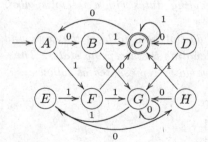

	A	B	C	D	E	F	G
B	×						
C	×	×					
D	×	×	×				
E		×	×	×			
F	×	×	×		×		
G	×	×	×	×	×	×	
H	×		×	×	×	×	×

Fig. 8.10   An example of a DFA and the corresponding table. Distinguishable states are marked by "×"; the table is only filled below the diagonal, as it is symmetric.

Problem 8.21. *Design the recursive table filling algorithm. Prove that in your algorithm, if two states are not distinguished by the algorithm, then the two states are equivalent.*

We now use the table filling algorithm to show both the equivalence of automata and to minimize them. Suppose D_1, D_2 are two DFAs. To see if they are equivalent, i.e., $L(D_1) = L(D_2)$, run the table-filling algorithm on their "union", and check if $q_0^{D_1}$ and $q_0^{D_2}$ are equivalent.

Note that the equivalence of states is an equivalence relation (see Section 9.3). We can use this fact to minimize DFAs. For a given DFA, we run the Table Filling Algorithm, to find all the equivalent states, and hence all the equivalence classes. We call each equivalence class a *block*. In the example in figure 8.10, the blocks would be:

$$\{E, A\}, \{H, B\}, \{C\}, \{F, D\}, \{G\}$$

The states within each block are equivalent, and the blocks are disjoint.

We now build a minimal DFA with states given by the blocks as follows: $\gamma(S, a) = T$, where $\delta(p, a) \in T$ for $p \in S$. We must show that γ is well defined; suppose we choose a different $q \in S$. Is it still true that $\delta(q, a) \in T$? Suppose not, i.e., $\delta(q, a) \in T'$, so $\delta(p, a) = t \in T$, and $\delta(q, a) = t' \in T'$. Since $T \neq T'$, $\{t, t'\}$ is a distinguishable pair. But then so is $\{p, q\}$, which contradicts that they are both in S.

Problem 8.22. *Show that we obtain a minimal DFA from this procedure.*

Problem 8.23. *Implement the minimization algorithm. Assume that the input is given as a transition table, where the alphabet is fixed to be $\{0, 1\}$, and the rows represent states, where the first row stands for the initial state. Indicate the rows that correspond to accepting states with a special symbol, for example, $*$.*

Note that with this convention you do not need to label the rows and columns of the input, except for the $*$ denoting the accepting states. Thus, the transition table given in figure 8.1 would be represented as follows:

$$2 \quad 0$$
$$1 \quad 1$$
$$* \quad 2 \quad 1$$

8.3.8 *Languages that are not regular*

It is easy to show that a language is regular; all we have to do is exhibit one of the models of computation that describe regular languages: a DFA, an NFA, or a regular expression. Thus, it is an *existential* proof, in that given an (alleged) regular language L, we have to show the existence of a machine A such that $L(A) = L$.

But how do we show that a language is *not* regular? Ostensibly, we have to show that for every machine A, $L(A) \neq L$, which *par contre* is a *universal* proof. This, intuitively, seems like a harder proposition because we cannot possibly list infinitely many machines, and check each one of them. Thus, we need a new technique; in fact, we propose two: the "Pumping Lemma," and the Myhill-Nerode Theorem. Thus, we enter a very challenging area of the theory of computation: proving impossibility results. Fortunately, impossibility results for regular languages, i.e., showing that a given language is not regular, are quite easy. This is because regular languages are described by relatively weak machines. The stronger a model of computation, the harder it is to give impossibility results for it.

We are interested in properties of regular languages because it is important to understand computation "without memory." Many embedded devices such as pacemakers do not have memory, or battery power to maintain a memory. Regular languages can be decided with devices without memory.

8.3.8.1 *Pumping Lemma*

Lemma 8.24 (Pumping Lemma). *Let L be a regular language. Then there exists a constant n (depending on L) such that for all $w \in L$, $|w| \geq n$, we can break w into three parts $w = xyz$ such that:*

(1) $y \neq \varepsilon$
(2) $|xy| \leq n$
(3) For all $k \geq 0$, $xy^k z \in L$

Proof. Suppose L is regular. Then there exists a DFA A such that $L = L(A)$. Let n be the number of states of A. Consider any $w = a_1 a_2 \ldots a_m$, $m \geq n$:

$$\underbrace{\underset{p_0}{\uparrow} a_1 \underset{p_1}{\uparrow} a_2 \underset{p_2}{\uparrow} a_3 \ldots a_i}_{x} \underset{p_i}{\uparrow} \underbrace{a_{i+1} \ldots a_j}_{y} \underset{p_j}{\uparrow} \underbrace{a_{j+1} \ldots a_m}_{z} \underset{p_m}{\uparrow} \qquad \square$$

Problem 8.25. *Show $L = \{0^n 1^n | n \geq 0\}$ is not regular.*

Problem 8.26. *Show $L = \{1^p | p$ is prime $\}$ is not regular.*

8.3.8.2 *Myhill-Nerode Theorem*

The Myhill-Nerode Theorem furnishes a definition of regular languages that is given without mention of a model of computation. It characterizes regular languages in terms of relational properties of strings. See Section 9.3 for a refresher on equivalence relations.

We start with some definitions and observations. Given a language $L \subseteq \Sigma^*$, let $\equiv_L$ be a relation on $\Sigma^* \times \Sigma^*$ such that $x \equiv_L y$ if for all z, $xz \in L \iff yz \in L$.

Problem 8.27. *Show that $\equiv_L$ is in fact an equivalence relation.*

Suppose some DFA D recognizes L, and $k = |Q_D|$. We say that X is a set that is *pairwise distinguishable by L* iff for every two distinct $x, y \in X$, $x \not\equiv_L y$. We show that if $|Q_D| = k$ then $|X| \leq k$. Suppose that $\{x_1, x_2, \ldots, x_{k+1}\} \subseteq X$. Since there are k states, there are two x_i, x_j, distinct, so that

$$\hat{\delta}_D(q_0, x_i) = \hat{\delta}(q_0, x_j)$$
$$\Rightarrow \forall z [\hat{\delta}_D(q_0, x_i z) = \hat{\delta}(q_0, x_j z)]$$
$$\Rightarrow \forall z [x_i z \in L \iff x_j z \in L]$$
$$\Rightarrow x_i \equiv_L x_j$$

Thus, it is not possible for $|X| > k$. We denote with $\text{index}(L)$ the cardinality $|X|$ of a largest pairwise distinguishable set $X \subseteq L$.

Theorem 8.28 (Myhill-Nerode). *L is regular iff $\text{index}(L)$ is finite. Furthermore, $\text{index}(L)$ is the size of the smallest DFA for L.*

Proof. Suppose that $\text{index}(L) = k$ and let $X = \{x_1, x_2, \ldots, x_k\}$; first note that for any $x \in \Sigma^*$, $x \equiv_L x_i$ for some (unique) $x_i \in X$; otherwise $X \cup \{x\}$ would be a bigger "pairwise distinguishable by L" set. Uniqueness follows by transitivity.

Let D be such that $Q_D = \{q_1, \ldots, q_k\}$ and

$$\delta_D(q_i, a) = q_j \iff x_i a \equiv_L x_j$$

The fact that a (unique) x_j exists such that $x_i a \equiv_L x_j$ follows from the above observation. Thus $\hat{\delta}(q_i, w) = q_j \iff x_i w \equiv_L x_j$.

Let $F_D = \{q_i \in Q_D : x_i \in L\}$ and let $q_0 := q_i$ such that $x_i \equiv_L \varepsilon$.

It is easy to show that our D works: $x \in L \iff x \equiv_L x_i$ for some $x_i \in L$. To see this note that $x \equiv_L x_i$ for a unique x_i, and if this $x_i \notin L$ then $x\varepsilon \in L$ while $x_i \varepsilon \notin L$, so we get the contradiction $x \not\equiv_L x_i$. Finally, $x \equiv_L x_i$ iff $\hat{\delta}(q_0, x) = q_i \in F_D$. $\square$

8.3.9 *Automata on terms*

See Section 9.4 for the necessary background in logic. In first order logic a *vocabulary*

$$\mathcal{V} = \{\mathbf{f}_1, \mathbf{f}_2, \mathbf{f}_3, \ldots; \mathbf{R}_1, \mathbf{R}_2, \mathbf{R}_3, \ldots\}$$

is a set of function (**f**) and relation (**R**) symbols. Each function and relation has an *arity*, i.e., "how many arguments it takes." A function of arity 0 is called a *constant*.

We define $\mathcal{V}$-*terms* (just *terms* when $\mathcal{V}$ is understood from the context) by structural induction as follows: any constant **c** (i.e., arity(**c**) = 0) is a term, and if $\mathbf{t}_1, \ldots, \mathbf{t}_n$ are n terms, and **f** is a function symbol of arity n, then $\mathbf{ft}_1 \ldots \mathbf{t}_n$ is also a term. That is, terms are constructed by juxtaposition. Let $\mathcal{T}$ be the set of all terms. Note that unlike in first order logic we do not introduce variables.

Problem 8.29. *Show that terms are "uniquely readable." (Hint: compare with Theorem 9.80.)*

A $\mathcal{V}$-*algebra* (just *algebra* when $\mathcal{V}$ is understood from the context) is an interpretation of a given vocabulary $\mathcal{V}$. That is, $\mathcal{A}$ is a $\mathcal{V}$-algebra if it consists of a non-empty set A (called the *universe* of $\mathcal{A}$), together with an interpretation of all the function and relation symbols of $\mathcal{V}$. That is, given $\mathbf{f} \in \mathcal{V}$ of arity n, $\mathcal{A}$ provides an interpretation for **f** in the sense that it assigns **f** a meaning $f : A^n \longrightarrow A$. We write $\mathbf{f}^{\mathcal{A}}$ to denote f, or just $\mathbf{f}^{\mathcal{A}} = f$.

$\mathcal{A}$ assigns each term **t** an interpretation $\mathbf{t}^{\mathcal{A}} \in A$.

Problem 8.30. *Define $\mathbf{t}^{\mathcal{A}}$ for arbitrary terms. What is the data structure that can be naturally associated with the carrying out of this interpretation? What is the natural interpretation for relations, i.e., what is $(\mathbf{Rt}_1 \ldots \mathbf{t}_n)^{\mathcal{A}}$? State explicitly the difference in "type" between $\mathbf{f}^{\mathcal{A}}$ and $\mathbf{R}^{\mathcal{A}}$.*

We say that an algebra $\mathcal{A}$ is an *automaton* if the universe A is finite and $\mathcal{V}$ has a single unary relation symbol **R**. We say that $\mathcal{A}$ *accepts* a term $\mathbf{t} \in \mathcal{T}$ if $\mathbf{t}^{\mathcal{A}} \in \mathbf{R}^{\mathcal{A}}$. Just like in the case of DFAs, we let $L(\mathcal{A})$ be the set of $\mathbf{t} \in \mathcal{T}$ that are accepted by $\mathcal{A}$.

Problem 8.31. *Let Σ be a finite alphabet, and let $\mathcal{V} = \Sigma' \cup \{\mathbf{c}\}$ where **c** is a new symbol denoting a function of arity 0, and each $a \in \Sigma$ is interpreted as a distinct unary function symbol **a** in Σ' (thus $|\Sigma| = |\Sigma'|$). Show that a language L over Σ is regular iff some automaton $\mathcal{A}$ accepts $L' = \{\mathbf{a}_n \ldots \mathbf{a}_2 \mathbf{a}_1 \mathbf{c} : a_1 a_2 \ldots a_n \in L\}$.*

We say that a subset $L \subseteq \mathcal{T}$ is *regular* if $L = L(\mathcal{A})$ for some automaton $\mathcal{A}$. Note that this a wider definition of regularity, as not all functions in $\mathcal{V}$ are necessarily unary (when they are, as problem 8.31. showed, this definition of "regular" corresponds to the classical definition of "regular").

Problem 8.32. *Show that regular languages (in this new setting), are closed under union, complementation and intersection.*

8.4   Context-free languages

In 1961 Chomsky promised to produce a complete grammar for English—half a year later he said that this was not possible, and abandoned the project. However, his PhD students continued to work in this area, and the different approaches to linguistics correspond to different stages of Chomsky's thinking and the students he had at the given time. Chomsky wanted to use grammars for *generating* speech; until his day, grammar was used only to analyze text. His approach is called *structural linguistics*, a trend to separate grammar from meaning (reminds me of Carnap's logical positivism). In computer science, grammar (computer) and meaning (human) are always separated; the interplay between syntax and semantics is one of the richest concepts in computer science.

The first language to be designed according to Chomsky's principles was ALGOL (the great grand-parent of C, C++, Pascal, etc.). ALGOL was based on Chomsky grammars, and hence unreadable for humans; hence first ALGOL programmers introduced the notion of *indentation*.

In the 1960s people did not think in terms of algorithms, but rather in terms of imaginary machines, i.e., in terms of hardware. *Pushdown automatons* (PDAs) are the machines corresponding to *Context-free grammars* (CFGs), just like DFAs correspond to regular languages. The main difference between DFAs and PDAs, is that DFAs are "algorithms" that do not require dynamic allocation of memory (no `malloc`), but PDAs allow for dynamic allocation of memory, albeit in the most primitive data structure type: a stack.

8.4.1 *Context-free grammars*

A *context-free grammar (CFG)* is expressed by the tuple $G = (V, T, P, S)$, where the letters stand for a set of variables, terminals, productions and the specified start variable.

For example, the grammar for the language of palindromes uses the following production: $P \longrightarrow \varepsilon|0|1|0P0|1P1$. And the grammar for the language of (reduced) algebraic expressions is $G = (\{E, T, F\}, \Sigma, P, E)$ where $\Sigma = \{a, +, \times, (,)\}$ and P is the following set of productions:

$$E \longrightarrow E + T | T$$
$$T \longrightarrow T \times F | F$$
$$F \longrightarrow (E) | a$$

Here we use E for expressions, T for terms, and F for factors. Under the normal interpretations of $+$ and $\times$, the three productions above respectively reflect the following structural facts about algebraic expressions:

- An expression is a term or the sum of an expression and a term;
- a term is either a factor or the product of a term and a factor;
- a factor is a either parenthesized expression or the terminal 'a'.

So the simplest expression would be one consisting of a single term, which in turn consists of a single factor: a.

Consider a string $\alpha A \beta$ over the alphabet $(V \cup T)^*$, where $A \in V$, and $A \longrightarrow \gamma$ is a production. Then we can say that $\alpha A \beta$ *yields* $\alpha \gamma \beta$, in symbols: $\alpha A \beta \Rightarrow \alpha \gamma \beta$. We use $\overset{*}{\Rightarrow}$ to denote 0 or more steps. We can now define the language of a grammar as: $L(G) = \{w \in T^* | S \overset{*}{\Rightarrow} w\}$.

Lemma 8.33. $L((\{P\}, \{0,1\}, \{P \longrightarrow \varepsilon|0|1|0P0|1P1\}, P))$ *is the set of Palindromes over* $\{0, 1\}$.

Proof. Suppose w is a palindrome. We show by induction on $|w|$ that $P \overset{*}{\Rightarrow} w$. Basis Case: $|w| \leq 1$, so $w = \varepsilon, 0, 1$, so use a single rule $P \longrightarrow \varepsilon, 0, 1$. Induction Step: For $|w| \geq 2$, $w = 0x0, 1x1$, and by the Induction Hypothesis $P \overset{*}{\Rightarrow} x$.

Suppose that $P \overset{*}{\Rightarrow} w$. We show by induction on the number of steps in the derivation that $w = w^R$. Basis Case: the derivation has one step. Induction Step:

$$P \Rightarrow 0P0 \overset{*}{\Rightarrow} 0x0 = w,$$

where the 0 can be replaced with a 1 instead. □

Suppose that we have a grammar $G = (V, T, P, S)$, and $S \overset{*}{\Rightarrow} \alpha$, where $\alpha \in (V \cup T)^*$. Then α is called a *sentential form* (of this particular grammar G). We let $L(G)$ be the set of those sentential forms which are in T^*. In other words, just as in the case of regular languages, $L(G)$ is the language of G. We define the *parse tree* for (G, w) as follows: it is a rooted tree, with S labeling the root, and the leaves are labeled left-to-right with the symbols of w. For each interior node, that is all the nodes except the leaves, the labels have the following form:

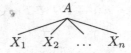

where $A \longrightarrow X_1 X_2 X_3 \ldots X_n$ is a rule in P.

There are a number of ways to demonstrate that a given word w can be generated with the grammar G, that is, to prove that $w \in L(G)$. These are: *recursive inference, derivation, left-most derivation, right-most derivation* and *yield of a parse tree*. A recursive inference is just like a derivation, except we generate the derivation from w to S. A left(right)-most derivation is a derivation which always applies the rule to the left(right)-most variable in the intermediate sentential form.

We say that a grammar is *ambiguous* if there are words which have two different parse trees. For example, $G = (\{E\}, [0-9], \{E \to E+E, E*E\}, E)$ is ambiguous as the parse trees corresponding to these two derivations are distinct:

$$E \Rightarrow E + E \Rightarrow E + E * E$$
$$E \Rightarrow E * E \Rightarrow E + E * E$$

The issue is that parse trees assign meaning to a string, and two different parse trees assign two possible meanings, hence the "ambiguity."

Problem 8.34. *Show that the extended regular languages, as defined in Section 8.3.9, are contained in the class of context free languages.*

8.4.2 *Pushdown automata*

A *Pushdown Automaton (PDA)* is an NFA with a stack. The formal definition of a PDA is given as follows: $P = (Q, \Sigma, \Gamma, \delta, q_0, F)$ where:

  i Q finite set of states
  ii Σ finite input alphabet
  iii Γ finite stack alphabet
  iv $\delta(q, x, a) = \{(p_1, b_1), \ldots, (p_n, b_n)\}$
  v q_0 initial state
  vi F accepting states

Problem 8.35. *What is a simple PDA for $\{ww^R | w \in \{0,1\}^*\}$?*

A P computes as follows: it accepts a given string w in Σ^* if $w = w_1 w_2 \ldots w_m$ where $w_i \in \Sigma_\varepsilon$, where $|w| = n \leq m$. That is, there exists a ε padding of w such that there exists a sequence of states $r_0, r_1, \ldots, r_m$ in Q, and a sequence of stack contents $s_0, s_1, \ldots, s_m \in \Gamma^*$ such that the following three hold:

i $r_0 = q_0$ and $s_0 = \varepsilon$

ii $(r_{i+1}, b) \in \delta(r_i, w_{i+1}, a)$, where $s_i = at$, $s_{i+1} = bt$ and $a, b \in \Gamma_\varepsilon$ and $t \in \Gamma^*$. That is, M moves properly according to state, stack and next input symbol.

iii $r_m \in F$.

A *configuration* is a tuple (q, w, γ): state, remaining input, contents of the stack. If $(p, \alpha) \in \delta(q, a, X)$, then $(q, aw, X\beta) \to (p, w, \alpha\beta)$

Lemma 8.36. *If $(q, x, \alpha) \overset{*}{\Rightarrow} (p, y, \beta)$, then $(q, xw, \alpha\gamma) \overset{*}{\Rightarrow} (p, yw, \beta\gamma)$.*

Problem 8.37. *Prove Lemma 8.36.*

There are two equivalent ways to define precisely what it meas for a PDA to accept an input word. There is acceptance by final state, where we let:

$$L(P) = \{w | (q_0, w, \$) \overset{*}{\Rightarrow} (q, \varepsilon, \alpha), q \in F\},$$

and there is acceptance by empty stack:

$$L(P) = \{w | (q_0, w, \$) \overset{*}{\Rightarrow} (q, \varepsilon, \varepsilon)\}.$$

When designing PDAs it might be more convenient to use one of these definitions rather than the other, but as the following Theorem demonstrates, both definitions capture the same set of languages.

Lemma 8.38. *L is accepted by PDA by final state iff it is accepted by PDA by empty stack.*

Problem 8.39. *Prove Lemma 8.38.*

Theorem 8.40. *CFGs and PDAs are equivalent.*

Proof. We show first how to translate a CFG to an equivalent PDA. A *left sentential form* is a particular way to express a configuration where:

$$\underbrace{x}_{\in T^*} \overbrace{A\alpha}^{\text{tail}}.$$

The tail appears on the stack, and x is the prefix of the input that has been consumed so far. The idea is that the input to the PDA is given by $w = xy$, and $A\alpha \overset{*}{\Rightarrow} y$.

Suppose that a PDA is in configuration $(q, y, A\alpha)$, and that it uses the rule $A \longrightarrow \beta$, and enters $(q, y, \beta\gamma)$. The PDA simulates the grammar as follows: the initial segment of β is parsed, and if there are terminal symbols, they are compared against the input and removed, until the first variable of β is exposed on top of the stack. This process is repeated, and the PDA accepts by empty stack.

For example, consider $P \longrightarrow \varepsilon|0|1|0P0|1P1$. The corresponding PDA has transitions:

$$\delta(q_0, \varepsilon, \$) = \{(q, P\$)\}$$
$$\delta(q, \varepsilon, P) = \{(q, 0P0), (q, 0), (q, \varepsilon), (q, 1P1), (q, 1)\}$$
$$\delta(q, 0, 0) = \delta(q, 1, 1) = \{(q, \varepsilon)\}$$
$$\delta(q, 0, 1) = \delta(q, 1, 0) = \emptyset$$
$$\delta(q, \varepsilon, \$) = (q, \varepsilon)$$

The computation is depicted in figure 8.11.

Z	P	1	P	0	P	0	P	0	0	1	Z
	Z	P	1	P	0	P	0	0	1	Z	
		1	Z	0	1	0	0	1	Z		
		Z		1	Z	0	1	Z			
				Z		1	Z				
						Z					

Fig. 8.11   The computation for $P \Rightarrow 1P1 \Rightarrow 10P01 \Rightarrow 100P001 \Rightarrow 100001$.

We now outline how to translate from a PDA to a CFG. The idea is that of "net popping" of one symbol of the stack, while consuming some input. The variables are: $A_{[pXq]}$, for $p, q \in Q$, $X \in \Gamma$. $A_{[pXq]} \overset{*}{\Rightarrow} w$ iff w takes PDA from state p to state q, and pops X off the stack. Productions: for all p, $S \longrightarrow A_{[q_0\$p]}$, and whenever we have:

$$(r, Y_1Y_2\ldots Y_k) \in \delta(q, a, X),$$

we bring aboard the rule:

$$A_{[qXr_k]} \longrightarrow aA_{[rY_1r_1]}A_{[r_1Y_2r_2]} \cdots A_{[r_{k-1}Y_kr_k]},$$

where $a \in \Sigma \cup \{\varepsilon\}$, $r_1, r_2, \ldots, r_k \in Q$ are all possible lists of states. If $(r, \varepsilon) \in \delta(q, a, X)$, then we have $A_{[qXr]} \longrightarrow a$.

Problem 8.41. *Show that* $A_{[qXp]} \overset{*}{\Rightarrow} w$ *iff* $(q, w, X) \overset{*}{\Rightarrow} (p, \varepsilon, \varepsilon)$.

This finishes the proof of the Lemma. □

A PDA is deterministic if $|\delta(q, a, X)| \leq 1$, and the second condition is that if for some $a \in \Sigma$ $|\delta(q, a, X)| = 1$, then $|\delta(q, \varepsilon, X)| = 0$. We call such machines DPDAs.

Lemma 8.42. *If L is regular, then $L = L(P)$ for some DPDA P.*

Proof. Simply observe that a DFA is a DPDA. □

Note that DPDAs that accept by final state are not equivalent to DPDAs that accept by empty stack. In order to examine the relationship between acceptance by state or empty stack in the context of DPDAs, we introduce the following property of languages: L has the *prefix property* if there exists a pair (x, y), $x, y \in L$, such that $y = xz$ for some z. For example, $\{0\}^*$ has the prefix property.

Lemma 8.43. *L is accepted by a DPDA by empty stack $\Longleftrightarrow$ L is accepted by a DPDA by final state* **and** *L does not have the prefix property.*

Lemma 8.44. *If L is accepted by a DPDA, then L is unambiguous.*

8.4.3 *Chomsky Normal Form*

In this section we show that every CFG can be put in an especially simple form, called the Chomsky Normal Form (CNF). A CFG is in *Chomsky Normal Form* if all the rules take one of the following three forms:

(1) $S \longrightarrow \varepsilon$, where S is the start variable;
(2) $A \longrightarrow BC$, where A, B, C are variables, possibly repeated;
(3) $A \longrightarrow a$, where A is a variable and a an alphabet symbol (not ε).

The CNF has many desirable properties, but one of the most important consequences is the so called CYK Algorithm (algorithm 8.1, Section 8.4.4), which is a dynamic programming algorithm for deciding $w \in L(G)$, for a given word w and CFG G.

We are now going to show how to convert an arbitrary CFG into CNF. In the discussion that follows, S is a variable, $X \in V \cup T$, $w \in T^*$ and $\alpha, \beta \in (V \cup T)^*$. We say that the symbol X is *useful* if there exists a derivation such that $S \overset{*}{\Rightarrow} \alpha X \beta \overset{*}{\Rightarrow} w$.

We say that X is *generating* if $X \overset{*}{\Rightarrow} w \in T^*$, and we say that X is *reachable* if there exists a derivation $S \overset{*}{\Rightarrow} \alpha X \beta$. A symbol that is useful will be both generating and reachable. Thus, if we eliminate non-generating symbols first, and then from the remaining grammar the non-reachable symbols, we will have only useful symbols left.

Problem 8.45. *Prove that if we eliminate non-generating symbols first, and then from the remaining grammar the non-reachable symbols, we will have only useful symbols left.*

This is how we establish the set of generating symbols, and the set of reachable symbols. Clearly every symbol in T is generating, and if $A \longrightarrow \alpha$ is a production, and every symbol in α is generating (or $\alpha = \varepsilon$) then A is also generating. Similarly, S is reachable, and if A is reachable, and $A \longrightarrow \alpha$ is a production, then every symbol in α is reachable.

Claim 8.46. *If L has a CFG, then $L - \{\varepsilon\}$ has a CFG without productions of the form $A \longrightarrow \varepsilon$, and without productions of the form $A \longrightarrow B$.*

Proof. A variable is *nullable* if $A \overset{*}{\Rightarrow} \varepsilon$. To compute nullable variables: if $A \longrightarrow \varepsilon$ is a production, then A is nullable, if $B \longrightarrow C_1 C_2 \ldots C_k$ is a production and all the C_i's are nullable, then so is B. Once we have all the nullable variables, we eliminate ε-productions as follows: eliminate all $A \longrightarrow \varepsilon$.

If $A \longrightarrow X_1 X_2 \ldots X_k$ is a production, and $m \leq k$ of the X_i's are nullable, then add the 2^m versions of the rule the the nullable variables present/absent (if $m = k$, do not add the case where they are *all* absent).

Eliminating unit productions: $A \longrightarrow B$. If $A \overset{*}{\Rightarrow} B$, then (A, B) is a unit pair. Find all unit pairs: (A, A) is a unit pair, and if (A, B) is a unit pair, and $B \longrightarrow C$ is a production, then (A, C) is a unit pair. To eliminate unit productions: compute all unit pairs, and if (A, B) is a unit pair and $B \longrightarrow \alpha$ is a non-unit production, add the production $A \longrightarrow \alpha$. Throw out all the unit productions. $\qquad \square$

Theorem 8.47. *Every CFL has a CFG in CNF.*

Proof. To convert G into CNF, start by eliminating all ε-productions, unit productions and useless symbols. Arrange all bodies of length ≥ 2 to consist of only variables (by introducing new variables), and finally break bodies of length ≥ 3 into a cascade of productions, each with a body of length exactly 2. $\qquad \square$

8.4.4 *CYK algorithm*

Given a grammar G in CNF, and a string $w = a_1 a_2 \ldots a_n$, we can test whether $w \in L(G)$ using the CYK[2] dynamic algorithm (algorithm 8.1). On input $G, w = a_1 a_2 \ldots a_n$ algorithm 8.1 builds an $n \times n$ table T, where each entry contains a subset of V. At the end, $w \in L(G)$ iff the start variable S is contained in position $(1, n)$ of T. The main idea is to put variable X_1 in position (i, j) if X_2 is in position (i, k) and X_3 is in position $(k+1, j)$ and $X_1 \longrightarrow X_2 X_3$ is a rule. The reasoning is that X_1 is in position (i, k) iff $X_1 \overset{*}{\Rightarrow} a_i \ldots a_k$, that is, the substring $a_i \ldots a_k$ of the input string can be generated from X_1. Let $V = \{X_1, X_2, \ldots, X_m\}$.

Algorithm 8.1 CYK
---
for $i = 1..n$ **do**
    for $j = 1..m$ **do**
        Place variable X_j in (i, i) iff $X_j \longrightarrow a_i$ is a rule of G
    end for
end for
for $1 \le i < j \le n$ **do**
    for $k = i..(j - 1)$ **do**
        if $(\exists X_p \in (i, k) \land \exists X_q \in (k+1, j) \land \exists X_r \longrightarrow X_p X_q)$ **then**
            Put X_r in (i, j)
        end if
    end for
end for

In the example in figure 8.12, we show which entries in the table we need to use to compute the contents of $(2, 5)$.

Problem 8.48. *Show the correctness of algorithm 8.1.*

Problem 8.49. *Implement the CYK algorithm. Choose a convention for representing CFGs, and document it well in your code. You may assume the grammar is given in CNF; or, you may check that explicitly. To make the project even more ambitious, you may implement a translation of a general grammar to CNF.*

---

[2]Named after the inventors: Cocke-Younger-Kasami.

×	(2,2)	(2,3)	(2,4)	(2,5)
×	×			(3,5)
×	×	×		(4,5)
×	×	×	×	(5,5)

Fig. 8.12 Computing the entry $(2,5)$: note that we require all the entries on the same row and column (except those that are below the main diagonal). Thus the CYK algorithm computes the entries dynamically by diagonals, starting with the main diagonal, and ending in the upper-right corner.

8.4.5 *Pumping Lemma for CFLs*

Lemma 8.50 (Pumping Lemma for CFLs). *There exists a p so that any s, $|s| \geq p$, can be written as $s = uvxyz$, and:*

(1) $uv^i xy^i z$ is in the language, for all $i \geq 0$,
(2) $|vy| > 0$,
(3) $|vxy| \leq p$.

Proof. Following the Pigeon Hole reasoning used to show the Pumping Lemma for regular languages (see Section 8.3.8.1, Lemma 8.24), figure 8.13 should be sufficient to convince the reader: It turns out that this argument

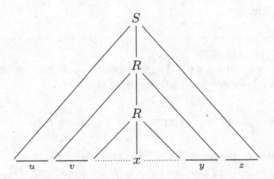

Fig. 8.13 If the word is long enough, the height of the parse tree is big enough to force the repetition of some variable (R) along some branch.

is best carried out with a translation of the grammar to CNF (Section 8.4.3). Then find the length of inputs that guarantees a tree height of at least $|V| + 1$. The details are left to the reader. $\qquad\square$

Problem 8.51. *Finish the proof of Lemma 8.50.*

Problem 8.52. *Show that $L = \{0^n1^n2^n|n \geq 1\}$ is not a CFL.*

8.4.6 *Further observations about CFL*

CFLs do not have the same wide closure properties as regular languages (see Section 8.3.5). CFLs are closed under union, concatenation, Kleene's star ($*$), homomorphisms and reversals. For homomorphism note that a homomorphism can be applied to a derviation. For reversals, just replace each $A \longrightarrow \alpha$ by $A \longrightarrow \alpha^R$.

CFLs are not closed under intersection or complement. To see that they are not closed under intersection, note that $L_1 = \{0^n1^n2^i|n, i \geq 1\}$ and $L_2 = \{0^i1^n2^n|n, i \geq 1\}$ are CFLs, but $L_1 \cap L_2 = \{0^n1^n2^n|n \geq 1\}$ is not.

To see that CFLs are not closed under complementation, note that the language $L = \{ww : w \in \{a, b\}^*\}$ is not a CFL, but L^c is a CFL. It turns out that it is not trivial to show that L^c is a CFL; designing the CFG is tricky: first note that no odd strings are of the form ww, so the first rule ought to be:

$$S \longrightarrow O|E$$
$$O \longrightarrow a|b|aaO|abO|baO|bbO$$

here O generates all the odd strings. On the other hand, E generates even length strings not of the form ww, i.e., all strings of the form:

$X =$	a	b		$Y =$	b	a

We need the rule:

$$E \longrightarrow X|Y$$

and now

$$X \longrightarrow PQ \quad Y \longrightarrow VW$$
$$P \longrightarrow RPR \quad V \longrightarrow SVS$$
$$P \longrightarrow a \qquad V \longrightarrow b$$
$$Q \longrightarrow RQR \quad W \longrightarrow SWS$$
$$Q \longrightarrow b \qquad W \longrightarrow a$$
$$R \longrightarrow a|b \qquad S \longrightarrow a|b$$

Note that R's can be replaced with any a or b, giving us the desirable property.

Problem 8.53. *Show that if L is a CFL, and R is a regular language, then $L \cap R$ is a CFL.*

Problem 8.54. *We know that CFL are closed under substitutions (a type of homomorphism): for every $a \in \Sigma$ we choose L_a, which we call $s(a)$. For any $w \in \Sigma^*$, $s(w)$ is the language of $x_1 x_2 \ldots x_n$, $x_i \in s(a_i)$. Show that if L is a CFL, and $s(a)$ is a CFL $\forall a \in \Sigma$, then $s(L) = \cup_{w \in L} s(w)$ is also a CFL.*

While the CYK algorithm allows us to decide whether a given string w is in the language of some given CFG G, there are many properties of CFG that are unfortunately undecidable. What does this mean? It means that there are computational problems regarding CFGs for which there are no algorithms. For example:

(1) Is a given CFG G ambiguous?
(2) Is a given CFL inherently ambiguous?
(3) Is the intersection of two CFL empty?
(4) Given G_1, G_2, is $L(G_1) = L(G_2)$?
(5) Is a given CFG equal to Σ^*?

It is difficult to show that a particular problem does not have an algorithm that solves it. In fact, we must introduce a new technique in order to show that the five questions above are "undecidable." We do so in Section 8.5. For the impatient, see Section 8.5.9.

8.4.7 *Other grammars*

Context-sensitive grammars (CSG) have rules of the form:

$$\alpha \to \beta$$

where $\alpha, \beta \in (T \cup V)^*$ and $|\alpha| \le |\beta|$. A language is *context-sensitive* if it has a CSG. In an elegant connection with complexity, CSLs turn out to describe precisely the set of those languages which can be decided by Nondeterministic TMs in linear time (see the next section).

A *rewriting system* (also called a *Semi-Thue system*) is a grammar where there are no restrictions; $\alpha \to \beta$ for arbitrary $\alpha, \beta \in (V \cup T)^*$.

Rewriting systems correspond to the most general model of computation, in the sense that anything that can be solved algorithmically can be solved with a rewriting system. Thus, a language has a rewriting system iff it is "computable," the topic of the next sections.

8.5 Turing machines

A Turing machine is an automaton with a finite control and an infinite tape, where the infinite tape captures the intuition of "unlimited space." Initially the input is placed on the tape, the head of the tape is positioned on the first symbol of the input, and the state is q_0. All the other squares contain blanks.

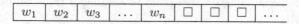

Fig. 8.14   Initial contents of the tape; the head is scanning w_1.

Formally, a *Turing machine* is a tuple $(Q, \Sigma, \Gamma, \delta, q_0, q_{\text{accept}}, q_{\text{reject}})$ where the input alphabet Σ is contained in the tape alphabet Γ, and $\square$ is the "blank" symbol, i.e., $\Sigma \cup \{\square\} \subseteq \Gamma$. The *transition function* $\delta(q, X) = (p, Y, D)$ where D is the direction of the motion of the tape, "left" or "right", sometimes denoted as "$\leftarrow$" or "$\rightarrow$."

A *configuration* is a string upv, where $u, v \in \Gamma^*$ and $p \in Q$, meaning that the state is p, the head is scanning the first symbol of v, and the tape contains only blanks following the last symbol of v. Initially, the configuration is $q_0 w$ where $w = w_1 w_2 \dots w_n$, $w_i \in \Sigma$, is the input, and the first symbol of w, w_1, is placed on the left-most square of the tape. In order to be extra careful, we say that the symbol immediately to the left of the last symbol of v has the property of being $\square$ and having the smallest index among all those squares in the tape satisfying two conditions: (i) it is to the right of the head; (ii) there are no symbols other than $\square$ to its right.

If $\delta(q_i, b) = (q_j, c, L)$ then configuration $uaq_i bv$ *yields* configuration $uq_j acv$, and if $\delta(q_i, b) = (q_j, c, R)$ then $uaq_i bv$ yields $uacq_j v$. Sometimes "C_1 yields C_2" is written as $C_1 \rightarrow C_2$. We assume that a TM halts when it enters an accepting or rejecting state, and we define the *language of a TM* M, denoted $L(M)$, as follows: $L(M) = \{w \in \Sigma^* | q_0 w \overset{*}{\Rightarrow} \alpha q_{\text{accept}} \beta\}$.

Problem 8.55. *Design a TM M such that $L(M)$ is the language of palindromes.*

Different variants of TMs are equivalent; this notion is called *robustness*. For example, the tape infinite in only one direction, or several tapes. It is easy to "translate" between the different models.

Languages accepted by TMs are called *recursively enumerable (RE)*, or *recognizable*, or *Turing-recognizable* (in Sipser). A language L is RE if there exists a TM M that halts in an accepting state for all $x \in L$, and does not accept $x \notin L$. In other words, L is RE if there exists an M such that $L = L(M)$ (but M does not necessarily halt on all inputs).

A language L is *recursive*, or *decidable*, or *Turing-decidable* (in Sipser), if there exists a TM M that halts in q_{accept} for all $x \in L$, and halts in q_{reject} for all $x \notin L$. In other words, L is decidable if there exists a TM M such that $L = L(M)$ (i.e., M recognizes/accepts L) and also M always halts. Recursive languages correspond to languages that can be recognized *algorithmically*.

8.5.1   *Nondeterministic TMs*

Recall that in Section 8.3.2 we defined NFA, Nondeterministic Finite Automata. Nondeterminism allows the possibility of several possible moves on the same configuration. This idea is now exploited in the context of Turing Machines.

A *Nondeterministic* TM is just like a normal TM except that the transition function is now a transition relation; thus there are several possible moves on a given state and symbol:

$$\delta(q, a) = \{(q_1, b_1, D_1), (q_2, b_2, D_2), \ldots, (q_k, b_k, D_k)\}.$$

Just like for NFA, nondeterminism does not strengthen the model of computation, at least not in the context of decidability. But it allows for a more convenient design formalism.

For example, consider the TM N which decides the following language $L(N) = \{w \in \{0,1\}^* | \text{ last symbol of } w \text{ is } 1 \}$. The description of N, together with a computation tree of N on input 011, can be found in Figure 8.15.

Theorem 8.56. *If N is a nondet TM, then there exists a det TM D such that $L(N) = L(D)$.*

Proof. D tries out all the possible moves of N, using "breadth-first" search. D maintains a sequence of configurations on tape 1:

$\cdots$	config$_1$	config$_2$	config$_3^*$	$\cdots$

and uses a second tape for scratch work. The configuration marked with '$*$' is the current config. D copies it to the second tape, and examines it to see if it is accepting. If it is, it accepts. If it is not, and N has k possible moves, D appends the k new configurations resulting from these

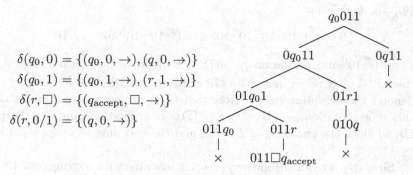

$$\delta(q_0, 0) = \{(q_0, 0, \rightarrow), (q, 0, \rightarrow)\}$$
$$\delta(q_0, 1) = \{(q_0, 1, \rightarrow), (r, 1, \rightarrow)\}$$
$$\delta(r, \square) = \{(q_{\text{accept}}, \square, \rightarrow)\}$$
$$\delta(r, 0/1) = \{(q, 0, \rightarrow)\}$$

Fig. 8.15 Definition of N together with a run on 011.

moves to tape 1, and marks the next config on the list as current. If maximum number of possible choices of N is m, i.e., m is the *degree of nondeterminism* of N, and N makes n moves before accepting, D examines $1 + m + m^2 + m^3 + \cdots + m^n \approx nm^n$ many configurations. $\square$

In effect, what is happening in the above proof is that D *simulates N*; the idea of simulation will be an important thread in the topic of computability. We can always have one Turing machine simulate another; the "other" Turing machine can be encoded in the states of the simulator. This is not surprising as a Turing machine is a "finite object" that can be "encoded" with finitely many symbols (more on that below). Alternatively, the description of the "other" machine can be placed on the tape, and the simulator checks this description to simulate each move on another dedicated tape. In short, the fact that this can be done should not be surprising, given that Turing machines capture what we understand to be the notion of a "computer." Further, we also have simulations in the "real world"—for example, we can use VMware software to simulate Windows OS on a Linux box.

Problem 8.57. *Show how M_1 can simulate M_2. One idea is to have states (s_{on}, p) and (s_{off}, p) where some of the p's are in Q_{M_2} and some correspond to the actions of M_1. Here $s_{\text{on}}, s_{\text{off}}$ indicate if the simulation is on or off, and the states of M_1 are such pairs.*

8.5.2 *Encodings*

Recall that a DFA B is just $(Q, \Sigma, \delta, q_0, F)$; we assume that $\Sigma = \{0, 1\}$ and $Q = \{q_1, q_2, \ldots, q_n\}$ where q_0 is always q_1. Assume also that $F =$

$\{q_{i_1}, \ldots, q_{i_k}\}$. Then,

$$\langle B \rangle := 0^n 10^{l_1^0} 10^{l_1^1} 10^{l_2^0} 10^{l_2^1} 1 \ldots 0^{l_n^0} 10^{l_n^1} 10^{i_1} 10^{i_2} 1 \ldots 10^{i_k}$$

where $0^{l_j^0} 10^{l_j^1}$ means that on q_j the DFA B moves to $q_{l_j^0}$ on 0 and to $q_{l_j^1}$ on 1, the initial 0^n denotes that there are n states, and the final $0^{i_1} 10^{i_2} 1 \ldots 10^{i_k}$ denotes the accepting states. Note that there are no two contiguous 1s in this representation, so $\langle B, w \rangle := \langle B \rangle 11w$ is a good encoding of the pair (B, w) since the encoding of B, $\langle B \rangle$, and the encoding of w are separated by 11.

Similarly, we can encode every Turing machine with a string over $\{0, 1\}$. For example, if M is a TM $(\{q_1, q_2\}, \{0, 1\}, \delta, \ldots)$ and $\delta(q_1, 1) = (q_2, 0, \to)$ is one of the transitions, then it could be encoded as:

$$\overset{\delta(q_1,1)=(q_2,0,\to)}{\underbrace{00}_{\text{2 states}} \; 11 \; \overbrace{\underbrace{0}_{q_1} \; 1 \; \underbrace{00}_{1} \; 1 \; \underbrace{00}_{q_2} \; 1 \; \underbrace{0}_{0} \; 1 \; \underbrace{0}_{\to}} \; 11 \; \underbrace{\ldots\ldots\ldots\ldots}_{\substack{\text{encoding of remaining} \\ \text{transitions}}}}$$

Not every string is going to be a valid encoding of a TM; for example the string 1 does not encode anything in our convention. We say that a string $x \in \{0, 1\}^*$ is a *well formed string (WFS)* if there exists a TM M and a string w so that $x = \langle M, w \rangle$; that is, x is a proper encoding of a pair (M, w). It is easy to see that we can design a decider that checks whether x is a WFS, or, in other words, the language of WFS is decidable.

8.5.3　*Decidability*

Theorem 8.58. *Regular languages are decidable and context-free languages are also decidable.*

The following are examples of decidable languages:

$A_{\text{DFA}} := \{\langle B, w \rangle : B \text{ is a DFA that accepts input string } w\}$

$A_{\text{NFA}} := \{\langle B, w \rangle : B \text{ is a NFA that accepts input string } w\}$

$A_{\text{REX}} := \{\langle R, w \rangle : R \text{ is a Reg Exp that accepts input string } w\}$

$E_{\text{DFA}} := \{\langle A \rangle : A \text{ is a DFA such that } L(A) = \emptyset\}$

$EQ_{\text{DFA}} := \{\langle A, B \rangle : A, B \text{ are DFAs such that } L(A) = L(B)\}$

$E_{\text{CFG}} := \{\langle G \rangle : G \text{ is a CFG such that } L(G) = \emptyset\}$

For EQ_{DFA} use symmetric difference: $C = (A \cap \overline{B}) \cup (\overline{A} \cap B)$.

Theorem 8.59. *If L is decidable, so is its complement.*

Proof. Let $\overline{L} = \Sigma^* - L$ be the complement of L, and suppose that L is decidable by M. Let M' be the following modification of M: on input x, M' runs just like M. However, when M is about to accept, M' rejects, and when M is about to reject, M' accepts. Clearly, $\overline{L} = L(M')$. Since M always halts, so does M', so by definition, $\overline{L}$ is decidable. $\qquad\square$

Theorem 8.60. *If both L and $\overline{L}$ are RE, then L is decidable.*

Proof. Let $L = L(M_1)$ and $\overline{L} = L(M_2)$. Let M be the following TM: on input x it simulates M_1 on x on one tape, and M_2 on x on another tape. Since $L \cup \overline{L} = \Sigma^*$, x must be accepted by one or the other. If M_1 accepts, so does M; if M_2 accepts, M rejects. $\qquad\square$

8.5.4 *Church-Turing thesis*

> *The intuitive notion of algorithm is captured by the formal definition of a TM.*

It is called a "thesis" because the notion of algorithm is intuitive, i.e., vague. We all have an intuitive understanding of the notion of "algorithm," as a recipe, a procedure, a set of instructions that for any input of a certain kind yields a desired outcome.

Consider the language:

$$\mathsf{A}_{\mathrm{TM}} = \{\langle M, w \rangle : M \text{ is a TM and } M \text{ accepts } w\}.$$

This language is sometimes called the *universal language*. It is recognizable because it is recognized by the *universal Turing machine (UTM)*; it is a machine that on input $\langle M, w \rangle$, where M is a TM and w is a string, checks that $\langle M, w \rangle$ is a WFS, and if it is, it simulates M on w, and answers accordingly to what $M(w)$ answers. Note, however, that U does *not* decide A_{TM}.

The UTM was a revolutionary idea of Turing; it was a concept that went against the engineering principles of his times. In Turing's epoch, the practice of engineering was to have "one machine to solve one problem." Thus, have a UTM that can solve "all" problems was to go against the grain. But our modern computers are precisely UTMs; that is, we do not build a computer to run *one* algorithm, but rather, our computers can run anything we *program* on them.

It is not difficult to see that a UTM can be constructed, but care must be taken to establish a convention of encoding TMs, and a convention for encoding $\langle M, w \rangle$. The UTM can have several tapes, one of them reserved for $\langle M \rangle$, i.e., a tape containing the "program," and another tape on which U simulates the computation $M(w)$. In the 1960s, Marvin Minsky, the head of the AI department at MIT, proposed the smallest UTM at the time: 7 states and 2 symbols. Currently, since 2008, the record is held by Alex Smith, who proposed a UTM with 2 states and 3 symbols.

It is really an important exercise for anyone seriously engaged in computer science to design a UTM. Such an exercise involves the design of a programming language (i.e., $\langle M \rangle$) and an interpreter/compiler (i.e., the U capable of *simulating* any M on any input). Such an exercise reifies many notions in computer science, and makes them more recognizable when they appear later on.

8.5.5   *Undecidability*

Theorem 8.61. $\mathsf{A_{TM}}$ *is undecidable.*

Proof.   Suppose that it is decidable, and that H decides it. Then, $L(H) = \mathsf{A_{TM}}$, and H always halts (observe that $L(H) = L(U)$, but U, as we already mentioned, is not guaranteed to be a decider). Define a new machine D (here D stands for "diagonal," since this argument follows Cantor's "diagonal argument"):

$$D(\langle M \rangle) := \begin{cases} \text{accept} & \text{if } H(\langle M, \langle M \rangle \rangle) = \text{reject} \\ \text{reject} & \text{if } H(\langle M, \langle M \rangle \rangle) = \text{accept} \end{cases}$$

that is, D does the "opposite." Then we can see that $D(\langle D \rangle)$ accepts iff it rejects. Contradiction; so $\mathsf{A_{TM}}$ cannot be decidable. $\square$

What is the practical consequence of this theorem? Imagine that you are developing a debugger for some programming language—something in the style of GDB for C. In the words of the "GNU Project" team, the GDB debugger allows you to see what is going on "inside" another program while it executes—or what another program was doing at the moment it crashed. A very useful feature would be to query the debugger whether your program is going to halt on a given input. For example, you run your program on some input x, and nothing happened for a long time until you pressed the CNTRL+D key to interrupt the execution. Did you press it too quickly? Perhaps if you waited longer your answer would have come; or, perhaps, it would never have halted on its own. The "halting feature" in your debugger would give you the answer. However, theorem 8.61 says that this feature *cannot* be implemented.

Let's make sure we understand what theorem 8.61 claims: it says that A_{TM} is undecidable, and so there is no TM that on any $\langle M, w \rangle$ halts with the right answer. This does not negate the possibility of developing a TM that halts on some (perhaps even infinitely many) $\langle M, w \rangle$ with the right answer. What theorem 8.61 says is that no algorithm exists that works correctly for every input.

See article by Moshe Vardi, regarding termination/unsolvability, from the July 2011 ACM Communications, "Solving the unsolvable."

Problem 8.62. *Is there a TM M such that $L(M) = A_{TM} - L'$ where $|L'| < \infty$? That is, M decides A_{TM} for all but finitely many $\langle M, w \rangle$.*

The *Busy Beaver (BB)* function, $\Sigma(n, m)$, outputs the maximum number of squares that can be written with a TM with n states and m alphabet symbols starting on empty tape. Fixing $m = 2$, and letting $\Sigma(n)$ be $\Sigma(n, 2)$, it is known that $\Sigma(2) = 4; \Sigma(3) = 6; \Sigma(4) = 13; \Sigma(5) \geq 4098; \Sigma(6) \geq 3.5 \times 10^{18267}$. The BB function is undecidable; suppose that it were decidable. Then we could use it to decide A_{TM} as follows: on input $\langle M, w \rangle$, construct a TM M' that on an empty tape writes w, and returns to the first square, and simulates M on w. Then compute $i = \Sigma(|Q_{M'}|, |\Gamma_{M'}|)$, and simulate M'. If M' ever crosses the i-th square, we know that $M(w)$ does not halt; if M' is circumscribed within the first i squares, then it will either halt or it will enter a "loop." We can detect this "loop" by keeping track of the different configurations, and making sure that they do not repeat. When the space is bounded by i, the number of configurations is bounded by $|Q_M| i |\Gamma|^i$.

Corollary 8.63. $\overline{A_{TM}}$ *is not RE.*

Proof. Since A_{TM} is RE (as $L(U) = A_{TM}$), by theorem 8.60 we know that if $\overline{A_{TM}}$ were also RE, then A_{TM} would be decidable, which by theorem 8.61 it is not. □

An *enumerator* is a TM that has a work tape, empty on input, and an output tape on which it writes strings, separated by some symbols, say #, never moving left. The idea is that it "enumerates" the strings in a language. A language is *enumerable* if there exists an enumerator E such that $L = L(E)$.

Theorem 8.64. *A language is recognizable iff it is enumerable.*

Proof. If L is enumerable, then let M on in input w simulate L's enumerator and accept if w appears in the output. For the other direction we have to be more careful: suppose L is recognizable by M. Let the enumerator E work as follows: in phase i it simulates M on the first i strings of Σ^* (in *lexicographic order*), each for i steps. When M accepts some string, E outputs it. This is the idea of "dovetailing." $\qquad\square$

8.5.6 *Reductions*

Using the notion of *reduction* we can show that many other languages are not RE or not decidable. Consider the language:

$$\text{HALT}_{\text{TM}} := \{\langle M, w\rangle : M \text{ is a TM that halts on } w\}.$$

This language is undecidable, and we can show it as follows: suppose that it *is* decidable, and that its decider is H. Consider H' which on input $\langle M, w\rangle$ runs $H(\langle M, w\rangle)$. If H accepts our H' simulates M on w and answers accordingly; otherwise, H' rejects. Clearly, $L(H') = \text{A}_{\text{TM}}$, but since H was a decider, so is H'. But this contradicts the undecidability of A_{TM}. Hence, we have just shown by contradiction that HALT_{TM} cannot be decidable, i.e., it is undecidable.

Consider now

$$E_{\text{TM}} := \{\langle M\rangle : M \text{ is a TM such that } L(M) = \emptyset\}.$$

This language is undecidable: suppose that E_{TM} is decidable; let R be the TM that decides it. Consider the TM R' designed as follows: on input $\langle M, w\rangle$, it first constructs a machine M_w where on x, M_w first checks whether $x = w$; if not, M_w rejects. Otherwise, M_w runs M on w and accepts if M accepts. Finally, R' simulates R on $\langle M_w\rangle$. Clearly, $L(R') = \text{A}_{\text{TM}}$, and since R' is a decider, this cannot be.

Consider the language

$$\text{REGULAR}_{\text{TM}} := \{\langle M\rangle : M \text{ is a TM and } L(M) \text{ is regular}\}.$$

This language is not decidable; suppose that it were, and R is its decider. We design S as follows: on input $\langle M, w\rangle$, S first constructs M' which works as follows: M' in input x checks if x has form $0^n 1^n$, and accepts if so. If x does not have this form, it runs M on w and accepts if M accepts. Finally, S runs R on $\langle M_2\rangle$. Note that $L(M')$ is either the nonregular language $\{0^n 1^n\}$ (if M rejects w) or the regular language $\{0, 1\}^*$ (if M accepts w).

8.5.7 *Rice's theorem*

It turns out that nontrivial properties of languages of Turing machines are undecidable. What do we mean by "nontrivial properties"? We mean, for example, the property of not accepting any strings, i.e., E_{TM}.

More formally, a *property* $\mathcal{P}$ is just a subset of $\{\langle M \rangle : M \text{ is a TM}\}$. We say that a property is nontrivial if $\mathcal{P} \neq \emptyset$ and $\overline{\mathcal{P}} \neq \emptyset$. Further, we require the following: given two TMs M_1 and M_2 such that $L(M_1) = L(M_2)$, then either both $\langle M_1 \rangle$ and $\langle M_2 \rangle$ are in $\mathcal{P}$ or both are not in $\mathcal{P}$. That is, whether $\langle M \rangle$ is in $\mathcal{P}$ depends only on the properties of the language of M, and not on, say, syntactic properties of the machine, such as the number of states.

Theorem 8.65 (Rice's). *Every nontrivial property is undecidable.*

8.5.8 *Post's Correspondence Problem*

Recall that the Myhill-Nerode Theorem (Section 8.3.8.2) provides a characterization of regular languages without mention of a model of computation. Post's problem does the same for undecidable languages; it provides an example of a concrete undecidable language without mention of Turing machines, or any other model of computation. This illustrates that undecidability is not a quirk of a particular model of computation, but an immutable property of certain languages.

An instance of the *Post's Correspondence Problem (PCP)* consists of two finite lists of strings over some alphabet Σ. The two lists must be of equal length:

$$A = w_1, w_2, \ldots, w_k$$
$$B = x_1, x_2, \ldots, x_k$$

For each i, the pair (w_i, x_i) is said to be a *corresponding pair*. We say that this instance of PCP has a solution if there is a sequence of one or more indices:

$$i_1, i_2, \ldots, i_m, \qquad m \geq 1,$$

where the indices can repeat, such that:

$$w_{i_1} w_{i_2} \ldots w_{i_m} = x_{i_1} x_{i_2} \ldots x_{i_m}.$$

The PCP is the following: given two lists (A, B) of equal length, does it have a solution? We can express PCP as a language:

$$L_{PCP} := \{\langle A, B \rangle | (A, B) \text{ instance of PCP with solution}\}.$$

For example, consider (A, B) given by:

$$A = 1, 10111, 10$$
$$B = 111, 10, 0$$

Then $i_1 = 2, i_2 = 1, i_3 = 1, i_4 = 3$ is a solution as:

$$\underbrace{10111}_{w_2} \underbrace{1}_{w_1} \underbrace{1}_{w_1} \underbrace{10}_{w_3} = \underbrace{10}_{x_2} \underbrace{111}_{x_1} \underbrace{111}_{x_1} \underbrace{0}_{x_3}.$$

Note that $i_1 = 2, i_2 = 1, i_3 = 1, i_4 = 3, i_5 = 2, i_6 = 1, i_7 = 1, i_8 = 3$ is another solution.

Problem 8.66. *Show that $A = 10, 011, 101$ and $B = 101, 11, 011$ does not have a solution.*

The *Modified Post's Correspondence Problem (MPCP)* has an additional requirement that the first pair in the solution must be the first pair of (A, B). So $i_1, i_2, \ldots, i_m$, $m \geq 0$, is a solution to the (A, B) instance of MPCP if:

$$w_1 w_{i_1} w_{i_2} \ldots w_{i_m} = x_1 x_{i_1} x_{i_2} \ldots x_{i_m}$$

We also say that $i_1, i_2, \ldots, i_r$ is a *partial solution* of (M)PCP if one of the following is the prefix of the other:

$$(w_1) w_{i_1} w_{i_2} \ldots w_{i_r} \qquad (x_1) x_{i_1} x_{i_2} \ldots x_{i_r}$$

In the case of MPCP, we further require that $i_1 = 1$.

With all these elements in place, we can now proceed to show that PCP is undecidable. We are going to do so in three steps: first, we show that if PCP is decidable, then so is MPCP. Second, we show that if MPCP is decidable, then so is A_{TM}. Third, since A_{TM} is *not* decidable, neither is (M)PCP.

Lemma 8.67. *If PCP is decidable then MPCP is decidable.*

Proof. We show that given an instance (A, B) of MPCP, we can construct an instance (A', B') of PCP such that:

$$(A, B) \text{ has solution} \iff (A', B') \text{ has solution}$$

Let (A, B) be an instance of MPCP over the alphabet Σ. Then (A', B') is an instance of PCP over the alphabet $\Sigma' = \Sigma \cup \{*, \$\}$, where $*, \$$ are new symbols.

If $A = w_1, w_2, w_3, \ldots, w_k$, then $A' = *\bar{w}_1*, \bar{w}_1*, \bar{w}_2*, \bar{w}_3*, \ldots, \bar{w}_k*, \$$.

If $B = x_1, x_2, x_3, \ldots, x_k$, then $B' = *\bar{x}_1, *\bar{x}_1, *\bar{x}_2, *\bar{x}_3, \ldots, *\bar{x}_k, *\$$, where if $x = a_1 a_2 a_3 \ldots a_n \in \Sigma^*$, then $\bar{x} = a_1 * a_2 * a_3 * \ldots * a_n$.

For example, if (A, B) is an instance if MPCP given as: $A = 1, 10111, 10$ and $B = 111, 10, 0$, then (A', B') is an instance of PCP given by the pair: $A' = *1*, 1*, 1*0*1*1*1*, 1*0*, \$$ and $B' = *1*1*1, *1*1*1, *1*0, *0, *\$$.

Problem 8.68 finishes the proof. $\square$

Problem 8.68. *Finish the proof of Lemma 8.5.8.*

Lemma 8.69. *If MPCP is decidable then* $\mathsf{A_{TM}}$ *is decidable.*

Proof. Given a pair (M, w) we construct an instance (A, B) of MPCP such that:

$$\text{TM } M \text{ accepts } w \iff (A, B) \text{ has a solution.}$$

The main idea is the following: the MPCP instance (A, B) simulates, in its partial solutions, the computation of M on w. That is, partial solutions will be of the form:

$$\#\alpha_1 \# \alpha_2 \# \alpha_3 \# \ldots$$

where α_1 is the initial config of M on w, and for all i, configuration α_i yields configuration α_{i+1}.

The partial solution from the B list will always be "one configuration ahead" of the A list; the A list will be allowed to "catch-up" only when M accepts w. For simplification, we assume that TMs do not print blank symbols (i.e., they do not print '$\square$'), so that the configurations are of the form $\alpha q \beta$ where $\alpha, \beta \in (\Gamma - \{\square\})^*$ and $q \in Q$.

Problem 8.70. *Show that TM that cannot print blank symbols are equivalent in power to those TM that can print them.*

Let M be a TM and $w \in \Sigma^*$; we construct an instance (A, B) of MPCP as follows:

(1) A: #

  B: #$q_0 w$#

(2) $A: a_1, a_2, \ldots, a_n, \#$

$B: a_1, a_2, \ldots, a_n, \#$

where the $a_i \in (\Gamma - \{\square\})^*$.

(3) To simulate a move of M, for all $q \in Q - \{q_{accept}\}$:

list A	list B	
qa	bp	if $\delta(q, a) = (p, b, \rightarrow)$
cqa	pcb	if $\delta(q, a) = (p, b, \leftarrow)$
$q\#$	$bp\#$	if $\delta(q, \square) = (p, b, \rightarrow)$
$cq\#$	$pcb\#$	if $\delta(q, \square) = (p, b, \leftarrow)$

(4) If the configuration at the end of B is accepting (i.e., of the form $\alpha q_{accept} \beta$), then we need to allow A to catch up with B. So, for all $a, b \in (\Gamma - \{\square\})^*$ we need the following corresponding pairs:

list A	list B
$a q_{accept} b$	q_{accept}
$a q_{accept}$	q_{accept}
$q_{accept} b$	q_{accept}

(5) Finally, after using 4 and 3 above, we end up with $x\#$ and $x\# q_{accept}\#$, where x is a long string. Thus we need $q_{accept}\#\#$ in A and $\#$ in B to complete the catching up.

$\square$

For example, consider the following TM M with states $\{q_1, q_2, q_3\}$ where q_1 abbreviates q_{init} and q_3 abbreviates q_{accept}, and where δ is given by the transition table:

	0	1	$\square$
q_1	$(q_2, 1, \rightarrow)$	$(q_2, 0, \leftarrow)$	$(q_2, 1, \leftarrow)$
q_2	$(q_3, 0, \leftarrow)$	$(q_1, 0, \rightarrow)$	$(q_2, 0, \rightarrow)$

From this M and input $w = 01$ we obtain the following MPCP problem:

Rule	list A	list B	Source
1	#	#$q_1$01#	
2	0	0	
	1	1	
	#	#	
3	$q_1$0	1q_2	$\delta(q_1,0)=(q_2,1,\rightarrow)$
	0$q_1$1	$q_2$00	$\delta(q_1,1)=(q_2,0,\leftarrow)$
	1$q_1$1	$q_2$10	$\delta(q_1,1)=(q_2,0,\leftarrow)$
	0q_1#	$q_2$01#	$\delta(q_1,B)=(q_2,1,\leftarrow)$
	1q_1#	$q_2$11#	$\delta(q_1,B)=(q_2,1,\leftarrow)$
	0$q_2$0	$q_3$00	$\delta(q_2,0)=(q_3,0,\leftarrow)$
	1$q_2$0	$q_3$10	$\delta(q_2,0)=(q_3,0,\leftarrow)$
	$q_2$1	0q_1	$\delta(q_2,1)=(q_1,0,\rightarrow)$
	q_2#	0q_2#	$\delta(q_2,B)=(q_2,0,\rightarrow)$

Rule	list A	list B	
4	0$q_3$0	q_3	
	0$q_3$1	q_3	
	1$q_3$0	q_3	
	1$q_3$1	q_3	
	0q_3	q_3	
	1q_3	q_3	
	$q_3$0	q_3	
	$q_3$1	q_3	
5	q_3##	#	

The TM M accepts the input $w = 01$ by the sequence of moves represented by the following chain of configurations:

$$q_1 01 \rightarrow 1q_2 1 \rightarrow 10q_1 \rightarrow 1q_2 01 \rightarrow q_3 101.$$

We examine the sequence of partial solutions that mimics this computation of M on w and eventually leads to a solution. We must start with the first pair (MPCP):

$$A: \quad \#$$
$$B: \quad \#q_1 01\#$$

The only way to extend this partial solution is with the corresponding pair $(q_1 0, 1q_2)$, so we obtain:

$$A: \quad \#q_1 0$$
$$B: \quad \#q_1 01\#1q_2$$

Now using copying pairs we obtain:

$$A: \quad \#q_1 01\#1$$
$$B: \quad \#q_1 01\#1q_2 1\#1$$

Next corresponding pair is $(q_2 1, 0q_1)$:

$$A: \quad \#q_1 01\#1q_2 1$$
$$B: \quad \#q_1 01\#1q_2 1\#10q_1$$

Now careful! We only copy the next two symbols to obtain:

$$A: \quad \#q_1 01 \#1 q_2 1 \#1$$
$$B: \quad \#q_1 01 \#1 q_2 1 \#10 q_1 \#1$$

because we need the $0q_1$ as the head now moves left, and use the next appropriate corresponding pair which is $(0q_1\#, q_2 01\#)$ and obtain:

$$A: \quad \#q_1 01 \#1 q_2 1 \#10 q_1 \#$$
$$B: \quad \#q_1 01 \#1 q_2 1 \#10 q_1 \#1 q_2 01 \#$$

We can now use another corresponding pair $(1q_2 0, q_3 10)$ right away to obtain:

$$A: \quad \#q_1 01 \#1 q_2 1 \#10 q_1 \#1 q_2 0$$
$$B: \quad \#q_1 01 \#1 q_2 1 \#10 q_1 \#1 q_2 01 \#q_3 10$$

and note that we have an accepting state! We use two copying pairs to get:

$$A: \quad \#q_1 01 \#1 q_2 1 \#10 q_1 \#1 q_2 01 \#$$
$$B: \quad \#q_1 01 \#1 q_2 1 \#10 q_1 \#1 q_2 01 \#q_3 101 \#$$

and we can now start using the rules in 4. to make A catch up with B:

$$A: \quad \ldots \#q_3 1$$
$$B: \quad \ldots \#q_3 101 \#q_3$$

and we copy three symbols:

$$A: \quad \ldots \#q_3 101 \#$$
$$B: \quad \ldots \#q_3 101 \#q_3 01 \#$$

And again catch up a little:

$$A: \quad \ldots \#q_3 101 \#q_3 0$$
$$B: \quad \ldots \#q_3 101 \#q_3 01 \#q_3$$

Copy two symbols:

$$A: \quad \ldots \#q_3 101 \#q_3 01 \#$$
$$B: \quad \ldots \#q_3 101 \#q_3 01 \#q_3 1 \#$$

and catch up:

$$A: \quad \ldots \#q_3 101 \#q_3 01 \#q_3 1$$
$$B: \quad \ldots \#q_3 101 \#q_3 01 \#q_3 1 \#q_3$$

and copy:

$$A: \quad \ldots \#q_3101\#q_301\#q_31\#$$
$$B: \quad \ldots \#q_3101\#q_301\#q_31\#q_3\#$$

And now end it all with the corresponding pair $(q_3\#\#, \#)$ given by rule 5. to get matching strings:

$$A: \quad \ldots \#q_3101\#q_301\#q_31\#q_3\#\#$$
$$B: \quad \ldots \#q_3101\#q_301\#q_31\#q_3\#\#$$

Thus, given an instance $\langle M, w \rangle$ of $\mathsf{A_{TM}}$, we construct an instance $(A, B)_{\langle M,w \rangle}$ of MPCP so that the following relationship holds:

$$M \text{ accepts } w \iff (A, B)_{\langle M,w \rangle} \text{ has a solution.} \tag{8.2}$$

In other words, we have reduced $\mathsf{A_{TM}}$ to MPCP, and our reduction is given by the (computable) function $f : \{0,1\}^* \longrightarrow \{0,1\}^*$ which is defined as follows: $f(\langle M, w \rangle) = \langle (A, B)_{\langle M,w \rangle} \rangle$. This shows that if MPCP is decidable so is $\mathsf{A_{TM}}$. To see that, suppose that MPCP is decidable; then, we have a decider for $\mathsf{A_{TM}}$: on input $\langle M, w \rangle$, our decider computes $x = f(\langle M, w \rangle)$ and runs the decider for MPCP on x. By (8.2) we know that a "yes" answer means that M accepts w.

8.5.9 *Undecidable properties of CFLs*

We can now use the fact that PCP is undecidable to show that a number of questions about CFLs are undecidable. Let (A, B) be an instance of the PCP, where $A = w_1, w_2, \ldots, w_k$ and $B = x_1, x_2, \ldots, x_k$. Let G_A and G_B be related CFGs given by:

$$A \longrightarrow w_1 A a_1 | w_2 A a_2 | \cdots | w_k A a_k | w_1 a_1 | w_2 a_2 | \cdots | w_k a_k$$
$$B \longrightarrow x_1 B a_1 | x_2 B a_2 | \cdots | x_k B a_k | x_1 a_1 | x_2 a_2 | \cdots | x_k a_k,$$

where $a_1, a_2, \ldots, a_k$ are *new* symbols not in the alphabet of (A, B).

Let $L_A = L(G_A)$ and $L_B = L(G_B)$, and so L_A and L_B consist of all the strings of the form:

$$w_{i_1} w_{i_2} \ldots w_{i_m} a_{i_m} \ldots a_{i_2} a_{i_1}$$
$$x_{i_1} x_{i_2} \ldots x_{i_m} a_{i_m} \ldots a_{i_2} a_{i_1},$$

respectively.

Theorem 8.71. *It is undecidable whether a CFG is ambiguous.*

Proof. Let G_{AB} be a CFG consisting of G_A, G_B, with the rule $S \longrightarrow A|B$ thrown in. Thus, G_{AB} is ambiguous $\Longleftrightarrow$ the PCP (A, B) has a solution. Note that the purpose of the new symbols a_i in G_A and G_B is to enforce that the corresponding pairs be in the same positions. $\qquad\square$

Theorem 8.72. *Suppose that G_1, G_2 are CFGs, and R is a regular expression, then the following are undecidable problems:*

(1) $L(G_1) \cap L(G_2) \overset{?}{=} \emptyset$

(2) $L(G_1) \overset{?}{=} L(G_2)$

(3) $L(G_1) \overset{?}{=} L(R)$

(4) $L(G_1) \overset{?}{=} T^*$

(5) $L(G_1) \overset{?}{\subseteq} L(G_2)$

(6) $L(R) \overset{?}{\subseteq} L(G_2)$

Proof. First we show that $\overline{L_A}$, where $L_A = L(G_A)$ defined above, is also a CFL; we show this by giving a PDA P. $\Gamma_P = \Sigma_A \cup \{a_1, a_2, \ldots, a_k\}$. As long as P sees a symbol in Σ_A it stores it on the stack. As soon as P sees a_i, it pops the stack to see if top of string is w_i^R. (i) if not, then accept no matter what comes next. (ii) if yes, there are two subcases: (iia) if stack is not yet empty, continue. (iib) if stack is empty, and the input is finished, reject. If after an a_i, P sees a symbol in Σ_A, it accepts.

Now we are ready to show that the six problems listed in the theorem are in fact undecidable:

(1) Let $G_1 = G_A$ and $G_2 = G_B$, then $L(G_1) \cap L(G_2) \neq \emptyset$ iff PCP (A, B) has a solution.

(2) Let G_1 be the CFG for $\overline{L_A} \cup \overline{L_B}$ (CFGs are closed under union). Let G_2 be the CFG for the regular language $(\Sigma \cup \{a_1, a_2, \ldots, a_k\})^*$. Note $L(G_1) = \overline{L_A} \cup \overline{L_B} = \overline{L_A \cap L_B}$ = everything but solutions to PCP (A, B).
$\therefore L(G_1) = L(G_2)$ iff (A, B) has no solution.

(3) Shown in 2., because $L(G_2)$ is a regular language.

(4) Again, shown in 2.

(5) Note that $A = B$ iff $A \subseteq B$ and $B \subseteq A$, so it follows from 2.

(6) By 3. and 5.

This shows that important properties of CFLs are undecidable. $\qquad\square$

8.6 Answers to selected problems

Problem 8.1. Σ_2^k is the set of unique strings of length k which can be constructed with Σ_2, i.e., a generic alphabet containing two symbols. A good example of Σ_2 is the standard binary alphabet, $\{0, 1\}$. In a string of length k on this alphabet, there are k symbols, each of which may be either 1 or 0; in other words, to construct a string of length k, k "choices" are made, each with two options. Thus there are 2^k possibilities. It can be shown very quickly that each of these possibilities is unique. Similarly, there are l^k unique words in Σ_l^k.

Next, we consider the set of strings over Σ_l, where no symbol can be repeated in any string. Let n be the length of such a string. Clearly it is simply a permutation of length n from the set Σ_l, without replacement, where $0 \leq n \leq l$. As such, the number of unique strings of length n is $\frac{l!}{(l-n)!}$. Thus, the total string count for lengths $n \in \{0, 1, 2, \ldots, l\}$ is $W(l) = \sum_{n=0}^{l} \frac{l!}{(l-n)!}$.

While this solution is correct, we can do better with a little analysis of our result. We start by factoring out $l!$.

$$W(l) = l! \cdot \sum_{n=0}^{l} \frac{1}{(l-n)!} = l! \cdot \sum_{n=0}^{l} \frac{1}{n!}$$

Recall that the Taylor expansion of e^x is $\sum_{n=0}^{\infty} \frac{x^n}{n!}$, so we can rewrite:

$$W(l) = l! \cdot \left(e - \sum_{n=(l+1)}^{\infty} \frac{1}{n!} \right) = l! \cdot \left(e - \left(\frac{1}{(l+1)!} + \frac{1}{(l+2)!} + \cdots \right) \right)$$

Next, we distribute:

$$W(n) = l! \cdot e - \left(\frac{1}{(l+1)} + \frac{1}{(l+1)(l+2)} + \cdots \right)$$

Consider the portion in parenthesis; it is clearly less than $(\frac{1}{l} + \frac{1}{l^2} + \cdots)$—a geometric series whose sum is $\frac{1}{(l-1)}$. Note that if $l > 2$, this sum is less than 1, so $W(l) > l! \cdot e - 1$. The sum is also positive, so $W(l) < l! \cdot e$. We have $l! \cdot e - 1 < W(l) < l! \cdot e$; this, combined with the fact that $W(l)$ is an integer, is enough to show that $W(l) = \lfloor l! \cdot e \rfloor$.

Problem 8.2. Consider a string S of the form $x01y$. After the last element of x has been "run", we are in one of the states q_0, q_1, q_2. Below we show that regardless of the state after x, we will be in state q_1 after the subsequent 01.

$$\delta(q_0, 0) = q_2 \text{ and } \delta(q_2, 1) = q_1$$

$$\delta(q_1, 0) = q_1 \text{ and } \delta(q_1, 1) = q_1$$

$$\delta(q_2, 0) = q_2 \text{ and } \delta(q_2, 1) = q_1$$

From here, each element a of y is either 0 or 1; in either case, $\delta(q_1, a) = q_1$, so after the 01 has been processed, we remain in state q_1 until the end of S. Since q_1 is a final state, S is accepted by A.

It remains to be seen that any string without a substring 01 is rejected by A. Consider such a string, S'. If it contains no 0's, then it is entirely composed of 1's. Moreover, we start in state q_0, and $\delta(q_0, 1) = q_0$, so the state is q_0 for the entirety of the string, and since q_0 is not a final state, S' is rejected. Similarly, if S' contains only one 0 and it is the final symbol, then S' looks like $1 \ldots 10$ with some arbitrary number of 1's in the gap. In this case we remain in state q_0 until the 0 at the end, so the ending state is q_2—which is not a final state either. If, on the other hand, S' contains at least one 0, not at the end of the string, then consider the first 0. There are no 1's after this first 0, as the first such 1 would necessarily be the end of a substring 01, which S' does not have. Thus, $S' = xy$ where x is a string of 1's (or the empty string) and y is a string of 0's. At the end of x, we are still in state q_0, as $\delta(q_0, 1) = q_0$ is still a fixed point. Then the first 0 in y results in $\delta(q_0, 0) = q_2$, and the remaining 0's do nothing because $\delta(q_2, 0) = q_2$ is also a fixed point. Thus, at the end of S', the state is q_2, which is not a final state; S' is rejected by A.

A much more efficient proof can be given via induction over the string's length—this is left to the reader.

Problem 8.3.

Problem 8.4.

Problem 8.5. For B_n, for each n, we want to build a (different) DFA D_n such that $L(D_n) = B_n$. Let D_n consist of states $Q = \{q_0, q_1, \ldots, q_{n-1}\}$ and let the transition function δ be defined by $\delta(q_i, 1) = q_{(i+1) \pmod n}$, and let $F = \{q_0\}$.

Problem 8.6. Let $Q = \{q_0, q_1, \ldots, q_{24}\}$, and define δ as follows:

$$\delta\left(q_i, \textcircled{1}\right) = q_{(i+1)} \pmod{25}$$
$$\delta\left(q_i, \textcircled{5}\right) = q_{(i+5)} \pmod{25}$$
$$\delta\left(q_i, \textcircled{10}\right) = q_{(i+10)} \pmod{25}$$
$$\delta\left(q_i, \textcircled{25}\right) = q_i$$

Finally, let $F = \{q_0\}$. This DFA will only accept multiples of 25. Of course, a vending machine needs to be able to deal with invalid inputs (say, arcade tokens or coins with unsupported values). Denote any invalid input as $\textcircled{I}$. Clearly,

$$\delta\left(q_i, \textcircled{I}\right) = q_i$$

Moreover, on such an input, δ should call an additional action to "spit out" the invalid coin.

Problem 8.7. Simply because ε could already be in L, and so if $\varepsilon \in L$ then $\varepsilon \in L^+$. On the other hand, remember the assumption that $\varepsilon \in \Sigma$, for any Σ.

Problem 8.9. The answer is $O(2^n)$. To see that note that the way to construct the DFA is as follows: a tree starting at q_0, branching on all the possible strings of n elements. Each leaf is a state q_w where $w \in \{0, 1\}^n$. The accepting leaves are those where w starts with 1. Suppose that we have the leaf q_{ax} (i.e., $w = ax$), then, $\delta(q_{ax}, b) = q_{xb}$. Note that it is much easier to design a DFA for L'_n, where L'_n is the set of strings where the n-th symbols from the *beginning* is 1.

Problem 8.13. For concatenation connect all the accepting states of the "first" DFA by ε-arrows to the starting state of the "second" DFA.

Problem 8.14. The base cases are as follows:

$$L(a) = \{a\}$$
$$L(\varepsilon) = \{\varepsilon\}$$
$$L(\emptyset) = \emptyset$$

Next, the induction rules:

$$L(E + F) = L(E) \cup L(F)$$
$$L(EF) = \{xy | x \in L(E) \wedge y \in L(F)\}$$
$$L(E^*) = \{x_0 x_1 \ldots x_n | \forall i (x_i \in L(E)) \wedge n \in \mathbb{N}\}$$

Problem 8.15. The set of binary strings without a substring 101 can be expressed:

$$0^*(1^*00(0^*))^*1^*0^*$$

The expression $(1^*00(0^*))^*$ denotes a concatenation of elements from the set of strings consisting of an arbitrary number of leading 1's, followed at least two 0's. The idea here is that every 1 (except for the last 1) is immediately followed either by another 1 or by at least two 0's, making the substring 101 impossible. The rest of the expression is just padding; the 0^* at the beginning denotes any leading 0's, and the 1^*0^* denotes any trailing substring of the form $11 \ldots 100 \ldots 0$.

Problem 8.17. We can intuitively construct a regular expression for all binary strings with substring 00—$(\varepsilon + 0 + 1)^*00(\varepsilon + 0 + 1)^*$, for instance. This method is useful in more complicated cases. Note that we need not compute R_{ij}^k for all k, i, j. The only final state is q_3, so $R = R_{13}^{(3)}$.

$$R_{13}^{(3)} = R_{13}^{(2)} + R_{13}^{(2)} \left(R_{33}^{(2)} \right)^* R_{33}^{(2)} \tag{8.3}$$

So we need to find $R_{13}^{(2)}$ and $R_{33}^{(2)}$.

$$R_{13}^{(2)} = R_{13}^{(1)} + R_{12}^{(1)} \left(R_{22}^{(1)} \right)^* R_{23}^{(1)} \tag{8.4}$$

$$R_{33}^{(2)} = R_{33}^{(1)} + R_{32}^{(1)} \left(R_{22}^{(1)} \right)^* R_{23}^{(1)} \tag{8.5}$$

So we must compute $R_{12}^{(1)}$, $R_{13}^{(1)}$, $R_{22}^{(1)}$, $R_{23}^{(1)}$, $R_{32}^{(1)}$, and $R_{33}^{(1)}$.

$$R_{12}^{(1)} = R_{12}^{(0)} + R_{11}^{(0)} \left(R_{11}^{(0)} \right)^* R_{12}^{(0)}$$
$$= 0 + (\varepsilon + 1)(\varepsilon + 1)^*0$$
$$= (\varepsilon + 1)^*0$$

Note that $(\varepsilon + 1)(\varepsilon + 1)^* = (\varepsilon + 1)^*$, because $\varepsilon \in L(\varepsilon + 1)$.

$$R_{13}^{(1)} = R_{13}^{(0)} + R_{11}^{(0)} \left(R_{11}^{(0)} \right)^* R_{13}^{(0)}$$
$$= \emptyset + (\varepsilon + 1)(\varepsilon + 1)^* \emptyset$$
$$= \emptyset$$

This last step is true because for any regular expression R, $R\emptyset = \emptyset R = \emptyset$.

$$R_{22}^{(1)} = R_{22}^{(0)} + R_{21}^{(0)} \left(R_{11}^{(0)} \right)^* R_{12}^{(0)}$$
$$= \varepsilon + 1(\varepsilon + 1)^*0$$
$$R_{23}^{(1)} = R_{23}^{(0)} + R_{21}^{(0)} \left(R_{11}^{(0)} \right)^* R_{13}^{(0)}$$
$$= 0 + 1(\varepsilon + 1)^*\emptyset$$
$$= 0$$
$$R_{32}^{(1)} = R_{32}^{(0)} + R_{31}^{(0)} \left(R_{11}^{(0)} \right)^* R_{13}^{(0)}$$
$$= \emptyset + \emptyset(\varepsilon + 1)^*0$$
$$= \emptyset$$

There are many shortcuts which can be taken with the right observations. For instance, $\delta(q_3, a) = q_3$ for all a, so it is impossible to leave state q_3. If $j \neq 3$ then $R_{3j}^{(n)} = \emptyset$.

$$R_{33}^{(1)} = R_{33}^{(0)} + R_{31}^{(0)} \left(R_{11}^{(0)} \right)^* R_{13}^{(0)}$$
$$= \varepsilon + 0 + 1 + \emptyset(\ldots)^* \ldots$$
$$= \varepsilon + 0 + 1$$

We can now find $R_{13}^{(2)}$ and $R_{33}^{(2)}$ with equations 8.4 and 8.5.

$$R_{13}^{(2)} = R_{13}^{(1)} + R_{12}^{(1)} \left(R_{22}^{(1)} \right)^* R_{23}^{(1)}$$
$$= \emptyset + (\varepsilon + 1)^*0(\varepsilon + 1(\varepsilon + 1)^*0)^*0$$
$$= (\varepsilon + 1)^*0(\varepsilon + 1(\varepsilon + 1)^*0)^*0$$
$$R_{33}^{(2)} = R_{33}^{(1)} + R_{32}^{(1)} \left(R_{22}^{(1)} \right)^* R_{23}^{(1)}$$
$$= \varepsilon + 0 + 1 + \emptyset(\ldots)^* \ldots$$
$$= \varepsilon + 0 + 1$$

Finally, we can use equation 8.3 to find $R_{13}^{(3)} = R$.

$$R_{13}^{(3)} = R_{13}^{(2)} + R_{13}^{(2)} \left(R_{33}^{(2)} \right)^* R_{33}^{(2)}$$
$$= (\varepsilon + 1)^*0(\varepsilon + 1(\varepsilon + 1)^*0)^*0$$
$$\quad + (\varepsilon + 1)^*0(\varepsilon + 1(\varepsilon + 1)^*0)^*0(\varepsilon + 0 + 1)^*(\varepsilon + 0 + 1)$$
$$= (\varepsilon + 1)^*0(\varepsilon + 1(\varepsilon + 1)^*0)^*0(\varepsilon + 0 + 1)^*$$

Of course, this expression is not simplified; the laws in table 8.3.4 can improve it. The result should not contain ε.

Problem 8.18. Union: $L = L(R)$ and $M = L(S)$, so $L \cup M = L(R + S)$. Complementation: $L = L(A)$, so $L^c = L(A')$, where A' is the DFA obtained from A as follows: $F_{A'} = Q - F_A$. Intersection: $L \cap M = \overline{\overline{L} \cup \overline{M}}$. Reversal: Given a RE E, define E^R by structural induction. The only trick is that $(E_1 E_2)^R = E_2^R E_1^R$. Homomorphism: given a RE E, define $h(E)$ suitably.

Problem 8.19. For i note that we require $O(n^3)$ steps for computing the ε closures of all the states, and there are 2^n states. For iii note that there are n^3 expressions $R_{ij}^{(k)}$, and at each stage the size quadruples (as we need four stage $(k-1)$ expressions to build one for stage k). iv the trick here is to use an efficient parsing method for the RE; $O(n)$ methods exist

Problem 8.20. For i use the automaton representation: Compute the set of reachable states from q_0. If at least one accepting state is reachable, then it is not empty. What if only the RE representation is given? For ii translate any representation to a DFA, and run the string on the DFA. For iii use equivalence and minimization of automata.

Problem 8.21. Here we present a generic proof for the "natural algorithm" that you should have designed for filling out the table. We use an argument by contradiction with the Least Number Principle (LPN). Let $\{p, q\}$ be a distinguishable pair, for which the algorithm left the corresponding square empty, and furthermore, of all such "bad" pairs $\{p, q\}$ has a shortest distinguishing string w. Let $w = a_1 a_2 \ldots a_n$, $\hat{\delta}(p, w)$ is accepting while $\hat{\delta}(q, w)$ is not. First, $w \neq \varepsilon$, as then p, q would have been found to be distinguishable in the basis case of the algorithm. Let $r = \delta(p, a_1)$ and $s = \delta(q, a_1)$. Then, $\{r, s\}$ are distinguished by $w' = a_2 a_3 \ldots a_n$, and since $|w'| < |w|$, they were found out by the algorithm. But then $\{p, q\}$ would have been found in the next stage.

Problem 8.22. Consider a DFA A on which we run the above procedure to obtain M. Suppose that there exists an N such that $L(N) = L(M) = L(A)$, and N has fewer states than M. Run the Table Filling Algorithm on M, N together (renaming the states, so they don't have states in common). Since $L(M) = L(N)$ their initial states are indistinguishable. Thus, each state in M is indistinguishable from at least one state in N. But then, two states of M are indistinguishable from the same state of N ...

Problem 8.25. Suppose it is. By PL $\exists p$ such that $|w| \geq p \implies w = xyz$ where $|xy| \leq p$ and $y \neq \varepsilon$. Consider $s = 0^p 1^p = xyz$. Since $|xy| \leq p$, $y \neq \varepsilon$, clearly $y = 0^j$, $j > 0$. And $xy^2 z = 0^{p+j} 1^p \in L$, which is a contradiction.

Problem 8.26. Suppose it is. By PL $\exists n \ldots$ Consider some prime $p \geq n+2$. Let $1^p = xyz$, $|y| = m > 0$. So $|xz| = p - m$. Consider $xy^{(p-m)}z$ which must be in L. But $|xy^{(p-m)}z| = |xz| + |y|(p-m) = (p-m) + m(p-m) = (p-m)(1+m)$. Now $1+m > 1$ since $y \neq \varepsilon$, and $p - m > 1$ since $p \geq n+2$ and $m = |y| \leq |xy| \leq n$. So the length of $xy^{(p-m)}z$ is not prime, and hence it cannot be in L — contradiction.

Problem 8.27. In order to show that $\equiv_L$ is an equivalence relation, we need to show that it is reflexive, symmetric and transitive. It is clearly reflexive; $xz \in L \iff xz \in L$ is true regardless of the context, so $x \equiv_L x$. Its symmetry and transitivity follow directly from symmetric and transitive nature of ' $\iff$ '.

Problem 8.29. We assign weights to the symbols in $\mathcal{V}$; any predicate symbol (i.e. function or relation symbol) of arity n has weight $n - 1$. The weight of a string $w = w_1 w_2 \ldots w_n$ is equal to the sum of its symbols. We make the following claims:

(1) Every term has weight -1
(2) Every proper initial segment weighs at least 0

Note: a proper initial segment is a string which is not a term, but can be extended to a term by concatenating extra symbol(s) on the right.

Base case: for 0-ary symbols, this is clearly true; they weigh -1, and the only proper initial segment is the empty string ε, which has weight 0.

This can be expanded, by structural induction, to include all terms. Consider the term $T = ft_1 \ldots t_n$, where f is an n-ary predicate symbol. f has weight $n - 1$, and each term t_i weighs -1, so T's net weight is $(n-1) + n \cdot (-1)$, or -1. Moreover, any proper initial segment of T consists of f (weight $n - 1$), the first i terms t_i (net weight $-i$) with $i < n$, and possibly a proper initial segment of t_{i+1}, whose weight is non-negative. Thus, the net weight of such a segment is at least $(n - 1) - i \geq 0$.

Let $T_1 = f_1 t_{11} \ldots t_{1n}$ and $T_2 = f_2 t_{21} \ldots t_{2m}$, and assume $T_1 \overset{\text{syn}}{=} T_2$ ($A \overset{\text{syn}}{=} B$ denotes that A and B are identical strings). Obviously, $f_1 = f_2 = f$; they are identical, single symbols, so they must represent the same function or relation. As such, $n = m$. Moreover, t_{11} and t_{21} start on the same index, and neither can be an initial segment of the other, so they must also end on the same index. This argument can be extended inductively over all of the remaining input terms for f. T_1 and T_2 represent the result of identical input terms in an identical order on the same function or relation.

Problem 8.30. Let $\mathbf{t}$ be $\mathbf{f}t_1 \ldots t_n$ for some n-ary function symbol $\mathbf{f}$ and terms $\mathbf{t}_i$. Then $\mathbf{t}^{\mathcal{A}} = \mathbf{f}^{\mathcal{A}}(\mathbf{t}_1^{\mathcal{A}}, \ldots, \mathbf{t}_n^{\mathcal{A}})$.

Similarly, $(\mathbf{R}t_1 \ldots t_n)^A$ is identical to $(\mathbf{t}_1^A, \ldots, \mathbf{t}_n^A) \in \mathbf{R}^A$. The difference is in the interpretation: a term with a leading relation symbol is either True or False, depending on whether the corresponding ordered sequence of terms is an element of the interpreted relation, while a term with a leading function symbol is simply the resulting element of A.

Problem 8.31. Suppose automaton $\mathcal{A}$ in finite universe A accepts $L' = \{\mathbf{a}_n \ldots \mathbf{a}_2 \mathbf{a}_1 \mathbf{c} : a_1 a_2 \ldots a_n \in L\}$. Clearly, $(\mathbf{a}_n \ldots \mathbf{a}_1 \mathbf{c})^A = \mathbf{a}_n^A(\mathbf{a}_{n-1}^A(\cdots(\mathbf{a}_1^A(\mathbf{c}^A))\cdots)) \in A$; in other words, $L(\mathcal{A}) \subseteq A$. We define an NFA for L: the initial state is $c = q_0$, and the remaining states $\{q_1, q_2, \ldots, q_m\}$ are the remaining elements of A—$|A|$ is finite so this NFA has finitely many states. We define the transition function as follows: $\delta(q_i, a) = \mathbf{a}^A(q_i)$. Finally, the accepting states F are simply those accepted by $\mathcal{A}$. L is recognized by an NFA, so it must be regular.

Given a regular language L, let D be the smallest DFA for L. We know index(L) and Q_D are finite and equal from theorem 8.28; let $A = Q_D$. We assign to q_0 the label $\mathbf{c}$ (i.e., $\mathbf{c}^A = q_0$) and choose the following interpretation: $\mathbf{a}^A(\mathbf{t}^A) = \delta(\mathbf{t}^A, a)$. Finally, we let $\mathbf{R}^A = F_D$. We have constructed an automaton which accepts L'.

Problem 8.32. The "method" of acceptance for automatons corresponds directly with intersections, unions, and complementation. Given automatons $\mathcal{A}$ and $\mathcal{B}$ with acceptance relations $\mathbf{R}^A$ and $\mathbf{R}^B$ and universes A and B, an automaton which accepts $L(\mathcal{A}) \cup L(\mathcal{B})$ is easily given with universe $A \cup B$ and relation $\mathbf{R}^A \cup \mathbf{R}^B$. The only nuance is that some symbols in $\mathcal{V}_A$ or $\mathcal{V}_B$ may need to be replaced with new symbols (with the same meaning as the symbols they are replacing) in order to avoid a double interpretation of a given symbol. Intersections can be handled in much the same way. Closure under complementation comes from the finite nature of A; $\mathbf{R}^A$ must contain finitely many elements of $\mathcal{P}(A)$, and it can simply be replaced with $\mathcal{P}(A) - \mathbf{R}^A$ to create an automaton for the complement of $L(\mathcal{A})$.

Problem 8.35. $P = \{Q, \Sigma, \Gamma, \delta, q_0, F\}$ where:

$$Q = \{q_0, q_1, q_2\}$$
$$\Sigma = \Gamma = \{1, 0\}$$
$$F = \{q_2\}$$

and the transition function δ is defined below. Note that ε as an element of Σ^* denotes ε-padding, while ε as an output of the stack (i.e., $\delta(q_n, x, \varepsilon)$)

denotes that the stack is empty.

$$\delta(q_0, 0, \varepsilon) = \{(q_0, 0)\}$$
$$\delta(q_0, 1, \varepsilon) = \{(q_0, 1)\}$$
$$\delta(q_0, \varepsilon, \varepsilon) = \{(q_2, \varepsilon)\}$$
$$\delta(q_0, 0, 1) = \{(q_0, 01)\}$$
$$\delta(q_0, 1, 0) = \{q_0, 10)\}$$
$$\delta(q_0, 0, 0) = \{(q_0, 00), (q_1, \varepsilon)\}$$
$$\delta(q_0, 1, 1) = \{(q_0, 11), (q_1, \varepsilon)\}$$
$$\delta(q_1, 1, 1) = \delta(q_1, 0, 0) = \{(q_1, \varepsilon)\}$$
$$\delta(q_1, \varepsilon, \varepsilon) = \{q_2, \varepsilon\}$$

Note that any undefined transitions are mapped to the implied "trash state". In the diagram below, an arrow from q_i to q_j with the label $a, b \to c$ means that $(q_j, c) \in \delta(q_i, a, b)$.

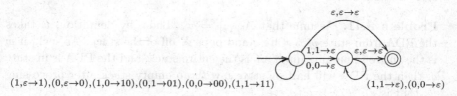

$(1, \varepsilon \to 1), (0, \varepsilon \to 0), (1, 0 \to 10), (0, 1 \to 01), (0, 0 \to 00), (1, 1 \to 11)$ 　　　　　 $(1, 1 \to \varepsilon), (0, 0 \to \varepsilon)$

Problem 8.37. Assume $(q, x, \alpha) \overset{*}{\Rightarrow} (p, y, \beta)$. We prove that $(q, x, \alpha\gamma) \overset{*}{\Rightarrow} (p, y, \beta\gamma)$ by induction on the number of steps.

Proof. Base case: $(q, x, \alpha) \to (p, y, \beta)$. Then $x = ay$ for some a such that $(p, b) \in \delta(q, a, \alpha_1)$ and $b\alpha_2\alpha_3 \cdots = \beta$. As such, $xw = ayw$ for any w, and $b\alpha_1\alpha_3 \ldots \gamma = \beta\gamma$. Thus, $(q, xw, \alpha\gamma) \to (q, xw, \beta\gamma)$.

Induction step: If $(q, x, \alpha) \overset{*}{\Rightarrow} (p, y, \beta)$ in n steps, than there is some tuple (o, z, σ) such that $(q, x, \alpha) \overset{*}{\Rightarrow} (o, z, \sigma)$ in $n - 1$ steps and $(o, z, \sigma) \to (p, y, \beta)$. The induction hypothesis grants that $(q, x, \alpha\gamma) \overset{*}{\Rightarrow} (o, z, \sigma\gamma)$, and another application of the base case grants that $(o, z, \sigma\gamma) \to (p, y, \beta\gamma)$. Thus, $(q, x, \alpha\gamma) \overset{*}{\Rightarrow} (p, y, \beta\gamma)$. □

Problem 8.39. Let P be a PDA which accepts by final state. We will modify P to accept the same language by empty stack. Let q_1 be P's initial state. For every a such that $\delta(q_1, a, \varepsilon) = \{(q_{i_1}, \beta_{i_1}), \ldots\}$ replace this transition with with $\delta(q_1, a, \varepsilon) = \{(q_{i_1}, \beta_{i_1}\$) \ldots\}$. For every accepting state q_f in P and every $s \in \Gamma_P \cup \{\$\}$ such that $\delta(q_f, \varepsilon, s)$ is empty, let $\delta(q_f, \varepsilon, s) = \{(q_f, \varepsilon)\}$. Clearly, if we run out of inputs on an accepting state, this modification allows P to "empty the stack" without leaving, resulting in acceptance by empty stack. For every rejecting state q_r and every $a \in \Sigma$, if $\delta(q_r, a, \varepsilon) = \{(q_{j_1}, \beta_{j_1}), \dots\}$ is defined, replace this definition with $\delta(q_r, a, \$) = \{(q_{j_1}, \beta_{j_1}\$)\}$; otherwise, leave $\delta(q_r, a, \$)$ undefined, so the stack cannot empty on a rejecting state. This altered PDA accepts $L(P)$ by empty stack.

Next, let P be a PDA which accepts by empty stack, and let q_1 be the initial state. For all a such that $\delta(q_1, a, \varepsilon)$ is defined to be some set of configurations $\{(q_{j_1}, \beta_{j_1}) \dots\}$, remove this transition and in its place let $\delta(q_1, a, \varepsilon) = \{(q_{j_1}, \beta_{j_1}\$) \dots\}$. Add a singular accepting state q_f, and for every state q_n, let $\delta(q_n, \varepsilon, \$) = \{(q_f, \varepsilon)\}$. Any input which would have been accepted by empty stack in the original P "lands" on q_f by construction, and moreover there is no other way to reach q_f (we just defined every transition to it) so no inputs are accepted which would have been rejected by P's initial definition. Thus, this modified PDA accepts the same language as P by final state.

Problem 8.41. Assume that $A_{[qXp]} \stackrel{*}{\Rightarrow} w$. Then, by definition, w takes the PDA from state p to state q and pops X off of the stack. As such, if w is the entire remaining input, X is the entire stack, and the PDA is in state q, then the PDA will halt on state p with an empty stack after processing w; that is, $(q, w, X) \stackrel{*}{\Rightarrow} (p, \varepsilon, \varepsilon)$.

Next, assume that $(q, w, X) \stackrel{*}{\Rightarrow} (p, \varepsilon, \varepsilon)$. Then w takes the PDA from state p to state q, and in the process it pops the entirety of X off of the stack; by definition, $A_{[qXp]} \stackrel{*}{\Rightarrow} w$. Thus, $\left(A_{[qXp]} \stackrel{*}{\Rightarrow} w\right) \iff \left((q, w, X) \stackrel{*}{\Rightarrow} (p, \varepsilon, \varepsilon)\right)$.

Problem 8.48. Let G be a CFG in CNF, and assume $w \in L(G)$, where $w = a_1 a_2 \dots a_n$. Clearly, for every terminal $a_l \neq \varepsilon$ in w, there must be a variable X_{i_l} such that $X_{i_l} \to \alpha a_l \beta$. Since G is in CNF and $a_l \neq \varepsilon$, it must be true that $\alpha = \beta = \varepsilon$, so $X_{i_l} \to a_l$ is a rule. Therefore, for all $i \in [1, n]$, (i, i) will be populated with a variable in the first for-loop.

But more can be gained from CNF; every rule is either of the form $A \to BC$ or $A \to a$; that is, every rule maps a variable either to a terminal or to two concatenated variables. Thus, if $S \stackrel{*}{\Rightarrow} a_1 a_2 \dots a_n$, then clearly $S \stackrel{*}{\Rightarrow} X_{i_1} X_{i_2} \dots X_{i_n}$, where $X_{i_l} \to a_l$ is a rule for all l.

Let us more closely examine the statement $S \stackrel{*}{\Rightarrow} X_{i_1} X_{i_2} \dots X_{i_n}$; we know that, in terms of variable introduction, the only available rules are of the form $S \to AB$, so the first '$\to$' from S in the derivation of $X_{i_1} X_{i_2} \dots X_{i_n}$ must be in this form. Clearly, there is an integer o such that $A \overset{*}{\Rightarrow} X_{i_1} X_{i_2} \ldots X_{i_o}$ and $B \overset{*}{\Rightarrow} X_{i_{o+1}} X_{i_{o+2}} \ldots X_{i_n}$. As such, if $(1, o)$ and $(o + 1, n)$ are populated with A and B then $(1, n)$ will subsequently be given S. We can continue this analysis recursively to show that A and B will be put in their correct places, and so S will eventually be in $(1, n)$ and w will be accepted. The only nuance here is the order in which the i, j pairs are checked; as figure 8.12 states, we start with the main diagonal and work toward the "top right", one diagonal at a time.

How do we know that no new words are accepted? That is, how can we be sure that there is no $w \notin L(G)$ which will be accepted by the CYK algorithm?

Problem 8.51. Let L be a CFL with grammar G for $L - \{\varepsilon\}$. Assume that G is in CNF, and furthermore that it has no nullable variables (see claim 8.46). Let G have n variables. Consider $s \in L(G)$ such that $|s| \geq 2^n$. Then s must have a path in the parse tree of length at least $n + 2$—a path of length $n + 1$ is necessary to reach a string of 2^n variables due to CNF, and an additional step is required to map these variables to terminals. As such, there is a path in the parse tree containing $n + 1$ variables; there are only n variables so at least one is repeated. That is, there is a variable R such that $R \overset{*}{\Rightarrow} vRy$ for $v, y \in \Sigma^*$; moreover, there is necessarily such a variable that this happens in at most n steps, so the result has length of at most 2^n. Due to the nature of variable to variable production in CNF and the absence of nullable variables, $|vy| > 0$. Since $R \overset{*}{\Rightarrow} vRy$, it is also true that $R \overset{*}{\Rightarrow} vvRyy$; we can keep "expanding" R in this way to get any (equal) number of repeated vs and ys. Finally, $R \overset{*}{\Rightarrow} x$ for some string of terminals x, finishing the proof. Note that u and z in the lemma are the (possibly empty) strings from the initial $S \overset{*}{\Rightarrow} uRz$ to reach the first R, where S is the starting variable. Thus, we have $S \overset{*}{\Rightarrow} uv^i xy^i z$ where $|vy| > 0$ and $|vxy| \leq 2^n$.

Problem 8.52. Assume, for contradiction, that $L = \{0^n 1^n 2^n | n \geq 1\}$ is a CFL. Let p be the pumping length for L. Consider $s = 0^p 1^p 2^p$. By lemma 8.50, s must be $uvxyz$... If v or y contains more than one unique terminal, concatenating it more than once creates a string which cannot be a substring of any element of L; for instance, if $v = 01$, then $v^2 = 0101$ which cannot appear in any $w \in L$. But if v and y are each concatenations of a single terminal, then only two of the three terminals gain an increase in length in their respective substrings. For instance, if $v = 11$ and $y = 22$, then $uv^2 xy^2 z = 0^p 1^{p+2} 2^{p+2} \notin L$. So, regardless of the composition of v

and y, they fail to meet the conditions of the pumping lemma.

Problem 8.53. Let L be a CFL and R a regular language, both on alphabet Σ. There is a PDA P for L, and a DFA D for R, both accepting by final state. We denote with d_i indexed states in D, and with p_j indexed states in P. For each state d_i in D, we create a PDA P_i which is a copy of P with two key differences: the final states in P_i are only final if d_i is a final state in D, and there are no transitions yet (so we've only really copied the states). We denote with q_{ij} the state in P_j which corresponds to d_i in D. Finally we define the transitions as follows: $(q_{kl}, t) \in \delta(q_{ij}, a, s)$ iff $\delta_D(d_i, a) = d_k$ and $(p_l, t) \in \delta_P(p_j, a, s)$. Note that by construction, q_{ij} is an accepting state iff d_i is in F_D and p_j is in F_P. This PDA, as such, accepts w iff $w \in L \wedge w \in R$. Thus, $L \cap R$ is accepted by a PDA, so it must be a CFL.

Problem 8.54. Let L be a CFL on Σ, represented by CFG G with terminals T. Note that $T = \Sigma$, assuming every element of Σ is reachable, and otherwise we can simply remove those that are unreachable. For each $a \in T$, we have a CFL L_a and a corresponding CFG $G_a = \{V_a, T_a, P_a, S_a\}$. We can assume without loss of generality that $V_a \cap V_b = \emptyset$ for all $a, b \in T$ such that $a \neq b$, because new variables can be introduced at will. In G, we can simply replace each terminal a in all productions with S_a, and add all productions in P_a. We have created a CFG for $s(L)$, so it must be a CFL.

Problem 8.55. We will design a TM M such that $L(M)$ is the language of binary palindromes. We have 8 states: $Q = \{q_0, q_1, q_2, q_3, q_4, q_5, q_{accept}, q_{reject}\}$, where q_0 is the initial state. We define δ as follows:

$$\delta(q_0, 1) = (q_1, \square, \rightarrow) \qquad \delta(q_0, 0) = (q_2, \square, \rightarrow) \qquad \delta(q_0, \square) = q_{accept}$$
$$\delta(q_1, 1) = (q_1, 1, \rightarrow) \qquad \delta(q_1, 0) = (q_1, 0, \rightarrow) \qquad \delta(q_1, \square) = (q_3, \square, \leftarrow)$$
$$\delta(q_2, 1) = (q_2, 1, \rightarrow) \qquad \delta(q_2, 0) = (q_2, 0, \rightarrow) \qquad \delta(q_2, \square) = (q_4, \square, \leftarrow)$$
$$\delta(q_3, 1) = (q_5, \square, \leftarrow) \qquad \delta(q_3, 0) = q_{reject} \qquad \delta(q_3, \square) = q_{accept}$$
$$\delta(q_4, 1) = q_{reject} \qquad \delta(q_4, 0) = (q_5, \square, \leftarrow) \qquad \delta(q_4, \square) = q_{accept}$$
$$\delta(q_5, 1) = (q_5, 1, \leftarrow) \qquad \delta(q_5, 0) = (q_5, 0, \leftarrow) \qquad \delta(q_5, \square) = (q_0, \square, \rightarrow)$$

Assume the input starts with 1. Then M will transition from q_0 to q_1 while rewriting this 1 as a blank space, and remain in q_1 going right until it hits the first blank space (just past the end of the input). At this space, it will go left (to the current right-most non-blank space) and into q_3. If this right-most input is a 1 (i.e., if it matches the 1 on the left), it will replace this 1 with a $\square$, transition to q_5 and keep going left until hitting the blank, at which point it will restart this process. If, on the other hand, it encounters a 0 here, then the input starts with 1 and ends with 0, so it is not a palindrome, and is rejected. Finally, if this value is $\square$, then every input has been written over with $\square$, indicating that the input was a palindrome and causing it to be accepted.

8.7 Notes

Regarding Babbages *Difference Engine* presented in the introduction of this chapter, students of business informatics might be interested to know that the ultimate failure of Babbage's undertaking was due to his lack of business acumen; see pp. 563–570, [Johnson (1991)].

The material in this chapter draws on the magnificent introduction to the theory of computation by [Sipser (2006)]. In particular, the proof of Theorem 8.65 can be founds in the solution to exercise 5.28 on page 215 of [Sipser (2006)], and Theorem 8.64 is Theorem 3.21 in [Sipser (2006)].

For further readings the reader is also directed to [Kozen (2006)]. In particular, Section 8.3.9 is based on pg. 109 in [Kozen (2006)].

The historical material in the first paragraph of Section 8.4, comes from Andrzej Ehrenfeucht's lectures at the University of Colorado at Boulder, in the Winter 2008. In 1971, Ehrenfeucht was a founding member of the Department of Computer Science at the University of Colorado. He formulated the Ehrenfeucht-Fraïssé game, using the back-and-forth method given by Roland Fraïssé in his thesis. The Ehrenfeucht-Mycielski sequence is also named after him. Two of his students, Eugene Myers and David Haussler, were prominent contributors to the sequencing of the human genome.

The regular language operations ix and x in Section 8.3.5 come from Problem 1.40 in [Sipser (2006)]. The material on the Myhill-Nerode Theorem, Section 8.3.8.2, is inspired by [Sipser (2006)][Exr. 1.51 & 1.52].

Context free grammars are the foundations of parsers. There are many tools that implement the ideas mentioned in this section; for example, `Lex`, `Yacc`, `Flex`, `Bison`, and others. you may read more about them here: `http://dinosaur.compilertools.net`.

Section 8.4.3 is based on §7.1 in [Hopcroft *et al.* (2007)].

In Section 8.2 we discuss ur-concepts such as symbols and words. An intriguing field that examines such objects is Semiotics, the study of signs and symbols and their use or interpretation. Since long ago "markings" have been used to store and process information. About 8,000 years ago, humans were using symbols to represent words and concepts. True forms of writing developed over the next few thousand years, and of special importance are cylinder seals. These were rolled across wet clay tablets to produce raised designs. Many museums have cylinder seals in lapis lazuli[3], belonging to the Assyrian culture, found in Babylon, Iraq, estimated to be 4,100–3,600 years old. The raised designs were cuneiform symbols that stood for concepts and later for sounds and syllables.

The reader is encouraged to visit, if only online, artifacts on display at the *Smithsonian Museum of Natural History*, Washington D.C. There one can find an engraved ocher[4] plaque with primitive markings, from Blombos Cave, South Africa, estimated to be 77,000–75,000 years old. Also, the *Ishango bone*, from the Congo, estimated to be 25,000–20,000 years old, which is a leg bone from a baboon, with three rows of tally marks, to *add* or *multiply* (archaeologists are not certain which). And finally, a reindeer antler with tally marks, from La Madeleine, France, estimated to be 17,000–11,500 years old.

In typesetting, the different shape styles of the English alphabet are called *fonts*. PostScript fonts are outline font specifications developed by Adobe Systems for professional digital typesetting, which uses PostScript file format to encode font information. Outline fonts (or vector fonts) are collections of vector images, i.e., a set of lines and curves to define the border of glyphs.

Algebraically, we can say that Σ^*, together with the concatenation operator $\cdot$, is a *monoid*, where $\cdot$ is an associative operation, and ε is the identity element. This is one of many points of contact between strings, and the beautiful area of Algebra known as *Group Theory* (see Section 9.2.3).

---

[3]Lapis lazuli is a rare semi-precious stone that has been prized since antiquity for its intense blue color.

[4]*Ocher* is an earthy pigment containing ferric oxide, typically with clay, varying from light yellow to brown or red.

Chapter 9

Mathematical Foundations

> And out of mathematical reasoning there arises the *true* philosophical question, the question that no amount of biology could ever solve: namely, what is mathematics *about*? What in the world *are* numbers, sets, and transfinite cardinals?
>
> Sir Roger Scruton [Scruton (2014)], pg. 6

9.1 Induction and Invariance

9.1.1 *Induction*

Let $\mathbb{N} = \{0, 1, 2, \ldots\}$ be the set of natural numbers. Suppose that S is a subset of $\mathbb{N}$ with the following two properties: first $0 \in S$, and second, whenever $n \in S$, then $n + 1 \in S$ as well. Then, invoking the *Induction Principle (IP)* we can conclude that $S = \mathbb{N}$.

We shall use the IP with a more convenient notation; let P be a property of natural numbers, in other words, P is a unary relation such that $\mathrm{P}(i)$ is either true or false. The relation P may be identified with a set S_{P} in the obvious way, i.e., $i \in S_{\mathrm{P}}$ iff $\mathrm{P}(i)$ is true. For example, if P is the property of being prime, then $\mathrm{P}(2)$ and $\mathrm{P}(3)$ are true, but $\mathrm{P}(6)$ is false, and $S_{\mathrm{P}} = \{2, 3, 5, 7, 11, \ldots\}$. Using this notation the IP may be stated as:

$$[\mathrm{P}(0) \wedge \forall n(\mathrm{P}(n) \rightarrow \mathrm{P}(n+1))] \rightarrow \forall m \mathrm{P}(m), \qquad (9.1)$$

for any (unary) relation P over $\mathbb{N}$. In practice, we use (9.1) as follows: first we prove that P(0) holds (this is the *basis case*). Then we show that $\forall n(P(n) \to P(n+1))$ (this is the *induction step*). Finally, using (9.1) and *modus ponens*, we conclude that $\forall m P(m)$.

As an example, let P be the assertion "the sum of the first i odd numbers equals i^2." We follow the convention that the sum of an empty set of numbers is zero; thus P(0) holds as the set of the first zero odd numbers is an empty set. P(1) is true as $1 = 1^2$, and P(3) is also true as $1 + 3 + 5 = 9 = 3^2$. We want to show that in fact $\forall m P(m)$ i.e., P is always true, and so $S_P = \mathbb{N}$.

Notice that $S_P = \mathbb{N}$ does not mean that all numbers are odd—an obviously false assertion. We are using the natural numbers to *index* odd numbers, i.e., $o_1 = 1, o_2 = 3, o_3 = 5, o_4 = 7, \ldots$, and our induction is over this indexing (where o_i is the i-th odd number, i.e., $o_i = 2i - 1$). That is, we are proving that for all $i \in \mathbb{N}$, $o_1 + o_2 + o_3 + \cdots + o_i = i^2$; our assertion $P(i)$ is precisely the statement "$o_1 + o_2 + o_3 + \cdots + o_i = i^2$."

We now use induction: the basis case is P(0) and we already showed that it holds. Suppose now that the assertion holds for n, i.e., the sum of the first n odd numbers is n^2, i.e., $1 + 3 + 5 + \cdots + (2n - 1) = n^2$ (this is our *inductive hypothesis* or *inductive assumption*). Consider the sum of the first $(n + 1)$ odd numbers,

$$\boxed{1 + 3 + 5 + \cdots + (2n - 1)} + (2n + 1) = \boxed{n^2} + (2n + 1) = (n + 1)^2,$$

and so we just proved the induction step, and by IP we have $\forall m P(m)$.

Problem 9.1. *Prove that* $1 + \sum_{j=0}^{i} 2^j = 2^{i+1}$.

Sometimes it is convenient to start our induction higher than at 0. We have the following generalized induction principle:

$$[P(k) \wedge (\forall n \geq k)(P(n) \to P(n+1))] \to (\forall m \geq k)P(m), \qquad (9.2)$$

for any predicate P and any number k. Note that (9.2) follows easily from (9.1) if we simply let $P'(i)$ be $P(i + k)$, and do the usual induction on the predicate $P'(i)$.

Problem 9.2. *Use induction to prove that for $n \geq 1$,*
$$1^3 + 2^3 + 3^3 + \cdots + n^3 = (1 + 2 + 3 + \cdots + n)^2.$$

Problem 9.3. *For every $n \geq 1$, consider a square of size $2^n \times 2^n$ where one square is missing. Show that the resulting square can be filled with "L" shapes—that is, with clusters of three squares, where the three squares do not form a line.*

Problem 9.4. *Suppose that we restate the generalized IP (9.2) as*

$$[P(k) \wedge \forall n(P(n) \to P(n+1))] \to (\forall m \geq k)P(m). \qquad (9.2')$$

What is the relationship between (9.2) and (9.2')?

Problem 9.5. *The* Fibonacci *sequence is defined as follows: $f_0 = 0$ and $f_1 = 1$ and $f_{i+2} = f_{i+1} + f_i$, $i \geq 0$. Prove that for all $n \geq 1$ we have:*

$$\begin{pmatrix} 1 & 1 \\ 1 & 0 \end{pmatrix}^n = \begin{pmatrix} f_{n+1} & f_n \\ f_n & f_{n-1} \end{pmatrix},$$

where the left-hand side is the n-th power of a 2×2 matrix.

Problem 9.6. *Write a program that computes the n-th Fibonacci number using the matrix multiplication trick of problem 9.5.*

Problem 9.7. *Prove the following: if m divides n, then f_m divides f_n, i.e., $m|n \Rightarrow f_m|f_n$.*

The *Complete Induction Principle* (CIP) is just like IP except that in the induction step we show that if $P(i)$ holds for all $i \leq n$, then $P(n+1)$ also holds, i.e., the induction step is now $\forall n((\forall i \leq n)P(i) \to P(n+1))$.

Problem 9.8. *Use the CIP to prove that every number (in $\mathbb{N}$) greater than 1 may be written as a product of one or more prime numbers.*

Problem 9.9. *Suppose that we have a (Swiss) chocolate bar consisting of a number of squares arranged in a rectangular pattern. Our task is to split the bar into small squares (always breaking along the lines between the squares) with a minimum number of breaks. How many breaks will it take? Make an educated guess, and prove it by induction.*

The *Least Number Principle (LNP)* says that every non-empty subset of the natural numbers must have a least element. A direct consequence of the LNP is that every decreasing non-negative sequence of integers must terminate; that is, if $R = \{r_1, r_2, r_3, \ldots\} \subseteq \mathbb{N}$ where $r_i > r_{i+1}$ for all i, then R is a *finite* subset of $\mathbb{N}$. We are going to be using the LNP to show termination of algorithms.

Problem 9.10. *Show that IP, CIP, and LNP are equivalent principles.*

There are three standard ways to list the nodes of a binary tree. We present them below, together with a recursive procedure that lists the nodes according to each scheme.

Infix: left sub-tree, root, right sub-tree.
Prefix: root, left sub-tree, right sub-tree.
Postfix: left sub-tree, right sub-tree, root.
See the example in figure 9.1.

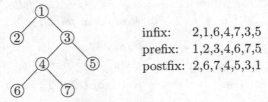

infix: 2,1,6,4,7,3,5
prefix: 1,2,3,4,6,7,5
postfix: 2,6,7,4,5,3,1

Fig. 9.1   A binary tree with the corresponding representations.

Note that some authors use a different name for infix, prefix, and postfix; they call it inorder, preorder, and postorder, respectively.

Problem 9.11. *Show that given any two representations we can obtain from them the third one, or, put another way, from any two representations we can reconstruct the tree. Show, using induction, that your reconstruction is correct. Then show that having just one representation is not enough.*

Problem 9.12. *Write a program that takes as input two of the three descriptions, and outputs the third. One way to present the input is as a text file, consisting of two rows, for example*

```
infix: 2,1,6,4,7,3,5
postfix: 2,6,7,4,5,3,1
```

and the corresponding output would be: `prefix: 1,2,3,4,6,7,5`. *Note that each row of the input has to specify the "scheme" of the description.*

9.1.2   *Invariance*

The *Invariance Technique (IT)* is a method for proving assertions about the outcomes of procedures. The IT identifies some property that remains true throughout the execution of a procedure. Then, once the procedure terminates, we use this property to prove assertions about the output.

As an example, consider an 8×8 board from which two squares from opposing corners have been removed (see figure 9.2). The area of the board

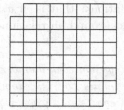

Fig. 9.2   An 8 × 8 board.

is $64 - 2 = 62$ squares. Now suppose that we have 31 dominoes of size 1×2. We want to show that the board *cannot* be covered by them.

Verifying this by *brute force* (that is, examining all possible coverings) is an extremely laborious job. However, using IT we argue as follows: color the squares as a chess board. Each domino, covering two adjacent squares, covers 1 white and 1 black square, and, hence, each placement covers as many white squares as it covers black squares. Note that the number of white squares and the number of black squares differ by 2—opposite corners lying on the same diagonal have the same color—and, hence, no placement of dominoes yields a cover; done!

More formally, we place the dominoes one by one on the board, any way we want. The invariant is that after placing each new domino, the number of covered white squares is the same as the number of covered black squares. We prove that this *is* an invariant by induction on the number of placed dominoes. The basis case is when zero dominoes have been placed (so zero black and zero white squares are covered). In the induction step, we add one more domino which, no matter how we place it, covers one white and one black square, thus maintaining the property. At the end, when we are done placing dominoes, we would have to have as many white squares as black squares covered, which is not possible due to the nature of the coloring of the board (i.e., the number of black and whites squares is not the same). Note that this argument extends easily to the $n \times n$ board.

Problem 9.13. *Let n be an odd number, and suppose that we have the set* $\{1, 2, \ldots, 2n\}$. *We pick any two numbers a, b in the set, delete them from the set, and replace them with* $|a - b|$. *Continue repeating this until just one number remains in the set; show that this remaining number must be odd.*

The next three problems have the common theme of social gatherings. We always assume that relations of likes and dislikes, of being an enemy or a friend, are symmetric relations: that is, if a likes b, then b also likes a, etc. See Section 9.3 for background on relations—symmetric relations are defined on page 242.

Problem 9.14. *At a country club, each member dislikes at most three other members. There are two tennis courts; show that each member can be assigned to one of the two courts in such a way that at most one person they dislike is also playing on the same court.*

We use the vocabulary of "country clubs" and "tennis courts," but it is clear that Problem 9.14 is a typical situation that one might encounter in computer science: for example, a multi-threaded program which is run on two processors, where a pair of threads are taken to be "enemies" when they use many of the same resources. Threads that require the same resources ought to be scheduled on different processors, to the extent that it is possible. In a sense, these seemingly innocent problems are parables of computer science.

Problem 9.15. *You are hosting a dinner party where $2n$ people are going to be sitting at a round table. As it happens in any social clique, animosities are rife, but you know that everyone sitting at the table dislikes at most $(n-1)$ people; show that you can make sitting arrangements so that nobody sits next to someone they dislike.*

Problem 9.16. *Handshakes are exchanged at a meeting. We call a person an* odd *person if he has exchanged an odd number of handshakes. Show that, at any moment, there is an even number of odd persons.*

9.2 Number Theory

In this section we work with the set of integers and natural numbers:

$$\mathbb{Z} = \{\ldots, -3, -2, -1, 0, 1, 2, 3, \ldots\}, \quad \mathbb{N} = \{0, 1, 2, \ldots\}.$$

9.2.1 *Prime numbers*

We say that x *divides* y, and write $x|y$ if $y = qx$. If $x|y$ we say that x is *divisor* (also *factor*) of y. Using the terminology introduced in Section 1.1.2, $x|y$ if and only if $y = \mathrm{div}(x, y) \cdot x$. We say that a number p is *prime* if its only divisors are itself and 1.

Claim 9.17. *If p is a prime, and $p|a_1a_2\ldots a_n$, then $p|a_i$ for some i.*

Proof. It is enough to show that if $p|ab$ then $p|a$ or $p|b$. Let $g = \gcd(a, p)$. Then $g|p$, and since p is a prime, there are two cases. Case 1, $g = p$, then since $g|a$, $p|a$. Case 2, $g = 1$, so there exist u, v such that $au + pv = 1$ (see algorithm 1.8), so $abu + pbv = b$. Since $p|ab$, and $p|p$, it follows that $p|(abu + pbv)$, so $p|b$. $\qquad\square$

Theorem 9.18 (Fundamental Theorem of Arithmetic). *Given an $a \geq 2$, a can be written as $a = p_1^{e_1}p_2^{e_2}\cdots p_r^{e_r}$, where p_i are prime numbers, and other than rearranging primes, this factorization is unique.*

Proof. We first show the existence of the factorization, and then its uniqueness. The proof of existence is by complete induction; the basis case is $a = 2$, where 2 is a prime. Consider an integer $a > 2$; if a is prime then it is its own factorization (just as in the basis case). Otherwise, if a is composite, then $a = b \cdot c$, where $1 < b, c < a$; apply the induction hypothesis to b and c.

To show uniqueness suppose that $a = p_1p_2\ldots p_s = q_1q_2\ldots q_t$ where we have written out all the primes, that is, instead of writing p^e we write $p \cdot p \cdots p$, e times. Since $p_1|a$, it follows that $p_1|q_1q_2\ldots q_t$. So $p_1|q_j$ for some j, by claim 9.17, but then $p_1 = q_j$ since they are both primes. Now delete p_1 from the first list and q_j from the second list, and continue. Obviously we cannot end up with a product of primes equal to 1, so the two list must be identical. $\qquad\square$

9.2.2 Modular arithmetic

Let $m \geq 1$ be an integer. We say that a and b are *congruent modulo m*, and write $a \equiv b \pmod{m}$ (or sometimes $a \equiv_m b$) if $m|(a - b)$. Another way to say this is that a and b have the same remainder when divided by m; using the terminology of section 1.1, we can say that $a \equiv b \pmod{m}$ if and only if $\text{rem}(a, m) = \text{rem}(b, m)$.

Problem 9.19. *Show that if $a_1 \equiv_m a_2$ and $b_1 \equiv_m b_2$, then $a_1 \pm b_1 \equiv_m a_2 \pm b_2$ and $a_1 \cdot b_1 \equiv_m a_2 \cdot b_2$.*

Proposition 9.20. *If $m \geq 1$, then $a \cdot b \equiv_m 1$ for some b if and only if $\gcd(a, m) = 1$.*

Proof. ($\Rightarrow$) If there exists a b such that $a \cdot b \equiv_m 1$, then we have $m|(ab-1)$

and so there exists a c such that $ab - 1 = cm$, i.e., $ab - cm = 1$. And since $\gcd(a, m)$ divides both a and m, it also divides $ab - cm$, and so $\gcd(a, m)|1$ and so it must be equal to 1.

($\Leftarrow$) Suppose that $\gcd(a, m) = 1$. By the extended Euclid's algorithm (see algorithm 1.8) there exist u, v such that $au + mv = 1$, so $au - 1 = -mv$, so $m|(au - 1)$, so $au \equiv_m 1$. So let $b = u$. $\qquad\square$

Let $\mathbb{Z}_m = \{0, 1, 2, \ldots, m-1\}$. We call $\mathbb{Z}_m$ the set of integers modulo m. To add or multiply in the set $\mathbb{Z}_m$, we add and multiply the corresponding integers, and then take the remainder of the division by m as the result. Let $\mathbb{Z}_m^* = \{a \in \mathbb{Z}_m | \gcd(a, m) = 1\}$. By proposition 9.20 we know that $\mathbb{Z}_m^*$ is the subset of $\mathbb{Z}_m$ consisting of those elements which have multiplicative inverses in $\mathbb{Z}_m$.

The function $\phi(n)$ is called the *Euler totient function*, and it is the number of elements less than n that are co-prime to n, i.e., $\phi(n) = |\mathbb{Z}_n^*|$.

Problem 9.21. *If we are able to factor, we are also able to compute $\phi(n)$. Show that if $n = p_1^{k_1} p_2^{k_2} \cdots p_l^{k_l}$, then $\phi(n) = \prod_{i=1}^l p_i^{k_i-1}(p_i - 1)$.*

Theorem 9.22 (Fermat's Little Theorem). *Let p be a prime number and $\gcd(a, p) = 1$. Then $a^{p-1} \equiv 1 \pmod{p}$.*

Proof.   For any a such that $\gcd(a, p) = 1$ the following products
$$1a, 2a, 3a, \ldots, (p-1)a, \qquad (9.3)$$
all taken mod p, are pairwise distinct. To see this suppose that $ja \equiv ka$ $\pmod{p}$. Then $(j - k)a \equiv 0 \pmod{p}$, and so $p|(j - k)a$. But since by assumption $\gcd(a, p) = 1$, it follows that $p \nmid a$, and so by claim 9.17 it must be the case that $p|(j - k)$. But since $j, k \in \{1, 2, \ldots, p-1\}$, it follows that $-(p - 2) \leq j - k \leq (p - 2)$, so $j - k = 0$, i.e., $j = k$.

Thus the numbers in the list (9.3) are just a reordering of the list $\{1, 2, \ldots, p-1\}$. Therefore
$$a^{p-1}(p-1)! \equiv_p \prod_{j=1}^{p-1} j \cdot a \equiv_p \prod_{j=1}^{p-1} j \equiv_p (p-1)!. \qquad (9.4)$$

Since all the numbers in $\{1, 2, \ldots, p-1\}$ have inverses in $\mathbb{Z}_p$, as $\gcd(i, p) = 1$ for $1 \leq i \leq p - 1$, their product also has an inverse. That is, $(p - 1)!$ has an inverse, and so multiplying both sides of (9.4) by $((p-1)!)^{-1}$ we obtain the result. $\qquad\square$

Problem 9.23. *Give a second proof of Fermat's Little theorem using the binomial expansion, i.e., $(x + y)^n = \sum_{j=0}^n \binom{n}{j} x^j y^{n-j}$ applied to $(a+1)^p$.*

9.2.3 *Group theory*

We say that $(G, *)$ is a *group* if G is a set and $*$ is an operation, such that if $a, b \in G$, then $a * b \in G$ (this property is called *closure*). Furthermore, the operation $*$ has to satisfy the following three properties:

(1) *identity law:* There exists an $e \in G$ such that $e * a = a * e = a$ for all $a \in G$.

(2) *inverse law:* For every $a \in G$ there exists an element $b \in G$ such that $a * b = b * a = e$. This element b is called an *inverse* and it can be shown that it is unique; hence it is often denoted as a^{-1}.

(3) *associative law:* For all $a, b, c \in G$, we have $a * (b * c) = (a * b) * c$.

If $(G, *)$ also satisfies the *commutative law*, that is, if for all $a, b \in G$, $a * b = b * a$, then it is called a *commutative* or *Abelian group*.

Typical examples of groups are $(\mathbb{Z}_n, +)$ (integers mod n under addition) and $(\mathbb{Z}_n^*, \cdot)$ (integers mod n under multiplication). Note that both these groups are Abelian. These are, of course, the two groups of concern for us; but there are many others: $(\mathbb{Q}, +)$ is an infinite group (rationals under addition), $\mathrm{GL}(n, \mathbb{F})$ (which is the group of $n \times n$ invertible matrices over a field $\mathbb{F}$), and S_n (the *symmetric group* over n elements, consisting of permutations of $[n]$ where $*$ is function composition).

Problem 9.24. *Show that $(\mathbb{Z}_n, +)$ and $(\mathbb{Z}_n^*, \cdot)$ are groups, by checking that the corresponding operation satisfies the three axioms of a group.*

We let $|G|$ denote the number of elements in G (note that G may be infinite, but we are concerned mainly with finite groups). If $g \in G$ and $x \in \mathbb{N}$, then $g^x = g * g * \cdots * g$, x times. If it is clear from the context that the operation is $*$, we use juxtaposition ab instead of $a * b$.

Suppose that G is a finite group and $a \in G$; then the smallest $d \in \mathbb{N}$ such that $a^d = e$ is called the *order* of a, and it is denoted as $\mathrm{ord}_G(a)$ (or just $\mathrm{ord}(a)$ if the group G is clear from the context).

Proposition 9.25. *If G is a finite group, then for all $a \in G$ there exists a $d \in \mathbb{N}$ such that $a^d = e$. If $d = \mathrm{ord}_G(a)$, and $a^k = e$, then $d | k$.*

Proof. Consider the list $a^1, a^2, a^3, \ldots$. If G is finite there must exist $i < j$ such that $a^i = a^j$. Then, $(a^{-1})^i$ applied to both sides yields $a^{j-i} = e$. Let $d = \mathrm{ord}(a)$ (by the LNP we know that it must exist!). Suppose that $k \geq d$, $a^k = e$; let q, r be the divisor and remainder, respectively. Then

$e = a^k = a^{dq+r} = (a^d)^q a^r = a^r$. Since $a^d = e$ it follows that $a^r = e$, contradicting the minimality of $d = \text{ord}(a)$, unless $r = 0$. $\square$

If $(G, *)$ is a group we say that H is a *subgroup* of G, and write $H \leq G$, if $H \subseteq G$ and H is closed under $*$. That is, H is a subset of G, and H is itself a group. Note that for any G it is always the case that $\{e\} \leq G$ and $G \leq G$; these two are called the *trivial subgroups* of G. If $H \leq G$ and $g \in G$, then gH is called a *left coset of* G, and it is simply the set $\{gh | h \in H\}$. Note that gH is not necessarily a subgroup of G.

Theorem 9.26 (Lagrange). *If G is a finite group and $H \leq G$, then $|H|$ divides $|G|$, i.e., the order of H divides the order of G.*

Proof. If $g_1, g_2 \in G$, then the two cosets $g_1 H$ and $g_2 H$ are either identical or $g_1 H \cap g_2 H = \emptyset$. To see this, suppose that $g \in g_1 H \cap g_2 H$, so $g = g_1 h_1 = g_2 h_2$. In particular, $g_1 = g_2 h_2 h_1^{-1}$. Thus, $g_1 H = (g_2 h_2 h_1^{-1})H$, and since it can be easily checked that $(ab)H = a(bH)$ and that $hH = H$ for any $h \in H$, it follows that $g_1 H = g_2 H$.

Therefore, for a finite $G = \{g_1, g_2, \ldots, g_n\}$, the collection of sets $\{g_1 H, g_2 H, \ldots, g_n H\}$ is a partition of G into subsets that are either disjoint or identical; from among all subcollections of identical cosets we pick a representative, so that $G = g_{i_1} H \cup g_{i_2} H \cup \cdots \cup g_{i_m} H$, and so $|G| = m|H|$, and we are done. $\square$

Problem 9.27. *Let $H \leq G$. Show that if $h \in H$, then $hH = H$, and that in general for any $g \in G$, $|gH| = |H|$. Finally, show that $(ab)H = a(bH)$.*

Problem 9.28. *If G is a group, and $\{g_1, g_2, \ldots, g_k\} \subseteq G$, then the set $\langle g_1, g_2, \ldots, g_k \rangle$ is defined as follows*
$$\{x_1 x_2 \cdots x_p | p \in \mathbb{N}, x_i \in \{g_1, g_2, \ldots, g_k, g_1^{-1}, g_2^{-1}, \ldots, g_k^{-1}\}\}.$$
Show that $\langle g_1, g_2, \ldots, g_k \rangle$ (called the subgroup generated by $\{g_1, g_2, \ldots, g_k\}$) is a subgroup of G. Also show that when G is finite $|\langle g \rangle| = \text{ord}_G(g)$.

9.2.4 *Applications of group theory to number theory*

Theorem 9.29 (Euler). *For every n and every $a \in \mathbb{Z}_n^*$, that is, for every pair a, n such that $\gcd(a, n) = 1$, we have $a^{\phi(n)} \equiv 1 \pmod{n}$.*

Proof. First it is easy to check that $(\mathbb{Z}_n^*, \cdot)$ is a group. Then by definition $\phi(n) = |\mathbb{Z}_n^*|$, and since $\langle a \rangle \leq \mathbb{Z}_n^*$, it follows by Lagrange's theorem that $\text{ord}(a) = |\langle a \rangle|$ divides $\phi(n)$. $\square$

Note that Fermat's Little theorem (already presented as theorem 9.22) is an immediate consequence of Euler's theorem, since when p is a prime, $\mathbb{Z}_p^* = \mathbb{Z}_p - \{0\}$, and $\phi(p) = (p-1)$.

Theorem 9.30 (Chinese Remainder). *Given two sets of numbers of equal size, $r_0, r_1, \ldots, r_n$ and $m_0, m_1, \ldots, m_n$, such that*

$$0 \le r_i < m_i \qquad 0 \le i \le n \tag{9.5}$$

and $\gcd(m_i, m_j) = 1$ for $i \ne j$, then there exists an r such that $r \equiv r_i$ (mod m_i) for $0 \le i \le n$.

Proof. The proof we give is by counting; we show that the distinct values of r, $0 \le r < \Pi m_i$, represent distinct sequences. To see this, note that if $r \equiv r'$ (mod m_i) for all i, then $m_i | (r - r')$ for all i, and so $(\Pi m_i) | (r - r')$, since the m_i's are pairwise co-prime. So $r \equiv r'$ (mod (Πm_i)), and so $r = r'$ since both $r, r' \in \{0, 1, \ldots, (\Pi m_i) - 1\}$.

But the total number of sequences $r_0, \ldots, r_n$ such that (9.5) holds is precisely Πm_i. Hence every such sequence must be a sequence of remainders of some r, $0 \le r < \Pi m_i$. $\qquad\square$

Problem 9.31. *The proof of theorem 9.30 (CRT) is non-constructive. Show how to obtain efficiently the r that meets the requirement of the theorem, i.e., in polytime in n—so in particular not using brute force search.*

Given two groups $(G_1, *_1)$ and $(G_2, *_2)$, a mapping $h : G_1 \longrightarrow G_2$ is a *homomorphism* if it respects the operation of the groups; formally, for all $g_1, g_1' \in G_1$, $h(g_1 *_1 g_1') = h(g_1) *_2 h(g_1')$. If the homomorphism h is also a bijection, then it is called an *isomorphism*. If there exists an isomorphism between two groups G_1 and G_2, we call them *isomorphic*, and write $G_1 \cong G_2$.

If $(G_1, *_1)$ and $(G_2, *_2)$ are two groups, then their product, denoted $(G_1 \times G_2, *)$ is simply $\{(g_1, g_2) : g_1 \in G_1, g_2 \in G_2\}$, where $(g_1, g_2) * (g_1', g_2')$ is $(g_1 *_1 g_1', g_2 *_2 g_2')$. The product of n groups, $G_1 \times G_2 \times \cdots \times G_n$ can be defined analogously; using this notation, the CRT can be stated in the language of group theory as follows.

Theorem 9.32 (Chinese Remainder Version II). *If $m_0, m_1, \ldots, m_n$ are pairwise co-prime integers, then*

$$\mathbb{Z}_{m_0 \cdot m_1 \cdots \cdot m_n} \cong \mathbb{Z}_{m_0} \times \mathbb{Z}_{m_1} \times \cdots \times \mathbb{Z}_{m_n}.$$

Problem 9.33. *Prove theorem 9.32.*

9.3   Relations

In this section we present the basics of relations. Given two sets X, Y, $X \times Y$ denotes the set of (ordered) pairs $\{(x, y)| x \in X \land y \in Y\}$, and a *relation* R is just a subset of $X \times Y$, i.e., $R \subseteq X \times Y$. Thus, the elements of R are of the form (x, y) and we write $(x, y) \in R$ (we can also write xRy, Rxy or $R(x, y)$). In what follows we assume that we quantify over the set X and that $R \subseteq X \times X$; we say that

(1) R is *reflexive* if $\forall x, (x, x) \in R$,

(2) R is *symmetric* if $\forall x \forall y, (x, y) \in R$ if and only if $(y, x) \in R$,

(3) R is *antisymmetric* if $\forall x \forall y$, if $(x, y) \in R$ and $(y, x) \in R$ then $x = y$,

(4) R is *transitive* if $\forall x \forall y \forall z$, if $(x, y) \in R$ and $(y, z) \in R$ then it is also the case that $(x, z) \in R$.

Suppose that $R \subseteq X \times Y$ and $S \subseteq Y \times Z$. The *composition* of R and S is defined as follows:

$$R \circ S = \{(x, y)|\exists z, xRz \land zSy\}. \tag{9.6}$$

Let $R \subseteq X \times X$; we can define $R^n := R \circ R \circ \cdots \circ R$ recursively as follows:

$$R^0 = \mathrm{id}_X := \{(x, x)|x \in X\}, \tag{9.7}$$

and $R^{i+1} = R^i \circ R$. Note that there are two different equalities in (9.7); "$=$" is the usual equality, and "$:=$" is a definition.

Theorem 9.34. *The following three are equivalent:*

(1) R is transitive,

(2) $R^2 \subseteq R$,

(3) $\forall n \geq 1, R^n \subseteq R$.

Problem 9.35. *Prove theorem 9.34.*

There are two standard ways of representing *finite* relations, that is, relations on $X \times Y$ where X and Y are finite sets. Let $X = \{a_1, \ldots, a_n\}$ and $Y = \{b_1, \ldots, b_m\}$, then we can represent a relation $R \subseteq X \times Y$:

(1) as a matrix $M_R = (m_{ij})$ where:

$$m_{ij} = \begin{cases} 1 & (a_i, b_j) \in R \\ 0 & (a_i, b_j) \notin R \end{cases},$$

(2) and as a directed graph $G_R = (V_R, E_R)$, where $V_R = X \cup Y$ and $a_i \bullet \longrightarrow \bullet b_j$ is an edge in E_R iff $(a_i, b_j) \in R$.

9.3.1 *Closure*

Let P be a property[1] of relations, for example transitivity or symmetry. Let $R \subseteq X \times X$ be a relation, with or without the property P. The relation S satisfying the following three conditions:

    (1) S has the property P

    (2) $R \subseteq S$ (9.8)

    (3) $\forall Q \subseteq X \times X$, "$Q$ has P" and $R \subseteq Q$ implies that $S \subseteq Q$

is called the *closure of R with respect to* P. Note that in some instances the closure may not exist. Also note that condition 3 may be replaced by

$$S \subseteq \bigcap_{Q \text{ has P}, \, R \subseteq Q} Q. \tag{9.9}$$

See figure 9.3 for an example of reflexive closure.

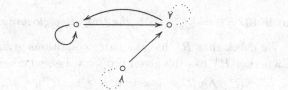

Fig. 9.3   Example of reflexive closure: without the dotted lines, this diagram represents a relation that is not reflexive; with the dotted lines it is reflexive, and it is in fact the smallest reflexive relation containing the three points and four solid lines.

Theorem 9.36. *For $R \subseteq X \times X$, $R \cup \text{id}_X$ is the reflexive closure of R.*

Problem 9.37. *Prove theorem 9.36.*

See figure 9.4 for an example of symmetric closure.

Theorem 9.38. *Given a relation $R \subseteq X \times Y$, the relation $R^{-1} \subseteq Y \times X$ is defined as $\{(x,y)|(y,x) \in R\}$. For $R \subseteq X \times X$, $R \cup R^{-1}$ is the symmetric closure of R.*

Problem 9.39. *Prove theorem 9.38.*

See figure 9.5 for an example of transitive closure.

---

[1]We have seen the concept of an abstract property in section 9.1.1. The only difference is that in section 9.1.1 the property $P(i)$ was over $i \in \mathbb{N}$, whereas here, given a set X, the property is over $Q \in \mathcal{P}(X \times X)$, that is, $P(Q)$ where $Q \subseteq X \times X$. In this section, instead of writing $P(Q)$ we say "Q has property P."

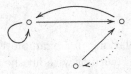

Fig. 9.4   Example of symmetric closure: without the dotted line, this diagram represents a relation that is not symmetric; with the dotted lines it is symmetric.

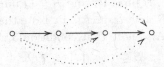

Fig. 9.5   Example of transitive closure: without the dotted line, this diagram represents a relation that is not transitive; with the dotted lines it is transitive.

Theorem 9.40. $R^+ := \bigcup_{i=1}^{\infty} R^i$ *is the transitive closure of R.*

Proof.   We check that R^+ has the three conditions given in (9.8). First, we check whether R^+ has the given property, i.e., whether it is transitive:

$$xR^+y \wedge yR^+z \iff \exists m, n \geq 1, xR^m y \wedge yR^n z$$
$$\implies \exists m, n \geq 1, x(R^m \circ R^n)z \qquad (\dagger)$$
$$\iff \exists m, n \geq 1, xR^{m+n}z$$
$$\iff xR^+z$$

so R^+ *is* transitive.

Second we check that $R \subseteq R^+$—this follows from the definition of R^+.

We check now the last condition. Suppose S is transitive and $R \subseteq S$. Since S is transitive, by theorem 9.34, $S^n \subseteq S$, for $n \geq 1$, i.e., $S^+ \subseteq S$, and since $R \subseteq S$, $R^+ \subseteq S^+$, so $R^+ \subseteq S$.   □

Problem 9.41. *Note that in the proof of theorem 9.40, when we show that R^+ itself is transitive, the second line, labeled with $(\dagger)$, is an implication, rather than an equivalence like the other lines. Why is it not an equivalence?*

Theorem 9.42. $R^* = \bigcup_{i=0}^{\infty} R^i$ *is the reflexive and transitive closure of R.*

Proof. $R^* = R^+ \cup \mathrm{id}_X.$ □

9.3.2   Equivalence relation

Let X be a set, and let I be an index set. The family of sets $\{A_i | i \in I\}$ is called a *partition* of X iff

(1) $\forall i,\ A_i \neq \emptyset$,
(2) $\forall i \neq j,\ A_i \cap A_j = \emptyset$,
(3) $X = \bigcup_{i \in I} A_i$.

Note that $X = \bigcup_{x \in X}\{x\}$ is the *finest* partition possible, i.e., the set of all singletons. A relation $R \subseteq X \times X$ is called an *equivalence relation* iff

(1) R is reflexive,
(2) R is symmetric,
(3) R is transitive.

For example, if x, y are strings over $\{0, 1\}^*$, then the relation given by $R = \{(x, y) \mid \text{length}(x) = \text{length}(y)\}$ is an equivalence relation. Another example is $xRy \iff x = y$, i.e., the equality relation is the equivalence relation *par excellence*. Yet another example: $R = \{(a, b) \mid a \equiv b \pmod{m}\}$ is an equivalence relation (where "$\equiv$" is the congruence relation defined on page 237).

Theorem 9.43. *Consider an equivalence relation. Then the following hold:*

(1) $a \in [a]$
(2) $a \equiv b \iff [a] = [b]$
(3) $a \not\equiv b$ *then* $[a] \cap [b] = \emptyset$
(4) *any two equivalence classes are either equal or disjoint.*

Theorem 9.44. *Let $F : X \longrightarrow X$ be any total function (i.e., a function defined on all its inputs). Then the relation R on X defined as: $xRy \iff F(x) = F(y)$, is an equivalence relation.*

Problem 9.45. *Prove theorem 9.44.*

Let R be an equivalence relation on X. For every $x \in X$, the set $[x]_R = \{y \mid xRy\}$ is the *equivalence class* of x with respect to R.

Theorem 9.46. *Let $R \subseteq X \times X$ be an equivalence relation. The following are equivalent:*

(1) aRb
(2) $[a] = [b]$
(3) $[a] \cap [b] \neq \emptyset$

Proof. (1) $\Rightarrow$ (2) Suppose that aRb, and let $c \in [a]$. Then aRc, so cRa (by symmetry). Since $cRa \wedge aRb$, cRb (transitivity), so bRc (symmetry), so $c \in [b]$. Hence $[a] \subseteq [b]$, and similarly $[b] \subseteq [a]$.

(2) $\Rightarrow$ (3) Obvious, since $[a]$ is non-empty as $a \in [a]$.

(3) $\Rightarrow$ (1) Let $c \in [a] \cap [b]$, so aRc and bRc, so by symmetry $aRc \wedge cRb$, so by transitivity aRb. $\qquad\square$

Corollary 9.47. *If R is an equivalence relation, then $(a, b) \notin R$ iff $[a] \cap [b] = \emptyset$.*

For every equivalence relation $R \subseteq X \times X$, let X/R denote the set of all equivalence classes of R.

Theorem 9.48. *X/R is a partition of X.*

Proof. Given theorem 9.46, the only thing that remains to be proven is that $X = \bigcup_{A \in X/R} A$. Since every $A = [a]$ for some $a \in X$, it follows that $\bigcup_{A \in X/R} A = \bigcup_{a \in X} [a] = X$. $\qquad\square$

Let R_1, R_2 be equivalence relations. If $R_1 \subseteq R_2$, then we say that R_1 is a *refinement* of R_2.

Lemma 9.49. *If R_1 is a refinement of R_2, then $[a]_{R_1} \subseteq [a]_{R_2}$, for all $a \in X$.*

If X/R is finite then $\text{index}(R) := |X/R|$, i.e., the *index* of R (in X) is the size of X/R.

Theorem 9.50. *If $R_1 \subseteq R_2$, then $\text{index}(R_1) \geq \text{index}(R_2)$.*

Problem 9.51. *Prove theorem 9.50.*

9.3.3 Partial orders

In this section, instead of using R to represent a relation over a set X, we are going to use the different variants of inequality: $(X, \preceq), (X, \sqsubseteq), (X, \leq)$.

A relation $\preceq$ over X, where $\preceq \subseteq X \times X$, is called a *partial order*, a *poset* for short, if it is:

(1) reflexive
(2) antisymmetric
(3) transitive

A relation "$\prec$" (where $\prec \subseteq X \times X$) is a *sharp partial order* if:

(1) $x \prec y \Rightarrow \neg(y \prec x)$
(2) transitive

These two standard relations, "$\preceq$" and "$\prec$", are linked in a natural manner by the following theorem.

Theorem 9.52. *A relation $\preceq$ defined as $x \preceq y \iff x \prec y \lor x = y$ is a partial order. That is, given a sharp partial order "$\prec$", we can extend it to a poset "$\preceq$" with the standard equality symbol "$=$".*

Let $(X, \preceq)$ be a poset. We say that x, y are *comparable* if $x \preceq y$ or $y \preceq x$. Otherwise, they are *incomparable*. Let $x \sim y$ be short for x, y are incomparable, i.e., $x \sim y \iff \neg(x \preceq y) \land \neg(y \preceq x)$. In general, for every pair x, y exactly one of the following is true

$$x \prec y, \quad y \prec x, \quad x = y, \quad x \sim y$$

Of course, in the context of posets represented by "$\preceq$" the meaning of "$\prec$" is as follows: $x \prec y \iff x \preceq y \land x \neq y$.

A poset $(X, \preceq)$ is *total* or *linear* if all x, y are comparable, i.e., $\sim = \emptyset$.

Some examples of posets: if X is a set, then $(\mathcal{P}(X), \subseteq)$ is a poset. For example, if $X = \{1, 2, 3\}$, then a *Hasse diagram* representation of this poset would be as given in figure 9.6.

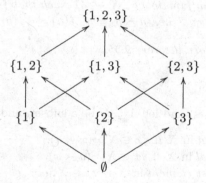

Fig. 9.6 Hasse diagram representation of the poset $(\{1, 2, 3\}, \subseteq)$. Hasse diagrams are transitive reductions—relations implied by transitivity are not included.

Let $\mathbb{Z}^+$ be the set of positive integers, and let $a|b$ be the "a divides b" relation (that we define on page 236). Then, $(\mathbb{Z}^+, |)$ is a poset.

If $(X_1, \preceq_1), (X_2, \preceq_2)$ are two posets, then the *component-wise order* is $(X_1 \times X_2, \preceq_C)$ defined as follows:

$$(x_1, x_2) \preceq (y_1, y_2) \iff x_1 \preceq_1 y_1 \land x_2 \preceq_2 y_2,$$

and it is also a poset.

The *lexicographic order* $(X_1 \times X_2, \preceq_L)$ is defined as follows:

$$(x_1, x_2) \preceq_L (y_1, y_2) \iff (x_1 \preceq_1 y_1) \vee (x_1 = y_1 \wedge x_2 \preceq_2 y_2).$$

Finally, $(X, \preceq)$ is a *stratified order* iff $(X, \preceq)$ is a poset, and furthermore $(x \sim y \wedge y \sim z) \Rightarrow (x \sim z \vee x = z)$. Define $a \approx b \iff a \sim b \vee a = b$.

Theorem 9.53. *A poset $(X, \preceq)$ is a stratified order iff $\approx \; = \; \sim \cup \; \mathrm{id}_X$ is an equivalence relation.*

In mathematics nomenclature can be the readers greatest scourge. The string of symbols "$\approx \; = \; \sim \cup \; \mathrm{id}_X$" is a great example of obfuscation; how to make sense of it? Yes, it is very succinct, but it takes practice to be able to read it. What we are saying here is that the order we called "$\approx$" is actually equal to the order that we obtain by taking the union of the order "$\sim$" and "id_X".

Problem 9.54. *Prove theorem 9.53.*

Theorem 9.55. *A poset $(X, \preceq)$ is a stratified order iff there exists a total order $(T, \preceq_T)$ and an function $f : X \longrightarrow T$ such that f is onto and f is an "order homomorphism," i.e., $a \preceq b \iff f(a) \preceq_T f(b)$.*

Problem 9.56. *Prove theorem 9.55.*

9.3.4 Lattices

Let $(X, \preceq)$ be a poset, and let $A \subseteq X$ be a subset, and $a \in X$. Then:

(1) a is *minimal* in X if $\forall x \in X, \neg(x \prec a)$.
(2) a is *maximal* in X if $\forall x \in X, \neg(a \prec x)$.
(3) a is the *least element* in X if $\forall x \in X, a \preceq x$.
(4) a is the *greatest element* in X if $\forall x \in X, x \preceq a$.
(5) a is an *upper bound* of A if $\forall x \in A, x \preceq a$.
(6) a is a *lower bound* if A if $\forall x \in A, a \preceq x$.
(7) a is the *least upper bound (supremum)* of A, denoted $\sup(A)$ if
    (a) $\forall x \in A, x \preceq a$
    (b) $\forall b \in X, (\forall x \in A, x \preceq b) \Rightarrow a \preceq b$
(8) a is the *greatest lower bound (infimum)* of A, denoted $\inf(A)$ if
    (a) $\forall x \in A, a \preceq x$
    (b) $\forall b \in X, (\forall x \in A, b \preceq x) \Rightarrow b \preceq a$

Problem 9.57. *Note that in the definitions 1–8 we sometimes use the definite article "the" and sometimes the indefinite article "a". In the former case this implies* uniqueness; *in the latter case this implies that there may be several candidates. Convince yourself of uniqueness where it applies, and provide an example of a poset where there are several candidates for a given element in the other cases. Finally, it is important to note that* $\sup(A), \inf(A)$ *may or may not exist; provide examples where they do not exist.*

A poset $(X, \preceq)$ is a *well-ordered* set if it is a total order and for every $A \subseteq X$, such that $A \neq \emptyset$, A has a least element.

A poset is *dense* if $\forall x, y$ if $x < y$, then $\exists z, x < z < y$. For example, $(\mathbb{R}, \leq)$, with a standard definition of "$\leq$", is a total dense order, but it is not a well ordered set; for example, the interval $(2, 3]$, which equals the subset of $\mathbb{R}$ consisting of those x such that $2 < x \leq 3$, does not have a least element.

A poset $(X, \preceq)$ is a *lattice* if $\forall a, b \in X$, $\inf(\{a, b\})$ and $\sup(\{a, b\})$ both exist in X. For example, every total order is a lattice, and $(\mathcal{P}(X), \subseteq)$ is a lattice for every X. This last example inspires the following notation: $a \sqcup b := \sup(\{a, b\})$ and $a \sqcap b := \inf(\{a, b\})$.

Problem 9.58. *Prove that for the lattice* $(\mathcal{P}(X), \subseteq)$ *we have:*

$$A \sqcup B = A \cup B$$
$$A \sqcap B = A \cap B$$

Not every poset is a lattice; figure 9.7 gives an easy example.

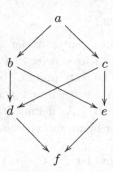

Fig. 9.7 An example of a poset that is *not* a lattice. While $\inf(\{b, c\}) = a$ and $\sup(\{d, e\}) = f$, the supremum of $\{b, c\}$ does not exist.

Theorem 9.59. *Let $(X, \preceq)$ be a lattice. Then, $\forall a, b \in X$,*

$$a \preceq b \iff a \sqcap b = a \iff a \sqcup b = b.$$

Problem 9.60. *Prove theorem 9.59.*

Theorem 9.61. *Let $(X, \preceq)$ be a lattice. Then, the following hold for all $a, b, c \in X$:*

(1) $a \sqcup b = b \sqcup a$ and $a \sqcap b = b \sqcap a$ (commutativity)
(2) $a \sqcup (b \sqcup c) = (a \sqcup b) \sqcup c$ and $a \sqcap (b \sqcap c) = (a \sqcap b) \sqcap c$ (associativity)
(3) $a \sqcup a = a$ and $a \sqcap a = a$ (idempotence)
(4) $a = a \sqcup (a \sqcap b)$ and $a = a \sqcap (a \sqcup b)$ (absorption)

Problem 9.62. *Prove the properties listed as theorem 9.61.*

A lattice $(X, \preceq)$ is *complete* iff $\forall A \subseteq X$, $\sup(A), \inf(A)$ both exist. We denote $\bot = \inf(X)$ and $\top = \sup(X)$.

Theorem 9.63. *$(\mathcal{P}(X), \subseteq)$ is a complete lattice, and the following hold $\forall \mathcal{A} \subseteq \mathcal{P}(X)$, $\sup(\mathcal{A}) = \bigcup_{A \in \mathcal{A}} A$ and $\inf(\mathcal{A}) = \bigcap_{A \in \mathcal{A}} A$, and $\bot = \emptyset$ and $\top = X$.*

Problem 9.64. *Prove theorem 9.63.*

Theorem 9.65. *Every finite lattice is complete.*

Proof. Let $A = \{a_1, \ldots, a_n\}$. Define $b = a_1 \sqcap \ldots \sqcap a_n$ (with parenthesis associated to the right). Then $b = \inf(A)$. Same idea for the supremum. $\square$

9.3.5 *Fixed point theory*

Suppose that F is a function, and consider the equation $\vec{x} = F(\vec{x})$. A solution $\vec{a}$ of this equation is a *fixed point of F*.

Let $(X, \preceq)$ and $(Y, \sqsubseteq)$ be two posets. A function $f : X \longrightarrow Y$ is *monotone* iff $\forall x, y \in X$, $x \preceq y \Rightarrow f(x) \sqsubseteq f(y)$. For example, $f_B : \mathcal{P}(X) \longrightarrow \mathcal{P}(X)$, where $B \subseteq X$, defined $\forall x \subseteq X$ by $f_B(x) = B - x$, is *not* monotone. On the other hand, $g_B(x) = B \cup x$ and $h_B(x) = B \cap x$ are both monotone.

Let $(X, \preceq)$ be a poset, and let $f : X \longrightarrow X$. A value $x_0 \in X$ such that $x_0 = f(x_0)$ is, as we saw, a fixed point of f. A fixed point may not exist; for example, f_B in the above paragraph does not have a fixed point when $B \neq \emptyset$, since the set equation $x = B - x$ does not have a solution in that case. There may also be many fixed points; for example, $f(x) = x$ has $|X|$ many fixed points.

Theorem 9.66 (Knaster-Tarski (1)). *Let $(X, \preceq)$ be a complete lattice, and let $f : X \longrightarrow X$ be a monotone function. Then the least fixed point of f exists and it is equal to $\inf(\{x | f(x) \preceq x\})$.*

Proof. Let $x_0 = \inf(\{x | f(x) \preceq x\})$. First we show that $x_0 = f(x_0)$. Let $B = \{x | f(x) \preceq x\}$, and note that $B \neq \emptyset$ because $\top = \sup(X) \in B$. Let $x \in B$, so we have $x_0 \preceq x$, hence since f is monotone, $f(x_0) \preceq f(x)$, i.e.,

$$f(x_0) \preceq f(x) \preceq x.$$

This is true for each x in B, so $f(x_0)$ is a lower bound for B, and since x_0 is the greatest lower bound of B, it follows that $f(x_0) \preceq x_0$.

Since f is monotone it follows that $f(f(x_0)) \preceq f(x_0)$, which means that $f(x_0)$ is in B. But then $x_0 \preceq f(x_0)$, which means that $x_0 = f(x_0)$.

It remains to show that x_0 is the least fixed point. Let $x' = f(x')$. This means that $f(x') \preceq x'$, i.e., $x' \in B$. But then $x_0 \preceq x'$. $\qquad\square$

Theorem 9.67 (Knaster-Tarski (2)). *Let $(X, \preceq)$ be a complete lattice, and let $f : X \longrightarrow X$ be a monotone function. Then the greatest fixed point of the equation $x = f(x)$ exists and it is equal to $\sup(\{x | f(x) \succeq x\})$.*

Note that these theorems are not constructive, but in the case of finite X, there is a constructive way of finding the least and greatest fixed points.

Theorem 9.68 (Knaster-Tarski: Finite Sets). *Let $(X, \preceq)$ be a lattice, $|X| = m$, $f : X \longrightarrow X$ a monotone function. Then $f^m(\bot)$ is the least fixed point, and $f^m(\top)$ is the greatest fixed point.*

Proof. Since $|X| = m$, $(X, \preceq)$ is a complete lattice, $\bot = \inf(X)$ and $\top = \sup(X)$ both exist. Since f is monotone, and $\bot \preceq f(\bot)$, we have $f(\bot) \preceq f(f(\bot))$, i.e., $f(\bot) \preceq f^2(\bot)$. Continuing to apply monotonicity we obtain:

$$f^0(\bot) = \bot \preceq f(\bot) \preceq f^2(\bot) \preceq f^3(\bot) \preceq \cdots \preceq f^i(\bot) \preceq f^{i+1}(\bot) \preceq \cdots.$$

Consider the above sequence up to $f^m(\bot)$. It has length $(m+1)$, but X has only m elements, so there are $i < j$, such that $f^i(\bot) = f^j(\bot)$. Since $\preceq$ is an order, it follows that

$$f^i(\bot) = f^{i+1}(\bot) = \cdots = f^j(\bot),$$

so $x_0 = f^i(\perp)$ is a fixed point as

$$f(x_0) = f(f^i(\perp)) = f^{i+1}(\perp) = f^i(\perp) = x_0.$$

Clearly $f^{j+1}(\perp) = f(f^j(\perp)) = f(x_0) = x_0$, so in fact $\forall k \geq i$, $x_0 = f^k(\perp)$, and so $f^m(\perp) = x_0$, so $f^m(\perp)$ is a fixed point.

We now suppose that x is another fixed point of f, i.e., $x = f(x)$. Since $\perp \preceq x$, and f is monotone, we conclude $f(\perp) \preceq f(x) = x$, i.e., $f(\perp) \preceq x$. Again, since f is monotone, $f(f(\perp)) \preceq f(x) = x$, so $f^2(\perp) \preceq x$. Hence, repeating this procedure sufficiently many times, we obtain $f^i(\perp) \preceq x$ for each i, so we get $x_0 = f^m(\perp) \preceq x$.

We do a similar argument for "greatest." $\qquad\square$

The situation is even better for the standard lattice $(\mathcal{P}(X), \subseteq)$, if X is finite.

Theorem 9.69. *Let X be a finite set, $|X| = n$, $f : \mathcal{P}(X) \longrightarrow \mathcal{P}(X)$ is monotone. Then $f^{n+1}(\emptyset)$ is the least fixed point, and $f^{n+1}(X)$ is the greatest fixed point.*

Proof. Note that the previous theorem says that $f^{2^n}(\emptyset)$ is the least fixed point, and $f^{2^n}(X)$ is the greatest fixed point, since $|\mathcal{P}(X)| = 2^n$, $\perp = \emptyset$ and $\top = X$, for the lattice $(\mathcal{P}(X), \subseteq)$. But this theorem claims $(n + 1)$ instead of 2^n. The reason is that $\emptyset \subseteq f(\emptyset) \subseteq f^2(\emptyset) \subseteq \cdots \subseteq f^{n+1}(\emptyset)$ *must* have two repeating sets (because $|X| = n$). $\qquad\square$

Problem 9.70. *Consider the lattice $(\mathcal{P}(\{a, b, c\}), \subseteq)$ and the functions $f(x) = x \cup \{a, b\}$ and $g(x) = x \cap \{a, b\}$. Compute their respective least/greatest fixed points.*

Let $(X, \preceq)$ be a complete lattice. A function $f : X \longrightarrow X$ is called

(1) *upward continuous* iff $\forall A \subseteq X$, $f(\sup(A)) = \sup(f(A))$,
(2) *downward continuous* iff $\forall A \subseteq X$, $f(\inf(A)) = \inf(f(A))$,
(3) *continuous* if it is both upward and downward continuous.

Lemma 9.71. *If $f : X \longrightarrow X$ is upward (downward) continuous, then it is monotone.*

Proof. Let f be upward continuous and $x \preceq y$, so $x = \inf(\{x, y\})$ and $y = \sup(\{x, y\})$, and

$$f(x) \preceq \sup(\{f(x), f(y)\}) = \sup(f(\{x, y\})) = f(\sup(\{x, y\})) = f(y).$$

A similar argument for downward continuous. $\qquad\square$

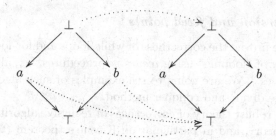

Fig. 9.8   An example of an ordering over $X = \{a, b, \bot, \top\}$, with a function $f : X \longrightarrow X$, indicated by the dotted lines. That is, $f(\bot) = \bot$ and $f(a) = f(b) = f(\top) = \top$. It can be checked by inspection that f is monotone, but it is not downward continuous.

Problem 9.72. *Show that the function f in figure 9.8 is not upward continuous. Give an example of a monotone function g that is neither upward nor downward continuous.*

Theorem 9.73 (Kleene). *If $(X, \preceq)$ is a complete lattice, $f : X \longrightarrow X$ is an upward continuous function, then $x_0 = \sup(\{f^n(\bot) | n = 1, 2, \ldots\})$ is the least fixed point of f.*

Proof.   Note that $\bot \preceq f(\bot)$, so by monotonicity of f, we have that

$$\bot \preceq f(\bot) \preceq f^2(\bot) \preceq f^3(\bot) \preceq \cdots \tag{9.10}$$

and,

$$f(x_0) = f(\sup(\{f^n(\bot) | n = 1, 2, \ldots\}))$$

and since f is upward continuous

$$= \sup(f(\{f^n(\bot) | n = 1, 2, \ldots\}))$$
$$= \sup(\{f^{n+1}(\bot) | n = 1, 2, \ldots\})$$

and by (9.10),

$$= \sup(\{f^n(\bot) | n = 1, 2, \ldots\}) = x_0$$

so $f(x_0) = x_0$, i.e., x_0 is a fixed point.

Let $x = f(x)$. We have $\bot \preceq x$ and f is monotone, so $f(\bot) \preceq f(x) = x$, i.e., $f(\bot) \preceq x$, $f^2(\bot) \preceq f(x) = x$, etc., i.e., $f^n(\bot) \preceq x$, for all n, so by the definition of sup,

$$x_0 = \sup(\{f^n(\bot) | n = 1, 2, \ldots\}) \preceq x,$$

so x_0 is the least fixed point. $\qquad\qquad\qquad\qquad\qquad\qquad\qquad\square$

9.3.6   *Recursion and fixed points*

So far we have proved the correctness of while-loops and for-loops, but there is another way of "looping" using *recursive* procedures, i.e., algorithms that "call themselves." We are going to see examples of such algorithms in the chapter on the divide and conquer method.

There is a robust theory of correctness of recursive algorithms based on fixed point theory, and in particular on Kleene's theorem (theorem 9.73). We briefly illustrate this approach with an example. Consider the recursive algorithm 9.1.

Algorithm 9.1 $F(x, y)$

1: **if** $x = y$ **then**
2:         **return** $y + 1$
3: **else**
4:         $F(x, F(x - 1, y + 1))$
5: **end if**

To see how this algorithm works consider computing $F(4, 2)$. First in line 1 it is established that $4 \neq 2$ and so we must compute $F(4, F(3, 3))$. We first compute $F(3, 3)$, recursively, so in line 1 it is now established that $3 = 3$, and so in line 2 y is set to 4 and that is the value returned, i.e., $F(3, 3) = 4$, so now we can go back and compute $F(4, F(3, 3)) = F(4, 4)$, so again, recursively, we establish in line 1 that $4 = 4$, and so in line 2 y is set to 5 and this is the value returned, i.e., $F(4, 2) = 5$. On the other hand it is easy to see that

$$F(3, 5) = F(3, F(2, 6)) = F(3, F(2, F(1, 7))) = \cdots,$$

and this procedure never ends as x will never equal y. Thus F is not a *total* function, i.e., not defined on all $(x, y) \in \mathbb{Z} \times \mathbb{Z}$.

Problem 9.74. *What is the* domain of definition *of F as computed by algorithm 9.1? That is, the domain of F is $\mathbb{Z} \times \mathbb{Z}$, while the domain of definition is the largest subset $S \subseteq \mathbb{Z} \times \mathbb{Z}$ such that F is defined for all $(x, y) \in S$. We have seen already that $(4, 2) \in S$ while $(3, 5) \notin S$.*

We now consider three different functions, all given by algorithms that are not recursive: algorithms 9.2, 9.3 and 9.4, computing functions f_1, f_2 and f_3, respectively.

Functions f_1 has an interesting property: if we were to replace F in algorithm 9.1 with f_1 we would get back F. In other words, given algorithm 9.1,

---

Algorithm 9.2 $f_1(x, y)$

---

   if $x = y$ **then**
        return $y + 1$
   else
        return $x + 1$
   end if

---

if we were to replace line 4 with $f_1(x, f_1(x-1, y+1))$, and compute f_1 with the (non-recursive) algorithm 9.2 for f_1, then algorithm 9.1 thus modified would now be computing $F(x, y)$. Therefore, we say that the function f_1 is a *fixed point* of the recursive algorithm 9.1.

For example, recall the we have already shown that $F(4, 2) = 5$, using the recursive algorithm 9.1 for computing F. Replace line 4 in algorithm 9.1 with $f_1(x, f_1(x - 1, y + 1))$ and compute $F(4, 2)$ anew; since $4 \neq 2$ we go directly to line 4 where we compute $f_1(4, f_1(3, 3)) = f_1(4, 4) = 5$. Notice that this last computation was not recursive, as we computed f_1 directly with algorithm 9.2, and that we have obtained the same value.

Consider now f_2, f_3, computed by algorithms 9.3, 9.4, respectively.

Algorithm 9.3 $f_2(x, y)$

---

   if $x \geq y$ **then**
        return $x + 1$
   else
        return $y - 1$
   end if

Algorithm 9.4 $f_3(x, y)$

---

   if $x \geq y \wedge (x - y$ is even$)$ **then**
        return $x + 1$
   end if

Notice that in algorithm 9.4, if it is not the case that $x \geq y$ and $x - y$ is even, then the output is undefined. Thus f_3 is a partial function, and if $x < y$ or $x - y$ is odd, then (x, y) is not in its domain of definition.

Problem 9.75. *Prove that f_1, f_2, f_3 are all fixed points of algorithm 9.1.*

The function f_3 has one additional property. For every pair of integers x, y such that $f_3(x, y)$ is defined, that is $x \geq y$ and $x - y$ is even, both $f_1(x, y)$

and $f_2(x, y)$ are also defined and have the same value as $f_3(x, y)$. We say that f_3 is *less defined than or equal to* f_1 and f_2, and write $f_3 \sqsubseteq f_1$ and $f_3 \sqsubseteq f_2$; that is, we have defined (informally) a partial order on functions $f : \mathbb{Z} \times \mathbb{Z} \longrightarrow \mathbb{Z} \times \mathbb{Z}$.

Problem 9.76. *Show that $f_3 \sqsubseteq f_1$ and $f_3 \sqsubseteq f_2$. Recall the notion of a domain of definition introduced in problem 9.74. Let S_1, S_2, S_3 be the domains of definition of f_1, f_2, f_3, respectively. You must show that $S_3 \subseteq S_1$ and $S_3 \subseteq S_2$.*

It can be shown that f_3 has this property, not only with respect to f_1 and f_2, but also with respect to all fixed points of algorithm 9.1. Moreover, $f_3(x, y)$ is the only function having this property, and therefore f_3 is said to be the *least (defined) fixed point of* algorithm 9.1. It is an important application of Kleene's theorem (theorem 9.73) that every recursive algorithm has a unique fixed point.

9.4   Logic

We present the foundations of propositional and predicate logic with the aim of defining Peano Arithmetic (PA). PA is the standard formalization of number theory, and it is the logical background for section 9.4.4—Formal Verification. Our treatment of logic is limited to providing this background, but the reader can find more resources in the Notes section.

9.4.1   *Propositional logic*

Propositional (Boolean) formulas are built from *propositional (Boolean) variables*[2] $p_1, p_2, p_3, \ldots$, and the logical connectives $\neg, \wedge, \vee$, listed in the preface on page 2.

We often use different labels for our variables (e.g., $a, b, c, \ldots, x, y, z, \ldots,$ $p, q, r, \ldots$, etc.) as "metavariables" that stand for variables, and we define propositional formulas by structural induction: any variable p is a formula, and if α, β are formulas, then so are $\neg\alpha, (\alpha \wedge \beta)$, and $(\alpha \vee \beta)$. For example, $p, (p \vee q), (\neg(p \wedge q) \wedge (\neg p \vee \neg q))$. Recall also from the preface, that $\rightarrow$ and $\leftrightarrow$ are the implication and equivalence connectives, respectively.

---

[2]Propositional variables are sometimes called *atoms*. A very thorough, and perhaps now considered a little bit old fashioned, discussion of "names" in logic (what is a "variable," what is a "constant," etc.), can be found in [Church (1996)], sections 01 and 02.

Problem 9.77. *Define propositional formulas with a context-free grammar.*

symbol	weight
$\neg$	0
$\wedge, \vee, ($	1
$), p$, for each variable p	-1

Fig. 9.9   Assignments of "weights" to symbols.

Lemma 9.78. *Assign weights to all symbols as in figure 9.9. The weight of any formula α is -1, but the weight of any proper initial segment is ≥ 0. Hence no proper initial segment of a formula is a formula.*

Proof. By structural induction on the length of α. The basis case is: $w(p) = -1$, for any variable p. The induction step has three cases: $\neg\alpha$, $(\alpha \wedge \beta)$ and $(\alpha \vee \beta)$. This shows that any well-formed formula has weight -1. We now show that any proper initial segment has weight ≥ 0. In the basis case (a single variable p) there are no initial segments; in the induction step, suppose that the claim holds for α and β (that is, any initial segment of α, and any initial segment of β, has weight ≥ 0). Then the same holds for $\neg\alpha$, as any initial segment of $\neg\alpha$ contains $\neg$ (and $w(\neg) = 0$) and some (perhaps empty) initial segment of α. □

Problem 9.79. *Finish the details of the proof of lemma 9.78.*

Let $\alpha \overset{\text{syn}}{=} \alpha'$ emphasize that α and α' are equal as string of symbols, i.e., we have a syntactic identity, rather than a semantic identity.

Theorem 9.80 (Unique Readability Theorem). *Suppose $\alpha, \beta, \alpha', \beta'$ are formulas, c, c' are binary connectives, and $(\alpha c \beta) \overset{\text{syn}}{=} (\alpha' c' \beta')$. Then $\alpha \overset{\text{syn}}{=} \alpha'$ and $\beta \overset{\text{syn}}{=} \beta'$ and $c \overset{\text{syn}}{=} c'$.*

Note that this theorem says that the grammar for generating formulas is unambiguous. Or, put another way, it says that there is only one candidate for the main connective, which means that the parse tree of any formula is unique. Recall that in problem 9.11 we compared infix, prefix, postfix notations; Boolean formulas are given in infix notation in the sense that the binary operators ($\wedge, \vee$) are placed in between the operands, and yet it is unambiguous (whereas problem 9.11 says that we need two out of three representations, from among {infix,prefix,postfix}, to represent a tree unambiguously). The difference is that in the case of Boolean formulas we have parentheses to delimit subformulas.

Problem 9.81. *Show that theorem 9.80 is a consequence of lemma 9.78. (Hint: define the weight of a formula to be the sum of the weights of all the symbols in it.)*

A *truth assignment* is a map τ : {variables} $\longrightarrow \{T, F\}$. Here $\{T, F\}$ represents "true" and "false," sometimes denoted 0,1, respectively. The truth assignment τ can be extended to assign either T of F to every formula as follows:

(1) $(\neg\alpha)^\tau = T$ iff $\alpha^\tau = F$
(2) $(\alpha \wedge \beta)^\tau = T$ iff $\alpha^\tau = T$ and $\beta^\tau = T$
(3) $(\alpha \vee \beta)^\tau = T$ iff $\alpha^\tau = T$ or $\beta^\tau = T$

The following are standard definitions: we say that the truth assignment τ *satisfies* the formula α if $\alpha^\tau = T$, and τ *satisfies* a set of formulas Φ if τ satisfies all $\alpha \in \Phi$. In turn, the set of formulas Φ is *satisfiable* if some τ satisfies it; otherwise, Φ is *unsatisfiable*. We say that α is a *logical consequence* of Φ, written $\Phi \vDash \alpha$, if τ satisfies α for every τ such that τ satisfies Φ. A formula α is *valid* if $\vDash \alpha$, i.e., $\alpha^\tau = T$ for all τ. A valid propositional formula is called a *tautology*. α and β are *equivalent* formulas (written $\alpha \iff \beta$) if $\alpha \vDash \beta$ and $\beta \vDash \alpha$. Note that ' $\iff$ ' and '$\leftrightarrow$' have different meanings: one is a semantic assertion, and the other is a syntactic assertion. Yet, one holds if and only if the other holds.

For example, the following are tautologies: $p \vee \neg p, p \rightarrow p, \neg(p \wedge \neg p)$. An instance of logical consequence: $(p \wedge q) \vDash (p \vee q)$. Finally, an example of equivalence: $\neg(p \vee q) \iff (\neg p \wedge \neg q)$. This last statement is known as the "De Morgan Law."

Problem 9.82. *Show that if $\Phi \vDash \alpha$ and $\Phi \cup \{\alpha\} \vDash \beta$, then $\Phi \vDash \beta$.*

Problem 9.83. *Prove the following* Duality Theorem: *Let α' be the result of interchanging $\vee$ and $\wedge$ in α, and replacing p by $\neg p$ for each variable p. Then $\neg\alpha \iff \alpha'$.*

Problem 9.84. *Prove the* Craig Interpolation Theorem: *Let α and β be any two propositional formulas. Let $Var(\alpha)$ be the set of variables that occur in α. Let $S = Var(\alpha) \cap Var(\beta)$. Assume S is not empty. If $A \rightarrow B$ is valid, then there exists a formula C such that $Var(C) = S$, called an "interpolant" such that $A \rightarrow C$ and $C \rightarrow B$ are both valid.*

One way to establish that a formula α with n variables is a tautology is to verify that $\alpha^\tau = T$ for all 2^n truth assignments τ to the variables of α. A similar exhaustive method can be used to verify that $\Phi \vDash \alpha$ (if Φ is finite). Another way, is to use the notion of a formal proof; here we present the PK proof system, due to the German logician Gentzen (PK abbreviates "Propositional Kalkül").

In the propositional sequent calculus system PK, each line in a proof is a *sequent* of the form:

$$S = \alpha_1, \ldots, \alpha_k \to \beta_1, \ldots, \beta_l$$

where $\to$ is a new symbol, and $\alpha_1, \ldots, \alpha_k$ and $\beta_1, \ldots, \beta_l$ are sequences of formulas ($k, l \geq 0$) called *cedents* (*antecedent* and *succedent*, respectively).

A truth assignment τ *satisfies* the sequent S iff τ falsifies some α_i or τ satisfies some β_i, i.e., iff τ satisfies the formula:

$$\alpha_S = (\alpha_1 \wedge \cdots \wedge \alpha_k) \to (\beta_1 \vee \cdots \vee \beta_l)$$

If the antecedent is empty, $\to \alpha$ is equivalent to α, and if the succedent is empty, $\alpha \to$ is equivalent to $\neg\alpha$. If both antecedent and succedent are empty, then $\to$ is false (unsatisfiable).

We have the analogous definitions of validity and logical consequence for sequents. For example, the following are valid sequents: $\alpha \to \alpha$, $\to \alpha, \neg\alpha$, $\alpha \wedge \neg\alpha \to$.

A formal *proof* in PK is a finite rooted tree in which the nodes are labeled with sequents. The sequent at the root (bottom) is what is being proved: the *endsequent*. The sequents at the leaves (top) are *logical axioms*, and must be of the form $\alpha \to \alpha$, where α is a formula. Each sequent other than the logical axioms must follow from its parent sequent(s) by one of the rules of inference listed in figure 9.10.

Problem 9.85. *Give PK proofs for each of the following valid sequents:* $\neg p \vee \neg q \to \neg(p \vee q)$, $\neg(p \vee q) \to \neg p \wedge \neg q$, *and* $\neg p \wedge \neg q \to \neg(p \vee q)$, *as well as* $(p_1 \wedge (p_2 \wedge (p_3 \wedge p_4))) \to (((p_1 \wedge p_2) \wedge p_3) \wedge p_4)$.

Problem 9.86. *Show that the contraction rules can be derived from the cut rule (with exchanges and weakenings).*

Problem 9.87. *Suppose that we allowed $\leftrightarrow$ as a primitive connective, rather than one introduced by definition. Give the appropriate left and right introduction rules for $\leftrightarrow$.*

Weak structural rules

exchange-left: $\dfrac{\Gamma_1, \alpha, \beta, \Gamma_2 \to \Delta}{\Gamma_1, \beta, \alpha, \Gamma_2 \to \Delta}$ exchange-right: $\dfrac{\Gamma \to \Delta_1, \alpha, \beta, \Delta_2}{\Gamma \to \Delta_1, \beta, \alpha, \Delta_2}$

contraction-left: $\dfrac{\Gamma, \alpha, \alpha \to \Delta}{\Gamma, \alpha \to \Delta}$ contraction-right: $\dfrac{\Gamma \to \Delta, \alpha, \alpha}{\Gamma \to \Delta, \alpha}$

weakening-left: $\dfrac{\Gamma \to \Delta}{\alpha, \Gamma \to \Delta}$ weakening-right: $\dfrac{\Gamma \to \Delta}{\Gamma \to \Delta, \alpha}$

Cut rule

$$\dfrac{\Gamma \to \Delta, \alpha \quad \alpha, \Gamma \to \Delta}{\Gamma \to \Delta}$$

Rules for introducing connectives

$\neg$-left: $\dfrac{\Gamma \to \Delta, \alpha}{\neg\alpha, \Gamma \to \Delta}$ $\neg$-right: $\dfrac{\alpha, \Gamma \to \Delta}{\Gamma \to \Delta, \neg\alpha}$

$\wedge$-left: $\dfrac{\alpha, \beta, \Gamma \to \Delta}{(\alpha \wedge \beta), \Gamma \to \Delta}$ $\wedge$-right: $\dfrac{\Gamma \to \Delta, \alpha \quad \Gamma \to \Delta, \beta}{\Gamma \to \Delta, (\alpha \wedge \beta)}$

$\vee$-left: $\dfrac{\alpha, \Gamma \to \Delta \quad \beta, \Gamma \to \Delta}{(\alpha \vee \beta), \Gamma \to \Delta}$ $\vee$-right: $\dfrac{\Gamma \to \Delta, \alpha, \beta}{\Gamma \to \Delta, (\alpha \vee \beta)}$

Fig. 9.10   PK rules. Note that Γ, Δ denote finite sequences of formulas.

For each PK rule, the sequent on the bottom is a logical consequence of the sequent(s) on the top; call this the *Rule Soundness Principle*. For example, in the case of $\vee$-right it can be shown as follows: suppose that τ satisfies the top sequent; suppose now that it satisfies Γ. Then, since τ satisfies the top, it has to satisfy one of Δ, α or β. If it satisfies Δ we are done; if it satisfies one of α, β then it satisfies $\alpha \vee \beta$ and we are also done.

Problem 9.88. *Check the Rule Soundness Principle: check that each rule is sound, i.e., the bottom of each rule is a logical consequence of the top.*

Theorem 9.89 (PK Soundness). *Each sequent provable in PK is valid.*

Proof. We show that the endsequent in every PK proof is valid, by induction on the number of sequents in the proof. For the basis case, the proof is a single line; an axiom $\alpha \to \alpha$, and it is obviously valid. For the induction step, one need only verify for each rule, if all top sequents are valid, then the bottom sequent is valid. This follows from the Rule Soundness Principle. □

The following is known as the *Inversion Principle*: for each PK rule, except weakening, if the bottom sequent is valid, then all top sequents are valid.

Problem 9.90. *Inspect each rule, and prove the Inversion Principle. Give an example, with the weakening rule, for which this principle fails.*

Theorem 9.91 (PK Completeness). *Every valid propositional sequent is provable in PK without using cut or contraction.*

Proof. We show that every valid sequent $\Gamma \to \Delta$ has a PK proof, by induction on the total number of connectives $\wedge, \vee, \neg$, occurring in $\Gamma \to \Delta$.

Basis case: zero connectives, so every formula in $\Gamma \to \Delta$ is a variable, and since it is valid, some variable p must be in both Γ and Δ. Hence $\Gamma \to \Delta$ can be derived from $p \to p$ by weakenings and exchanges.

Induction Step: suppose γ is not a variable, in Γ or Δ. Then it is of the form $\neg\alpha, (\alpha \wedge \beta), (\alpha \vee \beta)$. Then, $\Gamma \to \Delta$ can be derived by one of the connective introduction rules, using exchanges.

The top sequent(s) will have one fewer connective than $\Gamma \to \Delta$, and are valid by the Inversion Principle; hence they have PK proofs by the induction hypothesis. □

Problem 9.92. *What are the five rules not used in the induction step in the above proof?*

Problem 9.93. *Consider* PK$'$, *which is like* PK, *but where the axioms must be of the form* $p \to p$, *i.e.,* α *must be a variable in the logical axioms. Is* PK$'$ *still complete?*

Problem 9.94. *Suppose that* $\{\to \beta_1, \ldots, \to \beta_n\} \vDash \Gamma \to \Delta$. *Give a PK proof of* $\Gamma \to \Delta$ *where all the leaves are either logical axioms* $\alpha \to \alpha$, *or one of the non-logical axioms* $\to \beta_i$. *(Hint: your proof will require the use of the cut rule.) Now give a proof of the fact that given a finite* Φ *such that*

$\Phi \vDash \Gamma \to \Delta$, *there exists a PK proof of* $\Gamma \to \Delta$ *where all the leaves are logical axioms or sequents in* Φ. *This shows that* PK *is also* Implicationally Complete.

9.4.1.1 *Extended PK*

There is a natural extension of the PK system into what is called an Extended PK (EPK). A standard technique in mathematical proofs is to allow abbreviations of complex formulas which can then be utilized in the rest of the proof instead of rewriting the long formulas each time that they are needed. This can be done at the level of propositional logic by allowing axioms of the form:

$$p \leftrightarrow \alpha,$$

where p is a new variable that has not occurred in the proof yet, and α is any formula. The power of this construction arises from the nesting of these definitions, that is, α may employ some previously defined new variables.

Problem 9.95. *Show that any EPK proof can be rewritten as a PK proof. What happens, in general, to the size of the new PK proof?*

It is an interesting observation, beyond the scope of this book, that while PK corresponds to reasoning with Boolean formulas, EPK corresponds to reasoning with Boolean circuits. See [Cook and Nguyen (2010)], [Krajíček (1995)] or [Cook and Soltys (1999)].

9.4.2 *First Order Logic*

First Order Logic is also known as Predicate Calculus. We start by defining a *language* $\mathcal{L} = \{f_1, f_2, f_3, \ldots, R_1, R_2, R_3, \ldots\}$ to be a set of function and relation symbols. Each function and relation symbol has an associated *arity*, i.e., the number of arguments that it takes. $\mathcal{L}$-*terms* are defined by structural induction as follows: every variable is a term: $x, y, z, \ldots, a, b, c, \ldots$; if f is an n-ary function symbol and $t_1, t_2, \ldots, t_n$ are terms, then so is $f t_1 t_2 \ldots t_n$. A 0-ary function symbol is a constant (we use c and e as a metasymbols for constants). For example, if f is a binary (arity 2) function symbol and g is a unary (arity 1) function symbol, then $fgex, fxy, gfege$ are terms.

Problem 9.96. *Show the Unique Readability Theorem for terms. See theorem 9.80 for a refresher of unique readability in the propositional case.*

For example, the language of arithmetic, so called Peano Arithmetic, is given by $\mathcal{L}_A = [0, s, +, \cdot; =]$. We use infix notation (defined on page 234) instead of the formal prefix notation for $\mathcal{L}_A$ function symbols $\cdot, +$. That is, we write $(t_1 \cdot t_2)$ instead of $\cdot t_1 t_2$, and we write $(t_1 + t_2)$ instead of $+t_1 t_2$. For example, the following are $\mathcal{L}_A$-terms: $sss0, ((x + sy) \cdot (ssz + s0))$. Note that we use infix notation with parentheses, since otherwise the notation would be ambiguous.

We construct $\mathcal{L}$-formulas as follows:

(1) $Rt_1 t_2 \ldots t_n$ is an *atomic formula*, R is an n-ary predicate symbol, $t_1, t_2, \ldots, t_n$ are terms.
(2) If α, β are formulas, then so are $\neg\alpha, (\alpha \vee \beta), (\alpha \wedge \beta)$.
(3) If α is a formula, and x a variable, then $\forall x \alpha$ and $\exists x \alpha$ are also formulas.

For example, $(\neg \forall x Px \vee \exists x \neg Px)$, $(\forall x \neg Qxy \wedge \neg \forall z Q fyz)$ are first order formulas.

Problem 9.97. *Show that the set of $\mathcal{L}$-formulas can be given by a context-free grammar.*

We also use the infix notation with the equality predicate; that is, we write $r = s$ instead of $= rs$ and we write $r \neq s$ instead of $\neg = rs$.

An occurrence of x in α is *bound* if it is in a subformula of α of the form $\forall x \beta$ or $\exists x \beta$ (i.e., in the *scope* of a quantifier). Otherwise, the occurrence is *free*. For example, in $\exists y(x = y + y)$, x is free, but y is bound. In $Px \wedge \forall x Qx$ the variable x occurs both as free and bound. A term t or formula α are *closed* if they contain no free variables. A closed formula is called a *sentence*.

We now present a way of assigning meaning to first order formulas: *Tarski semantics*; we are going to use the standard terminology and refer to Tarski semantics as the *basic semantic definitions* (BSD).

A *structure* (or *interpretation*) gives meaning to terms and formulas. An $\mathcal{L}$ structure $\mathcal{M}$ consists of:

(1) A nonempty set M, called the *universe of discourse*.
(2) For each n-ary f, $f^{\mathcal{M}} : M^n \longrightarrow M$.
(3) For each n-ary P, $P^{\mathcal{M}} \subseteq M^n$.

If $\mathcal{L}$ contains $=$, $=^{\mathcal{M}}$ must be the usual $=$. Thus equality is special—it must always be the true equality. On the other hand, $<^{\mathcal{M}}$ could be anything, not necessarily the order relation we are used to.

Every $\mathcal{L}$-sentence becomes either true or false when interpreted by an $\mathcal{L}$-structure $\mathcal{M}$. If a sentence α becomes true under $\mathcal{M}$, we say $\mathcal{M}$ *satisfies* α, or $\mathcal{M}$ is a *model* for α, and write $\mathcal{M} \vDash \alpha$.

If α has free variables, then they must get values from M (the universe of discourse), before α can get a truth value under $\mathcal{M}$. An *object assignment* σ for a structure $\mathcal{M}$ is a mapping from variables to the universe M. In this context, $t^{\mathcal{M}}[\sigma]$ is an element in M—given by the structure $\mathcal{M}$ and the object assignment σ. $\mathcal{M} \vDash \alpha[\sigma]$ means that $\mathcal{M}$ satisfies α when its free variables are assigned values by σ.

This has to be defined very carefully; we show how to compute $t^{\mathcal{M}}[\sigma]$ by structural induction:

(1) $x^{\mathcal{M}}[\sigma]$ is $\sigma(x)$

(2) $(ft_1t_2\ldots t_n)^{\mathcal{M}}[\sigma]$ is $f^{\mathcal{M}}(t_1^{\mathcal{M}}[\sigma], t_2^{\mathcal{M}}[\sigma], \ldots, t_n^{\mathcal{M}}[\sigma])$

If x is a variable, and m is in the universe of discourse, i.e., $m \in M$, then $\sigma(m/x)$ is the same object assignment as σ, except that x is mapped to m. Now we present the definition of $\mathcal{M} \vDash \alpha[\sigma]$ by structural induction:

(1) $\mathcal{M} \vDash (Pt_1\ldots t_n)[\sigma]$ iff $(t_1^{\mathcal{M}}[\sigma], \ldots, t_n^{\mathcal{M}}[\sigma]) \in P^{\mathcal{M}}$.

(2) $\mathcal{M} \vDash \neg\alpha[\sigma]$ iff $\mathcal{M} \nvDash \alpha[\sigma]$.

(3) $\mathcal{M} \vDash (\alpha \overset{(\vee)}{\wedge} \beta)[\sigma]$ iff $\mathcal{M} \vDash \alpha[\sigma]$ $\overset{(\text{or})}{\text{and}}$ $\mathcal{M} \vDash \beta[\sigma]$.

(4) $\mathcal{M} \vDash (\overset{(\exists)}{\forall} x\alpha)[\sigma]$ iff $\mathcal{M} \vDash \alpha[\sigma(m/x)]$ for $\overset{(\text{some})}{\text{all}}$ $m \in M$.

If t is closed, we write $t^{\mathcal{M}}$; if α is a sentence, we write $\mathcal{M} \vDash \alpha$.

For example, let $\mathcal{L} = [; R, =]$ (R binary predicate) and let $\mathcal{M}$ be an $\mathcal{L}$-structure with universe $\mathbb{N}$ and such that $(m, n) \in R^{\mathcal{M}}$ iff $m \leq n$. Then, $\mathcal{M} \vDash \exists x\forall y Rxy$, but, $\mathcal{M} \nvDash \exists y\forall x Rxy$.

The *standard structure* $\underline{\mathbb{N}}$ for the language $\mathcal{L}_A$ has universe $M = \mathbb{N}$, $s^{\underline{\mathbb{N}}}(n) = n+1$, and $0, +, \cdot, =$ get their usual meaning on the natural numbers. For example, $\underline{\mathbb{N}} \vDash \forall x\forall y\exists z(x + z = y \vee y + z = x)$, but $\underline{\mathbb{N}} \nvDash \forall x\exists y(y + y = x)$.

We say that a formula α is *satisfiable* iff $\mathcal{M} \vDash \alpha[\sigma]$ for some $\mathcal{M}$ & σ. Let Φ denote a set of formulas; then, $\mathcal{M} \vDash \Phi[\sigma]$ iff $\mathcal{M} \vDash \alpha[\sigma]$ for all $\alpha \in \Phi$. $\Phi \vDash \alpha$ iff $(\forall \mathcal{M}, \sigma), (\mathcal{M} \vDash \Phi[\sigma] \to \mathcal{M} \vDash \alpha[\sigma])$, i.e., α is a *logical consequence* of Φ. We say that a formula α is *valid*, and write $\vDash \alpha$, iff $\mathcal{M} \vDash \alpha[\sigma]$ for all $\mathcal{M}$ & σ. We say that α and β are *logically equivalent*, and write $\alpha \iff \beta$, iff for all $\mathcal{M}$ & σ, $(\mathcal{M} \vDash \alpha[\sigma]$ iff $\mathcal{M} \vDash \beta[\sigma])$.

Note that $\vDash$ is a symbol of the "meta language" (English), as opposed to $\wedge, \vee, \exists, \ldots$ which are symbols of first order logic. Also, if Φ is just one formula, i.e., $\Phi = \{\beta\}$, then we write $\beta \vDash \alpha$ in place of $\{\beta\} \vDash \alpha$.

Problem 9.98. *Show that* $(\forall x\alpha \vee \forall x\beta) \vDash \forall x(\alpha \vee \beta)$, *for all formulas* α *and* β.

Problem 9.99. *Is it the case that* $\forall x(\alpha \vee \beta) \vDash (\forall x\alpha \vee \forall x\beta)$?

Suppose that t, u are terms. Then:

$t(u/x)$ result of replacing all occurrences of x in t with u

$\alpha(u/x)$ result of replacing all *free* occurrences of x in α with u

Semantically, $(u(t/x))^{\mathcal{M}}[\sigma] = u^{\mathcal{M}}[\sigma(m/x)]$ where $m = t^{\mathcal{M}}[\sigma]$.

For example, let $\mathcal{M}$ be $\underline{\mathbb{N}}$ (the standard structure) for $\mathcal{L}_A$. Suppose $\sigma(x) = 5$ and $\sigma(y) = 7$. Let:

$$u \quad \text{be the term } x + y$$
$$t \quad \text{be the term } ss0$$

Then:

$$u(t/x) \text{ is } ss0 + y \text{ and so } (u(t/x))^{\underline{\mathbb{N}}}[\sigma] = 2 + 7 = 9$$

Similarly, $m = t^{\underline{\mathbb{N}}} = 2$, so $u^{\underline{\mathbb{N}}}[\sigma(m/x)] = 2 + 7 = 9$.

Problem 9.100. *Prove* $(u(t/x))^{\mathcal{M}}[\sigma] = u^{\mathcal{M}}[\sigma(m/x)]$ *where* $m = t^{\mathcal{M}}[\sigma]$, *using structural induction on* u.

Problem 9.101. *Does the result in problem 9.100 apply to formulas* α? *That is, is it true that* $\mathcal{M} \vDash \alpha(t/x)[\sigma]$ *iff* $\mathcal{M} \vDash \alpha[\sigma(m/x)]$, *where* $m = t^{\mathcal{M}}[\sigma]$?

For example, suppose α is $\forall y \neg(x = y + y)$. This says "$x$ is odd". But $\alpha(x + y/x)$ is $\forall y \neg(x + y = y + y)$ which is always false, regardless of the value of $\sigma(x)$. The problem is that y in the term $x + y$ got "caught" by the quantifier $\forall y$.

A term t is *freely substitutable for* x *in* α iff no free occurrence of x in α is in a subformula of α of the form $\forall y\beta$ or $\exists y\beta$, where y occurs in t.

Theorem 9.102 (Substitution Theorem). *If* t *is freely substitutable for* x *in* α *then for all structures* $\mathcal{M}$ *and all object assignments* σ, *it is the case that* $\mathcal{M} \vDash \alpha(t/x)[\sigma]$ *iff* $\mathcal{M} \vDash \alpha[\sigma(m/x)]$, *where* $m = t^{\mathcal{M}}[\sigma]$.

Problem 9.103. *Prove the Substitution Theorem. (Hint. Use structural induction on* α *and the BSDs.)*

If a term t is not freely substitutable for x in α, it is because some variable y in t gets caught by a quantifier $\forall y$ or $\exists y$ in α. One way to fix this is simply rename the bound variable y in α to some new variable z. This renaming does not change the meaning of α.

Let $a, b, c, \ldots$ denote free variables and let $x, y, z, \ldots$ to denote bound variables. A first order formula α is called a *proper formula* if it satisfies the restriction that it has no free occurrence of any "bound" variable and no bound occurrence of any "free" variable. Similarly a *proper term* has no "bound" variable. Notice that a subformula of a proper formula is not necessarily proper, and a proper formula may contain terms which are not proper.

The sequent system LK is an extension of the propositional system PK where now all formulas in the sequent $\alpha_1, \ldots, \alpha_k \to \beta_1, \ldots, \beta_l$ must be proper formulas. The system LK is PK together with the four rules for introducing quantifiers given in figure 9.11.

$$\forall \text{ introduction:} \qquad \frac{\alpha(t), \Gamma \to \Delta}{\forall x \alpha(x), \Gamma \to \Delta} \qquad \frac{\Gamma \to \Delta, \alpha(b)}{\Gamma \to \Delta, \forall x \alpha(x)}$$

$$\exists \text{ introduction:} \qquad \frac{\alpha(b), \Gamma \to \Delta}{\exists x \alpha(x), \Gamma \to \Delta} \qquad \frac{\Gamma \to \Delta, \alpha(t)}{\Gamma \to \Delta, \exists x \alpha(x)}$$

Fig. 9.11   Extending PK to LK.

There are some restrictions in the use of the rules given in figure 9.11. First, t is a proper term, and $\alpha(t)$ (respectively, $\alpha(b)$) is the result of substituting t (respectively, b) for all free occurrences of x in $\alpha(x)$. Note that t, b can be freely substituted for x in $\alpha(x)$ because $\forall x \alpha(x), \exists x \alpha(x)$ are proper formulas. The free variable b must not occur in the conclusion in $\forall$ right and $\exists$ left.

Problem 9.104. *Show that the four new rules are sound.*

Problem 9.105. *Give a specific example of a sequent $\Gamma \to \Delta, \alpha(b)$ which is valid, but the bottom sequent $\Gamma \to \Delta, \forall x \alpha(x)$ is not valid, because the restriction on b is violated (b occurs in Γ or Δ or $\forall x \alpha(x)$). Do the same for $\exists$ left.*

An LK proof of a valid first order sequent can be obtained using the same method as in the propositional case. Write the goal sequent at the bottom, and move up using the introduction rules in reverse. If there is a choice about which quantifier to remove next, choose $\forall$ right or $\exists$ left (working backward), since these rules carry a restriction.

9.4.3 *Peano Arithmetic*

Recall the language of arithmetic, $\mathcal{L}_A = [0, s, +, \cdot ; =]$. The axioms for PA are the following

P1 $\forall x(sx \neq 0)$
P2 $\forall x \forall y(sx = sy \rightarrow x = y)$
P3 $\forall x(x + 0 = x)$
P4 $\forall x \forall y(x + sy = s(x + y))$
P5 $\forall x(x \cdot 0 = 0)$
P6 $\forall x \forall y(x \cdot sy = x \cdot y + x)$

plus the *Induction Scheme:*

$$\forall y_1 \dots \forall y_k[(\alpha(0) \wedge \forall x(\alpha(x) \rightarrow \alpha(sx))) \rightarrow \forall x \alpha(x)] \qquad (9.11)$$

where α is any $\mathcal{L}_A$-formula, and (9.11) is a sentence. Note that this is the formal definition of induction given in section 9.1.1.

We also have a scheme of equality axioms.

E1 $\forall x(x = x)$
E2 $\forall x \forall y(x = y \rightarrow y = x)$
E3 $\forall x \forall y \forall z((x = y \wedge y = z) \rightarrow x = z)$
E4 $\forall x_1 \dots \forall x_n \forall y_1 \dots \forall y_n(x_1 = y_1 \wedge \dots \wedge x_n = y_n) \rightarrow fx_1 \dots x_n = fy_1 \dots y_n$
E5 $\forall x_1 \dots \forall x_n \forall y_1 \dots \forall y_n(x_1 = y_1 \wedge \dots \wedge x_n = y_n) \rightarrow Px_1 \dots x_n \rightarrow Py_1 \dots y_n$

where E4 and E5 hold for all n-ary function and predicate symbols. In $\mathcal{L}_A$, which is our language of interest, s is unary, $+, \cdot$ are binary, and $=$ is binary.

Let LK-PA be LK where the leaves are allowed to be P1-6 and E1-5, besides the usual axioms $\alpha \rightarrow \alpha$. For example, $\rightarrow \forall x(x = x)$ would be a valid leaf.

Problem 9.106. *Show that LK-PA proves that all nonzero elements have predecessor.*

Problem 9.107. *Show that LK-PA proves the following: the associative and commutative law of addition, the associative and commutative laws* *of multiplication and that multiplication distributes over addition. Specify carefully which axioms you are using.*

9.4.4 *Formal verification*

The proofs of correctness we have been giving thus far are considered to be "informal" mathematical proofs. There is nothing wrong with an informal proof, and in many cases such a proof is all that is necessary to convince oneself of the validity of a small "code snippet." However, there are many circumstances where extensive formal code validation is necessary; in that case, instead of an informal paper-and-pencil type of argument, we often employ computer assisted software verification. For example, the US Food and Drug Administration requires software certification in cases where medical devices are dependent on software for their effective and safe operation. When formal verification is required everything has to be stated explicitly, in a formal language, and proven painstakingly line by line. In this section we give an example of such a procedure.

Let $\{\alpha\}P\{\beta\}$ mean that if formula α is true before execution of P, P is executed and terminates, then formula β will be true, i.e., α, β, are the precondition and postcondition of the program P, respectively. They are usually given as formulas in some formal theory, such as first order logic over some language $\mathcal{L}$. We assume that the language is Peano Arithmetic; see Section 9.4.

Using a finite set of rules for program verification, we want to show that $\{\alpha\}P\{\beta\}$ holds, and conclude that the program is correct *with respect to the specification* α, β. As our example is small, we are going to use a limited set of rules for program verification, given in figure 9.12

The "If" rule is saying the following: suppose that it is the case that $\{\alpha \wedge \beta\}P_1\{\gamma\}$ and $\{\alpha \wedge \neg\beta\}P_2\{\gamma\}$. This means that P_1 is (partially) correct with respect to precondition $\alpha \wedge \beta$ and postcondition γ, while P_2 is (partially) correct with respect to precondition $\alpha \wedge \neg\beta$ and postcondition γ. Then the program "**if** β **then** P_1 **else** P_2" is (partially) correct with respect to precondition α and postcondition γ because if α holds before it executes, then either β or $\neg\beta$ must be true, and so either P_1 or P_2 executes, respectively, giving us γ in both cases.

The "While" rule is saying the following: suppose it is the case that $\{\alpha \wedge \beta\}P\{\alpha\}$. This means that P is (partially) correct with respect to precondition $\alpha \wedge \beta$ and postcondition α. Then the program "**while** β **do** P" is (partially) correct with respect to precondition α and postcondition

Consequence left and right

$$\frac{\{\alpha\}P\{\beta\} \qquad (\beta \to \gamma)}{\{\alpha\}P\{\gamma\}} \qquad \frac{(\gamma \to \alpha) \qquad \{\alpha\}P\{\beta\}}{\{\gamma\}P\{\beta\}}$$

Composition and assignment

$$\frac{\{\alpha\}P_1\{\beta\} \qquad \{\beta\}P_2\{\gamma\}}{\{\alpha\}P_1P_2\{\gamma\}} \qquad \frac{x := t}{\{\alpha(t)\}x := t\{\alpha(x)\}}$$

If

$$\frac{\{\alpha \wedge \beta\}P_1\{\gamma\} \qquad \{\alpha \wedge \neg\beta\}P_2\{\gamma\}}{\{\alpha\} \text{ if } \beta \text{ then } P_1 \text{ else } P_2 \{\gamma\}}$$

While

$$\frac{\{\alpha \wedge \beta\}P\{\alpha\}}{\{\alpha\} \text{ while } \beta \text{ do } P \{\alpha \wedge \neg\beta\}}$$

Fig. 9.12   A small set of rules for program verification.

$\alpha \wedge \neg\beta$ because if α holds before it executes, then either β holds in which case the while-loop executes once again, with $\alpha \wedge \beta$ holding, and so α still holds after P executes, or β is false, in which case $\neg\beta$ is true and the loop terminates with $\alpha \wedge \neg\beta$.

As an example, we verify which computes $y = A \cdot B$. Note that in algorithm 9.5, which describes the program that computes $y = A \cdot B$, we use "=" instead of the usual "←" since we are now proving the correctness of an actual program, rather than its representation in pseudo-code.

Algorithm 9.5 mult(A,B)

Pre-condition: $B \geq 0$

$a = A$;
$b = B$;
$y = 0$;
while $b > 0$ **do**
    $y = y + a$;
    $b = b - 1$;
end while

Post-condition: $y = A \cdot B$

We want to show:

$$\{B \geq 0\}\text{mult}(A,B)\{y = AB\} \tag{9.12}$$

Each pass through the while-loop adds a to y, but $a \cdot b$ decreases by a because b is decremented by 1. Let the loop invariant be: $(y + (a \cdot b) = A \cdot B) \wedge b \geq 0$. To save space, write tu instead of $t \cdot u$. Let $t \geq u$ abbreviate the $\mathcal{L}_A$-formula $\exists x (t = u + x)$, and let $t \leq u$ abbreviate $u \geq t$.

1 $\{y + a(b - 1) = AB \wedge (b - 1) \geq 0\}$b=b-1;$\{y + ab = AB \wedge b \geq 0\}$
assignment

2 $\{(y+a)+a(b-1) = AB \wedge (b-1) \geq 0\}$y=y+a;$\{y+a(b-1) = AB \wedge (b-1) \geq 0\}$
assignment

3 $(y + ab = AB \wedge b - 1 \geq 0) \rightarrow ((y + a) + a(b - 1) = AB \wedge b - 1 \geq 0)$
theorem

4 $\{y + ab = AB \wedge b - 1 \geq 0\}$y=y+a;$\{y + a(b - 1) = AB \wedge b - 1 \geq 0\}$
consequence left 2 and 3

5 $\{y + ab = AB \wedge b - 1 \geq 0\}$y=y+a;b=b-1;$\{y + ab = AB \wedge b \geq 0\}$
composition on 4 and 1

6 $(y + ab = AB) \wedge b \geq 0 \wedge b > 0 \rightarrow (y + ab = AB) \wedge b - 1 \geq 0$
theorem

7 $\{(y + ab = AB) \wedge b \geq 0 \wedge b > 0\}$y=y+a; b=b-1;$\{y + ab = AB \wedge b \geq 0\}$
consequence left 5 and 6

```
                         while (b>0)
```
8 $\{(y+ab = AB) \wedge b \geq 0\}$ `y=y+a;` $\{y+ab = AB \wedge b \geq 0 \wedge \neg(b > 0)\}$
`                         b=b-1;`

while on 7

9 $\{(0 + ab = AB) \wedge b \geq 0\}$ y=0; $\{(y + ab = AB) \wedge b \geq 0\}$
assignment

```
                    y=0;
                    while (b>0)
```
10 $\{(0+ab = AB) \wedge b \geq 0\}$ `    y=y+a;` $\{y+ab = AB \wedge b \geq 0 \wedge \neg(b > 0)\}$
`                    b=b-1;`

composition on 9 and 8

11 $\{(0 + aB = AB) \wedge B \geq 0\}$ b=B; $\{(0 + ab = AB) \wedge b \geq 0\}$
assignment

```
                    b=B;
                    y=0;
```
12 $\{(0+aB = AB) \wedge B \geq 0\}$ `while (b>0)` $\{y+ab = AB \wedge b \geq 0 \wedge \neg(b > 0)\}$
`                    y=y+a;`
`                    b=b-1;`

composition on 11 and 10

13 $\{(0 + AB = AB) \wedge B \geq 0\}$ `a=A;` $\{(0 + aB = AB) \wedge B \geq 0\}$

assignment

14 $\{(0 + AB = AB) \wedge B \geq 0\}$ `mult(A,B)` $\{y + ab = AB \wedge b \geq 0 \wedge \neg(b > 0)\}$

composition on 13 and 12

15 $B \geq 0 \rightarrow ((0 + AB = AB) \wedge B \geq 0)$

theorem

16 $(y + ab = AB \wedge b \geq 0 \wedge \neg(b > 0)) \rightarrow y = AB$

theorem

17 $\{B \geq 0\}$ `mult(A,B)` $\{y + ab = AB \wedge b \geq 0 \wedge \neg(b > 0)\}$

consequence left on 15 and 14

18 $\{B \geq 0\}$ `mult(A,B)` $\{y = AB\}$

consequence right on 16 and 17

Problem 9.108. *The following is a project, rather than an exercise. Give formal proofs of correctness of the division algorithm and Euclid's algorithm (algorithms 1.1 and 1.2). To give a complete proof you will need to use Peano Arithmetic, which is a formalization of number theory—exactly what is needed for these two algorithms. The details of Peano Arithmetic are given in Section 9.4.*

9.5 Answers to selected problems

Problem 9.1. Clearly, the basis case holds: $1 + \sum_{j=0}^{0} 2^j = 1 + 1 = 2^{0+1}$ (i.e., P(0)). For induction, assume that it holds for some $n \in \mathbb{N}$; that is, $1 + \sum_{j=0}^{n} 2^j = 2^{n+1}$. Then:

$$1 + \sum_{j=0}^{n+1} 2^j = 2^{n+1} + 1 + \sum_{j=0}^{n} 2^j$$

here we apply the induction hypothesis:

$$= 2^{n+1} + 2^{n+1} = 2^{n+2}$$

We have shown that P(0) is true, and moreover that $P(n) \rightarrow P(n+1)$. Therefore, $\forall m P(m)$.

Problem 9.2. Basis case: $n = 1$, then $1^3 = 1^2$. For the induction step:

$$(1 + 2 + 3 + \cdots + n + (n+1))^2$$
$$= (1 + 2 + 3 + \cdots + n)^2 + 2(1 + 2 + 3 + \cdots + n)(n+1) + (n+1)^2$$

and by the induction hypothesis,

$$= (1^3 + 2^3 + 3^3 + \cdots + n^3) + 2(1 + 2 + 3 + \cdots + n)(n+1) + (n+1)^2$$
$$= (1^3 + 2^3 + 3^3 + \cdots + n^3) + 2\frac{n(n+1)}{2}(n+1) + (n+1)^2$$
$$= (1^3 + 2^3 + 3^3 + \cdots + n^3) + n(n+1)^2 + (n+1)^2$$
$$= (1^3 + 2^3 + 3^3 + \cdots + n^3) + (n+1)^3$$

Problem 9.3. It is important to interpret the statement of the problem correctly: when it says that one square is missing, it means that *any* square may be missing. So the basis case is: given a 2×2 square, there are four possible ways for a square to be missing; but in each case, the remaining squares form an "L." These four possibilities are drawn in figure 9.13.

Fig. 9.13   The four different "L" shapes.

Suppose the claim holds for n, and consider a square of size $2^{n+1} \times 2^{n+1}$. Divide it into four quadrants of equal size. No matter which square we choose to be missing, it will be in one of the four quadrants; that quadrant can be filled with "L" shapes (i.e., shapes of the form given by figure 9.13) by induction hypothesis. As to the remaining three quadrants, put an "L" in them in such a way that it straddles all three of them (the "L" wraps around the center staying in those three quadrants). The remaining squares of each quadrant can now be filled with "L" shapes by induction hypothesis.

Problem 9.4. Since $\forall n(P(n) \to P(n+1)) \to (\forall n \geq k)(P(n) \to P(n+1))$, then $(9.2) \Rightarrow (9.2')$. On the other hand, $(9.2') \not\Rightarrow (9.2)$.

Problem 9.5. The basis case is $n = 1$, and it is immediate. For the induction step, assume the equality holds for exponent n, and show that it holds for exponent $n + 1$:

$$\begin{pmatrix} 1 & 1 \\ 1 & 0 \end{pmatrix}^n \begin{pmatrix} 1 & 1 \\ 1 & 0 \end{pmatrix} = \begin{pmatrix} f_{n+1} & f_n \\ f_n & f_{n-1} \end{pmatrix} \begin{pmatrix} 1 & 1 \\ 1 & 0 \end{pmatrix} = \begin{pmatrix} f_{n+1} + f_n & f_{n+1} \\ f_n + f_{n-1} & f_n \end{pmatrix}$$

The right-most matrix can be simplified using the definition of Fibonacci numbers to be as desired.

Problem 9.7. $m|n$ iff $n = km$, so show that $f_m | f_{km}$ by induction on k. If $k = 1$, there is nothing to prove. Otherwise, $f_{(k+1)m} = f_{km+m}$. Now, using a separate inductive argument, show that for $y \geq 1$, $f_{x+y} =$

$f_y f_{x+1} + f_{y-1} f_x$, and finish the proof. To show this last statement, let $y = 1$, and note that $f_y f_{x+1} + f_{y-1} f_x = f_1 f_{x+1} + f_0 f_x = f_{x+1}$. Assume now that $f_{x+y} = f_y f_{x+1} + f_{y-1} f_x$ holds. Consider

$$\begin{aligned} f_{x+(y+1)} = f_{(x+y)+1} &= f_{(x+y)} + f_{(x+y)-1} = f_{(x+y)} + f_{x+(y-1)} \\ &= (f_y f_{x+1} + f_{y-1} f_x) + (f_{y-1} f_{x+1} + f_{y-2} f_x) \\ &= f_{x+1}(f_y + f_{y-1}) + f_x(f_{y-1} + f_{y-2}) \\ &= f_{x+1} f_{y+1} + f_x f_y. \end{aligned}$$

Problem 9.8. Note that this is almost the *Fundamental Theorem of Arithmetic*; what is missing is the fact that up to reordering of primes this representation is unique. The proof of this can be found in Section 9.2, theorem 9.18.

Problem 9.9. Let our assertion $P(n)$ be: the minimal number of breaks to break up a chocolate bar of n squares is $(n-1)$. Note that this says that $(n-1)$ breaks are sufficient, and $(n-2)$ are not. Basis case: only one square requires no breaks. Induction step: Suppose that we have $m+1$ squares. No matter how we break the bar into two smaller pieces of a and b squares each, $a + b = m + 1$.

By induction hypothesis, the "a" piece requires $a - 1$ breaks, and the "b" piece requires $b - 1$ breaks, so together the number of breaks is

$$(a - 1) + (b - 1) + \boxed{1} = a + b - 1 = m + 1 - 1 = m,$$

and we are done. Note that the **1** in the box comes from the initial break to divide the chocolate bar into the "a" and the "b" pieces.

So the "boring" way of breaking up the chocolate (first into rows, and then each row separately into pieces) is in fact optimal.

Problem 9.10. Let IP be: $[P(0) \wedge (\forall n)(P(n) \to P(n+1))] \to (\forall m)P(m)$ (where n, m range over natural numbers), and let LNP: *Every non-empty subset of the natural numbers has a least element.* These two principles are equivalent, in the sense that one can be shown from the other. Indeed:

LNP$\Rightarrow$IP: Suppose we have $[P(0) \wedge (\forall n)(P(n) \to P(n+1))]$, but that it is *not* the case that $(\forall m)P(m)$. Then, the set S of m's for which $P(m)$ is false is non-empty. By the LNP we know that S has a least element. We know this element is not 0, as $P(0)$ was assumed. So this element can be expressed as $n + 1$ for some natural number n. But since $n + 1$ is the least such number, $P(n)$ must hold. This is a contradiction as we assumed that $(\forall n)(P(n) \to P(n+1))$, and here we have an n such that $P(n)$ but not $P(n+1)$.

IP⇒LNP: Suppose that S is a non-empty subset of the natural numbers. Suppose that it does not have a least element; let $P(n)$ be the following assertion "all elements up to and including n are not in S." We know that $P(0)$ must be true, for otherwise 0 would be in S, and it would then be the least element (by definition of 0). Suppose $P(n)$ is true (so none of $\{0, 1, 2, \ldots, n\}$ is in S). Suppose $P(n+1)$ were false: then $n+1$ would necessarily be in S (as we know that none of $\{0, 1, 2, \ldots, n\}$ is in S), and thereby $n+1$ would be the smallest element in S. So we have shown $[P(0) \wedge (\forall n)(P(n) \to P(n+1))]$. By IP we can therefore conclude that $(\forall m)P(m)$. But this means that S is empty. Contradiction. Thus S must have a least element.

IP⇒CIP: For this direction we use the LNP which we just showed equivalent to the IP. Suppose that we have IP; assume that $P(0)$ and $\forall n((\forall i \leq n)P(i) \to P(n+1))$. We want to show that $\forall n P(n)$, so we prove this with the IP: the basis case, $P(0)$, is given. To show $\forall j(P(j) \to P(j+1))$ suppose that it does not hold; then there exists a j such that $P(j)$ and $\neg P(j)$; let j be the smallest such j; one exists by the LNP, and $j \neq 0$ by what is given. So $P(0), P(1), P(2), \ldots, P(j)$ but $\neg P(j+1)$. But this contradicts $\forall n((\forall i \leq n)P(i) \to P(n+1))$, and so it is not possible. Hence $\forall j(P(j) \to P(j+1))$ and so by the IP we have $\forall n P(n)$ and hence we have the CIP.

The last direction, CIP⇒IP, follows directly from the fact that CIP has a "stronger" induction step.

Problem 9.11. We use the example in figure 9.1. Suppose that we want to obtain the tree from the infix (2164735) and prefix (1234675) encodings: from the prefix encoding we know that 1 is the root, and thus from the infix encoding we know that the left sub-tree has the infix encoding 2, and so prefix encoding 2, and the right sub-tree has the infix encoding 64735 and so prefix encoding 34675, and we proceed recursively.

Problem 9.13. Consider the following invariant: the sum S of the numbers currently in the set is odd. Now we prove that this invariant holds. Basis case: $S = 1 + 2 + \cdots + 2n = n(2n+1)$ which is odd. Induction step: assume S is odd, let S' be the result of one more iteration, so

$$S' = S + |a - b| - a - b = S - 2\min(a, b),$$

and since $2\min(a, b)$ is even, and S was odd by the induction hypothesis, it follows that S' must be odd as well. At the end, when there is just one number left, say x, $S = x$, so x is odd.

Problem 9.14. To solve this problem we must provide both an algorithm and an invariant for it. The algorithm works as follows: initially divide the club into any two groups. Let H be the total sum of enemies that each member has in his own group. Now repeat the following loop: while there is an m which has at least two enemies in his own group, move m to the other group (where m must have at most one enemy). Thus, when m switches houses, H decreases. Here the invariant is "H decreases monotonically." Now we know that a sequence of positive integers cannot decrease for ever, so when H reaches its absolute minimum, we obtain the required distribution.

Problem 9.15. At first, arrange the guests in any way; let H be the number of neighboring hostile pairs. We find an algorithm that reduces H whenever $H > 0$. Suppose $H > 0$, and let (A, B) be a hostile couple, sitting side-by-side, in the clockwise order A, B. Traverse the table, clockwise, until we find another couple (A', B') such that A, A' and B, B' are friends. Such a couple must exist: there are $2n - 2 - 1 = 2n - 3$ candidates for A' (these are all the people sitting clockwise after B, which have a neighbor sitting next to them, again clockwise, and that neighbor is neither A nor B). As A has at least n friends (among people other than itself), out of these $2n - 3$ candidates, at least $n - 1$ of them are friends of A. If each of these friends had an enemy of B sitting next to it (again, going clockwise), then B would have at least n enemies, which is not possible, so there must be an A' friends with A so that the neighbor of A' (clockwise) is B' and B' is a friend of B; see figure 9.14.

Note that when $n = 1$ no one has enemies, and so this analysis is applicable when $n \geq 2$, in which case $2n - 3 \geq 1$.

Now the situation around the table is $\ldots, A, \boxed{B, \ldots, A'}, B', \ldots$. Reverse everyone in the box (i.e., mirror image the box), to reduce H by 1. Keep repeating this procedure while $H > 0$; eventually $H = 0$ (by the LNP), at which point there are no neighbors that dislike each other.

$$A, B, c_1, c_2, \ldots, c_{2n-3}, c_{2n-2}$$

Fig. 9.14 List of guests sitting around the table, in clockwise order, starting at A. We are interested in friends of A among $c_1, c_2, \ldots, c_{2n-3}$, to make sure that there is a neighbor to the right, and that neighbor is not A or B; of course, the table wraps around at c_{2n-2}, so the next neighbor, clockwise, of c_{2n-2} is A. As A has at most $n - 1$ enemies, A has at least n friends (not counting itself; self-love does not count as friendship). Those n friends of A are among the c's, but if we exclude c_{2n-2} it follows that A has at least $n - 1$ friends among $c_1, c_2, \ldots, c_{2n-3}$. If the clockwise neighbor of c_i, $1 \leq i \leq 2n - 3$, i.e., c_{i+1} was in each case an enemy of B, then, as B already has an enemy of A, it would follow that B has n enemies, which is not possible.

Problem 9.16. We partition the participants into the set E of even persons and the set O of odd persons. We observe that, during the hand shaking ceremony, the set O cannot change its parity. Indeed, if two odd persons shake hands, $|O|$ decreases by 2. If two even persons shake hands, $|O|$ increases by 2, and, if an even and an odd person shake hands, $|O|$ does not change. Since, initially, $|O| = 0$, the parity of the set is preserved.

Problem 9.19. If $a_1 \equiv_m a_2$, then there is some $a \in \{0, 1, 2, \ldots, m - 1\}$ such that $a_1 = \alpha_1 m + a$ and $a_2 = \alpha_2 m + a$, where α_1 and α_2 are integers. Similarly, we have $b_1 = \beta_1 m + b$ and $b_2 = \beta_2 m + b$. Thus,

$$a_1 \pm b_1 = (\alpha_1 \pm \beta_1)m + (a \pm b)$$
$$\equiv_m a \pm b$$
$$\equiv_m (\alpha_2 \pm \beta_2)m + (a \pm b)$$
$$= a \pm b_2$$

and

$$a_1 \cdot b_1 = (\alpha_1 m + a) \cdot (\beta_1 m + b)$$
$$= \alpha_1 \beta_1 \cdot m^2 + (\alpha_1 b + \beta_1 a) \cdot m + a \cdot b$$
$$\equiv_m a \cdot b$$
$$\equiv_m \alpha_2 \beta_2 \cdot m^2 + (\alpha_2 b + \beta_2 a) \cdot m + a \cdot b$$
$$= a_2 \cdot b_2$$

where every "$\equiv_m$" is true because extra multiples of m are 0; that is, $\forall k \in \mathbb{Z}, \, k \cdot m \equiv_m 0$.

Problem 9.21. Base case: let n be a prime number. Clearly, $n = n^1$ is n's prime factorization, and every element of $\mathbb{Z}_n - \{0\}$ is co-prime to n (that is, for every positive integer $i < n$, $\gcd(n, i) = 1$ because n is prime). Therefore, $\phi(n) = |\mathbb{Z}_n| - 1 = n - 1 = n^{1-1}(n - 1)$, concluding the base case. Consider any composite $n = p_1^{k_1} \cdot \cdots \cdot p_i^{k_i}$. Obviously we can divide out a prime factor p to get n_0 such that $n = p \cdot n_0$. We consider two cases:

Case 1: $p | n_0$. Let $m \in \mathbb{Z}_{n_0}^*$. Clearly, $\gcd(m, p) = \gcd(m, n_0) = 1$, as otherwise m and n_0 would share the common factor p and we know $m \in \mathbb{Z}_{n_0}^*$. Assume, for contradiction, that $\exists i \in \{0, 1, 2, \ldots, p - 1\}$ such that $\gcd(m + in_0, pn_0) = o > 1$. $o | pn_0$, so $o = p$ or $o | n_0$, but $o < p$, so $o | n_0$. Therefore, $o | in_0$, and we already know that $o \nmid m$, as $\gcd(m, n_0) = 1$, so $o \nmid (m + in_0)$. We've found our contradiction, o cannot be a divisor of $m + in_0$ if it doesn't divide $m + in_0$ evenly, by definition. Thus, $\forall i \in \mathbb{Z}_p$, $\gcd(m + in_0, pn_0) = 1$. Moreover, m was an arbitrary element of $\mathbb{Z}_{n_0}^*$, so this works for every such m—$\phi(n) \geq p \cdot \phi(n_0)$. Clearly, for any $q \in \mathbb{Z}_{n_0} - \mathbb{Z}_{n_0}^*$,

$q + in_0 \notin \mathbb{Z}_n^*$, so $\mathbb{Z}_n^*$ doesn't have any "extra" elements; $\phi(n) = p \cdot \phi(n_0)$. This completes induction for this case.

Case 2: $p \nmid n_0$. This case is very similar to the one before; the only difference is that, at the end, we must remove every multiple of p, as these elements share the factor p with n. There are exactly $\phi(n_0)$ such multiples of p, as every other multiple shared a different factor with n_0 itself and as such wasn't included. Thus, $\phi(n) = p \cdot \phi(n_0) - \phi(n_0) = (p - 1) \cdot \phi(n_0)$, completing induction.

To clarify why these recurrences prove induction, consider what happens to $\prod_{i=1}^{l} p_i^{k_i - 1}(p_i - 1)$ when either the power of a prime is increased by 1 (Case 1) or when a new prime is included (Case 2).

Problem 9.23. $(a + 1)^p \equiv_p \sum_{j=0}^{p} \binom{p}{j} a^{p-j} 1^j \equiv_p (a^p + 1) + \sum_{j=1}^{p-1} \binom{p}{j} a^{p-j}$. Note that $\binom{p}{j}$ is divisible by p for $1 \leq j \leq p - 1$, and so we have that $\sum_{j=1}^{p-1} \binom{p}{j} a^{p-j} \equiv_p 0$. Thus we can prove our claim by induction on a. The case $a = 1$ is trivial, and for the induction step we use the above observation to conclude that $(a+1)^p \equiv_p (a^p + 1)$ and we apply the induction hypothesis to get $a^p \equiv_p a$. Once we have proven $a^p \equiv_p a$ we are done since for a such that $\gcd(a, p) = 1$ we have an inverse a^{-1}, so we multiply both sides by it to obtain $a^{p-1} \equiv_p 1$.

Problem 9.24. First, we consider $(\mathbb{Z}_n, +)$. Clearly, closure is met, as addition in $\mathbb{Z}_n$ is done modulus n, so the result of addition must be in $\mathbb{Z}_n$. The identity is 0; $0 + i \equiv_n i$ for any $i \in \mathbb{Z}_n$. We can also find an inverse easily: $i^{-1} = n - i$, because $i + (n - i) = n \equiv_n 0$. Finally, addition modulus n is associative for any n so all three axioms are met.

Next, consider $(\mathbb{Z}_n^*, \cdot)$. Given $a, b \in \mathbb{Z}_n^*$, $\gcd(a \cdot b, n) = 1$ with regular multiplication, so $\gcd(a \cdot b, n) = 1$ with modular multiplication as well—the only difference is the removal of any "extra" multiples of n. Thus, we have closure. $\gcd(n, 1) = 1$ regardless of n's value, so $1 \in \mathbb{Z}_n^*$. Clearly, 1 meets the requirements of an identity element under multiplication. Given any element $a \in \mathbb{Z}_n^*$, we know $\gcd(a, n) = 1$, so we can find integers x, y such that $ax + ny = 1$. Moreover, $ny \equiv_n 0$, so $ax \equiv_n 1$. If $x \notin \mathbb{Z}_n$, there is an $x' \in \mathbb{Z}_n$ such that $x' \equiv_n x$. $ax' \equiv_n 1$ as well; from ax we have only removed a multiple of an, so the effect (mod n) is 0. Since $ax' \equiv_n 1$, x' must not share any factors with n, so $x' \in \mathbb{Z}_n^*$. Thus, we have an inverse. Again, associativity is trivial, as it is guaranteed by the chosen operation, multiplication modulus n.

Problem 9.27. Let $H \leq G$ and assume $h \in H$. Since H is a group, we know $h^{-1} \in H$ as well. We also know that $e \in H$, where e is the identity element of G (and, of course, of H), again simply because H is a group. Since H is closed, we know that for all $a \in H$, $h^{-1}a \in H$ as well, and as such $hh^{-1}a = a \in hH$. Thus, $H \subseteq hH$. Next, consider any $a' \in hH$; clearly $a' = ha$ for some $a \in H$. Since $h \in H$ as well, and H is closed, a' must be in H. Therefore $hH \subseteq H$, finishing our proof that $hH = H$.

Let $g \in G$, and consider gH; obviously $|gH| \leq |H|$, as each element of gH requires a unique $h \in H$. Assume that $|gH| < |H|$. Then there are two unique elements of H, h_1 and h_2, such that $gh_1 = gh_2$. But G is a group, so g has an inverse, g^{-1}. So $g^{-1}gh_1 = g^{-1}gh_2$, or identically $h_1 = h_2$—a contradiction. Thus, $|gH| = |H|$.

Assume $h' \in (ab)H$. Then $\exists h \in H$ such that $(ab)h = h'$. Groups are associative, so $h' = a(bh)$, and as such $h' \in H$. Proving that any element of $a(bH)$ is also in $(ab)H$ is nearly identical.

Problem 9.28. We will use the term "product" to mean the result of the given group's operation. Notice that $\langle g_1, g_2, \ldots, g_k \rangle$ is simply the collection of products of an arbitrary permutation of elements of $G' = \{g_1, \ldots, g_k, g_1^{-1}, \ldots, g_k^{-1}\}$ with replacement. Clearly, if we multiply any $g \in G'$ by itself, or another element of G, the result is in the generated subgroup (which forces inclusion of the identity, given that inverses are included in G'). Moreover, given any two generated elements $x_1 x_2 \cdots x_{p_1}$ and $y_1 y_2 \cdots y_{p_2}$, the product $x_1 \cdots x_{p_1} y_1 \cdots y_{p_2}$ meets the requirements to be included in $\langle g_1, g_2, \ldots, g_k \rangle$. Thus, the generated subgroup is closed. It clearly includes inverses as well, as the inverse of a product $x_1 \cdots x_k$ is simply the product $x_k^{-1} \cdots x_1^{-1}$. Associativity is provided by the encompassing group G. Thus, the generated subgroup is, indeed, a group. As for $|\langle g \rangle|$, note that any element can be written as a product of g's and g^{-1}'s. In other words, every element of $|\langle g \rangle|$ can be written in the form g^n for some integer n. But $g^{\text{ord}(G)} = 1$, so $g^n = g^{(n \mod \text{ord}(G))}$. As there are only $\text{ord}(G)$ distinct elements in $\mathbb{Z}_{\text{ord}(G)}$, there are also only $\text{ord}(G)$ distinct elements of $\langle g \rangle$.

Problem 9.31. Construct the r in stages, so that at stage i it meets the first i congruences, that is, at stage i we have that $r \equiv r_j \pmod{m_j}$ for $j \in \{0, 1, \ldots, i\}$. Stage 1 is simple: just set $r \longleftarrow r_0$. Suppose that the first i stages have been completed; let $r \longleftarrow r + (\Pi_{j=0}^i m_j)x$, where x satisfies

$$x \equiv (\Pi_{j=0}^i m_j)^{-1}(r_{i+1} - r) \pmod{m_{i+1}}.$$

We know that the inverse of $(\Pi_{j=0}^i m_j)$ exists (in $\mathbb{Z}_{m_{i+1}}$) since $\gcd(m_{i+1}, (\Pi_{j=0}^i m_i)) = 1$, and furthermore, this inverse can be obtained efficiently with the extended Euclid's algorithm.

Problem 9.33. We will prove that if $m_0, m_1, \ldots, m_n$ are pairwise co-prime integers, then

$$\mathbb{Z}_{m_0 \cdot m_1 \cdot \ldots \cdot m_n} \cong \mathbb{Z}_{m_0} \times \mathbb{Z}_{m_1} \times \cdots \times \mathbb{Z}_{m_n}$$

through induction over n. Let $M = m_0 \cdot m_1 \cdot \ldots \cdot m_n$. Theorem 9.30 provides a convenient bijection from $\mathbb{Z}_M$ to $\mathbb{Z}_{m_0} \times \cdots \times \mathbb{Z}_{m_n}$:

$$f(r) = (r \bmod m_0, r \bmod m_1, \ldots, r \bmod m_n)$$

for all $r \in \mathbb{Z}_M$. Note that the operations in these two groups is unspecified because they are implied by the context; for $\mathbb{Z}_M$, the operation is addition modulus M. We will denote this as "$+_M$" (in fact for any natural number n, we will denote addition modulus n as "$+_n$" when convenient). For $\mathbb{Z}_{m_0} \times \cdots \times \mathbb{Z}_{m_n}$, it is element-wise modular addition—that is, given $x, y \in \mathbb{Z}_{m_0} \times \cdots \times \mathbb{Z}_{m_n}$, "$x * y$" will denote $(x_0 +_{m_0} y_0, \ldots, x_n +_{m_n} y_n)$.

$$\begin{aligned}
f(r +_M r') &= (r_0 +_M r_0 \bmod m_0, \ldots, r_n +_M r'_n \bmod m_n) \\
&= (r + r' \bmod m_0, \ldots, r + r' \bmod m_n) \\
&= f(r) * f(r')
\end{aligned}$$

where we are able to use normal addition instead of modular addition because for all i, $m_i | M$. We already knew f was a bijection; we now know it is an isomorphism, so the two groups are isomorphic.

Problem 9.35. $(1) \Rightarrow (2)$ Suppose that R is transitive, and let $(x, y) \in R^2$. Then, by definition (9.6) we know that there exists a z such that xRz and zRy. By transitivity we have that $(x, y) \in R$. $(2) \Rightarrow (3)$ Suppose that $R^2 \subseteq R$. We show by induction on n that $R^n \subseteq R$. The basis case, $n = 1$, is trivial. For the induction step, suppose that $(x, y) \in R^{n+1} = R^n \circ R$, so by definition (9.6) there exists a z such that $xR^n z$ and zRy. By the induction assumption this means that xRz and zRy, so $(x, y) \in R^2$, and, since $R^2 \subseteq R$, it follows that $(x, y) \in R$, and we are done. $(3) \Rightarrow (1)$ Suppose that for all n, $R^n \subseteq R$. If xRy and yRz then $xRz \in R^2$, and so $xRz \in R$, and so R is transitive.

Problem 9.37. Given $R \subseteq X \times X$, let $S = R \cup \mathrm{id}_X$. Clearly S is reflexive, as id_X alone contains every pair necessary to ensure reflexiveness. Consider any S' for which there is a pair x, y such that xSy and $\neg xS'y$. If xRy, then $R \not\subseteq S'$. Otherwise, $(x, y) \in \mathrm{id}_X$, so $x = y$; there is an element x such that $\neg xS'x$, so S' is not reflexive. In either case, S' is not the reflexive closure of R. So $R \subseteq S$, S is reflexive, and any set that meets these two conditions contains every element of S. Therefore, S is the reflexive closure of R.

Problem 9.39. Let $S = R \cup R^{-1}$. Obviously $R \subseteq S$, and S is clearly symmetric. Consider S' such that $S \nsubseteq S'$. There is a pair $(x, y) \in S$ such that $(x, y) \notin S'$. If $(x, y) \in R$, then $R \nsubseteq S'$. Otherwise, $(y, x) \in R$; if $(y, x) \in S'$ then S' is not symmetric, but if $(y, x) \notin S'$, then $R \nsubseteq S'$. In any case, S' is either not closed or does not contain R. S, on the other hand, contains R, is symmetric, and is a subset of any set which meets these conditions. Therefore, it is the symmetric closure of R.

Problem 9.41. The reason is that in the first line we chose a *particular* y: $xR^{+}y \wedge yR^{+}z \iff \exists m, n \geq 1, xR^{m}y \wedge yR^{n}z$. On the other hand, from the statement $\exists m, n \geq 1, x(R^{m} \circ R^{n})z$ we can only conclude that there exists some y' such that $\exists m, n \geq 1, xR^{m}y' \wedge y'R^{n}z$, and it is not necessarily the case that $y = y'$.

Problem 9.45. R is reflexive since $F(x) = F(x)$; R is symmetric since $F(x) = F(y)$ implies $F(y) = F(x)$ (equality is a symmetric relation); R is transitive because $F(x) = F(y)$ and $F(y) = F(z)$ implies $F(x) = F(z)$ (again by transitivity of equality).

Problem 9.51. We know from lemma 9.49 that $\forall a \in X, [a]_{R_1} \subseteq [a]_{R_2}$. Therefore the mapping $f : X/R_1 \longrightarrow X/R_2$ given by $f([a]_{R_1}) = [a]_{R_2}$ is surjective, and hence $|X/R_1| \geq |X/R_2|$.

Problem 9.54. We show the left-to-right direction. Clearly $\approx$ is reflexive as it contains id_X. Now suppose that $a \approx b$; then $a \sim b$ or $a = b$. If $a = b$, then $b = a$ (as equality is obviously a symmetric relation), and so $b \approx a$. If $a \sim b$, then by definition of incomparability, $\neg(a \preceq b) \wedge \neg(b \preceq a)$, which is logically equivalent to $\neg(b \preceq a) \wedge \neg(a \preceq b)$, and hence $b \sim a$, and so $b \approx a$ in this case as well. Finally, we want to prove transitivity: suppose that $a \approx b \wedge b \approx c$; if $a = b$ and $b = c$, then $a = c$ and we have $a \approx c$. Similarly, if $a = b$ and $b \sim c$, then $a \sim c$, and so $a \approx c$, and if $a \sim b$ and $b = c$, and $a \sim c$, and also $a \approx c$. The only case that remains is $a \sim b$ and $b \sim c$, and it is here where we use the fact that $\preceq$ is a stratified order, as this implies that $a \sim c \vee a = c$, which gives us $a \approx c$.

Problem 9.56. We show the left-to-right direction. The natural way to proceed here is to let T be the set consisting of the different equivalence classes of X under $\sim$. That is, $T = \{[a]_{\sim} : a \in X\}$. Then T is totally ordered under $\preceq_T$ defined as follows: for $X, X' \in T$, such that $X \neq X'$ and $X = [x]$ and $X' = [x']$, we have that $X \preceq_T X'$ iff $x \preceq x'$. Note also that given two distinct X, X' in T, and any pair of representatives x, x', it is always the case that $x \preceq x'$ or $x' \preceq x$, since if neither was the case, we would have $x \sim x'$, and hence $[x] = [x']$ and so $X = X'$. Then the function $f : X \longrightarrow T$ given as $f(x) = [x]$ satisfies the requirements.

Problem 9.57. Let $X = \{a, b, c, d, e\}$. Consider the poset given by the ordered pairs $\{(a, c), (a, d), (a, e), (b, c), (b, d), (b, e), (c, d), (c, e)\}$ (where the reflexive pairs (i.e. $(a, a), (b, b) \ldots$) have been omitted. Clearly a is minimal, as there is no element $x \neq a$ such that $x \preceq a$. Similarly, b is minimal, and d, e are maximal. However, there is no least element or greatest element; our minimal elements a, b are incomparable, as are the maximal d, e. Note that in the case of a finite linear poset, this would not be possible, because every element would be comparable. X also has no supremum or infimum, again because no minimal or maximal element can be compared to the others. There are easy examples of linear posets without an infimum or supremum as well. Consider, for example, the poset $(\mathbb{R}^+, \preceq)$, where $\mathbb{R}^+$ is the positive real numbers and $x \preceq y$ if and only if $x, y \in \mathbb{R}^+ \wedge x \leq y$. It is obvious that this poset has no supremum—there is always a larger real number. Less obvious is that it has no infimum! There is an intuitive candidate for the infimum: 0. However, $\preceq$ is only defined for pairs of elements in $\mathbb{R}^+$, so 0 is incomparable to everything. If, we use the poset $(\mathbb{R}, \leq)$ instead, then $\mathbb{R}^+ \subset \mathbb{R}$ does have an infimum: 0.

Let $A \subset X$ be $\{b, c, d\}$. The portion of our poset on X which applies to A: $\{(b, c), (b, d), (c, d)\}$. Unlike X, A has a clear infimum, supremum, greatest element and least element, even though its encompassing X is not linear.

Problem 9.58. Let X be a set, and consider the poset $(\mathcal{P}(X), \subseteq)$. Given $A, B \in \mathcal{P}(X)$, we aim to prove that $A \sqcup B = A \cup B$. Clearly, $A, B \subseteq A \cup B$. Moreover, any proper subset of $A \cup B$ is necessarily missing an element of A or B, so for all $C \in \mathcal{P}(X)$, $A, B \subseteq C \implies A \cup B \subseteq C$. Thus, $A \cup B = \inf(\{A, B\})$. The proof that $A \sqcap B = A \cap B$ follows approximately the same process, but with subsets and supersets reversed.

Problem 9.60. We prove the following part: $a \preceq b \iff a \sqcap b = a$. Suppose that $a \preceq b$. As $(X, \preceq)$ is a lattice, it is a poset, and so $a \preceq a$ (reflexivity), which means that a is a lower bound of the set $\{a, b\}$. Since $(X, \preceq)$ is a lattice, $\inf\{a, b\}$ exists, and thus $a \preceq \inf\{a, b\}$. On the other hand, $\inf\{a, b\} \preceq a$, and so, by the antisymmetry of a poset, we have $a = \inf\{a, b\} = a \sqcap b$. For the other direction, $a \sqcap b = a$ means that $\inf\{a, b\} = a$, and so $a \preceq \inf\{a, b\}$, and so $a \preceq b$.

Problem 9.62. (1) follows directly from the observation that $\{a, b\}$ and $\{b, a\}$ are the same set. (2) follows from the observation that $\inf\{a, \inf\{b, c\}\} = \inf\{a, b, c\} = \inf\{\inf\{a, b\}, c\}$, and same for the supremum. (3) follows directly from the observation that $\{a, a\} = \{a\}$ (we are dealing with sets, not with "multi-sets"). For (4), the absorption law, we show that $a = a \sqcup (a \sqcap b)$. First note that $a \preceq \sup\{a, *\}$ (where "$*$" denotes anything, in particular $a \sqcap b$). On the other hand, $a \sqcap b \preceq a$ by definition, and $a \preceq a$ by reflexivity, and so a is upper bound for the set $\{a, a \sqcap b\}$. Therefore, $\sup\{a, a \sqcap b\} \preceq a$ and hence, by antisymmetry, $a = \sup\{a, a \sqcap b\}$, i.e., $a = a \sqcup (a \sqcap b)$. The other absorption law can be proven similarly.

Problem 9.64. To show that $(\mathcal{P}(X), \subseteq)$ is complete, it is enough to prove the other properties listed in theorem 9.63, as a formula for the supremum and infimum are stronger than their existence. We first prove that $\forall \mathcal{A} \subseteq \mathcal{P}(X)$, $\sup(\mathcal{A}) = \bigcup_{A \in \mathcal{A}} A$. Clearly, it meets the requirement of being an upper bound. Moreover, any proper subset of $\bigcup_{A \in \mathcal{A}} A$ is missing at least one of the elements in an $A \in \mathcal{A}$, so it is not an upper bound of $\mathcal{A}$. Thus, $\bigcup_{A \in \mathcal{A}} A$ is the supremum of $\mathcal{A}$. Note that this follows directly from the results of problem 9.58. The proof that $\inf(\mathcal{A}) = \bigcap_{A \in \mathcal{A}} A$ is very similar (and also follows directly from problem 9.58). The remaining facts, $\bot = \emptyset$ and $\top = X$, should be very intuitive; they are also immediate conclusions that can be drawn from the supremum and infimum formulas in this problem.

Problem 9.70. For example, the least fixed point of f is given by $f^4(\emptyset) = f^3(\{a, b\}) = f^2(\{a, b\}) = f(\{a, b\}) = \{a, b\}$.

Problem 9.72. Note that $\sup\{a, b\} = \top$, and so $f(\sup\{a, b\}) = f(\top) = \top$. On the other hand, $f(\{a, b\}) = \{\bot\}$, as $f(a) = f(b) = \bot$. Therefore, $\sup(f(\{a, b\}) = \sup(\{\bot\}) = \bot$. See figure 9.15 for a function g that is monotone, but is neither upward nor downward continuous.

Problem 9.74. Let $S \subseteq \mathbb{Z} \times \mathbb{Z}$ be the set consisting precisely of those pairs of integers (x, y) such that $x \geq y$ and $x - y$ is even. We are going to prove that S is the domain of definition of F. First, if $x < y$ then $x \neq y$ and so we go on to compute $F(x, F(x - 1, y + 1))$, and now we must compute $F(x - 1, y + 1)$; but if $x < y$, then clearly $x - 1 < y + 1$; this condition is preserved, and so we end up having to compute $F(x - i, y + i)$ for all i, and so this recursion never "bottoms out." Suppose that $x - y$ is odd. Then $x \neq y$ (as 0 is even!), so again we go on to $F(x, F(x - 1, y + 1))$; if $x - y$ is odd, so is $(x - 1) - (y + 1) = x - y - 2$. Again we end up having to compute $F(x - i, y + i)$ for all i, and so the recursion never terminates. Clearly, all the pairs in S^c are not in the domain of definition of F.

Suppose now that $(x, y) \in S$. Then $x \geq y$ and $x - y$ is even; thus, $x - y = 2i$ for some $i \geq 0$. We show, by induction on i, that the algorithm terminates on such (x, y) and outputs $x + 1$. Basis case: $i = 0$, so $x = y$, and so the algorithm returns $y + 1$ which is $x + 1$. Suppose now that $x - y = 2(i + 1)$. Then $x \neq y$, and so we compute $F(x, F(x - 1, y + 1))$.

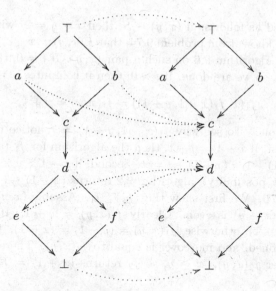

Fig. 9.15 An example of an ordering over $X = \{a, b, c, d, e, f, \bot, \top\}$, with a function $g : X \longrightarrow X$, indicated by the dotted lines. While g is monotone, it is neither upward now downward continuous.

But

$$(x - 1) - (y + 1) = x - y - 2 = 2(i + 1) - 2 = 2i,$$

for $i \geq 0$, and so by induction $F(x - 1, y + 1)$ terminates and outputs $(x - 1) + 1 = x$. So now we must compute $F(x, x)$ which is just $x + 1$, and we are done.

Problem 9.75. We show that f_1 is a fixed point of algorithm 9.1. Recall that in problem 9.74 we showed that the domain of definition of F, the function computed by algorithm 9.1, is $S = \{(x, y) : x - y = 2i, i \geq 0\}$. Now we show that if we replace F in algorithm 9.1 by f_1, the new algorithm, which is algorithm 9.6, still computes F albeit not recursively (as f_1 is defined by algorithm 9.2 which is not recursive).

Algorithm 9.6 Algorithm 9.1 with F replaced by f_1.

1: **if** $x = y$ **then**
2:        **return** $y + 1$
3: **else**
4:        $f_1(x, f_1(x - 1, y + 1))$
5: **end if**

We proceed as follows: if $(x, y) \in S$, then $x - y = 2i$ with $i \geq 0$. On such (x, y) we know, from problem 9.74, that $F(x, y) = x+1$. Now consider the output of algorithm 9.6 on such a pair (x, y). If $i = 0$, then it returns $y + 1 = x + 1$, so we are done. If $i > 0$, then it computes

$$f_1(x, f_1(x - 1, y + 1)) = f_1(x, x) = x + 1,$$

and we are done. To see why $f_1(x - 1, y + 1) = x$ notice that there are two cases: first, if $x - 1 = y + 1$, then the algorithm for f_1 (algorithm 9.2) returns $(y + 1) + 1 = (x - 1) + 1 = x$. Second, if $x - 1 > y + 1$ (and that is the only other possibility), algorithm 9.2 returns $(x - 1) + 1 = x$ as well.

Problem 9.76. We first show that $f_3 \sqsubseteq f_1$. Assume $(x, y) \in S_3$. Then $x \geq y$, and $(x - y)$ is even. Clearly $f_3(x, y) = x + 1$. If $x \neq y$, then $f_1(x, y) = (x + 1)$; otherwise, $f_1(x, y) = (y + 1) = (x + 1)$. In either case, $f_1(x, y)$ is defined, and moreover is equal to $f_3(x, y)$. Therefore, $f_3 \sqsubseteq f_1$. Next, consider $f_2(x, y)$. $x \geq y$, so f_2 returns $(x + 1) = f_3(x, y)$. Thus, $f_3 \sqsubseteq f_2$.

Problem 9.77. Let the grammar G_{prop} have the alphabet $\{p, 1, \wedge, \vee, \neg (,)\}$, and of the set of rules given by

$$S \longrightarrow pX | \neg S | (S \wedge S) | (S \vee S)$$
$$X \longrightarrow 1 | X1$$

The variables are $\{p1, p11, p111, p1111, \ldots\}$, i.e., they are encoded in unary notation.

Problem 9.79. By the induction hypothesis, $w(\alpha) = w(\beta) = 1$, so $w(\neg\alpha) = 0 + (-1) = -1$ and since the left and right parentheses balance each other out, in the sense that $w((t)) = w(() + w(t) + w()) = 1 + w(t) + (-1) = w(t)$, the result quickly follows for $(\alpha \wedge \beta)$ and $(\alpha \vee \beta)$. To show that any proper initial segment of $(\alpha \circ \beta)$ (where $\circ \in \{\wedge, \vee\}$) has weight ≥ 0, we write it as follows:

$$(\alpha \circ \beta) \overset{\text{syn}}{=} (\alpha_1\alpha_2 \ldots \alpha_m \circ \beta_1\beta_2 \ldots \beta_n)$$

where α_i and β_j are the symbols of α and β, respectively. Several cases naturally present themselves: if the initial segment consists only of (, then its weight is 1. If the initial segment ends in the α_i's, but does not end at α_m, then by induction it has weight ≥ 1. If it ends exactly at α_m, then by induction it has weight 0. If it ends at $\circ$, then it has weight 1. Similarly, we deal with the initial segment ending in the middle of the β_j's, at β_n, and at the last parenthesis).

Problem 9.81. Suppose $\alpha \overset{\text{syn}}{\neq} \alpha'$. Then, since $\alpha c \beta \overset{\text{syn}}{=} \alpha' c' \beta'$, α and α' are both initial segments of the same string. As such, one must be an initial segment of the other; we assume without loss of generality that α is the first n elements of α', and that α' contains more than n elements. Clearly, α is a proper initial segment, as α' is a valid formula. Lemma 9.78 grants that the weight of α is non-negative—but α is a formula, so its weight is -1. The assumption that $\alpha \overset{\text{syn}}{\neq} \alpha'$ leads to a contradiction, so $\alpha \overset{\text{syn}}{=} \alpha'$. As such, c and c' share the same index in identical strings; they are the same binary connective. Furthermore, β and β' must then start on the same index of $\alpha c \beta \overset{\text{syn}}{=} \alpha' c' \beta'$, and continue until the end, so $\beta \overset{\text{syn}}{=} \beta'$.

Problem 9.82. Suppose that we have $\Phi \vDash \alpha$ and $\Phi \cup \{\alpha\} \vDash \beta$. And suppose that τ is a truth assignment that satisfies Φ. Then, by the first assumption it must satisfy α, and so τ satisfies $\Phi \cup \{\alpha\}$, and hence by the second assumption it must satisfy β.

Problem 9.83. By structural induction on α. Clearly, if α is just a variable p, then α' is $\neg p$, and $\neg \alpha \iff \alpha'$. The induction step follows directly from De Morgan Laws.

Problem 9.84. Let the variables of α be $\alpha(\bar{x}, \bar{y})$ and the variables of β be $\beta(\bar{y}, \bar{z})$. The notation $\bar{x}$ denotes a set of Boolean variables; using this convention, the set $S = \text{Var}(\alpha) \cap \text{Var}(\beta) = \{\bar{y}\}$. We define the Boolean function f as follows:

$$f(\bar{y}) = \begin{cases} 1 & \text{if } \exists \bar{x} \text{ such that } \alpha(\bar{x}, \bar{y}) = 1 \\ 0 & \text{otherwise} \end{cases}$$

We are abusing notation slightly here, by mixing Boolean functions and Boolean formulas; $\bar{y}$ is working over-time: it is both an argument to f and a truth assignment to α. But the meaning is clear. Let $C_f(\bar{y})$ be the Boolean formula associated with f; it can be obtained, for example, by conjunctive normal form. The C_f is our formula: suppose that $\tau \vDash \alpha$; then τ clearly satisfies C_f (by its definition). If $\tau \vDash C$, then there must be an $\bar{x}$ such that $\alpha(\bar{x}, \tau)$ is true, and hence $\beta(\tau, \bar{z})$ is true by the original assumption.

Note that we could have defined f dually with β; how?

Problem 9.85. We offer proof that $\neg(p \vee q) \to \neg p \wedge \neg q$. Justification of each step is provided to the right. The "weaken" and "exchange" rules are denoted "w" and "e" respectively. Similarly, "left" and "right" are denoted "l" and "r".

$$\cfrac{\cfrac{\cfrac{\cfrac{p \to p}{p \to p,q}\ \text{w}}{p \to p \vee q}\ \vee\ \text{r}}{\neg(p \vee q) \to \neg p}\ \neg\ \text{l,r} \qquad \cfrac{\cfrac{\cfrac{q \to q}{q \to p,q}\ \text{w,e}}{q \to p \vee q}\ \vee\ \text{r}}{\neg(p \vee q) \to \neg q}\ \neg\ \text{l,r}}{\neg(p \vee q) \to \neg q \wedge \neg q}\ \wedge\ \text{r}$$

Problem 9.86. The following is a PK proof of the left contraction; as such, we assume that $\Gamma, \alpha, \alpha \to \Delta$ is true.

$$\cfrac{\cfrac{\alpha \to \alpha}{\Gamma, \alpha \to \Delta, \alpha} \qquad \cfrac{\Gamma, \alpha, \alpha \to \Delta}{\alpha, \Gamma, \alpha \to \Delta}}{\Gamma, \alpha \to \Delta}$$

Problem 9.87. A right-introduction rule for $\leftrightarrow$:

$$\cfrac{\alpha, \Gamma \to \Delta, \beta \qquad \beta, \Gamma \to \Delta, \alpha}{\Gamma \to \Delta, (\alpha \leftrightarrow \beta)}$$

Problem 9.88. Recall that each sequent is written in the form *antecedent* $\to$ *succedent*, where the antecedent is a conjunction and the succedent a disjunction. The *exchange* rules result directly from the commutativity and associativity of the "and" and "or" operators. Similarly, the *weakening* rules result from the properties of these operators. Considering an extra formula in the antecedent might make it evaluate to *false* when it was otherwise *true*, but this cannot cause the sequent to become *false* when it was otherwise *true*. Similarly, including a new formula in the succedent may cause the resulting disjunction to newly evaluate to *true*, but this again cannot cause an otherwise true sequent to be *false*.

Assume $\Gamma \to \Delta, \alpha$ and $\alpha, \Gamma \to \Delta$. That is, $\Gamma \to (\Delta \vee \alpha)$ and $(\alpha \wedge \Gamma) \to \Delta$. Assume Γ is true, and assume for the sake of contradiction that Δ is false. Then *true* $\to$ (*false* $\vee$ α), so α is *true*. So (*true* $\wedge$ *true*) $\to \Delta$, therefore Δ must be *true*. Clearly we've found a contradiction; Δ must be *true* whenever Γ is *true*, proving the *cut* rule.

We show in problem 9.86 that the *contraction* rules can be proven correct given use of the *exchange*, *weakening* and *cut* rules.

We now begin the introduction rules. For $\neg$-left, let $\Gamma \to \Delta \vee \alpha$. Assume that Γ and $\neg\alpha$ are *true*—and assume for contradiction that Δ is *false*. Then we have: *true* $\to$ *false* $\vee$ *false*; this assignment of values contradicts the hypothesis. Thus, $\neg\alpha \wedge \Gamma \to \Delta$. A similar argument can be given for the $\neg$-right rule.

The ∧-left and ∨-right rules follow from the commutative and associative natures of the antecedent and succedent. The ∧-right and ∨-left rules can be proven by quickly via proof by contradiction, similar to the ¬ rules.

Problem 9.90. Each of the exchange rules is its own inverse, so each is invertible as a result of its own correctness. Similarly, the ¬-introduction rules are each other's inverses. The contraction rules are proven directly by the assertions that $(\Gamma \wedge \alpha \wedge \alpha) \iff (\Gamma \wedge \alpha)$ and $(\Delta \vee \alpha \vee \alpha) \iff (\Delta \vee \alpha)$. Similarly, the cut rule results from two clearly true observations: $(\alpha \wedge \Gamma) \to \Gamma$ and $\Delta \to (\Delta \vee \alpha)$.

The ∧-left and ∨-right rules clearly don't change the meaning of the sequent given that conjunctions and disjunctions are commutative and associative.

For ∧-right, let $\Gamma \to \Delta, (\alpha \wedge \beta)$. If Γ is *false*, then both top sequents are *true* regardless of the value of their succedents. Assume Γ is *true*. Again, if Δ is *true* then we're done— assume Δ is *false*. Then $(\alpha \wedge \beta)$ are both *true* by the hypothesis so $\Delta \vee \alpha$ and $\Delta \vee \beta$ are *true*. Thus, $\Gamma \to \Delta, \alpha$ and $\Gamma \to \Delta, \beta$, and we're done.

To prove that the ∨-left rule is invertible, let $(\alpha \vee \beta), \Gamma \to \Delta)$ be *true*. Assume α and Γ are both *true*. Then $(\alpha \vee \beta) \wedge \Gamma$ is *true*, so Δ must be *true*. Thus, $\alpha, \Gamma \to \Delta$ is *true*. An identical argument can be made to prove that $\beta, \Gamma \to \Delta$, completing the argument.

Finally, we offer an example for which inversion of the weakening rule fails. Let $\alpha, \Gamma \to \Delta$ be *true*. Clearly, if α is *false* and Γ is *true*, then no conclusion can be drawn about Δ—it may be either *true* or *false*. In the case that Δ is *false*, we find a contradiction to the assertion that $\Gamma \to \Delta$.

Problem 9.92. Five rules are not needed: the contraction, weakening and cut rules. We need the exchange rules to make the proofs match the exact order of the given rules, and we need whichever connective introduction rule is applicable.

Problem 9.93. Any non-trivial formula can be written in one of the following forms: $\alpha \wedge \beta$, $\alpha \vee \beta$, or $\neg \alpha$. To prove that PK′ is complete, we need only show that formulas in these forms can be introduced from their component parts. We provide a constructions of them. First, ∧:

$$\frac{\dfrac{\alpha \to \alpha}{\alpha, \beta \to \alpha} \qquad \dfrac{\beta \to \beta}{\alpha, \beta \to \beta}}{\dfrac{\alpha, \beta \to \alpha \wedge \beta}{\alpha \wedge \beta \to \alpha \wedge \beta}}$$

Next, ∨:

$$\frac{\dfrac{\alpha \to \alpha}{\alpha \to \alpha, \beta} \qquad \dfrac{\beta \to \beta}{\beta \to \alpha, \beta}}{\dfrac{\alpha \vee \beta \to \alpha, \beta}{\alpha \vee \beta \to \alpha \vee \beta}}$$

And finally, $\neg\alpha \to \neg\alpha$ results from two quick applications of $\neg$ introduction rules to $\alpha \to \alpha$.

Problem 9.96. We assign weight to each symbol in a fashion similar to figure 9.9. Every n-ary predicate symbol has weight equal $(n-1)$. For example, a 4-ary function symbol has weight 3. As an extension of this rule, constants (which are really just 0-ary function symbols) have weight -1. Variables, which (like constants) represent complete terms, also have weight -1. We claim that every term weighs -1, and that every proper initial segment weighs at least 0. First we consider the trivial case: a term consisting of a single constant or variable. It's weight is -1 and the only proper initial segment is the empty segment, which has 0 weight.

Moreover, this property is clearly inductive. Any non-trivial term is an n-ary predicate symbol, with weight $(n-1)$, followed by n terms. If each of these terms has weight -1, then the resulting term has weight $(n-1) - n = -1$. Any initial segment is composed of this n-ary symbol, less than n complete terms and up to 1 incomplete term; this term weighs ≥ 0, and clearly there aren't enough complete terms to overwhelm the $(n-1)$ weight imposed by the initial predicate—any proper initial segment must have weight ≥ 0. It follows that two identical strings cannot represent the same predicate and series of terms, as this would imply that some included term is a proper initial segment of another; for a more detailed explanation of this last step, see the solution to problem 9.81.

Problem 9.98. We prove this using BSDs: Let $\mathcal{M}$ be any structure, and σ any object assignment. Suppose $\mathcal{M} \vDash (\forall x\alpha \vee \forall x\beta)[\sigma]$. Then, $\mathcal{M} \vDash \forall x\alpha[\sigma]$ or $\mathcal{M} \vDash \forall x\beta[\sigma]$.

Case (1): $\mathcal{M} \vDash \forall x\alpha[\sigma]$. Then, $\mathcal{M} \vDash \alpha[\sigma(m/x)]$ for all $m \in M$. Then, $\mathcal{M} \vDash (\alpha \vee \beta)[\sigma(m/x)]$ for all $m \in M$. So, $\mathcal{M} \vDash \forall x(\alpha \vee \beta)[\sigma]$.

Case (2): $\mathcal{M} \vDash \forall x\beta[\sigma]$; same idea as above.

Therefore, $\mathcal{M} \vDash \forall x(\alpha \vee \beta)[\sigma]$. By the definition of logical consequence, $(\forall x\alpha \vee \forall x\beta) \vDash \forall x(\alpha \vee \beta)$

Problem 9.99. No, not necessarily. We use the def of logical consequence to prove this. To prove that the RHS is *not* a logical consequence of the

LHS, we must exhibit a model $\mathcal{M}$, an object assignment σ and formulas α, β such that: $\mathcal{M} \vDash \forall x(\alpha \vee \beta)[\sigma]$, but $\mathcal{M} \nvDash (\forall x\alpha \vee \forall x\beta)[\sigma]$.

Let α and β be Px and Qx, respectively (P, Q unary predicates). Now define $\mathcal{M}$ and σ. Since the formulas are sentences, no need to define σ. $\mathcal{M}$: let the universe of discourse be $M = \mathbb{N}$. We still need to give meaning in $\mathcal{M}$ to P, Q. Let $P^{\mathcal{M}} = \{0, 2, 4, \ldots\}$, and $Q^{\mathcal{M}} = \{1, 3, 5, \ldots\}$. Then: $\mathcal{M} \vDash \forall x(Px \vee Qx)$ (because every number is even or odd).

But, $\mathcal{M} \nvDash (\forall x Px \vee \forall x Qx)$ (because it is not true that either all numbers are even or all numbers are odd).

Problem 9.100. Base case: let $u = ft_1 t_2 \ldots t_n$, where some of f's input terms t_i may be x, but none of them otherwise include x. If none of the terms are x, then clearly

$$(u(t/x))^{\mathcal{M}}[\sigma] = u^{\mathcal{M}}[\sigma] = u^{\mathcal{M}}[\sigma(m/x)]$$

for any m; x doesn't occur in u so the substitutions do nothing when applied to u. Otherwise, there are some i such that $t_i = x$; below we assume x is present once in the terms, but this detail is irrelevant.

$$
\begin{aligned}
(u(t/x))^{\mathcal{M}}[\sigma] &= ((ft_1 \ldots x \ldots t_n)(t/x))^{\mathcal{M}}[\sigma] \\
&= (ft_1 \ldots t \ldots t_n)^{\mathcal{M}}[\sigma] \\
&= f^{\mathcal{M}}(t_1^{\mathcal{M}}[\sigma], \ldots t^{\mathcal{M}}[\sigma], \ldots t_n^{\mathcal{M}}[\sigma])
\end{aligned}
$$

Similarly,

$$
\begin{aligned}
u^{\mathcal{M}}[\sigma(m/x)] &= (ft_1 \ldots x \ldots t_n)^{\mathcal{M}}[\sigma(m/x)] \\
&= f^{\mathcal{M}}(t_1^{\mathcal{M}}[\sigma(m/x)], \ldots, x^{\mathcal{M}}[\sigma(m/x)], \ldots, t_n^{\mathcal{M}}[\sigma(m/x)])
\end{aligned}
$$

here we use the knowledge that the non-x terms don't contain x.

$$
\begin{aligned}
&= f^{\mathcal{M}}(t_1^{\mathcal{M}}[\sigma], \ldots, m, \ldots t_n^{\mathcal{M}}[\sigma]) \\
&= f^{\mathcal{M}}(t_1^{\mathcal{M}}[\sigma], \ldots t^{\mathcal{M}}[\sigma], \ldots t_n^{\mathcal{M}}[\sigma])
\end{aligned}
$$

So $(u(t/x))^{\mathcal{M}}[\sigma] = u^{\mathcal{M}}[\sigma(m/x)]$ in this case.

Induction is very easy in comparison: if this applies to each term which is input into a any given function, it then applies to the function's output as well due to the recursive nature of term evaluation.

Problem 9.101. For example, suppose α is $\forall y \neg(x = y + y)$. This says "$x$ is odd". But $\alpha(x + y/x)$ is $\forall y \neg(x + y = y + y)$ which is always false, regardless of the value of $\sigma(x)$. The problem is that y in the term $x + y$ got "caught" by the quantifier $\forall y$.

Problem 9.103. If α is an atomic formula, then it is of the form $Pt_1 \ldots t_n$. We show in problem 9.100 that if t_i is a term, then $(t_i(t/x))^{\mathcal{M}}[\sigma] = t_i^{\mathcal{M}}[\sigma(m/x)]$, where $m = t^{\mathcal{M}}[\sigma]$. Thus, the following are equivalent:

$$\mathcal{M} \vDash \alpha(t/x)[\sigma]$$
$$\mathcal{M} \vDash ((Pt_1 \ldots t_n)(t/x))[\sigma]$$
$$(t_1(t/x)^{\mathcal{M}}[\sigma], \ldots, t_n(t/x)^{\mathcal{M}}[\sigma]) \in P^{\mathcal{M}}$$
$$(t_1^{\mathcal{M}}[\sigma(m/x)], \ldots, t_n^{\mathcal{M}}[\sigma(m/x)]) \in P^{\mathcal{M}}$$
$$\mathcal{M} \vDash (Pt_1 \ldots t_n)[\sigma(m/x)]$$
$$\mathcal{M} \vDash \alpha[\sigma(m/x)]$$

As such, for any atomic formula α, $\mathcal{M} \vDash \alpha(t/x)[\sigma]$ iff $\mathcal{M} \vDash \alpha[\sigma(m/x)]$.

Let α, β be any two formulas with this property. The following are equivalent:

$$\mathcal{M} \vDash ((\alpha \wedge \beta)(t/x))[\sigma]$$
$$\mathcal{M} \vDash (\alpha(t/x))[\sigma] \text{ and } \mathcal{M} \vDash (\beta(t/x))[\sigma]$$
$$\mathcal{M} \vDash \alpha[\sigma(m/x)] \text{ and } \mathcal{M} \vDash \beta[\sigma(m/x)]$$
$$\mathcal{M} \vDash (\alpha \wedge \beta)[\sigma(m/x)]$$

Moreover, the same can be said of $\vee$ as $\wedge$. Finally, we have the following equivalences:

$$\mathcal{M} \vDash (\forall y(\alpha(t/x)))[\sigma]$$
$$\mathcal{M} \vDash \alpha(t/x)[\sigma(n/y)] \text{ for all } n \in \mathcal{M}$$

We apply that y does not occur in t to equate the two above and two below:

$$\mathcal{M} \vDash \alpha[\sigma(m/x)(n/y)] \text{ for all } n \in \mathcal{M}$$
$$\mathcal{M} \vDash (\forall y \alpha)[\sigma(m/x)]$$

Here the first two are identical to the second two because y does not occur in t (otherwise t would not be freely substitutable for x), so the two substitutions are disjoint (i.e., they do not affect any common terms). The same argument can be applied to $\exists$ as $\forall$.

Problem 9.104. There are two rules which require no justification:

$$\frac{\alpha(t), \Gamma \to \Delta}{\forall x \alpha(x), \Gamma \to \Delta}$$

and

$$\frac{\Gamma \to \Delta, \alpha(t)}{\Gamma \to \Delta, \exists x \alpha(x)}$$

Clearly, $\forall x \alpha(x) \implies \alpha(t)$, so if $\alpha(t) \wedge \Gamma$ implies that Δ is true, then so does $\forall x \alpha(x) \wedge \Gamma$. Similarly, if Γ implies that $\Delta \vee \alpha(t)$ is true, then it also implies $\Delta \vee \exists x \alpha(x)$, as $\alpha(t) \implies \exists x \alpha(x)$.

The other two are less trivial; it is not immediately clear that they are correct at first glance. The key insight comes from our previously defined nomenclature; where t in the above is a specific term, b is a free variable, so we can consider it to be an arbitrary element of M (or identically *any* element of M). Let us first look at the right introduction rule for $\forall$:

$$\frac{\Gamma \to \Delta, \alpha(b)}{\Gamma \to \Delta, \forall x \alpha(x)}$$

Since b is arbitrary (i.e., no assignment σ is listed to further specify b's meaning), the top must be true with any applicable x assigned to b, hence the result.

Next we look at the left introduction rule for $\exists$:

$$\frac{\alpha(b), \Gamma \to \Delta}{\exists x \alpha(x), \Gamma \to \Delta}$$

Again, the key is that b is unassigned. The premise, then, is that for any b, $\alpha(b) \wedge \Gamma \implies \Delta$. As such, the existence of an x meeting the condition $\alpha(x)$ implies that said x can be "plugged into" b in the premise, so that $\alpha(x) \wedge \Gamma \implies \Delta$.

Problem 9.105. Let M be the natural numbers. σ is irrelevant for our purposes here, so we leave it undefined. Consider the following sequent: $(b = y + y) \to \alpha(b)$, where $\alpha(b)$ denotes "b is even". Clearly, this sequent is true. Consider, then, the result of $\forall$-right: $(b = y + y) \to \forall x \alpha(x)$. This sequent states, "if b is even then every x is even", which is obviously false.

Next, consider the trivial sequent $\beta(b) \to (b > 2)$, where $\beta(b)$ denotes "$b \geq 3$" It is obviously true, but if we apply $\exists$-left, we get: $\exists x \beta(x) \to (b > 2)$. In other words, the existence of a natural number $x \geq 3$ implies that $b > 2$; but b is a free variable, it could be 1 or 0 depending on σ.

Problem 9.106. Let $\alpha(x)$ be $(x = 0 \vee \exists y(x = sy))$. We outline the proof informally, but the proof can of course be formalized in LK-PA. Basis case: $x = 0$, and LK-PK proves $\alpha(0)$ easily:

$$\frac{\dfrac{\dfrac{\to \forall x(x = x)}{\to 0 = 0, \forall x(x = x)} \text{ weak \& exch} \quad \dfrac{0 = 0 \to 0 = 0}{\forall x(x = x) \to 0 = 0} \text{ } \forall\text{-left}}{\to 0 = 0} \text{ Cut}}{\dfrac{\to 0 = 0, \exists y(0 = sy)}{\to 0 = 0 \vee \exists y(0 = sy)} \text{ } \vee\text{-right}} \text{ weak}$$

Induction Step: Show that LK-PA proves $\forall x(\alpha(x) \to \alpha(sx))$, i.e., we must give an LK-PA proof of the sequent:

$$\to \forall x(\neg(x = 0 \lor \exists y(x = sy)) \lor (sx = 0 \lor \exists y(sx = sy)))$$

This is not difficult, and it is left to the reader. From the formulas $\alpha(0)$ and $\forall x(\alpha(x) \to \alpha(sx))$, and using the axiom:

$$\to (\alpha(0) \land \forall x(\alpha(x) \to \alpha(sx))) \to \forall x \alpha(x)$$

we can now conclude (in just a few steps): $\to \forall x \alpha(x)$ which is what we wanted to prove. Thus, LK-PA proves $\forall x \alpha(x)$.

9.6　Notes

The epigraph for this chapter is a quote from the prolific philosopher writer Sir Roger Scruton. *Drinks in Helsinki*, a chapter in [Scruton (2005)], is as funny as it is possible in serious writing, and it reminds this author of his own experience in Turku, Finland (presenting [Soltys (2004)]).

$\mathbb{N}$ (the set of natural numbers) and IP (the induction principle) are very tightly related; the rigorous definition of $\mathbb{N}$, as a set-theoretic object, is the following: it is the *unique* set satisfying the following three properties: (i) it contains 0, (ii) if n is in it, then so is $n + 1$, and (iii) it satisfies the induction principle (which in this context is stated as follows: if S is a subset of $\mathbb{N}$, and S satisfies (i) and (ii) above, then in fact $S = \mathbb{N}$).

The references in this paragraph are with respect to Knuth's seminal *The Art of Computer Programming*, [Knuth (1997)]. For an extensive study of Euclid's algorithm see §1.1. Problem 9.2 comes from §1.2.1, problem #8, pg. 19. See §2.3.1, pg. 318 for more background on tree traversals. For the history of the concept of pre and post-condition, and loop invariants, see pg. 17. In particular, for material related to the extended Euclid's algorithm , see page 13, algorithm E, in [Knuth (1997)], page 937 in [Cormen et al. (2009)], and page 292, algorithm A.5, in [Delfs and Knebl (2007)]. We give a recursive version of the algorithm in section 3.4.

See [Zingaro (2008)] for a book dedicated to the idea of invariants in the context of proving correctness of algorithms. A great source of problems on the invariance principle, that is section 9.1.2, is chapter 1 in [Engel (1998)]

The example about the 8×8 board with two squares missing (figure 9.2) comes from [Dijkstra (1989)].

For more algebraic background, see [Dummit and Foote (1991)] or [Alperin and Bell (1995)]. For number theory, especially related to cryptography, see [Hoffstein *et al.* (2008)]. A classical text in number theory is [Hardy and Wright (1980)].

The section on relations is based on hand-written lecture slides of Ryszard Janicki. A basic introduction to relations can be found in chapter 8 of [Rosen (2007)], and for a very quick introduction to relations (up to the definition of equivalence classes), the reader is invited to read the delightful section 7 of [Halmos (1960)].

A different perspective on partial orders is offered in [Mendelson (1970)], chapter 3. In this book the author approaches partial orders from the point of view of *Boolean algebras*, which are defined as follows: a set B together with two binary operations $\curlywedge, \curlyvee$ (normally denoted $\wedge, \vee$, but we use these for "and","or", and so here we use the "curly" version to emphasize that "$\curlywedge$" and "$\curlyvee$" are not necessarily the standard Boolean connectives) on B, a singularity operation $'$ on B, and two specific elements 0 and 1 of B, and satisfying a set of axioms: $x \curlywedge y = y \curlywedge x$ and $x \curlyvee y = y \curlyvee x$, distributivity of $\curlywedge$ over $\curlyvee$, and vice-versa, as well as $x \curlywedge 1 = x$ and $x \curlyvee 0 = x$, $x \curlyvee x' = 1$ and $x \curlywedge x' = 0$, and finally $0 \neq 1$. A Boolean algebra is usually denoted by the sextuple $\mathcal{B} = \langle B, \curlywedge, \curlyvee, ', 0, 1 \rangle$, and it is assumed to satisfy the axioms just listed.

Given a Boolean algebra $\mathcal{B}$, we define a binary relation $\preceq$ as follows:

$$x \preceq y \iff x \curlywedge y = x.$$

This turns out to be equivalent to our notion of a lattice order. Mendelson then abstracts the three properties of reflexivity, antisymmetry and transitivity, and says that any relation that satisfies all three is a partial order—and not every partial order is a lattice.

There are many excellent introductions to logic; for example, [Buss (1998)] and [Bell and Machover (1977)]. This section follows the logic lectures given by Stephen Cook at the University of Toronto.

Problem 9.83 is of course an instance of the general Boolean "Duality Principle." A proof-theoretic version of this principle is given, for example, as theorem 3.4 in [Mendelson (1970)], where the *dual* of a proposition concerning a Boolean algebra B is the proposition obtained by substituting $\curlyvee$ for $\curlywedge$ and $\curlywedge$ for $\curlyvee$ (see page 293 where we defined these symbols). We also substitute 0 for 1 and 1 for 0. Then, if a proposition is derivable from the usual axioms of Boolean algebra, so is its dual.

Section 9.3.6 on the correctness of recursive algorithms is based on chapter 5 of [Manna (1974)].

Bibliography

Agrawal, M., Kayal, N. and Saxena, N. (2004). Primes is in P, *Annals of Mathematics* **160**, 2, pp. 781–793.

Aleknovich, M., Borodin, A., Buresh-Oppenheim, J., Impagliazzo, R., Magen, A. and Pitassi, T. (2005). Toward a model of backtracking and dynamic programming, .

Alford, W. R., Granville, A. and Pomerance, C. (1994). There are infinitely many Carmichael numbers, *Annals of Mathematics* **139**, 3, pp. 703–722.

Allan Borodin, C. R., Morten N. Nielsen (2003). (incremental) priority algorithms, *Algorithmica* **37**, 4, pp. 295–326.

Alperin, J. L. and Bell, R. B. (1995). *Groups and Representations* (Springer).

Arrow, K. (1951). *Social Choice and Individual Values* (J. Wiley).

Austrin, P. (2010). How hard is unshuffling a string (reply), CS Theory Stack Exchange reply to [Erickson (2010)]. http://cstheory.stackexchange.com/q/692.

Bell, J. and Machover, M. (1977). *A course in mathematical logic* (North-Holland).

Berkowitz, S. J. (1984). On computing the determinant in small parallel time using a small number of processors, *Information Processing Letters* **18**, 3, pp. 147–150.

Borodin, A. and El-Yaniv, R. (1998). *Online Computation and Competitive Analysis* (Cambridge University Press).

Bozóki, S. and Rapcsák, T. (2008). On saaty's and koczkodaj's inconsistencies of pairwise comparison matrices, *Journal of Global Optimization* **42**, 2, pp. 157–175, doi:10.1007/s10898-007-9236-z.

Brin, S. and Page, L. (1998). The anatomy of a large-scale hypertextual web search engine, in *Proceedings of the seventh international conference on World Wide Web 7*, WWW7 (Elsevier Science Publishers B. V., Amsterdam, The Netherlands, The Netherlands), pp. 107–117, URL http://dl.acm.org/citation.cfm?id=297805.297827.

Bush, V. (1945). As we may think, *The Atlantic Monthly* .

Buss, S. R. (1998). An introduction to proof theory, in S. R. Buss (ed.), *Handbook of Proof Theory* (North Holland), pp. 1–78.

Buss, S. R. and Soltys, M. (2013). Unshuffling a square is NP-hard, *Journal of Computer and System Sciences* **80**, 4, pp. 766–776, doi:http://dx.doi.org/10.1016/j.jcss.2013.11.002, URL http://www.sciencedirect.com/science/article/pii/S002200001300189X.

Cenzer, D. and Remmel, J. B. (2001). Proof-theoretic strength of the stable marriage theorem and other problems, *Reverse Mathematics*, pp. 67–103.

Christian, B. and Griffiths, T. (2016). *Algorithms to Live By: the Computer Science of Human Decisions* (Henry Holt and Company, LLC).

Church, A. (1996). *Introduction to Mathematical Logic* (Princeton University Press).

Clarke, R. A. and Knake, R. (2011). *Cyber War: The Next Threat to National Security and What to Do About It* (Ecco; Reprint edition).

Condorcet (1785). Essai sur l'application de l'analyse 'a la probabilité des décisions rendues à la pluralité des vois, Paris.

Cook, S. A. and Nguyen, P. (2010). *Logical Foundations of Proof Complexity* (Cambridge Univeristy Press).

Cook, S. A. and Soltys, M. (1999). Boolean programs and quantified propositional proof systems, *Bulletin of the Section of Logic* **28**, 3, pp. 119–129.

Cormen, T. H., Leiserson, C. E., Rivest, R. L. and Stein, C. (2009). *Introduction to Algorithms*, 3rd edn. (McGraw-Hill Book Company), third Edition.

Delfs, H. and Knebl, H. (2007). *Introduction to Cryptography* (Springer).

Dickens, C. (1850). *David Copperfield* (Penguin Classics).

Dickens, C. (1854). *Hard Times* (Everyman's Library).

Dierbach, C. (2013). *Introduction to Computer Science using Python: A computational problem solving focus* (Wiley).

Dijkstra, E. W. (1989). On the cruelty of really teaching computing science, *Communications of the ACM* **32**, 12.

Doctorow, E. L. (1971). *The Book of Daniel* (Plume Penguin).

Dorrigiv, R. and López-Ortiz, A. (2009). On developing new models, with paging as a case study, *ACM SIGACT News* **40**, 4.

Downey, A. (2015). *Think Python: How to Think Like a Computer Scientist*, 2nd edn. (Green Tea Press).

Duda, H. (1977). *Zajęcia pozalekcyjne z matematyki w szkole podstawowej. Zbiory i relacje* (Wydawnictwa Szkolne i Pedagogiczne).

Dummit, D. S. and Foote, R. M. (1991). *Abstract Algebra* (Prentice Hall).

Dyer, J. S. (1990). Remarks on the analytic hierarchy process, *Manage. Sci.* **36**, 3, pp. 249–258, doi:10.1287/mnsc.36.3.249, URL http://dx.doi.org/10.1287/mnsc.36.3.249.

Easley, D. and Kleinberg, J. (2010). *Networks, crowds, and markets: reasoning about a highly connected world* (Cambridge).

Engel, A. (1998). *Problem-Solving Strategies* (Springer).

Erickson, J. (2010). How hard is unshuffling a string? CS Theory Stack Exchange posting. http://cstheory.stackexchange.com/questions/34/how-hard-is-unshuffling-a-string.

Faliszewski, P., Hemaspaandra, E. and Hemaspaandra, L. A. (2010). Using complexity to protect elections, *Communications of the ACM* **53**, 11,

p. 74, doi:10.1145/1839676.1839696, URL http://dx.doi.org/10.1145/1839676.1839696.

Fernández, A. G. and Soltys, M. (2013). Feasible combinatorial matrix theory, in K. Chatterjee and J. Sgall (eds.), *Mathematical Foundations of Computer Science 2013, Lecture Notes in Computer Science*, Vol. 8087 (Springer Berlin Heidelberg), ISBN 978-3-642-40312-5, pp. 777–788, doi:10.1007/978-3-642-40313-2_68, URL http://dx.doi.org/10.1007/978-3-642-40313-2_68.

Franceschet, M. (2011). Pagerank: standing on the shoulders of giants, *Communications of the ACM* **54**, 6.

Fred D. Taylor, J. (2011). Software: The broken door of cyberspace security, *Harvard Law School National Security Journal* URL http://harvardnsj.org/2011/02/software-the-broken-door-of-cyberspace-security/.

Gale, D. and Shapley, L. S. (1962). College admissions and the stability of marriage, *American Mathematical Monthly* **69**, pp. 9–14.

Ginsburg, S. and Spanier, E. (1965). Mapping of languages by two-tape devices, *Journal of the Association of Computing Machinery* **12**, 3, pp. 423–434.

Gischer, J. (1981). Shuffle languages, Petri nets, and context-sensivite grammars, *Communications of the ACM* **24**, 9, pp. 597–605.

Gruber, H. and Holzer, M. (2009). Tight bounds on the descriptional complexity of regular expressions, in *Proc. Intl. Conf. on Developments in Language Theory (DLT)* (Springer Verlag), pp. 276–287.

Hägele, G. and Pukelsheim, F. (2001). Llull's writings on electoral systems, *Studia Lulliana* **41**, pp. 3–38, URL https://www.math.uni-augsburg.de/htdocs/emeriti/pukelsheim/2001a.html.

Halmos, P. R. (1960). *Naive Set Theory* (Springer-Verlag).

Halmos, P. R. (1995). *Linear algebra problem book* (The mathematical association of America).

Hardy, G. H. and Wright, E. M. (1980). *An Introduction to the Theory of Numbers*, 5th edn. (Oxford University Press).

Harel, D. (1987). *Algorithmics: The Spirit of Computing* (The Addison-Wesley Publishing Company), ISBN 0-201-19240-3.

Harris, R. (1996). *Enigma* (Ballantine Books).

Henshall, D., Rampersad, N. and Shallit, J. (2012). Shuffling and unshuffling, *Bulletin of the EATCS* **107**, pp. 131–142.

Hoffman, P. (1998). *The Man Who Loved Only Numbers: The Story of Paul Erdős and the Search for Mathematical Truth* (Hyperion).

Hoffstein, J., Pipher, J. and Silverman, J. H. (2008). *An Introduction to Mathematical Cryptography* (Springer).

Hutton, G. (2007). *Programming in Haskell* (Cambridge University Press, New York, NY, USA), ISBN 0521871727, 9780521871723.

Janicki, R. (2011). Approximations of arbitrary relations by partial orders: Classical and rough set models, in J. F. P. et al (ed.), *Transactions on Rough Sets XIII, LNCS*, Vol. 6499 (Springer-Verlag Berlin Heidelberg).

Janicki, R. and Zhai, Y. (2011). Remarks on pairwise comparison numerical and non-numerical rankings, *Lecture Notes in Computer Science* **6954**, pp. 290–300.

Jantzen, M. (1981). The power of synchronizing operations on strings, *Theoretical Computer Science* **14**, pp. 127–154.

Jantzen, M. (1985). Extending regular expressions with iterated shuffle, *Theoretical Computer Science* **38**, pp. 223–247.

Jedrzejowicz, J. (1999). Structural properties of shuffle automata, *Grammars* **2**, 1, pp. 35–51.

Jedrzejowicz, J. and Szepietowski, A. (2001). Shuffle languages are in P, *Theoretical Computer Science* **250**, 1-2, p. 31=53.

Jedrzejowicz, J. and Szepietowski, A. (2005). On the expressive power of the shuffle operator matched with intersection by regular sets, *Theoretical Informatics and Applications* **35**, pp. 379–388.

Johnson, P. (1991). *The Birth of the Modern* (Phoenix Giant).

Kakiashvili, T., Koczkodaj, W. W. and Woodbury-Smith, M. (2012). Improving the medical scale predictability by the pairwise comparisons method: evidence from a clinical data study, *Comput Methods Programs Biomed* **105**, 3, pp. 210–6, doi:10.1016/j.cmpb.2011.09.011.

Karp, R. M. and Rabin, M. O. (1987). Efficient randomized pattern-matching algorithms, *IBM Journal of Research and Development* **31**, 2, pp. 249–260.

Katajainen, J. and Träff, J. L. (1997). A meticulous analysis of mergesort programs, in *Proceedings of the Third Italian Conference on Algorithms and Complexity*, CIAC '97 (Springer-Verlag, London, UK, UK), ISBN 3-540-62592-5, pp. 217–228, URL http://dl.acm.org/citation.cfm?id=648256.752881.

Kimball, R. (2012). *The fortunes of permanence: Culture and anarchy in an Age of Amnesia* (St. Augustine's Press).

Kleinberg, J. and Tardos, É. (2006). *Algorithm Design* (Pearson Education).

Knuth, D. E. (1997). *The Art of Computer Programming*, Vol. 1, Fundamental Algorithms, 3rd edn. (Addison Wesley).

Koczkodaj, W. (1993). A new definition of consistency of pairwise comparisons, *Mathematical and Computer Modelling* **18**, 7, pp. 79–84, doi:http://dx.doi.org/10.1016/0895-7177(93)90059-8, URL http://www.sciencedirect.com/science/article/pii/0895717793900598.

Koczkodaj, W. W., Kułakowski, K. and Ligęza, A. (2014). On the quality evaluation of scientific entities in poland supported by consistency-driven pairwise comparisons method, *Scientometrics* **99**, pp. 911–926, doi:10.1007/s11192-014-1258-y.

Kozen, D. (2006). *Theory of Computation* (Springer).

Krajíček, J. (1995). *Bounded Arithmetic, Propositional Logic, and Complexity Theory* (Cambridge).

Lehtonen, E. (2008). Two undecidable variants of collatz's problems, *Theoretical Computer Science* **407**, 1-3, pp. 596–600, doi:10.1016/j.tcs.2008.08.029, URL http://dx.doi.org/10.1016/j.tcs.2008.08.029.

Manna, Z. (1974). *Mathematical Theory of Computation* (McGraw-Hill Computer Science Series).

Mansfield, A. (1982). An algorithm for a merge recognition problem, *Discrete Applied Mathematics* **4**, 3, pp. 193 – 197, doi:http://dx.doi.org/10.1016/

0166-218X(82)90039-7, URL http://www.sciencedirect.com/science/article/pii/0166218X82900397.

Mansfield, A. (1983). On the computational complexity of a merge recognition problem, *Discrete Applied Mathematics* **1**, 3, pp. 119–122.

Mayer, A. J. and Stockmeyer, L. J. (1994). The complexity of word problems — this time with interleaving, *Information and Computation* **115**, pp. 293–311.

Mendelson, E. (1970). *Boolean algebra and switching circuits* (McGraw Hill).

Mhaskar, N. and Soltys, M. (2015). String shuffle: Circuits and graphs, *Journal of Discrete Algorithms* **31**, 0, pp. 120 – 128, doi:http://dx.doi.org/10.1016/j.jda.2015.01.003, URL http://www.sciencedirect.com/science/article/pii/S1570866715000040, 24th International Workshop on Combinatorial Algorithms (IWOCA 2013).

Miller, G. A. (1995). Wordnet: A lexical database for english, *Communications of the ACM* .

Ogden, W. F., Riddle, W. E. and Rounds, W. C. (1978). Complexity of expressions allowing concurrency, in *Proc. 5th ACM Symposium on Principles of Programming Languages (POPL)*, pp. 185–194.

Papadimitriou, C. H. (1994). *Computational Complexity* (Addison-Wesley).

Papadimitriou, C. H. and Steiglitz, K. (1998). *Combinatorial Optimization: Algorithms and Complexity* (Dover).

Press, W. H., Vetterling, W. T., Teukolsky, S. A. and Flannery, B. P. (2007). *Numerical Recipes: The Art of Scientifc Computing*, 3rd edn. (Cambridge University Press).

Reingold, O. (2005). Undirected st-connectivity in log-space, in *STOC'05: Proceedings of the thirty-seventh annual ACM symposium on Theory of computing*, pp. 376–385.

Renatus, P. F. V. (4th or 5th century AD). De re militari, .

Riddle, W. E. (1973). A method for the description and analysis of complex software systems, *SIGPLAN Notices* **8**, 9, pp. 133–136.

Riddle, W. E. (1979). An approach to software system modelling and analysis, *Computer Languages* **4**, 1, pp. 49–66.

Rosen, K. H. (2007). *Discrete Mathematics and Its Applications*, 6th edn. (McGraw Hill).

Saaty, T. L. (1977). A scaling method for priorities in hierarchical structures, *Journal of Mathematical Psychology* **15**, pp. 234–281.

Schwartz, R. L., Foy, B. D. and Phoenix, T. (2011). *Learning Perl*, 6th edn. (O'Reilly Media, Inc.), ISBN 1449303587, 9781449303587.

Scruton, R. (2005). *Gentle Regrets: Thoughts from a Life* (Continuum).

Scruton, R. (2011). *Beauty: A Very Short Introduction* (Oxford University Press).

Scruton, R. (2014). *The soul of the world* (Princeton University Press).

Scruton, R. (2015). Living with a mind, *First Things* .

Shaw, A. C. (1978). Software descriptions with flow expressions, *IEEE Transactions on Software Engineering* **SE-4**, 3, pp. 242–254.

Shoudai, T. (1992). A P-complete language describable with iterated shuffle, *Information Processing Letters* **41**, 5, pp. 233–238.

Shustek, L. (2009). Interview, *Communications of the ACM* **52**, 3, pp. 38–41.

Singh, S. (1999). *The Code Book: The evolution of secrecy, from Mary, Queen of Scots, to Quantum Cryptography* (Doubleday).

Sipser, M. (2006). *Introduction to the Theory of Computation* (Thompson), second Edition.

Solovay, R. and Strassen, V. (1977). A fast monte-carlo test for primality, *SIAM Journal of Computing* **6**, pp. 84–86.

Soltys, M. (2002a). Berkowitz's algorithm and clow sequences, *Electronic Journal of Linear Algebra* **9**, pp. 42–54.

Soltys, M. (2002b). Extended Frege and Gaussian Elimination, *Bulletin of the Section of Logic* **31**, 4, pp. 1–17.

Soltys, M. (2004). LA, permutations, and the Hajós calculus, in J. Díaz, J. Karhumäki, A. Lepistö and D. Sannella (eds.), *Automata, Languages and Programming, 31st International Colloquium (ICALP)*, *Lecture Notes in Computer Science*, Vol. 3142, European Association of Theoretical Computer Science, University of Turku (Springer), pp. 1176–1187, doi: http://dx.doi.org/10.1007/978-3-540-27836-8_97.

Soltys, M. (2005). Feasible proofs of matrix properties with Csanky's algoritm, in C.-H. L. Ong (ed.), *Computer Science Logic, 19th International Workshop (CSL)*, *Lecture Notes in Computer Science*, Vol. 3634, Oxford University Computing Laboratory (Springer), pp. 493–508, doi:http://dx.doi.org/10.1007/11538363_34.

Soltys, M. (2009). *An introduction to computational complexity* (Jagiellonian University Press).

Soltys, M. (2013). Circuit complexity of shuffle, in T. Lecroq and L. Mouchard (eds.), *International Workshop on Combinatorial Algorithms 2013*, *Lecture Notes in Computer Science*, Vol. 8288 (Springer), pp. 402—411, doi:10.1007/978-3-642-45278-9_34.

Soltys, M. and Cook, S. (2004). The proof complexity of linear algebra, *Annals of Pure and Applied Logic* **130**, 1–3, pp. 207–275, doi:http://dx.doi.org/10.1016/j.apal.2003.12.005.

Su, F. E. (2010). Teaching research: encouraging discoveries, *American Mathematical Monthly* .

Thurstone, L. L. (1927). A law of comparative judgement, *Psychological Review* **34**, 278–286.

van Vliet, H. (2000). *Software Engineering: Principles and Practice*, 2nd edn. (Wiley).

Velleman, D. J. (2006). *How To Prove It*, 2nd edn. (Cambridge University Press).

von zur Gathen, J. (1993). Parallel linear algebra, in J. H. Reif (ed.), *Synthesis of Parallel Algorithms* (Morgan and Kaufman), pp. 574–617.

von zur Gathen, J. and Gerhard, J. (1999). *Modern computer algebra* (Cambridge University Press).

Warmuth, M. K. and Haussler, D. (1984). On the complexity of iterated shuffle, *Journal of Computer and System Sciences* **28**, 3, pp. 345–358.

Whitman, W. (1892). Song of myself, .

Zhai, Y. (2010). *Pairwise comparisons based non-numerical ranking*, Ph.D. thesis, McMaster University.

Zingaro, D. (2008). *Invariants: A generative approach to programming* (College Publications).

Index

Printed in the United States
By Bookmasters